COVERED
WITH
GLORY

Also by Rod Gragg

Confederate Goliath: The Battle of Fort Fisher
The Illustrated Confederate Reader
The Old West Quiz and Fact Book
The Civil War Quiz & Fact Book
Planters, Pirates, and Patriots
Bobby Bagley: P. O. W.

Covered
with
Glory

THE 26TH NORTH CAROLINA INFANTRY
AT THE BATTLE OF GETTYSBURG

Rod Gragg

Perennial

An Imprint of HarperCollinsPublishers

This work is dedicated to three mountaineers from the Globe:

Charles Lemuel Gragg (1891–1974)

Coma Adelaide Gragg (1891–1971)

and their son,

Lemuel Wallace Gragg (1914–1998)

First Perennial edition published 2001.

Designed by Adam W. Cohen

Maps by Mark Stein

The Library of Congress has catalogued the hardcover edition as follows:

Gragg, Rod.
    Covered with glory : the 26th North Carolina Infantry at Gettysburg / Rod Gragg.—1st ed.
      p. cm.
    Includes bibliographical references and index.
    ISBN 0–06–017445–5
    1. Gettysburg (Pa.), Battle of, 1863. 2. Confederate States of America. Army. North Carolina Infantry Regiment, 26th. 3. North Carolina—History—Civil War, 1861–1865—Regimental Histories. 4. United States—History—Civil War, 1861–1865—Regimental Histories. I. Title.

E475.53 .G72 2000
973.7'349—dc21   99-089035

ISBN 0-06-093477-8 (pbk.)

01 02 03 04 05 ❖/RRD 10 9 8 7 6 5 4 3 2 1

Time, like an ever-rolling stream,

Bears all its sons away;

They fly forgotten as a dream

Dies at the opening day.

—"O God, Our Help in Ages Past,"
a hymn popular during the Civil War

Contents

Acknowledgments

Even in the late 1950s, the fireplace was the only source of heat in my grandparents' farmhouse parlor. Upstairs there was *no* heat—and winter nights could be icy cold in North Carolina's Blue Ridge Mountains. Layers of quilts on the upstairs beds would eventually overcome the chill, but the inevitable shock of cold sheets was a sensation that deserved to be delayed as long as possible. Knowing that you soon would have to brave that cold upstairs bedroom made sitting around the parlor fire even more appealing. Many houses in the Globe, the mountain farming community that was our ancestral home, were still heated solely by fireplaces in the late fifties. America was plotting a space race to the moon, but most folks in my grandparents' isolated mountain community were still without telephones, central heat or indoor plumbing. If my grandparents felt underprivileged by the absence of such conveniences, they never complained around us grandchildren.

Like many of his generation, my father had left the mountains during the Great Depression to find a paying job. After a stint in the Civilian Conservation Corps and military service for the duration in World War II, he had pursued postwar success in a small town far away from the family farm. Raised in town, I eagerly seized every opportunity to visit my mountain grandparents. Not only did I treasure time with Granny and Granddaddy, who doted on all their grandchildren, but a visit to their Appalachian community was like time travel backward to another century. The nearest place with street lights, supermarkets and telephones was almost an hour's drive away on winding mountain roads.

In the summer we splashed in the creek or fished for trout. In the fall and winter we squirrel-hunted on the mountain ridges or tracked rabbits in the snow. There were jars of fruit in the smokehouse, honey fresh from the hives, and warm biscuits waiting on the cast-iron wood-stove. We romped with the hunting dogs, rode bareback on the plow-horse, played on the hay bales in the barn loft, and cheerfully gathered eggs and firewood. Daytime offered a variety of adventures, but our most memorable pastime occurred only at night. After the supper dishes were cleared, the grownups would pull the straight-back chairs from the table and sit in a semi-circle around the parlor fireplace, where a blaze was habitually kept alive. On every visit my brother and I would routinely prolong the climb to the cold upstairs bedrooms. We were mesmerized not only by the parlor fire—but also by the old-timers' tales. Talk of politics, baseball, the doings in Blowing Rock or Lenoir, and local news from the surrounding farm families was always just a prelude. Eventually, the talk would turn to "the War." Talk about World War II exploits was apparently deemed too fresh, too modern or too immodest; tales of "the War" were always about *that* war—the War Between the States. My wiry, craggy-faced grandfather had a fascinating repertoire of stories about mountain folks and the war. Blessed with the Southerner's pleasant drawl, he would verbally unfold his accounts at a mountaineer's natural pace—slow and steady—as he methodically opened a cherry-red tin of Prince Albert smoking tobacco and constructed a roll-your-own cigarette. His captivating cadence was usually interrupted only by an appropriate chuckle or an appreciative grunt from other grownups, although my great-grandfather—in his nineties and wearing a white handlebar mustache—occasionally exercised family rank with a terse comment while leaning on his walking stick.

Staring trancelike into the flames, I heard tales about hard men and hard times—tales of bushwhackers and battle scars, of Southern soldiers bound to do their duty, of local Unionists hiding from the Home Guard in the mountain wilds, and resourceful farm wives who thwarted Yankee raiders by burying the family valuables beneath the collard patch. There were stories about Keese Blalock the renegade, and tales about Stoneman's Raid—when the Yankees reportedly carried off pro-South menfolk and shot loyal slaves. There were also whimsical tales about Scalawags and Carpetbaggers, and serious stories that conveyed respect for the common Southern soldier. I don't remember hearing specific references to the Hibriten Guards, which included many boys from the Globe community, or even direct mention of the 26th North Carolina, but there were comments aplenty about men who had served in the regiment. As a boy at the turn of the century, my grandfather had known many of them and their families—Moores, Coffeys, Esteses, Crumps, and others. Hearing such stories left me amazed at the grit of these Tarheel soldiers—gumption, they called it in the mountains—and it did even more. It made me deeply aware of the proximity of "the War"—so close that my grandfather and even my father had actually seen and touched and talked to men who had *been there*. The men and women whose stories I heard while sitting before the fire were not one-dimensional characters on the page of a book. They were real people, who had *lived* history. I was left with the notion that comprehending history—an era, an event, a war, a battle—required discovering the details about the real people involved.

So, I am indebted to my grandparents on my father's side, Charles and Adelaide Gragg, and to my maternal grandparents, Oak and Lula Lunsford, for kindling my curiosity about history. In a way, this book had its origin in the firelit parlor of that long gone home-place near the headwaters of John's River, when old men bequeathed heartfelt history to young boys. Others made fundamental contributions. My father, Lemuel Wallace Gragg—reticent, responsible, knowledgeable and always faithful to his family—had a mountaineer's quiet gumption and a scholar's devotion to reading. Without saying a word, he taught me to love books. My mother, Elizabeth Lunsford Gragg—joyful, selfless, and devout—happily placed book after book in my hands, transported me to historic sites far and near, and implanted in me a lifelong devotion to faith, family, history, travel and the Blue Ridge. When our family transportation consisted of a single pickup truck my father used in his work, she made a mile-long march to the library seem like a great adventure. Equipped with a limited budget, a station wagon, air mattresses and a road map, she cheerfully organized, promoted and directed a family vacation in 1958 that introduced me to Gettysburg. This book and everything else I've written bears her positive, behind-the-scenes encouragement. My brother Ted and my cousins Bob and Charles were my boyhood mentors. They fueled my interest in the Civil War, fostered my respect for the soldiers in blue and gray and kindled interests that eventually led to this book.

M. S. "Buz" Wyeth Jr., now retired from his post of executive editor at HarperCollins, was instrumental in developing this project. He has been a valuable mentor and friend, and I learned a lot from him while writing five books under his editorship. I'm grateful also to publisher Cathy Hemming for supporting this work, and to book editors Paul McCarthy and Tim Duggan for their professional direction. Thanks are also due to John Atkins, Sue Llewellyn, Elina Nudelman, and Bob Spizer at HarperCollins.

I owe a unique debt to Paul Fowler, a superb professional researcher and a faithful friend, for an immeasurable contribution to this work. Without his assistance, this book probably could not have been written. I'm indebted also to Keith Toney of Winchester, Virginia—a Gettysburg expert and a licensed guide with the National Park Service—for sharing his broad knowledge of the field of battle. Long before I began work on the 26th's role at Gettysburg, gifted historians like Randall Garrison, Clint Johnson, Greg Mast, David McGee, Skip Smith and Jeff Stepp had skillfully researched and recorded the regiment's remarkable history. Their excellent work in *Company Front* and other published works set both a precedent and a high standard for study of the regiment. Likewise, the members of the Society for the Preservation of the 26th North Carolina Troops and the 26th Regiment of North Carolina Troops (Reactivated) have faithfully preserved the history and the legacy of the regiment through living history and publications like the *Home Front,* the *Rebel Boast* and the *Skirmish Line.* Susan Albert, Dennis Brooks, and Dr. Brooks W. Gilmore Jr. also provided knowledgeable advice. Key documents and photographs related to Colonel John R. Lane were graciously shared with me by his descendant, J. R. Gorrell of Raleigh.

A select group of historical collections were of key importance to this work, and I'm especially grateful to the personnel of these institutions: Duke University's Special Collections Library, the Eleanor Brockenbrough Library at the Museum of the Confederacy, the Gettysburg National Military Park, the Library of Congress, the National Archives, the North Carolina Department of Archives and History, the North Carolina Museum of History, the Southern Historical Collection at the University of North Carolina, the U.S. Military Academy Library at West Point, and the U.S. Army Military History Institute at Carlisle Barracks.

I'm also thankful for the assistance I received from the following: Adams County Historical Society, Alderman Library at the University of Virginia, Antietam National Battlefield, Bentley Historical Library at the University of Michigan, Caldwell County Public Library, Civil War Library and Museum of Philadelphia, Georgia Historical Society, Greensboro Historical Museum, Handley Public Library, High Point Public Library, Horry County Memorial Library, Kimbel Library at Coastal Carolina University, Moravian Music Foundation, Moravian Archives, New Jersey Historical Society, Oakwood Cemetery, Pack Memorial Library, Presbyterian Department of History at Montreat, Preston Library at the Virginia Military Institute, South Carolina State Archives Department, South Caroliniana Library, Washington County

Free Library, Wilson Library at the University of North Carolina-Chapel Hill and the Winchester-Frederick County Historical Society.

The remarkable image of the 26th North Carolina on the march to Gettysburg that graces the jacket of this book is the artwork of Mort Kunstler, who is America's premier historical artist. I appreciate his work and his friendship. I'm grateful too for the personal and professional support I've received from Mort Kunstler's art publishers, Ted and Mary Sutphen of the American Print Gallery, who are pioneers in their own field of history. Thanks are also due to Beth Rogers Williams, Debbie Shaub and Theresa Horne for bearing with me during the daunting challenges posed by this work. I'm thankful too for the encouragement I received from Ted and Connie Gragg, Margaret Outlaw, Newt and Deborah, Jimmy and Gail, John and Tina, Doug and Jackie, Joe and Margaret, and from my friends at Grace Presbyterian Church, P.C.A., and Conway Christian School.

Many other individuals helped with this work. Some of them are: Edison B. Allen, Col. Joseph Alexander, Ted Alexander, Joe Bilby, Tim Barnwell, John Bass, Edna Bellamy, Tom Belton, Robert Brewer, Keven Brown, Kathy Budnie, William B. Bynum, Stephen Catlett, Mike Cavenaugh, William M. Clark, John Coski, Blake L. Deegan, Becky Ebert, John Emerson, Jim Enos, Ronnie W. Faulkner, Joseph Freed, Lisabeth M. Holloway, Diane B. Jacob, Bobbie S. Johnson, Ervin Jordan Jr., David A. Keogh, Dr. Nola R. Knouse, Alan C. Leonard, Don Leonard, Frances Allgood Peed, Marchita J. Phifer, Tracy Powers, Joel Reese, Rob Richardson, Verna G. Richardson, Judith Sibley, Jack Simpson, Rita Simpson, Dr. Lynne Smith, Herman Starnes, Randy Tarlton, Mark Terry, Sharon A. Tully, Forest Turner, H. Preston Williams and Steven Wright.

Thanks also go to my children—Faith, Rachel, Elizabeth, Joni, Penny, Matt, and Skip—for bearing with me through a long and challenging project that sometimes (rarely, of course) left me tired and grumpy. Special honor is due my wife Cindy, a Civil War widow of sorts, whose quiet and gentle spirit personifies the biblical role model of Proverbs 31. Most of all, I'm eternally grateful for the lasting truth of Romans 10:9–11.

"I Was Once a Soldier"

He still looked strong and robust, but he was an old man now. His dark, chest-length beard was flecked with gray and his face bore the wrinkles of almost seven decades. Tomorrow would be his sixty-eighth birthday. Dressed in a suit of gray, he stood ramrod straight on an outdoor stage amid American flags and bunting of red, white and blue. His attire was formal and his manner was dignified, but he had the weathered face of a farmer. His body bore the scars of battle, and on his coat was pinned the Southern Cross of Honor. Below him were the upturned faces of an audience numbering more than a thousand. As the crowd watched expectantly, he turned to greet another bearded old man, who walked sprightly across the stage. He too wore a suit, but it was dark and on it was pinned a different badge. The two grasped hands like friends of old, and the crowd roared its approval. Said the man in the dark suit: "I thank God I did not kill you."[1]

Moments later the old man in gray addressed the audience. "I was once a soldier," he told them, "never a speaker. Besides, our good friends the enemy took good care on this field of Gettysburg that I should never become an orator, for a Yankee bullet ruined my throat and took away part of my tongue and deprived me of my teeth." Despite his humble manner—and his speech impediment—he spoke confidently. From the speaker's platform this July afternoon in 1903, he could see a panorama of green fields, shady glades and burly ridges. He knew, however, that the serene appearance was deceptive. In his memory, the same pastoral scenery was transformed into the fierce fury of battle—with images of smoke and flame, gunfire and confusion, the screams of the wounded and the shouts of desperate men. In his memory, too, were so many faces—the faces of young men who fought and fell and bloodied the rich soil of Pennsylvania. He pointed to his right, over the crowd, beyond the fields, and in the direction of a faraway tree-topped ridge. Then he began. "Forty years ago," he told his hushed audience, "on the first of July at 10 o'clock A.M., our regiment lay over there facing McPherson's hill, in line of battle. . . ."[2]

CHAPTER 1

Good, Honest
American Stock

U<small>P</small> ahead, death awaited some of them.

Lieutenant Colonel John Randolph Lane understood that grim fact, but at the moment he was distracted by a wave of nausea. After a bone-wearying two-week march from Virginia to Pennsylvania, his regiment and the rest of General Robert E. Lee's army were finally about to fight the Yankees on Northern soil. A mile or so up the road now crowded with Confederate troops, the smoke of battle was rising from a crossroads hamlet called Gettysburg. In the distance, Lane could hear the sputtering roll of small arms fire and the slam-slam-slam of artillery fire. The men of his regiment were moving steadily toward the sound of the guns, but Lane feared his nausea might force him to fall out. Was it bad water or a case of pre-battle jitters? He was unsure. He had been up all night overseeing the brigade picket line, had eaten practically nothing for breakfast and had unwisely gulped down several big swallows of muddy water. Now he felt so nauseous he wondered if he could do his job in the fighting that lay ahead.[1]

Tall and erect, Lane was a robust man with a stocky build. He was three days away from his twenty-eighth birthday, but a chest-length black beard made him look older. Despite his uniform of Confederate gray, he looked more like a farmer than an army officer. Before the war, he *was* a farmer, turning over the sod every spring in the rolling fields of central North Carolina's Chatham County. He had the hardy look of a man accustomed to the outdoors—a strong face with rough-hewn features—but he also projected a natural dignity that befitted his current occupation. Lieutenant Colonel Lane was now second-in-command of the 26th North Carolina—one of the largest infantry regiments in the Army of Northern Virginia. His men revered him, and he returned their esteem. Most of the regiment's shirkers were gone now; the last handful had been shaken loose by the hard march north and the prospect of battle. What remained was a regiment of more than 800 well-drilled fighting men.[2]

A year earlier, Lane had endured a hellish night on the battlefield at Malvern Hill with these men. Now, exactly one year later—Wednesday, July 1, 1863—he was heading with them into what appeared to be an even greater battle. Would he be too ill to exercise command? They were approaching Gettysburg from the west, marching on a well-used highway called the Chambersburg Turnpike. Up the road before them they could see a series of ridges, and from atop the crest of a distant ridge, on the outskirts of Gettysburg, Federal troops appeared to be pouring fire into the Confederate troops ahead. In response, the Confederates—Third Corps troops of Heth's Division—were spreading out in a long battle line on both sides of the pike. The men of the 26th advanced up the road in formation as the chaotic sounds of heavy fighting increased, muffling the rhythmic tread of the marching men. As the troops leading the regiment crested a ridge, Federal artillery fire suddenly shrieked down from the morning sky and exploded on the road just steps ahead. It was their first fire of the battle, and it came unexpectedly, jarring the marching column with a concussion and a loud blast of smoke, flame and debris. The men in front wavered, and the column seemed to hesitate.[3]

"Steady, men!" boomed a calm but authoritative voice. It belonged to the regiment's commanding officer, Colonel Henry King Burgwyn Jr. Moving alongside the column on horseback, Burgwyn shouted encouragement to the troops, and they regained their step. "Steady, boys, steady," he urged them, and the measured tread of the march resumed. Moments later, Burgwyn ordered the men off the road. They deployed along to their right behind a row of Confederate artillery pieces, and prepared to form a line of battle.[4]

The cool-headed response to the incoming artillery fire was typical of Colonel Burgwyn. He had a reputation in the 26th as a steady man in a time of danger—and one who always put his troops first. He was also known for his youth: Colonel Henry King Burgwyn Jr. was twenty-one years old. Even in an army of so many young men, such youthfulness was exceptional. Yet, Burgwyn's troops followed him devotedly. The Colonel was "cool under fire," proclaimed one of his men, and always knew "exactly what to do." A year earlier, a brigade commander had sparked protests when he tried to block Burgwyn's promotion because of his youthfulness. Soon afterwards the 26th had transferred to another brigade. Now, as the regiment moved into battle at Gettysburg, Burgwyn enjoyed even greater loyalty from his men, who knew he would never send them anywhere he would not go. The young officer had not always enjoyed such enthusiastic support. Lieutenant Colonel Lane could remember when Burgwyn was the most despised man in the regiment.[5]

Lane was a fresh recruit the first time he saw Burgwyn. It was a warm August morning in 1861. He and his company—the Chatham Boys—had just arrived at Camp Carolina, a large training post established about three miles northwest of Raleigh at Crabtree Plantation. The Chatham Boys had arrived by train in the night and could see little in the darkness. In the morning, Lane awoke to a sprawling encampment—rows of tents, smoking campfires and hordes of coughing, laughing, yelling recruits. Looking at the rifle-toting sentries patrolling the boundaries of the camp, Lane suddenly realized the four-month-old war that had seemed so distant was a serious reality. In their fumbling adjustment to soldiering that morning, the Chatham Boys somehow failed to join the rest of the camp for roll call. Soon afterwards, a message arrived from the camp commandant—Major Henry K. Burgwyn Jr.—demanding to know why the company had failed to report. The company commander, Captain William S. McLean, summoned Lane, who was already a corporal, and ordered him to pick three "soldierly-looking" privates and go face the major.[6]

Lane reported to headquarters, wondering what fate awaited him. He was soon confronted by Major Burgwyn, who was then nineteen years old and fresh from the Virginia Military Institute. Despite his youthfulness, Burgwyn acted authoritatively and decisively. Lane was immediately impressed. "At first sight," he later admitted, "I both feared and admired him." Burgwyn said nothing about the failure to report but assigned the three Chatham Boys a hefty chore. "Corporal, take these three men and thoroughly police this camp," he ordered. "Don't leave a watermelon rind or anything filthy in camp." Lane made certain his first order was followed to perfection—and the Chatham Boys, which became Company G of the 26th North Carolina, never missed another roll call.[7]

Although he displayed a professional's command presence and confidence, Burgwyn was well aware of his youthfulness. A few weeks after his first meeting with Lane, the 26th North Carolina was organized and the troops elected Burgwyn their lieutenant colonel. In a personal journal marked

"Strictly Private," Burgwyn confided his concerns: "I am now 19 years, 9 months & 27 days old & probably the youngest Lt. Col. in the Confederate or U.S. service. . . . May Almighty God lend me his aid in discharging my duty to him and to my country."[8]

Discharging his duty was a character trait Burgwyn learned early. Before his twelfth birthday, he reportedly memorized four volumes of Virgil's *Aeneid*— paid per stanza by his parents—and earned enough money to buy the gold watch he later carried as a Confederate officer. Such an academic accomplishment was typical of Burgwyn, whose intellect was carefully nurtured by both parents. His mother, Anna Greenough Burgwyn, was a Bostonian raised in nineteenthth-century New England affluence. She met Burgwyn's father while both were visiting relatives in New York City in 1838. A member of a prominent North Carolina family from New Bern, Henry Senior also had Northern ancestors—including eighteenth-century New England theologian Jonathan Edwards, who had helped launch the Great Awakening. When married, Henry Senior and Anna chose to raise their family in North Carolina, although Anna Burgwyn treasured her Northern roots and returned to Massachusetts to bear her children. Unlike most Southern gentlemen, Henry Junior was a Northerner by birth. The oldest son in a large family, he was born in Jamaica Plains, Massachusetts, on October 3, 1841.[9]

He was raised at Thornbury plantation, which lay along North Carolina's Roanoke River near the Virginia state line in Northampton County. His father had inherited the property from a bachelor uncle before Harry was born, and although they had not been raised for a life of agriculture, Burgwyn's parents had become successful planters. They had also inherited more than a hundred slaves, although Burgwyn's father was uncomfortable with slavery and his mother detested it. They tried to replace their slaves with Irish field hands imported from the North, but the experiment failed. The Burgwyns kept their slaves, reportedly earning a reputation as benevolent masters. Burgwyn's slave villages were known for their "good framed buildings with a garden attached to each, and 'regular hospitals' maintained for the sick." Observed the local Episcopal bishop in 1849: "Mr. Burgwyn is making very laudable efforts to Christianize his slaves which thus far have proved eminently successful."[10]

Although his family was not as affluent as many Southern planters, Harry Burgwyn grew up in an atmosphere unknown to the yeomen farmers who composed the vast majority of the free Southern population. He was tended by a governess and a tutor, enjoyed comforts available to few and was granted the time and encouragement to study and learn. He was especially close to his mother, who was well-educated, disciplined and attentive to her children. His father was intellectual and innovative. Henry Senior served as vice president of the U.S. Agricultural Society and was recognized as one of the South's leading planters by the time Harry was in his teens.[11]

Raised in such an environment, Burgwyn could have grown selfish and aloof, but his parents balanced privilege with discipline and responsibility. Like most Southern boys, he learned to hunt as a child and also came to be an accomplished horseman. Burgwyn's father believed a Southern gentleman should be more than just charming: He was expected to excel in a profession and return something to his community. As preparation, ten-year-old Harry was enrolled in a prep school near Baltimore, and afterwards he attended an Episcopal college near Philadelphia. He proved to be an exceptionally bright student, completing advanced courses of study at a remarkably young age. His father wanted Burgwyn to attend the U.S. Military Academy, but at age fifteen he was deemed too young by U.S. Secretary of War Jefferson Davis, who was an old friend of Harry's father. To prepare for admission, Burgwyn was sent to West Point for private tutoring by an Academy professor. When the officer was transferred to another post, Burgwyn enrolled in the University of North Carolina at age sixteen. Two years later, he graduated with top honors. He then joined the corps of cadets at the Virginia Military Institute, where he again compiled an excellent academic record. At V.M.I., he was a member of the cadet detachment detailed to guard John Brown while the radical abolitionist was awaiting execution for his raid on the Federal arsenal at Harpers Ferry.[12]

Burgwyn graduated from V.M.I. near the top of his class in April of 1861—as war fever engulfed America. V.M.I. Professor Thomas J. Jackson, who would soon earn fame as "Stonewall" Jackson, gave Burgwyn an official recommendation describing him as "a high-toned Southern gentleman" known for "the highly practical as well as scientific character of his mind." Although his family initially opposed secession—his father termed it a "calamity"—Harry Burgwyn had come to see Southern independence as a solution to the decades of tension between North and South. Many Southerners feared Northern leaders were determined to enlarge the Federal government, centralize power in Washington, reduce the autonomy of the states and dominate the South's economy and politics. Meanwhile, the controversy over slavery, an institution that gradually had been discarded by other Western nations, became an explosive fuel for the smoldering flames of sectional distrust and rivalry. The new Republican Party, feared by many in the South as anti-Southern, captured the White House in the 1860 presidential election. South Carolina responded by seceding. Other Southern states followed and formed the Confederate States of America. The American political crisis deteriorated into warfare at Fort Sumter in April of 1861. Newly inaugurated as president, Abraham Lincoln refused Confederate demands to remove Federal troops from the Charleston fort and chose instead to resupply the post. When Confederate forces bombarded Fort Sumter into surrender, Lincoln responded with a public call for "volunteers to suppress the insurrection"— which prompted four other Southern states—including North Carolina—to join the Confederacy.[13]

Burgwyn fervently believed in state sovereignty—that any state had the right to secede from a voluntary union—and he saw Lincoln's call for an invasion of the South as "coercion." A year and a half earlier, his father had returned from a fact-finding visit to the North convinced that there was no way "by which our great Union is to be preserved." Even so, Henry Senior had predicted a peaceful separation. While admitting that few Northern leaders supported "full and equal rights" for the South, he had remained confident that the seceded states would be "free from any molestation from the North." The Yankees, Henry Senior had assured friends and family, would "make the best treaty with us they could to continue their present advantageous trade with the South." Events had proven him wrong. For Harry Burgwyn, Lincoln's call to arms had ended all debate: His homeland faced invasion, and he would defend it.[14]

From V.M.I., Burgwyn had been dispatched to Richmond to drill recruits, but he was soon summoned back home to North Carolina, where he was commissioned as a captain and sent to recruit troops from the state's western mountains. Meanwhile, he had waged an unsuccessful campaign to obtain command of the newly organized 12th North Carolina. Finally, on July 5, 1861, he had been granted a major's rank with appointment by the governor as commander of Camp Carolina. He was a masterful drill instructor. Six feet tall, erect, slim and dignified, he fit perfectly the nineteenth-century American image of a military officer. He conducted himself with an authoritative, reserved manner, and insisted on discipline. A slight speech impediment caused his "Forward, march!" to sound like "forward mollop," but he struggled determinedly with the pronunciation until he could voice the order precisely. He had cultivated a fashionable French-style mustache and a slight goatee, which—along with his polite but commanding attitude—gave him an appearance of maturity beyond his years. He was deemed handsome by his peers, some of whom described him as "beautiful," and he bore a reputation as "a ladies' man" in a gentlemanly fashion. Harry Burgwyn looked like a leader capable of converting ragamuffins to soldiers, and at Camp Carolina he went to work with zeal.[15]

Pouring into the camp were thousands of anxious, excited recruits, who were eager for battle but generally unprepared for war. "We arrived safely last Thursday evening at this place," a young officer in the Chatham Boys advised the folks back home. "[We] are pleasantly situated with our tents pitched in regular style in a pine grove hardly surpassed in the line of beauty. We were complimented very much as we marched through the city as being one among the finest companies they had seen." Soldier life at Camp Carolina seemed like a great adventure to some recruits. "I am better satisfied than I expected to be," a volunteer in the Chatham Independents wrote home. "Our camp is right on the side of the railroad where we can see the cars every day." The new soldiers were drilled thoroughly, organized into regiments and then mustered into Confederate service. Among their ranks were ten companies of volunteers who, on August 27, 1861, became the 26th Regiment North Carolina Troops.[16]

They had come to Camp Carolina from the red clay country of Union and Anson Counties, from the rolling farmland of Moore, Chatham and Wake Counties, and from the hollows and high ridges of Caldwell, Wilkes and Ashe. Most were young and strong, toughened by countless hours spent behind a mule or swinging an ax. They had turned away from the plow and the wheat cradle, the barnyard chores of splitting stove wood, slopping hogs, milking cows and toting water from the springhouse. They had left behind frame farmhouses with river-rock fireplaces, corn-shuck mattresses and Sunday dinner tables laden with cured hams, collard greens, sweet potatoes, cut corn, biscuits and rhubarb pie. Behind them lay the familiarities of boyhood: a favorite fishing hole, a one-room schoolhouse, a deep woods hunting trail, corn cribs, haylofts, berry patches, a tail-wagging coon dog and pew-filled sanctuaries that rang with hymns and preaching on Sunday mornings. Left behind too in the outburst of Southern patriotism and pride were fretful mothers, solemn-faced fathers, teary-eyed sweethearts and, among the older recruits, anxious wives and children—all hoping the boys would win the war quickly and soon return home.[17]

There were few aristocrats among them. The great majority owned neither slaves nor plantations. For most of them, home was a small farm where they worked from sunup to sundown raising corn, oats, wheat, beans, hogs and a few cows. Although many had limited schooling, they were generally bright, observant and self-reliant. Lane liked to describe them as "the great middle class that owned small farms." They were men who "earned their living with honest sweat," he would say, "and owed not any man." Most were also seasoned outdoorsmen who were comfortable with firearms and who were trained from childhood to shoot with deadly precision. Represented in their ranks was a sampling of common nineteeth-century American occupations: blacksmiths, carpenters, merchants, mechanics, harness-makers, painters, teachers, millwrights and servants. A few were laborers, and some were students who happily put aside books and slates for the adventure of war. At least one was a bartender, another was a printer, one was a postmaster and at least one was a well-digger. The overwhelming majority, however, was composed of small farmers—"good, honest American stock," Lieutenant Colonel Lane liked to call them.[18]

Most were also reluctant secessionists. Their ancestors had battled the British on famous fields such as King's Mountain and Guilford Court House, and like most North Carolinians, they had been slow to give up on the Union. Not until President Lincoln had called for 75,000 volunteers to invade the South in the wake of Fort Sumter, did they rally for Southern independence. Although wary of secession, they refused to join the North in making war upon their Southern brothers. "You will get no troops from North Carolina," Governor John W. Ellis had boldly advised President Lincoln when the Federal government petitioned North Carolina for troops to invade the seceding states. "I can be no party to this wicked violation of the laws of the country and to this war on the liberties of a free people," he had proclaimed, echoing the sentiments of many North Carolinians. And so the Tarheel volunteers had gone to war, convinced—said one of them—"that the cause for which [we were] fighting was just."[19]

They had assembled in county seats and farmers' market towns such as Lenoir, Holly Springs and Wilkesboro, where they had signed up for twelve months of war with the bravado of prizefighters and a romantic notion of a quick and heroic conquest. Vowed one Tarheel volunteer: "I'm willing to undergo any necessary hardship or privation, short of starving, for my country's cause, which is the foremost and dearest companion of my heart, save my darling." Assembled into the 26th North Carolina were the Jeff Davis Mountaineers from Ashe County, which became Company A; the Waxhaw Jackson Guards of Union County, Company B; the Wilkes Volunteers from Wilkes County, Company C; the Wake Guards of Wake County, Company D; the Independent Guards from Chatham County, Company E; the Hibriten Guards from Caldwell County, Company F; the Chatham Boys of Chatham County, Company G; the Moore Independents from Moore County, Company H; the Caldwell Guards of Caldwell County, Company I; and the Pee Dee Wild Cats from Anson County, which became Company K.[20]

Typical was the experience of the Hibriten Guards of Caldwell County, who took their company name from a nearby mountain peak. When President Lincoln declared his intent to invade the South, a public call for defenders was issued from the county seat of Lenoir, a bustling, dirt-lane market town in the foothills of the Blue Ridge Mountains. Although the residents of western North Carolina had few slaves and little initial enthusiasm for secession, a flood of volunteers surged into Lenoir in response to the threatened Northern invasion. By May 25, 1861, the Hibriten Guards were organized and drilling in Lenoir under the command of Captain Nathaniel P. Rankin, an instructor from a local military school.[21]

To properly outfit the company, supporters organized a community effort. With the spirit of a barn-raising, Caldwell County residents handcrafted uniforms, knapsacks, tents and other items deemed necessary for a well-equipped company of troops. Like most volunteer companies in the Civil War, the Guards consisted primarily of men recruited from the same region, which meant soldiers were going off to war with brothers, cousins, neighbors, schoolmates and friends. Such familiarity unquestionably encouraged a spirit of community and devotion in the ranks, but it also held a grim potential: Battlefield casualties would be grievously personal.[22]

In the heady excitement of the war's early days, however, the gruesome reality of warfare was unimaginable to an enthusiastic, untested company of young recruits like the farm boys from Caldwell County. After a couple of months of organization and drill, the Guards were called to Camp Carolina. On July 31, 1861, the company assembled in Lenoir's town square for a farewell ceremony. Applauded by a crowd of family, friends and well-wishers, the Guards stood at attention while a contingent of young ladies attired in white dresses presented the company with a hand-crafted state flag. Captain Rankin officially received the presentation, and the Guards marched off to Hickory Tavern and the nearest rail station. There they boarded a Raleigh-bound train, in what was the first rail trip for most and the first time away from home for many. "We had a jolly time on the train," Private William C. Davis wrote home. "All was tearfully saluted by all from the finest ladies to the blackest negroes. The ladies would wave their handkerchiefs at half a mile distance."[23]

At Camp Carolina, recruits were issued muskets, rifles and "altered muskets" and were put to work drilling for hours at a time. Major Burgwyn was a demanding drillmaster, and the volunteers soon learned how to assemble, move and respond to command. Life was dictated by the roll of the drum and regulated by an established routine. Even hardy farm boys grew tougher and leaner, changing from boys to men. "We get plenty to eat," a soldier in the Chatham Independents wrote home. "We have bacon, beef, corn meal and flour, sugar, coffee, molasses and rice." Some recruits thrived. "i am well and well satisfied," one Camp Carolina trainee assured his parents. "i weigh one hundred and 40 . . . i am much of a man." Others found military life difficult. "Camp life I find to be hard," one young volunteer wrote his mother. "I will make the best of it." Although surrounded by hundreds of other recruits, many volunteers became homesick. "Some of the boys are ancious to come home," wrote one soldier, "for they say they want to see there folks." Chaplains held worship services on Sundays and occasional week-night prayer meetings, but along with men of character and self-discipline, the sprawling encampment also included a sampling of rogues and rascals. "i have bin in and at many places," confided a recruit to the folks back home, "but this is the . . . damnest place that i ever seen. some fusses, some sings, some curses, some plays cards and all sorts of devilment."[24]

Major Burgwyn intended to allow little time for "devilment." He was determined that the new soldiers at Camp Carolina would be properly drilled and prepared for service. "We drill . . . twice a day—once in the morning at 8 o'clock to ten o'clock and from 3 in the evening until 5," a recruit told his folks. "[In] the evening we [go] out on dress parade which continues until about seven in the evening." Despite his obvious skills as a drillmaster, however, Burgwyn did not want to spend the war training recruits. He expected the war to be brief, and he wanted a field command. He got his wish:

When the 26th North Carolina was organized on August 27th, the troops elected Burgwyn as their lieutenant colonel and second-in-command. Captain Abner B. Carmichael, commander of the Wilkes Volunteers, was elected the 26th's major. Picked as the regiment's new colonel and commander, however, was one of North Carolina's most prominent political leaders: Zebulon Baird Vance.[25]

An affable, ambitious thirty-one-year-old mountaineer with dark hair, a thick dark mustache and a youthful, puffy-looking face, Vance was a native of North Carolina's Buncombe County, where he was born in a log house on Reems Creek north of Asheville. Bright and assertive, he studied law at the University of North Carolina at age twenty-one and barely a year later was serving as Asheville's solicitor. After a year of prosecuting lawbreakers, he entered private practice. Vance was perceptive, energetic and witty—a master of "jokes and broad humor," noted a contemporary—and he retained a down-home manner despite his achievements. "He is a fine specimen of a true son of the soil," observed a British diplomat. His competence, ambition and personality propelled him toward his passion: politics. At age twenty-four, he won a seat in the North Carolina House of Representatives and assumed the editor's post at the *Asheville Spectator*. Four years later, he was elected to the U.S. Congress. There, reflecting the sentiments of his mountaineer constituents, he emerged as a vocal opponent of secession—until the Confederate bombardment of Fort Sumter. Congressman Vance had been assured by U.S. Secretary of State William H. Seward that Lincoln would withdraw Fort Sumter's Federal garrison. When Lincoln did otherwise, Vance felt betrayed. He left Congress and endorsed secession.[26]

Although urged by friends to campaign for the Confederate Congress, Vance instead went home to Buncombe County, where he raised a company of volunteers—the Rough and Ready Guards—and was commissioned captain. In June of 1861, he accompanied the Guards to Virginia, where they joined the 14th North Carolina. Vance's tour of duty as a company commander was brief: He yearned to lead—and he got his chance when offered command of the 26th North Carolina. He hurried back to North Carolina and took command of the regiment, despite his lack of military training. So unsoldierly did he appear when he joined the 26th—attired in civilian garb and sporting shoulder-length hair—that he was at first mistaken for a chaplain. Despite appearances, Vance's affable personality and politician's skills quickly earned him popularity with the troops. "In the first place he had the keenest sympathy with his men," a Tarheel soldier would later recall. "They soon came to feel that Colonel Vance loved them and made their troubles his own. In the next place, Colonel Vance was able to inspire his men with the belief that he had confidence in them."[27]

Lieutenant Colonel Burgwyn had no such political skills. He was a professionally trained officer, and his approach was strictly military. He was determined to transform the regiment's raw recruits into good soldiers—and that meant at least six hours of drill a day. Before he could begin, however, shocking news arrived at Camp Carolina: Federal forces had captured Fort Hatteras on North Carolina's Outer Banks. "It makes every vein ready to burst with indignation," bristled a North Carolinian in a typical response. "When I think of such vile feet treading the soil of the Proud old North State." After the celebrated Confederate victory at First Manassas a month earlier, Burgwyn had expected the regiment to be shipped to the Virginia front. Instead, the day after the regiment was officially organized, the 26th was ordered to the North Carolina coast.[28]

The train carrying the regiment rolled into the coastal hamlet of Morehead City in the dark of night on September 2nd. It had been a wearying, all-day trip, so the troops were allowed to sleep through the night on the railroad cars. After a one-day bivouac, Burgwyn and some other officers crossed the sound to the beach and picked a campsite for the regiment. The troops were moved to a camp on the eastern end of North Carolina's Bogue Banks, which was little more than a long, narrow island of sand dunes and sea oats just off the southern tip of the Outer Banks. On the island's northeastern point, however, an imposing prewar masonry fortification called Fort Macon loomed over the Atlantic shore. To the rear, across a wide and picturesque sound, lay the tiny but bustling seaport of Beaufort—which was known to seafarers for its excellent harbor.[29]

On the island, the men of the 26th scrambled to set up camp. Their inexperience was obvious to Burgwyn, who penned a lament—"such a scene of confusion"—in his journal that night. Burgwyn had been charged with getting the troops to the coast, where Colonel Vance would join them. Burgwyn had directed the move skillfully, but his professional demeanor had disguised a nineteen-year-old's anxiety. "I am myself very desirous for the Colonel to take charge and relieve me of what is truly a very [heavy] responsibility," he had confided to his journal at one point. Vance soon arrived, and the troops were put to work organizing their new camp, digging wells and standing ready to do battle with the Yankees. Burgwyn was anxious for a taste of combat, but the opportunity did not arise: the Federal forces which had landed up the coast on Hatteras Island were busy readying their new post as a staging point for further incursions. The port of Beaufort presented an irresistible target for the Yankees, however, which put Fort Macon under constant threat and required the 26th to maintain a state of readiness. The regiment shifted its campsite several times, eventually establishing winter quarters across the sound on the mainland but remained posted on or near Bogue Banks through the rest of the year.[30]

Army life was still an adventure for the troops in those early days, and the seashore was a novelty to country boys from the North Carolina hills. They gathered seashells for the folks back home and marveled over the appearance of the sandy shore—which some declared to be "white as snow." The constant drill caused many to lose weight, regain it and toughen in the outdoor life. They quickly grew weary of army bacon and hardtack and tried to supplement their diet by buying local produce or catching fish from the ocean or sound. "their was four fish caut the other day between the fort and [Beaufort] on the sound that weighed a thousand lbs a peace," one soldier swore to the home folks. "they calde them black fish. the largest one was 17 feet long, the smallest one was twelve feet long."[31]

They built rough-hewn huts for winter quarters and swept the sandy floors to a state of military tidiness. Occasionally they found time to fiddle or dance around the campfire and engage in boyish horseplay. "i will haft to stop Riting," complained one private, "for tha keep so much [racket] no man [can] rite. Some singing, some holering, some pestering a body." Away from camp, especially in Beaufort's sailor bars, some found mischief. "I and G.T. Powell went over to Buford the other day and george got tite, and he was the [funniest] feller i hav ever seen," a Caldwell County soldier admitted in a letter home. Reported another: "some of our men must spend their Christmas in the guard house for their misbehavior—but I can boast so far that none of my tent mates or mess mates has got in the guard house yet." They assured each other—and perhaps anyone else who would listen—that they would whip the Yankees by the score at the first opportunity. "if they attempt to land here they will find that there is trouble before them," vowed one. "the boys is all anxious for a fight," bragged another. "We think we can whip six thousand Yankees. the bois sais they can whip five a peace. i think i can whip six myself."[32]

The adventure and novelties of army life—along with the monotony and aggravation—were often shared with folks back home. Letter writing was unfamiliar to many soldiers, who were away from home for the first time. Some tried to be properly formal on paper: "Dear Sister—I now take my pen in hand to drop you a few lines to let you know that I am well at this time." Others wrote as they spoke: "I want you [to] tell all of my kin and friends howdy for me." They described their duties, speculated on their futures, inquired about the folks and the crops, and asked for quilts, shirts, pants, socks—and food from home. Many struggled with homesickness: "You cannot think how much pleasure it would give me could I get back to Moore County again [and] there to remain in peace." For married men with wives and children left to cope at home, army life included a special burden. "I know that if I was a single man as I once was, I could stay here more contented than I do," wrote one husband, "for there ain't a day, no hardly an hour, but what I am thinking of you and the children." Unmarried soldiers fretted over girlfriends, hoping they would not be lost to "cowards" who chose to sit out the war. "There is a great many young fellows that have no cares to keep them from going out in defense of their country, but are such cowards that they would suffer subjugation rather than fight," complained a private in the 26th. "I trust the ladies will not countenance such fellows."[33]

Letters from home were prized treasures in camp. The writers spoke of family and friends, of crops and work, sick children, neighborhood news, church services, camp meetings and any unusual event. They traded news from other relatives and teased the single men about their girlfriends: "Tell Cousin Neill that I saw his gal last Sunday . . . at church and she looks as well as ever." Mothers updated fathers on their children and occasionally included a note from a child. "Pappy—I had one pig, and I give that to brother," wrote a son to his soldier father. "Mother give me her little sheep, and I will have the wool to make you some stockings."[34]

Home folks generally presented a brave front in their letters, shielding the men at war from bad news if possible. Sometimes, however, the loneliness and hardship of the home front were difficult to stifle: "O, if this war was over you and all the soldiers could come home and stay at home in peace," lamented one spouse. "I would be so glad so we both [could] be with our children."

As soldiers and the distant families began to realize the war would be lengthy and dangerous, the exchanged letters began to reflect a sober determination. "The times are going to be awfully hard—harder than we have expected, and harder than we have ever seen," a private in the 26th candidly advised his wife in January of 1862. "Notwithstanding the numerous reports of the danger with which we are threatened here now, rest assured that I am confident in the belief that I shall survive . . . and come home safely." Confided another: "i dont no wether i will come home or not, but i think i will."[35]

The buoyant optimism of the war's early days was soon tempered by a sobering amount of illness-related death in the ranks. Like most Southern regiments, the 26th was composed of country boys fresh from the farm who had never been exposed to urban illnesses. In the confined conditions of camp, contagious diseases spread easily and rapidly. Soldiers eager and ready for battle could be struck down without firing a shot, sickened or killed by measles, pneumonia, typhoid fever, dysentery or a mysterious, deadly ailment known only as "the fever," which would later be identified as malaria. On the coast, mosquitoes sometimes appeared in swarms. "[Of] all the nights I ever spent in the neighborhood of musketoes last night was the worst," Burgwyn noted. "No sleep visited my weary eyes until very late." Measles and "the fever" swept through the regiment while it was posted to the coast. "R.P. Wilcox has the Typhoid Fever but he is mending," one enlisted man wrote home. "S.P. Short was taken sick yesterday. [The] Dr. said he had the fever. [T]here is a few slight cases of mumps in our co." Nine soldiers died in one week. Before it spent itself, the wave of illnesses also killed two officers and an assistant surgeon.[36]

The men had little free time on the coast. When not assigned guard duty—"guard mounting," they called it—or doing camp chores, they spent most of their time drilling. "Colonel Burgwyn was emphatically a worker in camp . . . constantly drilling," a junior officer would later recall. "[He] believed in discipline and endeavored to bring his regiment to the highest state of efficiency." Conscious of his limited military experience, Colonel Vance delegated drill and discipline to Burgwyn. The constant drill and Burgwyn's strict professionalism contrasted sharply with Colonel Vance's winsome ways. Burgwyn's popularly began to wear thin and was replaced by growing bitterness among the regiment's enlisted men.[37]

The spirit of self-sacrifice and the willingness to endure sustained hardship that would come to characterize the Southern soldier were not immediately evident. In the war's opening months, Southern volunteers sometimes displayed attitudes that bordered on insubordination. A Confederate veteran would later try to explain the fiercely independent mindset held by Southerners like the soldiers of the 26th:

> *The men who volunteered went to war of their own accord, and were wholly unaccustomed to acting on any other than their own notion. . . . [They] were not used to control of any sort, and were not disposed to obey anybody except for good and sufficient reason given. . . . These men were the people of the South, and the war was their own; therefore they fought to win it of their own accord, and not at all because their officers commanded them to do so. Their personal spirit and their intelligence were their sole elements of strength. Death has few terrors for such men, as compared with dishonor, and so they needed no officers at all, and no discipline, to insure their personal and good conduct on the field of battle. The same elements of character, too, made them accept hardship with the utmost cheerfulness, as soon as hardship became a necessary condition to the successful prosecution of a war that every man of them regarded as his own.*[38]

By New Year's Day of 1862, six months of army discipline and relentless drill—both dispensed with a perfectionist's zest by Lieutenant Colonel Burgwyn—had provoked some soldiers to mutter threats. A few even bragged that they would take care of Burgwyn when the time for fighting finally came. A few weeks later, they got their chance.[39]

CHAPTER 2

Into the Jaws
of Certain Death

Bonfires lit the night sky to signal the alarm: the Yankees were coming. Commanded by Major General Ambrose E. Burnside, approximately 10,000 Federal troops had been ferried from their staging area on the Outer Banks and across Pamlico Sound to the North Carolina mainland. Aboard their troopships, they waited in darkness near the mouth of the Neuse River. Meanwhile, Confederate scouts lit signal fires to announce the enemy's arrival. On March 13, 1862, they came ashore and began a drive inland toward New Bern, a strategic railroad shipping point and coastal river port. Capturing New Bern would give the Federals a key base on the North Carolina mainland and would pierce the heart of the state's coastal region. Fearing such a move, Confederate authorities had been concentrating troops around New Bern for weeks. Among the forces defending the town was the 26th North Carolina, which had been hurried inland from the regiment's winter camp on the coast.[1]

In steadily moving blue columns, Burnside's Federal army advanced toward New Bern along the road from Beaufort and over the tracks of the Atlantic & North Carolina Railroad, which ran parallel to the road. Their route of march would bring them straight into the Confederate defensive line, which was manned by 4,500 North Carolina troops under Brigadier General Lawrence O'Bryan Branch. The line stretched from Fort Thompson, an earthen fortification on the Neuse River, to a distant wagon trail called Weathersby Road. Between the two points the line extended through a cleared patch of timber, an abandoned brickyard, another thin stand of timber and a section of swampland. The railroad and the Beaufort Road ran through the middle of the line, and the 26th North Carolina defended the Confederate right—manning a long line of hastily dug earthworks just to the right of the railroad.[2]

Colonel Vance posted himself near the center of the regiment's line. Major Abner B. Carmichael, a popular young officer from the Wilkes Volunteers, commanded the 26th's left, while Lieutenant Colonel Burgwyn commanded the right. Finally they were about to see action—after more than six months of camp duty. "The ball is about to open," as the troops would say, and Burgwyn was about to have a wish fulfilled: He had once feared the war might end before he could experience combat. "I am anxious to be in at least one battle before I go out of service," he had confided to his journal, "& my reputation will greatly depend on my conduct on that occasion."[3]

With the Yankees just a few hours' march away, the regiment was assembled, and Burgwyn made a brief speech. "Soldiers! [The] enemy are before you, and you will soon be in combat," he announced in his commanding voice. "You have the reputation of being one of the best drilled regiments in the service. Now I wish you to prove yourselves one of the best fighting." He had been pushing the men hard for months. He had expected a call to battle and wanted his men to be ready. Furloughs had been suspended, the troops had been restricted to camp, and their days had been consumed by relentless drill. Despite the resentment his demands had sparked, the men standing before him were now disciplined soldiers. Looking at the mass of gray-clad troops, Burgwyn made a promise. "Men," he told the assembled ranks, "stand by me and I will by you."[4]

From downriver came a distant rumbling: Federal gunboats were shelling the riverbanks. In this somber setting, the men of the 26th received Burgwyn's exhortation seriously. No one cheered, and Burgwyn could see by their faces that they understood the gravity of the moment and the dangers that lay before them. "[Every] eye brightened [and] every arm grew nervous & the most deadly determination is on all," he wrote in a last-minute letter home. "You may rely upon a hard fight; but God's providence is over us all."[5]

The attack came early in the morning on March 14, 1862, as mist cloaked the field. Although outnumbered, the Confederate defenders stood firm against repeated assaults by Northern troops. "The severest fighting was on my extreme left, the enemy advancing under the shelter of woods to within easy range of our lines," Colonel Vance later reported. "Whenever they left the woods and entered among the fallen timber of the swamp in our front they were driven back in confusion by the most deadly and well-directed fire from our lines." The center of the Confederate took a severe pounding, where several companies of the 26th were posted, but the men of the regiment withstood their baptism of fire and responded with volleys of gunfire. The weakest point in the line lay just left of center, where a force of poorly armed militia defended the brickyard alongside the railroad. After several hours of fierce fighting, Federal troops pierced the Confederate line at the brickyard and stampeded the militia, who scrambled for the rear, taking several companies of the 35th North Carolina with them.[6]

Attempts to restore order failed, and Federal troops rushed to exploit the breakthrough. As Confederate troops on his left began falling back in large numbers, Colonel Vance realized his side of the line was now exposed. Ordering a retreat, he concluded, was his only option. "Without hesitation I gave the order," he would later explain. "My men jumped out of the trenches, rallied, and formed in the woods without panic or confusion." One large force of defenders, including dozens of men from three companies of the 26th, fell back through a stand of timber behind the Confederate lines—and walked into the guns of Federal infantry and artillery. Mercifully, a Federal officer called for the North Carolinians to surrender, and the men laid down their arms.[7]

Seventy-two men from the 26th were captured or missing; ten were wounded, and five were killed. Among the dead was Major Carmichael, who had gone into action with his kepi adorned by a tiny Confederate flag given to him by a female admirer. In the heat of the fight, as Carmichael was conferring with another officer, he took a bullet through the mouth. "I was standing at his side when he fell," another officer would later recall. "He died instantly. A feeling of bitter grief ran through the trenches as he fell, for there was not a man in the Twenty-Sixth who was not devotedly attached to him." Dead too of a head wound was Captain William P. Martin, the commander of Company H, who had joined the regiment at the head of the Moore Independents.[8]

Despite his yearning for battle, Lieutenant Colonel Burgwyn saw practically none of it. The deadly swirl of combat did not reach the far right of the line, where Burgwyn held immediate command. Burgwyn heard the roar of battle and braced for an enemy attack—but it never came his way. Instead, he received an order from Colonel Vance to retreat immediately. He reacted like a seasoned professional. Showing no signs of panic despite the impending danger of being overrun by Federal forces, Burgwyn coolly ordered his troops to form behind their earthworks. So calm did he remain that a junior officer assumed the men were assembling to pursue a defeated enemy—until he learned that a retreat was underway. "Going to him for orders," the officer later recalled, "he informed me that we had been defeated on the left and must try to beat the enemy to New Berne."[9]

Burgwyn mounted his horse and led his men back toward the railroad—but was stopped by a cavalryman sounding the alarm: The Yankees were moving up the railroad in force just minutes away. Still calm, Burgwyn immediately dismissed his artillerists, who hurriedly limbered up their two pieces of field artillery and hauled them away. He ordered his small support force of cavalry to scatter and save themselves, and then he put out a scout, shifted direction and led his men toward the nearby Trent River. Once all of General Branch's army was safely across, the bridges could be burned to slow the Yankee advance. The scout soon returned with more bad news, however: The bridges had been set afire already and were now blazing. Burgwyn then turned his men toward Bryce's Creek, struck the trail left by Colonel Vance and the rest of the regiment and followed it to the creek. There he found the rest of the 26th near panic.[10]

A deep, swift waterway, Bryce's Creek was impossible to ford. When Colonel Vance and his command had reached the flooded creek, Vance had impulsively spurred his mount into the waters. Immediately unhorsed, he had disappeared beneath the surface of the dark waters. Some men on the other side had managed to rescue him, however, and had hoisted him to the opposite bank. When he had recovered from his near-drowning, the thoroughly soaked colonel had disappeared in search of boats. Some of the troops had tried to swim across, but when several drowned, the swimming had stopped. By the time Burgwyn arrived, hundreds of them were milling in confusion along the riverbank, waiting for the Yankees to arrive. Certain of capture, some had thrown their muskets into the creek.[11]

Burgwyn promptly instilled order. He called the regiment's officers together, reminded them that they were responsible for their men and ordered them to form ranks. Someone had found a three-man skiff, which Burgwyn put to work slowly ferrying the troops across the flooded river. Knowing he had to do more—a round trip in the skiff required ten minutes—he dispatched troops to look for more boats. The men rounded up two more, but before they returned a slave appeared on the opposite bank and hallooed across to the Confederates that he could help. He led them downstream to a larger boat, which could hold eighteen men, and the troops quickly put it into service. With his makeshift fleet in place, Burgwyn and another officer stood by the boats and ordered the men to file in, counting them as they got aboard.

A few panicky soldiers tried to force their way aboard, but backed up when Burgwyn drew his sword.[12]

For hours the boats were rowed back and forth across the dark waters as the men waited their turns, wondering if the Yankees would suddenly rush them from the rear. Burgwyn, who had been offered the first seat in the boat, insisted on being the last man across. "I will never cross until the last man of my regiment is over," he vowed. He kept his word, remaining by the boats and counting off the troops who filed past one by one. His actions instilled confidence in the bewildered soldiers, who suppressed their panic and obediently waited in line for their boat ride to safety. Privately, Burgwyn was fearful: He expected the enemy to appear at any moment. "When I arrived at Brice's creek my heart sank within me," he confided later. "An impassable creek was behind me & the enemy not far from us on our right." He kept his fears to himself. Instead, he projected cool professionalism and maintained rigid discipline. Near dusk, with all his men safely on the opposite bank, Burgwyn finally boarded a boat, towing his two horses, and crossed Bryce's Creek. He was the last man across. Minutes later, Federal skirmishers appeared on the opposite shore.[13]

Burgwyn had saved the regiment from disaster. After the narrow escape, the attitude of the men toward Burgwyn appeared to undergo a dramatic change. Even his critics had to admit that he had put the safety of his men before his own. Gradually, the resentment toward Burgwyn diminished—and was replaced by admiration. In New Bern, meanwhile, the defeat provoked panic. "There was great excitement in the city," recalled an eyewitness. "Citizens were flocking to the station; train after train was run up the road. . . . Meanwhile the booming of the cannon became louder, and presently several bombs screamed over our heads, completing the work of demoralization that had been going on in us all the morning." Later that day, triumphant Federal forces occupied the town and thoroughly pillaged it. Following up his victories at Hatteras, Roanoke Island and New Bern, Burnside moved a large force of troops to the Bogue Banks and directed a siege that forced the surrender of Fort Macon. The Federal navy promptly utilized Beaufort's harbor by establishing a principal naval base and refueling station there for the North Atlantic Blockading Squadron. New Bern, meanwhile, became a key Federal post and a staging area for Federal operations in the region. Except for the heavily defended Cape Fear area around Wilmington, Northern forces held all of coastal North Carolina by the spring of 1862. To prevent Federal advances into the interior of the state, thousands of Confederate troops were posted to the eastern region of the state—including the 26th North Carolina.[14]

Although many Southerners were unnerved by the loss of the North Carolina coast, the men of the 26th North Carolina were not demoralized by the defeat at New Bern. Instead of suffering shame, the regiment was praised for its disciplined conduct. "No troops could have behaved better than the Twenty-Sixth," exulted General Branch. Seeking a bright spot in a cloud of defeat, North Carolina newspapers celebrated the regiment's performance. One exaggerated newspaper account described Colonel Vance standing in his stirrups and shouting, "[We] can die but never surrender." Lieutenant Colonel Burgwyn, who was chagrined that the fighting did not come his way, was reported to have charged the enemy "very handsomely and effectively." In a letter home, Burgwyn observed: "You will see a great many accounts of the battle, but they are all exaggerated." Privately, he blamed the defeat on General Branch and Colonel Vance. Branch had done a poor job of deploying his forces, confided Burgwyn, who bluntly dismissed the popular Vance as "no sort of a commander." Vance would have disagreed with Burgwyn's assessment: "I believe," he wrote his wife, "they would every one follow me into the jaws of certain death if I lead the way." Although its baptism of fire ended in defeat, the regiment's reputation was boosted by reports of its conduct at New Bern. The Yankees had captured the regiment's tents, knapsacks, cooking equipment, overcoats and hundreds of weapons—but morale remained high. Posted to a camp near the hamlet of Kinston, the men of the 26th were welcomed into town by cheering residents who treated the troops to a home-cooked feast on the courthouse grounds.[15]

Escorting the regiment as it marched into Kinston was a new addition: the 26th North Carolina Regimental Band. Composed of Moravian musicians from Salem, North Carolina, the band had joined the regiment shortly before the battle of New Bern. It had been originally organized for another North Carolina unit, Wheeler's Battalion, but the battalion had been captured by the Yankees on Roanoke Island. Determined that his musicians would enter Confederate service, the band's director, Samuel T. Mickey, had traveled to New Bern to see if the band could join the 26th North Carolina. Mickey parked himself in a hotel lobby to wait for Colonel Vance. The dark-haired colonel soon strode in with a loaf of bread under each arm, and Mickey made his bid to join the 26th. "You are the very man I am looking for," Vance proclaimed, and the deal was done. Nattily attired in new gray uniforms adorned with brass buttons, the bandsmen joined the regiment at New Bern. There, quartered in tents adjacent to the officers, they were assigned their official duties: a morning performance to announce the changing of the guard, a nightly concert to entertain the troops, performance at Sunday inspection and play during brigade reviews.[16]

The adjustment to military life was jarring for the musicians. They drilled on a freshly cleared parade ground littered with stumps and roots—which caused some men to stumble or fall as they tried to coordinate marching and music. About the time they learned the drill, the entire band was almost captured when New Bern was overrun by the Yankees. They escaped, however, and rejoined the regiment at Kinston, where they provided a welcome boost in morale. Renowned for their long-standing musical tradition, the Moravians brightened regiment's daily routine and soon acquired a reputation as one of the best bands in Confederate service. "On nearly every evening there would come out to our camp numbers of ladies and gentlemen from Kinston," a band member would later recall, "and we were vain enough to imagine that our music was a large part of the attraction."[17]

At Kinston, the 26th was assigned to a brigade commanded by Brigadier General Samuel G. French, who replaced Brigadier General Branch. A few days later, French was transferred to Virginia, and command of the brigade went to Brigadier General Robert Ransom Jr. A thirty-four-year-old North Carolinian, Ransom was a West Pointer known for outspoken opinions and demanding drill. Soon the men of the 26th found themselves back on a parade ground, drilling for hours a day. Meanwhile, Colonel Vance issued a public plea for uniforms and camp equipment—and was rewarded with an outpouring of donations from the citizens of North Carolina. The Colonel also issued a public call for volunteers to replace the loss of troops at New Bern. Lured by the regiment's newfound reputation—and a $65 enlistment bounty—a wave of new recruits flooded the regiment.[18]

Among them were McKesson and "Sam" Blalock, who had come to the regiment from Caldwell County. McKesson Blalock, who called himself "Kesse," was a strapping twenty-six-year-old mountaineer; his companion was small and unusually good-looking. Both performed acceptably for about two months, but each harbored a secret life. Kesse was really a Unionist who had joined the army hoping for a chance to desert to Northern forces. After weeks of long, rigorous drill with no opportunity to join the Yankees, he slipped into the swamp one day and rubbed poison oak all over his body. The regimental surgeon misdiagnosed the resultant rash and issued Blalock a medical discharge. "Sam" Blalock then shocked the regiment by announcing she was really Kesse's wife, Malinda. "Finally to the great merriment of the whole army, she made herself known," a veteran would later recall. "Then, after having returned the bounty money, and replacing the suit of Dixie gray with a woman's gown, she went back in a happy mood and with an enlarged acquaintance, to her mountain home." Kesse went with her, leaving the regiment with a peculiar legacy.[19]

On April 21, 1862, the 26th North Carolina was officially reorganized. Gone was the illusion that the war would be quickly won. Like countless other regiments in the Federal and Confederate armies, the 26th North Carolina had been filled by men who had volunteered to serve twelve-month enlistments. As those enlistments neared expiration, Colonel Vance had encouraged his troops to do their patriotic duty as Southerners and reenlist for the duration of war. "Our colonel, Vance, was a very fluent and eloquent speaker, and was asked to visit the various regiments and address the men, bringing his [band] with him," one of the bandsmen would recall. "Of course we felt flattered and consented to blow as much war spirit into the men as we could." In the 26th, most soldiers did reenlist and were supported by new recruits. Reorganization meant the regiment was composed of volunteers who vowed to remain in uniform for the duration of the war—and one of their first acts was the election of regimental staff officers.[20]

Aided by his political skills, Colonel Vance won handily. John R. Lane retained his captaincy of Company G, but several companies received new captains. Lieutenant Colonel Burgwyn was reelected—but barely. Had the election occurred before Burgwyn's cool actions in the retreat at New Bern, he almost certainly would have been turned out of office. Enough men realized his demanding discipline had saved them, however, to provide the support he needed for reelection. "A large number of . . . officers were turned out & some of the best we had were thrown aside," Burgwyn wrote his parents. "I am secure of my position for the war."[21]

"Fellow soldiers," proclaimed Colonel Vance on June 19th, "it gives me pleasure to announce to you that we will leave for Richmond, Virginia, tomorrow morning by daylight to take part in the vital struggle now pending before its walls." The men of the regiment undoubtedly understood the full meaning of the Colonel's announcement: a struggle for the life of the fledgling

Confederacy was underway outside the Confederate capital—and they would be joining it. Led by Major General George B. McClellan, the 105,000-man Army of the Potomac—the principal Federal army in the East—had been transported from the Washington, D.C., area to Virginia's Peninsula and was now threatening Richmond from the east. General Joseph E. Johnston, commander of the Confederate army defending the Southern capital, had steadily withdrawn toward Richmond until the advancing Federal forces were within sight of the city's church spires. Then, at the battle of Seven Pines on May 31st, General Johnson had been seriously wounded, and command of the Confederate army had gone to President Davis's chief military advisor: General Robert E. Lee.[22]

After shoring up Richmond's defenses and reorganizing his forces into the newly named Army of Northern Virginia, Lee had developed an offensive strategy designed not to merely defend Richmond, but to destroy McClellan's huge Federal army—or at least force it to retreat. The son of Henry ("Light-Horse Harry") Lee—Revolutionary war hero, governor of Virginia, U.S. Congressman—Lee was a Mexican War veteran, a former superintendent at West Point and, according to some, had been the most capable officer in the prewar American army. Ironically, at the outbreak of war he had turned down an offer to command the Federal forces now facing him as enemies. He disliked secession, deplored slavery and had hoped to avoid military service when the Union had begun to unravel in early 1861. After prayerfully pondering his options, however, he had concluded that his first duty lay with his native Virginia, although he had refused to bear arms until Virginia had seceded and was threatened by invasion. Given command of Virginia's state troops, he had directed organization of Virginia's defenses, then had accepted a general's commission in the Confederate army. After holding brief field command in western Virginia, he had been dispatched to strengthen coastal defenses in South Carolina and Georgia until recalled to Richmond to act as the president's military chief of staff. Lee had proven to be so essential that Davis had immediately turned to him when in need of a new commander. Combined with a series of serious Confederate losses in the war's Western Theater, the imposing Federal advance on Richmond seemed to threaten impending destruction of the Southern nation. By late June, however, Lee was prepared to strike McClellan's huge, lumbering army in what would become known as the Seven Days Campaign, and among the troops summoned for the offensive was Ransom's Brigade—which included the 26th North Carolina.[23]

Bolstered by reorganization, strict training and their new reputation, the men of the regiment were eager and confident. The fighting which lay ahead might determine the fate of the Confederacy, believed Lieutenant Henry Clay Albright, a nineteen-year-old officer who had left college to join the Chatham Boys. "We leave in the morning at daybreak for Richmond to participate in the great battles soon to be fought in that section," he wrote home the night before departure. "Col. Vance addressed us this evening under arms a few touching remarks and I don't think I divert far from the truth when I say that I felt like rushing headlong to victory or death."[24]

In Virginia, some men encountered death quickly. After a wearying train ride to Petersburg and on to Richmond, the 26th and the rest of Ransom's Brigade joined Major General Benjamin Huger's division several miles east of Richmond near a rural community called King's School House. Their first night on the battlefield, June 25th, the troops were ordered to relieve another regiment and moved forward in the night through dense woods and swamp. Hampered by darkness, the regiment unknowingly deployed only a few paces from a line of Federal troops waiting in ambush. "We took our position on one side of a rail fence and hedgerow," a survivor would recall. "The enemy was in line on the other side . . . biding their time, and as soon as the 26th Regiment had quieted down in entire ignorance of the presence of the enemy, [the Yankees] suddenly thrust their guns through the fence and opened fire. So close were they to our men that the beards of some were singed." Many of the men panicked and scrambled away, but three companies stood firm. The regiment recovered from the shock attack—three men were killed and eight were wounded—and helped drive out the enemy the next day. During the following days, the 26th was engaged in several other "heavy skirmishes," which, one soldier groused, would have been considered "battles" in North Carolina.[25]

An even deadlier test of fire came five days later on July 1, 1862, when Ransom's Brigade was rushed into action at the bloody battle of Malvern Hill. For six days Lee had battered McClellan's army with uncoordinated but punishing assaults, driving the huge Federal army back down the Peninsula in retreat. Hoping one more assault would destroy or severely cripple McClellan's army before it could withdraw, Lee ordered an attack on the Federal defensive line atop Malvern Hill, a strongly fortified slope defended by more than 200 pieces of field artillery. Swampland and ravines on the slope's flanks funneled the attacking Confederates up the front of the rise through an open area that became a killing field. Sheets of artillery fire tore through the Confederate ranks as brigade after brigade tried—and failed—to break the Federal line. It was near twilight when Ransom's Brigade was ordered up, and the 26th North Carolina was the last regiment of the brigade to go into action. Already the Seven Days Campaign had exposed the men of the regiment to battlefield horrors exceeding anything they had seen at New Bern. "In places the Yankees were lying almost in heaps," Burgwyn would later report. "Their wounded had not even been moved & groans & lamentations filled the putrid air."[26]

As they moved toward the action, the troops of the 26th flushed a rabbit from the brush. It bounded wildly in retreat as the men whooped and laughed. "Go it, Mollie Cottontail," Vance yelled. "If I had no more reputation to lose than you have, I would run too." Marching forward along a country lane, as artillery shells fell around them like pelting rain, the regiment took a wrong turn. As they moved forward in search of the front lines, the 26th was confronted by a stream of panicky soldiers, retreating toward the rear and babbling that their regiments had been "cut to pieces." Adding to the confusion, Federal artillery shells began bursting in the treetops, dropping large, leafy limbs to the ground. Determined to get the regiment to the front, Burgwyn drew his sword, grabbed a fleeing skulker and threatened to kill him unless he guided the 26th into battle. More afraid of Burgwyn than the Yankees, the soldier obeyed. As they neared Malvern Hill, the sound of the massed Federal artillery grew louder. The roar reminded Burgwyn of a stormy surf. "I can liken nothing to it," he would later recall. "It seemed as if the discharges of artillery were like the angry surf beating upon the beach, except the intervals between the discharges were much shorter than between the beating of the waves."[27]

It was dark by the time they reached the front, which was eerily lit by flashes from the Federal artillery fire. Formed in a line of battle, the regiment advanced at the quick-step through the darkness. About three quarters of a mile from the Federal line, they were ordered to charge the flashing guns. It was a chaotic assault. "[We] could not distinguish friend from foe," Burgwyn would recall, "& judged of the enemy's position solely by the flashes of his cannons & they were fast enough not to leave any doubt." As the regiment charged over the bodies of the fallen Southerners who had gone before them, many of the wounded sat up, waved their hats and cheered. Several hundred yards from the blazing Federal line, the 26th was ordered to halt and open fire. "[We] were pouring volley after volley into them with dreadful effect," a junior officer would later report. Suddenly, shouts came from the front, warning that friendly troops were lying in the line of fire. The regiment ceased fire immediately, and the advance stalled. Moments later, the men were commanded to lie down. The order somehow failed to reach one company, whose troops continued the advance until turned back within fifteen yards of the blazing line. Miraculously, they suffered only a handful of casualties before they too took to the ground. As the Federal artillery swept the field inches above their heads, Vance and Burgwyn kept all the men on their bellies, holding their fire as ordered.[28]

Lying among his troops, Burgwyn fished his watch out of his pocket and peered at it in the darkness, trying to count the enemy artillery fire. By his estimate, about 44 guns were firing every minute. The men of the 26th hunkered down on the darkened slopes of Malvern Hill, lying among the dead and wounded, and waited for orders to advance. Exhausted by marching, charging and the stress of battle, some men fell asleep. "I was so completely broken down that I never slept sounder than I did there amongst the dead and wounded," remembered a survivor. The order to resume the charge never came. At about ten o'clock that night, the Federal batteries suddenly ceased fire. An ear-ringing silence settled over the battlefield, broken only by the moans of the wounded.[29]

Burgwyn sent a courier back to General Ransom for instructions, and at about 11:30 the regiment was ordered to quietly withdraw. Like well-trained veterans, the men of the 26th silently obeyed. As the regiment left the field, Burgwyn could hear wounded Southern troops crying in the night: "3rd Alabama come & take me off; 2nd Louisiana give me some water." He appointed a detail to remove the 26th's wounded and did not leave the field until every man alive in his regiment had been taken to safety.[30]

To his frustration, Burgwyn later learned that the report of friendly troops in the front was a mistake: Nothing lay between the regiment and the enemy when the 26th was ordered to the ground. Optimistically, Burgwyn believed his regiment could have broken the death-dealing Federal line where others had failed. However, the order to halt may have spared the 26th the carnage that befell other regiments. Malvern Hill produced some of the war's highest casualties to date—more than 8,500—but the 26th North Carolina came off the bloody field more than 90 percent intact. Such light casualties amid a bloodbath spurred some muttering about "cowardice" from other regiments, but the men of the 26th noted that their dead lay nearer the Federal line than those of any other regiment. Colonel Vance, who considered the Confederate assault at Malvern Hill "murderous and ill-advised," believed his troops had "acted gloriously." Burgwyn, however, eventually concluded that he and his men had narrowly avoided slaughter. "I can only attribute my escape to an all merciful Providence," he wrote home.[31]

When morning came, McClellan's army abandoned the field and resumed its retreat back down the Peninsula to waiting troop transports. Lee's army followed, sweeping up Yankee prisoners of war and gathering discarded arms and equipment. "The track of their retreat for 15 miles is strewn with immense amounts of clothing of every description, knapsacks, canteens, guns, ammunition, provisions, etc. etc.," a soldier in the 26th wrote home. "Were I to describe the roads with the destruction, I would hardly be believed. The Yankees are daily coming in, by scores and hundreds to our men, saying that they will not fight any longer." The Federal army had escaped destruction, but Richmond had been rescued, and throughout the Confederacy, Lee and his army were celebrated as the saviors of the South. "When this bloody war will end, is for our enemies to say," observed an officer in the 26th. "We will, by the help of God, contend for our rights and maintain them. As a good old lady said the other day, until our enemies let us alone, we must 'Trust in God and our Southern boys.'"[32]

Though the 26th had suffered relatively light casualties in the Seven Days Campaign—six dead, forty wounded, twenty-five missing—the men had witnessed the slaughter of war firsthand, and the experience was sobering. "The dead reminded me more of the sheaves behind the reaper . . . making it the most horrible sight you can behold," reported one member of the 26th. Recalled another: "In one piece of pinewoods the trees had been cut off by the shells as though the ground had been cleared. It seemed miraculous that any one should have escaped annihilation. Twenty dead bodies lay together awaiting burial, and within a short distance, seven hundred more were in the same condition, the enemy having left them for our men to put away."[33]

One who escaped death at Malvern Hill was John R. Lane, although he experienced a narrow escape. Lane, then a captain, lay on the field with the rest of the regiment in the darkness. During the night he dozed off. When he awakened, he discovered the men on both sides of him had been killed. Harry Burgwyn was also affected by the reality of war. After Malvern Hill, his letters home no longer expressed a longing for combat. "I saw many instances of the battle on Wednesday," Burgwyn solemnly wrote home. "Trees struck by balls

& cut off by shells & solid shot, guns & equipment & bits of clothing, & finally unburied ghastly bodies of dead Yankees met our gaze at every step. . . . I often wished that Lincoln & his cabinet could behold some of the scenes to be met with at every step we took. Not that I believe it would have any such effect upon them as would make them stop the war, but it could but influence them if they were men."[34]

A few weeks after the Seven Days Campaign, Colonel Vance left the regiment—and ignited a chain of events that eventually placed the 26th North Carolina on the road to Gettysburg. Vance had been elected Governor of North Carolina. He had been nominated for the office in June by North Carolina's newly formed Conservative Party, and with little public politicking he had successfully defeated the Confederate Party candidate, a Charlotte railroad executive named William J. Johnston. The originator and mastermind of Vance's campaign was William W. Holden, the editor of Raleigh's influential *North Carolina Standard,* who promoted Vance as a "patriot, soldier and statesman" too busy defending the homeland to engage in politics. Aided by the army vote, Vance won by a landslide. He was soon packing his bags for Raleigh and an inauguration ceremony that would include a performance by the 26th North Carolina Regimental Band.[35]

He resigned from the regiment in mid-August, while the 26th and the rest of Ransom's Brigade were still encamped near Richmond. His farewell ceremony included presentation of a ceremonial sword from the 26th's officers and a rousing departure speech. "It is fight to the end," Vance urged the men. "All you can expect is War! War! War!" Lieutenant Colonel Burgwyn, meanwhile, was back home on medical leave with what appeared to be a bout of dysentery. As second-in-command of the regiment, Burgwyn had every reason to be confident that army policy would result in his promotion to colonel and regimental commander. Instead, however, Burgwyn received startling news: General Ransom appeared ready to appoint a new commander from outside the regiment.[36]

The General's choice was Colonel Thomas Ruffin Jr., who was the son of a prominent North Carolina judge and former U.S. Congressman. Before leaving for Raleigh, Vance had warned the regiment's junior officers of Ransom's plans. In response, they had promptly formed a committee and had submitted a slate of recommended officers to Ransom—with Burgwyn's name heading the list as colonel. Ransom was adamant: He wanted no "boy colonels" in his brigade. Alarmed, some of the officers dispatched letters to Burgwyn, advising him to return to camp quickly. "Please come to us as quickly as you can," urged Captain Joseph J. Young, the regiment's assistant quartermaster. "I wish for you to resist to the last this usurpation of power. I am too angry to act."[37]

Anger did not stymie Burgwyn. He promptly left for camp—and also enlisted his father's powerful political clout. Henry Senior contacted influential friends in the army, indignantly denouncing the "decided slur" upon his son, and then headed to Richmond for a personal conference with the Confederate Secretary of War. Back in camp, Burgwyn sat down face-to-face with General Ransom, who admitted that he did not want a twenty-year-old colonel in his brigade and had taken the issue all the way to President Davis. The President, he acknowledged, had advised him that the law protected Burgwyn's promotion. "So . . . you are Colonel of the 26th [Regiment]," Ransom told Burgwyn.[38]

Although the dispute was settled, Ransom and Burgwyn were left with a difficult arrangement: A youthful officer had triumphed in a command struggle with his superior. Burgwyn politely proposed a way out. Would General Ransom entertain a request to transfer the 26th North Carolina to another brigade? Ransom recognized Burgwyn's proposal as an easy solution to an awkward dilemma and promptly accepted it. Within the week Colonel Henry K. Burgwyn Jr. and the 26th North Carolina were transferred. Some members of the regiment welcomed the news. Declared one private: "[We] will git oute from under olde Ranssom cond found him." On August 26, 1862, the regimental band played a spirited tune as the assembled troops of the 26th watched Ransom's Brigade march away to a new station. "General Ransom told us goodbye as he rode past," noted one soldier. On the same day the 26th North Carolina received orders to march south to Petersburg, where the regiment would join Pettigrew's Brigade.[39]

When Colonel Burgwyn stood before Brigadier General James Johnston Pettigrew, he met a match in intellect and youthful accomplishment. Dark-haired, dark-eyed, lean and immaculately groomed, the thirty-four-year-old North Carolinian cut a dashing figure. Recently exchanged as a prisoner-of-war, Pettigrew was still sore from wounds he had received back in the summer at the battle of Seven Pines. Like Burgwyn, Pettigrew was an alumnus of the University of North Carolina—which he had attended at age fourteen—and, like Burgwyn, Pettigrew displayed ample evidence of genius. Family told tales of his poring over the works in his father's 3,000-volume library as a mere four-year-old. Raised on his family's Bonarva Plantation in Tyrell County, North Carolina, Pettigrew received a Southern gentleman's upbringing much like Burgwyn's. Despite a sickly childhood, Pettigrew became an accomplished fencer and boxer. He was also a mathematics genius. Upon his graduation from college—where he was class valedictorian—Pettigrew was invited by President James K. Polk and U.S. Navy Secretary John Mason to become professor of astronomy at the National Observatory. He accepted and quickly attained proficiency as a professional astronomer; however, the job bored him and he resigned after six months. With equal ease he acquired an education in the law, joined a prestigious Charleston law firm for a while, and then in 1849 left for further study in Europe.[40]

There he promptly mastered six languages, including Hebrew and Arabic, became an accomplished pianist, studied Prussian and French military science and immersed himself in the culture of Spain, which was his favorite country. He viewed the Spanish as Europe's Southerners: friendly, courageous and chivalrous. He grew Spanish-style whiskers, dressed like a Spanish nobleman and adopted Latin manners, all of which he considered appropriate for a Southern cavalier. Back in Charleston, he gained prominence as an attorney and, at age thirty, was given $50,000 by a family friend so that he could devote himself to public service. He almost died ministering to yellow fever victims in Charleston, was elected to the state legislature and stirred a nationwide debate with an official report condemning proposals to reopen the foreign slave trade. Pettigrew believed Southern slavery had evolved as a relatively benevolent institution compared to slavery in other nations, and he feared a renewed slave trade would harm both Southern slaves and Southern society. A second trip to Europe enabled him to publish a book on Spanish culture, and to conclude that war with the North was not only likely, but would be bloody and desperate—a prophecy that caused some Southerners to brand him "eccentric & crack-brained." As a world traveler and serious student of foreign cultures, Pettigrew concluded that radical Northern politicians were much like the Prussian militarists he had met in Berlin: quite willing to launch a war to achieve their political goals. He believed that anti-Southern Northerners—newly organized as Republicans—would eventually seize control of the Federal government some day soon and then provoke war with the South.[41]

Pettigrew prepared to meet the coming war like a Spanish knight of old. He studied European military theory, mastered the elements of military engineering and artillery and was elected colonel of a Charleston militia regiment. When the crisis at Fort Sumter erupted, South Carolina Governor Francis Pickens sent Pettigrew and his troops to seize the abandoned Federal post at Castle Pinckney. Soon afterwards, with war underway, he was elected colonel of the 22nd North Carolina then organizing in Raleigh. Within months, he was offered a brigadier's commission, but he considered himself undeserving of "so flattering a position" and turned it down. His humility impressed President Davis, and when the commission was offered a second time, Pettigrew was ordered to accept it. At Seven Pines, on the first day of his first battle, he was shot in the throat and left for dead on the battlefield, where he was shot again and bayoneted. He somehow survived his wounds and months of captivity in a Northern prison. Exchanged and back in uniform, he was assigned command of a new brigade—which now included the 26th North Carolina. By the time he met young Colonel Burgwyn, Pettigrew was viewed by close associates as "the truest—the purest and the bravest of men—a fine scholar, and amongst the noblest of patriots."[42]

Pettigrew's Brigade was composed entirely of North Carolina troops. It included four regiments—the 26th, the 44th, the 47th and the 52nd—and at year's end would also include the 11th North Carolina. Pettigrew's Brigade was posted to Camp French near Petersburg, Virginia, and charged with protecting the vital railway line into North Carolina. Although some troops in the 26th yearned for a return to North Carolina, others were relieved to be posted away from the swampland of the coast. Confessed one soldier: "I had a heape druther stay here than in the eastern parte of North Carolina in among them frog pons." If the men of the 26th were glad to serve under one of North Carolina's famous sons, Pettigrew had good reason to welcome the 26th to his brigade. Not only was the 26th one of the largest regiments in Confederate service—boasting a peak strength of more than 800 troops—it was also recognized as one of the best-trained. Like Burgwyn, Pettigrew advocated constant drill. He also exercised command with an obvious cheerfulness. At his direction, the 26th's band was kept busy playing at parade and serenading the troops at night. "The whole regiment is marched out into the field & the Colonel inspects one company after the other while we play," Musician J. Edward Peterson wrote home. "This takes about ¾ of an hour. In the evening at ½ past 5 dress parade comes off. At this we play about 4 pieces. The regiment is formed into line and we march down the line in slow time, coming back in quick time. This closes the performances of the day." Pettigrew seemed pleased with the 26th Band. "General Pettigrew [became] very kindly disposed toward us," reported one bandsman, "and gave us the piano music of The Rifle Regiment Quickstep, which he . . . regarded as his favorite piece."[43]

While posted to Camp French, Captain Lane was promoted to lieutenant colonel to fill the vacancy left by Burgwyn's advancement. Burgwyn had hoped second-in-command would go to Captain Oscar Rand, who had been captured at the battle of New Bern but recently freed in a prisoner swap. Lane held seniority over Rand, however, and was also favored by the troops. They viewed Lane as one of their own: He had reached lieutenant colonel by rising through the ranks from corporal. Apparently unaffected by his achievement, he seemed devoid of the pompous pride that afflicted some officers. Born on Independence Day in 1835, Lane was descended from one of North Carolina's leading Revolutionary War patriots, but he had been raised in a farming family of modest means. Although his formal education was meager, he was intelligent, resourceful and articulate. A devout Christian, he was respected within the regiment for his fairness, sincerity and devotion to duty. Despite his preference for another officer, Burgwyn soon viewed his new second-in-command as indispensable.[44]

The regiment spent the next nine months shifting back and forth between Petersburg and sites in eastern North Carolina, sometimes providing detached companies for guard duty, expeditions and military actions. On November 2, 1862, back in North Carolina, the 26th engaged Federal forces led by General John G. Foster at Rawls' Mill. In March of 1863, Pettigrew's Brigade was assigned a key role in General D.H. Hill's campaign to retake New Bern from the Federals. Colonel Burgwyn and the 26th were charged with assaulting a well-defended Federal earthwork called Fort Anderson. At daylight on March 14th, the regiment drove back the Federal pickets and then stood by to make the main assault after Confederate field artillery bombarded the fortification. The plan went awry, however, when artillery ammunition proved defective, and two of Pettigrew's four field pieces were disabled. Federal gunboats soon unleashed a ferocious return fire, and without artillery support Pettigrew reluctantly decided to abort the assault. "We were drawn up in line in an open field in full view of the town and stood the shells from five boats for six hours," reported Captain Isaac A. Jarratt of Company C. The attempt to recapture New Bern failed, but Pettigrew had high praise for the 26th. "The 26th had been in waiting since daylight," he advised Hill afterwards, "and would have [captured the enemy position] in five minutes. . . . I cannot too highly express my admiration of the manner in which they stood the furious shelling of the enemy without flinching."[45]

In late March, Hill shifted his forces to the river town of Washington, North Carolina, which was also occupied by Federal forces, and placed the town's Federal garrison under a siege. On April 11th, the 26th Regiment was engaged in action at Blount's Creek, where the regiment helped turn back a Federal relief column dispatched to raise the siege. After a two-week campaign failed to take the town, Hill finally withdrew. "The place could have been taken easily," observed one of the regiment's officers, "but as the Yankee commander would not let the women & children out Gen. Hill was unwilling to shell it." Privately, Colonel Burgwyn was critical of Hill's tactics at Washington. "He set out without any definite plan," Burgwyn confided to his father. "He should have made up his mind to storm the place at once, or he should have been prepared to undertake a regular siege." Despite the lack of victories, the regiment had enhanced its reputation in the months of campaign. However, the numerous marches, bad weather and scanty rations had tested the troops. "Times ar very hard," one soldier wrote home. "[We] cant hardly Get a nuff to eat. I have Saw the Devil since I come from home, marching through the mud and wading creeks. . . . I am gitting tired of Old Bacon and Crackers." As they moved around the rim of Federally occupied North Carolina, the troops of the 26th also witnessed the destruction sometimes wrought by invading Northern troops. "The Yankees reduced Hamilton to ashes," reported Lieutenant Henry Albright, "destroyed any amount of property in and about Williamston and ran off large numbers of slaves. It is said they damaged Martin County $100,000." The enemy activity kept the regiment constantly on the march. Company C's Captain Jarratt complained that Pettigrew's Brigade was dispatched any time a regional commander got the jitters. "Our brigade is on halfway ground," he griped, "and every time [they] get scared, away we go to help them."[46]

From his headquarters in an abandoned North Carolina church, Colonel Burgwyn penned his parents a description of the regiment's on-call activity: "Much to my surprise as I was enjoying my morning nap this morning an order came round to leave in the direction of Greenville in half an hour. I jumped up, dressed, [ate] my breakfast, mounted my horse & set the Rgt. in motion at the appointed time. The cause of this order was that the Yankees had come out to the Cross Roads near Washington." In one long stretch of hard campaigning, the 26th stayed on the march for six weeks. Burgwyn and his regiment were exposed to punishing weather, meager rations and—he groused in a letter home—"6 weeks . . . without a change of underclothing." By the end of April, he calculated, "we have marched 300 miles over the worst kind of swampy roads, fording swamp after swamp, subsisting on one pound of meal or crackers a day & a half pound of meat." In his journal, Burgwyn penned a record of fatigue: "All of us exceedingly tired. For about 2 nights I had not had any sleep & had been working hard all the time. In march last night I would fall asleep on my horse & even when I got down to walk I would nod." Everyone—officers as well as enlisted men—suffered from lice. "I myself (your son) found one upon the outside of my pantaloons," Burgwyn admitted to his mother. But amid the hardships, Burgwyn believed, his men had proved their mettle. "[The] men [endured] all this," he proudly observed, "without a murmur or complaint or any criticism except that so much hardship should be borne & so little fruit produced." The soldiers of the 26th North Carolina had come a long way, he realized, from the days when mere drill produced murmurs of mutiny. "I feel very certain," Burgwyn vowed to his father, "that we can whip any number of Yankees."[47]

On May 1, 1863, Burgwyn received an order that made the prospect of fighting Yankees seem extremely likely. While in the field near Kinston, the troops of the 26th were ordered to cook rations and prepare to leave for Virginia, where the battle of Chancellorsville was underway. The order came as no surprise to Burgwyn: Major General Joseph Hooker, the current commander of the Army of the Potomac, had been readying an attack on Lee's army, which was positioned near Fredericksburg. Although Hooker boasted that he commanded the "finest army on the planet," Burgwyn believed the Yankees would suffer a devastating defeat. "Lee will administer to him a most tremendous thrashing," Burgwyn predicted in a letter home. Such success would allow Lee to invade the North, Burgwyn believed, in search of a great victory that would end the war. If his predictions proved correct, Burgwyn advised his parents, Lee would need to strengthen his army—and the call for reinforcements would almost certainly include Pettigrew's Brigade and the 26th North Carolina. "So I expect to see Old Virginny once more," Burgwyn wrote home. He was right. By late afternoon on May 1st, Burgwyn and his men were on railroad cars rolling toward Virginia.[48]

CHAPTER 3

We Are on Our Way

It was a gorgeous day for a parade. Julius Lineback could look up into the Virginia sky that Monday afternoon, June 15, 1863, and see nothing but cloudless blue expanse. Virginia was gripped by a summer heat wave, and it was unusually hot, but skies were cheerfully bright, and the men of the 26th North Carolina were equipped with crisp new uniforms. They stood in line— more than 800 of them—on a field just outside Fredericksburg. They had been in Virginia six weeks, awaiting a momentous campaign. Now, in just a few moments they would receive orders to march, following the rest of Lee's army northwestward to the Shenandoah Valley and parts unknown. Already, the drummers had sounded the "long roll," calling the troops to marching order. Lineback stood with the other members of the regimental band, his cornet in hand, ready to play.[1]

At twenty-eight, he was skinny and a bit on the small side, but so far he had been able to meet the demands of army life. For awhile he had even carried the E-flat bass—a tuba-like instrument that had dwarfed him—until he had been able to switch to the cornet. He was not a soldier and did not pretend to be one. In civilian life he had been a bookkeeper, but he loved music, and he had eagerly joined the regimental band—which had allowed him to do his patriotic duty while making music. It was obvious that a hard campaign lay ahead, but he had already seen hard times. During battle the bandsmen were detailed as litter bearers and hospital attendants, and at battlefields like Malvern Hill he had seen gore and suffering aplenty. If this new campaign led to more fighting, the band would be there to do its duty as needed. Meanwhile, he and the other bandsmen would give the troops the proper musical send-off.[2]

Since their arrival in Virginia, the soldiers of the 26th North Carolina had been awaiting the order to march. They had detrained in Richmond

after an unnerving rail trip from North Carolina—a train wreck en route
had killed two men in the regiment and had injured several others. From
Richmond they had been dispatched northward to Hanover Junction to
protect a vital section of railroad. There they had spent most of the month
of May guarding the tracks. Meanwhile, at the battle of Chancellorsville,
Lee had given Hooker's Federal army the "tremendous thrashing" that
Burgwyn had predicted. "From all I can learn the battle of the Wilderness
or Chancellorsville was the most glorious victory of the war," Burgwyn
wrote home. It had been costly victory, however: General Thomas J. ("Stonewall") Jackson, Lee's irreplaceable "right arm," had suffered the wound
that led to his death by pneumonia. In early June, after weeks of guard
duty, the 26th had been moved to Hamilton's Crossing near Fredericksburg, where Pettigrew's Brigade joined Lee's Army of Northern Virginia. As
Burgwyn had suspected, Lee was strengthening his army for an invasion of
the North.[3]

Looking beyond the glow of success at Chancellorsville, Lee knew that
the South had to do something to win the war soon or final defeat was
inevitable. In the year since he had driven McClellan's army away from
Richmond—while the 26th North Carolina had marched and counter-
marched in eastern North Carolina—Lee had saved the South and gained
the attention of the world with a succession of brilliant victories over
Northern forces. In August of 1862, he had boldly marched his army into
northern Virginia, where he had scored a dramatic victory over Major General John Pope and another Federal army at the battle of Second Manassas.
Following up on his success, he had marched his army northward in September, hoping to win a major victory on Northern soil. Instead, he had
been stopped in Maryland at the battle of Sharpsburg, where he had fought
General McClellan and the Army of the Potomac to a standstill on the
war's bloodiest day. He had managed to save his army from destruction, but
his invasion plans were shattered, and he had been forced to retreat back to
Virginia.[4]

Three months later, however, he had inflicted a staggering defeat on the
Army of the Potomac and its new commander—Major General Ambrose E.
Burnside—at the battle of Fredericksburg. Afterwards, Burnside had been
replaced by Hooker, who had launched another Federal offensive against Lee
in the spring of 1863. Following a well-devised strategy, Hooker had sought

to envelop and destroy Lee's army in the forest thickets west of Fredericksburg. "My plans are perfect," Hooker had boasted, "and when I start to carry them out, may God have mercy on General Lee, for I will have none." The end result of Hooker's grand plan, however, was the three-day contest at Chancellorsville—and Hooker too was left defeated and disgraced by Lee and his army.[5]

The battle had bolstered the Army of Northern Virginia's image of invincibility. By mid-June of 1863, Lee was feared in the North, revered in the South and respected abroad. Admiration for his military genius was matched by appreciation of his character. "General Lee is, almost without exception, the handsomest man of his age I ever saw," reported a British military observer. "He is fifty-six years old, tall, broad-shouldered, very well made, well set up—a thorough soldier in appearance; and his manners are most courteous and full of dignity. He is a perfect gentleman in every respect. . . . He has none of the small vices, such as smoking, drinking, chewing or swearing, and his bitterest enemy has never accused him of any of the greater ones."[6]

Unaffected by such acclaim, Lee could evaluate the South's chances of survival with the seasoned judgment of a uniquely gifted strategist—and what he foresaw was probable doom. The war had gone poorly for the South in the Western Theater. Kentucky and most of Tennessee had been overrun by Northern forces, who also controlled most of the Mississippi River—the artery of the Southern heartland. On the lower end of the waterway, New Orleans was occupied by Northern troops, who also held the river port of Memphis to the north. In between, the key Confederate bastion of Vicksburg was now besieged by a powerful Federal army commanded by Major General Ulysses S. Grant. If Vicksburg fell, Federal forces would control the Mississippi, and the South would be split. Meanwhile, an increasingly effective Federal naval blockade was slowly sealing one Southern seaport after another, and choking off the importation of vitally needed arms and equipment. Most damaging, perhaps, was the war's unprecedented casualties—13,000 Confederate losses at Chancellorsville alone—which bled the South of its fighting men.[7]

It was just a matter of time, Lee believed, before the North's superior manpower and resources overwhelmed the hard-fighting South. "We should not, therefore, conceal from ourselves that our resources in men are constantly diminishing," Lee wrote President Davis on June 10th, "and the disproportion in this respect between us and our enemies, if they continue united in their efforts to subjugate us, is steadily augmenting." Unless he took the offense, Lee argued, he and his army would eventually be forced back within the defenses of Richmond, where the Army of Northern Virginia—and the Confederacy—would be systematically whittled to death by the overpowering resources of the North. "I think it is worth a trial to prevent such a catastrophe," he wrote Secretary of War James A. Seddon in early June. To win at all, Lee believed, the South had to win soon—and that meant taking the war to the North.[8]

Grave risks were involved: The North had the manpower to confront Lee's army in Maryland or Pennsylvania while still protecting Washington. Or Hooker could simply ignore Lee's invasion, trust Washington's formidable defenses to protect the capital, and launch a quick strike on Richmond while Lee's army was moving northward. There was also the possibility that Lee's army might be trapped in the North and destroyed. Lee believed that risks were unavoidable, however, and that the best way to protect Richmond was to draw the enemy away. He counted on the Lincoln administration to continue its policy of protecting Washington at all costs. Threatening Washington or Philadelphia, he believed, would lure Hooker and his army away from Richmond and out of Virginia. Taking the war to the North would give war-weary Virginia desperately needed relief—and would allow him to better supply his poorly rationed army.[9]

Lee's troops could barely survive on the scanty rations available to the army by mid-1863. They had to constantly forage for additional food, and Virginia's farms were severely depleted. Even the once-bountiful Shenandoah Valley had been gleaned in many places by Northern and Southern forces. Taking his army to the rich farmland of Pennsylvania would solve the immediate need of feeding the troops. His men could live off the land during the campaign, and army quartermasters would likely round up a lot of beef for future rations. Observed one of Lee's officers: "The hungry hosts of Israel did not look across Jordan to the vine-clad hills of Canaan with more longing eyes than did Lee's braves contemplate the yellow grain-fields of Pennsylvania beyond the Potomac." At the very least, invading the North would disrupt Federal plans for a summer offensive against Richmond and would clear the Shenandoah Valley of Federal forces. Those alone were worthwhile campaign goals.[10]

A successful invasion, moreover, might spark a financial panic in the North and strengthen the growing Northern peace movement. Capture of Washington, Philadelphia or even a state capital like Harrisburg might be a mortal blow to the Northern war effort. The North had the power to wage a long and bloody war, but did it have the will? The sight of armed men in gray and butternut on the streets of Washington or Philadelphia might have a major demoralizing effect on Northerners. So might a major battlefield victory on Northern soil. A Confederate victory like Chancellorsville or Fredericksburg in the North might at least spur Great Britain and France to declare official recognition of the Confederacy. If Hooker's army could be routed again and pursued toward Washington, a panicked North might even force the Lincoln administration to call for a negotiated peace. Then this bloodiest of all American wars could end, and Southern nationhood might be assured.[11]

To prepare for the proposed invasion, Lee strengthened the Army of Northern Virginia with fresh troops and reorganized it into three army corps, each consisting of three divisions. The First Corps was commanded by Lieutenant General James Longstreet; Second Corps, which formerly belonged to Stonewall Jackson, was headed by Lieutenant General Richard Ewell; and Third Corps was placed under the command of Lieutenant General Ambrose Powell Hill. In an attempt to provide a greater concentration of firepower, the army's artillery was also restructured, giving each corps five battalions of artillery. Lee's cavalry corps, commanded by Major General J.E.B. Stuart— whom Lee called the "eyes of the army"— was boosted to a troop strength of about 10,000. The reorganization created some weaknesses: Ewell and Hill were new to corps command; three division commanders and a handful of brigade commanders were newly promoted; and, most obvious, Stonewall Jackson was gone. Even so, the Army of Northern Virginia was more formidable than ever. Strengthened and restructured, it numbered about 75,000 troops and stood in peak fighting condition. "There were never such men in an army before," Lee observed. "They will go anywhere and do anything if properly led." They would be led into the North, Lee finally decided, and there he hoped they would win the war.[12]

"Taking all things into consideration," Colonel Burgwyn wrote his father on May 21st, "my opinion is that 6 weeks will find Gen. Lee's army in Maryland. I must confess it seems to me that it would be quite as well, if we are going to lose Vicksburg, to concentrate everything in the valley of Va. & advance upon Philadelphia." Burgwyn shared Lee's confidence in the army. "I believe they will compare favorably with those of the Romans or of Napoleon's Old Guard," he told his father. "The army that he has now can not be whipped by anything in Yankeedom."[13]

On Wednesday, June 3rd, the lead division of Longstreet's Corps left Lee's Fredericksburg lines and marched northwestward. Ewell's Corps followed the next day. Lee planned to concentrate most of his forces at Culpeper Court House, which was located about halfway between Fredericksburg and the Shenandoah Valley. At the proper time he would slip his army into the Shenandoah Valley, neutralize the Federal forces posted there, and then— using the Blue Ridge Mountains to shield his movements—advance across the Maryland panhandle into Pennsylvania. Hill's Corps, designated last to leave, would remain behind at Fredericksburg as a decoy to deceive Hooker into believing Lee's army was still in line. When the other two corps were properly positioned in the Valley, Hill's Corps would join them. By then, Lee hoped, his army would have the jump on the Federals.[14]

On Sunday, June 7th, troops of Pettigrew's Brigade boarded trains and were taken to Hamilton's Crossing five miles south of Fredericksburg. One regiment, the 44th North Carolina, remained at Hanover Junction to guard the railroad, leaving four regiments in the brigade: the 11th North Carolina, the 26th, the 47th and the 52nd. Pettigrew's Brigade joined the Army of Northern Virginia in Hill's III Corps and was assigned to Major General Henry Heth's division. Heth—known to friends as "Harry"—was a thirty-seven-year-old career army officer with a reputation for courage and, according to some, a tendency toward impulsiveness. An affable, well-mannered Virginian, he had graduated last in his class at West Point sixteen years earlier. He had missed service in the Mexican War but had fought Indians on the Western frontier and had risen to captain in the prewar army. Upon entering Confederate service, he had quickly received a brigadier's commission. After commands in Kentucky and western Virginia, he had been granted a brigade in Lee's army on the eve of Chancellorsville. He had handled his command admirably in the battle, and when the army was reorganized Heth had been promoted to divisional command. Hill's Corps consisted of three divisions: Heth's Division; one commanded by Major General William Dorsey Pender; and another under Major General Richard H. Anderson. Heth's division was composed of Brigadier General James Jay

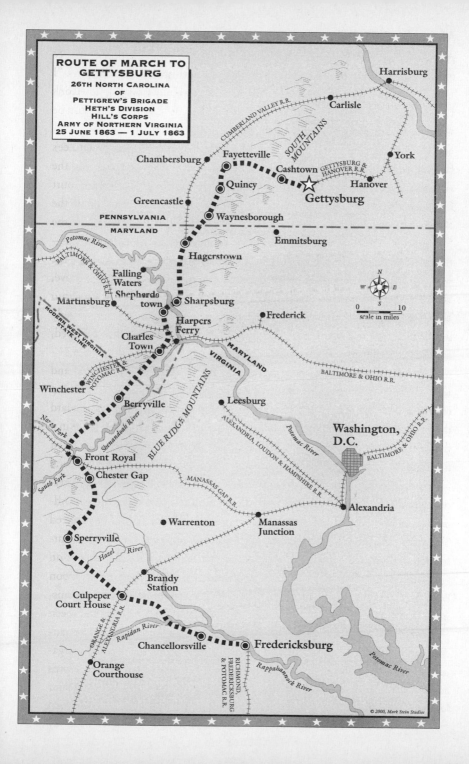

ROUTE OF MARCH TO
GETTYSBURG
26TH NORTH CAROLINA
OF
PETTIGREW'S BRIGADE
HETH'S DIVISION
HILL'S CORPS
ARMY OF NORTHERN VIRGINIA
25 JUNE 1863 — 1 JULY 1863

Harrisburg

Carlisle

CUMBERLAND VALLEY R.R.

SOUTH MOUNTAINS

York

Chambersburg

Fayetteville

Cashtown

GETTYSBURG & HANOVER R.R.

Hanover

Quincy

Gettysburg

Greencastle

Waynesborough

PENNSYLVANIA

MARYLAND

Emmitsburg

Potomac River

BALTIMORE & OHIO R.R.

Hagerstown

Falling Waters

Frederick

Shepherdstown

Martinsburg

Sharpsburg

MODERN WEST VIRGINIA STATE LINE

Harpers Ferry

MARYLAND

Charles Town

VIRGINIA

BALTIMORE & OHIO R.R.

WINCHESTER & POTOMAC R.R.

Winchester

Leesburg

Berryville

Washington, D.C.

ALEXANDRIA, LOUDON & HAMPSHIRE R.R.

Potomac River

BALTIMORE & OHIO R.R.

Nor. Fork

Shenandoah River

BLUE RIDGE MOUNTAINS

Front Royal

Chester Gap

MANASSAS GAP R.R.

South Fork

Sperryville

Warrenton

Manassas Junction

Alexandria

Hazel River

Brandy Station

Culpeper Court House

ORANGE & ALEXANDRIA R.R.

Rapidan River

Chancellorsville

Fredericksburg

RICHMOND, FREDERICKSBURG & POTOMAC R.R.

Rappahannock River

Potomac River

Orange Courthouse

N
W E
S

0   10
scale in miles

© 2000, Mark Stein Studios

Archer's brigade of Alabama and Tennessee troops; Colonel John M. Brock-enbrough's Virginians; a brigade of Mississippi and North Carolina troops under Brigadier General Joseph R. Davis; and Pettigrew's brigade of North Carolinians.[15]

The troops of Hill's Corps occupied the positions vacated by Longstreet and Ewell's corps along the south bank of the Rappahannock near Fredericks-burg. The 26th North Carolina was posted to a line along the river heights about four miles below Hamilton's Crossing. As soon as the regiment was bivouacked, Julius Lineback and the bandsmen sauntered over to a bluff on the riverbank to take in the view. "Far below us," Lineback would recall, "extending for miles up and down within the range of our vision, lay the valley of the Rappahannock, several miles wide, lovely in its spring dress of green, with the river flowing peacefully thru it. The city of Fredericksburg lay in full view, and excited our pity for the place and its helpless occupants, when we saw how completely it was at the mercy of the enemy's guns on the opposite heights." A few months earlier, Colonel Burgwyn had asked his father to loan him a small pair of binoculars—"opera glasses," he called them—and he used them to study the distant riverbank with remarkable results. "[I] can see the Yankee pickets easily with the naked eye & distinguish their accou-trements with my glass," he wrote home. "I use it constantly to see whether the Yankees are throwing up breastworks or not or whether they are preparing positions for batteries, etc. At night I can also observe their fires much more distinctly."[16]

For more than a week, the troops of Hill's Corps displayed their presence, occasionally exchanging artillery fire with the Federals or trading fire with the enemy pickets. On at least one occasion, Northern and Southern bands—including the 26th's—engaged in impromptu competition, sending the sounds of alternating performances wafting across the wide Rappahannock. "The Yankees . . . keep up the most tremendous racket & beating of drums that you can conceive of," Burgwyn wrote. "Our men think 2/3 of their army must be drummers."[17]

Then one day they were gone. Burgwyn studied the opposite riverbank on the morning of June 15th and saw nothing—even the Yankee pickets had disappeared. Hooker's Army of the Potomac was on the move, paral-leling Lee's northward advance. The ruse conducted by Hill's Corps was no longer necessary, but it had been successful. Not until June 14th, when

Ewell and his II Corps routed Federal forces in the Shenandoah Valley at Winchester, did Hooker realize that Lee and his Army of Northern Virginia had slipped into the Valley and stood poised to invade the North. Prompted by alarmed officials in Washington, Hooker hurriedly got his army up and moving northward, intending to somewhere, somehow block Lee's threatened invasion. Now Hill's Corps had no reason to remain in line near Fredericksburg and could move to catch up with the rest of Lee's army.[18]

Even before they realized the Yankees had withdrawn, the men of the 26th North Carolina knew something was happening. Orders were issued for the troops to cook enough field rations for three days, and officers were told to pack their personal baggage for shipment to the rear. Company captains and lieutenants began preparing their camp trunks for transporting to Richmond. Burgwyn had most of his personal effects packed up for shipment home to North Carolina. Worried about their music library, Lineback and other band members persuaded the regimental quartermaster to bend the rules and allow a box of music and some of the band's mess equipment to be stowed away on the 26th's wagon train. The intent of the orders was obvious to the troops: They were preparing for a long, hard march. Burgwyn figured the much-discussed invasion was now underway, but even he was unsure of the actual destination. He dashed off a quick note to his father: "I suppose we will go up towards Culpeper to join the main body though no body knows. Gen Lee keeps his own counsel so well that no major general knows any more than I do about his plans."[19]

Orders for the 26th North Carolina to begin the march were given at 1 P.M. that 15th day of June. As Lineback and the other bandsmen played a rousing tune, the well-drilled soldiers stepped off as if in a review. For some, the scene was unforgettable. "The Regiment made a fine appearance," one private would recall, "with the men beaming in their splendid grey uniforms, the colors flying, and the band playing; everything seemed positive of success."[20]

In the sweltering summer heat wave, the march soon lost the appearance of a parade. Trailed by the regimental wagon train, the men tramped along the dusty road toward Culpeper Court House, which lay about 30 miles to the northwest. Lee's army now stretched for more than a hundred miles, from the advance elements in the Shenandoah Valley to the last of Hill's Corps leaving Fredericksburg. Its position on the extreme right of Hill's line at Fredericksburg placed Pettigrew's Brigade near the rear of the army as it spread in serpentine fashion over the roads from Fredericksburg, past Culpeper Court House, over the Blue Ridge and down the Valley toward Maryland and Pennsylvania. As the 26th North Carolina marched away from Fredericksburg on the afternoon of June 15th, the lead column of Ewell's Corps was fording the Potomac at Williamsport, Maryland.[21]

Unlike the men of the 26th North Carolina, most of Lee's troops did not have "splendid grey uniforms" of recent issue. Their worn, ragged appearance made them look less than imposing. "Their clothing is serviceable, so also are their boots; but there is the usual utter absence of uniformity as to color and shape of their garments and hats . . . [gray] of all shades, and brown clothing, with felt halts," noted an observer. "Hundreds had no shoes," a veteran of the march would recall, "[and] thousands were as ragged as they could be, some with the bottom of their pants in long frazzles, others with their knees sticking out, others out at their elbows, and their hair sticking through holes in their hats. Some of the men patched their clothing . . . one man having the seat of his pants patched with bright red, his knees patched with black, another with a piece of gray or a brown blanket." Few had knapsacks like the Northern soldiers, but many had blankets rolled and looped over one shoulder and worn across the chest with the ends tied together on one side of the waist. They carried a variety of black leather cap and cartridge boxes—including many that were U.S. issue. They generally marched four abreast, although their files sometimes became irregular as the day's march wore on.[22]

Despite their ragged appearance—dusty and dirty from the march— Lee's troops radiated an air of professionalism. They had the look of men who were confident—who knew who they were and what they could do. After settling into a measured pace—the "route step" they called it—they moved in a steady but seemingly casual manner. A foreign military observer called it "a slow, dragging pace," but even he conceded that the men in gray and butternut often managed to cover an impressive distance in a day's march. Most of these troops were veterans. They had shed the timid men in a ripple of desertion on the eve of the march. Now their ranks were largely composed of committed fighters. None knew for sure where they were going, but few fretted about their eventual destination. "We are on the side of the road . . . on our way to some place," wrote one Private James W. Wright of the 26th. "Some think we are going to Maryland, some to Winchester, but we don't know." They trusted General Lee—"Uncle Robert" or "the Old Man" as some reverently called him—and they acted like soldiers who were used to winning.[23]

They had fought the Army of the Potomac repeatedly, usually outnumbered and at a disadvantage, and most expected to fight and win again. "The staff officers spoke of the battle as a certainty," a witness to the march would recall, "and the universal feeling in the army was one of profound contempt for an enemy whom they have beaten so constantly, and under so many disadvantages." Observed a soldier in the ranks: "We whip the Yankees every time we catch up with them and we get half a chance at them." Noted another: "It does not seem possible to defeat [our] army now with General Lee at its head." Even the enemy appeared at times to view Lee and his troops as unbeatable. "The Yankees are certainly very tired of this war," reported a Confederate surgeon in Lee's army. "All the prisoners I have talked with express themselves as completely worn out and disgusted with it. [The] Yankees say they are very anxious to have peace and get home." Some Southern soldiers, however, harbored a few doubts. "It is said that Gen Lee is going to . . . give Hooker [another] battle," confided a North Carolinian in a letter home. "Lee had better let that alone if he dont want his men cut up."[24]

Most men in the 26th North Carolina apparently did not expect to be "cut up"—their morale was high. "[A] finer body of men never gathered for battle," vouched one of their officers. "[These] men were patriots; they loved their country, they loved liberty. . . . They were quick to see, quick to understand, quick to act. [And] every man of them had been trained from boyhood to shoot a rifle with precision." Thanks to Governor Vance, their former commander, they were also among the best-uniformed troops in Lee's army. A few were barefooted, but all had new uniforms. As governor, Vance had established a factory in Raleigh to manufacture uniforms and overcoats for North Carolina's soldiers, and he had encouraged blockade-running to supply Tarheel troops with uniforms, arms and equipment from Great Britain. Ten days before the 26th began its march, a shipment of new uniforms from North Carolina had reached the regiment in Virginia. The troops were issued new kepis, trousers and jackets. The kepis were received without enthusiasm: Like most Southern troops, the men of the 26th preferred common broad-brimmed hats, which offered protective shade. The trousers varied in color and quality, but they were clean and lice-free. The prize of the lot was the issue of jackets. There were hundreds of them—all alike and all of the same variation of Confederate gray. Tramping along with the rest of Lee's army, the troops of the 26th may have groused about having "pantaloons of every color," but the new uniforms gave them a fresh start in ridding themselves of the lice that plagued troops in the field—and now they were surely one of the best-uniformed regiments in the Army of Northern Virginia.[25]

They were also marching under a new battle flag—an Army of Northern Virginia pattern similar to the battle flags carried by other regiments in Lee's army. It was a square version of the Confederate "Starry Cross" and was not yet adorned with the regiment's numerical designation. Colonel Burgwyn planned to send the regiment's old flag back home for safe-keeping. Although not as experienced as some regiments in Lee's army, the 26th North Carolina had braved Yankee shot and shell at New Bern, King's School House, Malvern Hill and in heavy skirmishes in eastern North Carolina. They still held the reputation as one of the best-drilled regiments in Confederate service, and they had endured heat, mud, storms, scanty rations, fatigue and vermin in countless hard marches.[26]

They were as capably led as other regiments. In every action, Burgwyn had been with them when they advanced, and in control during retreat. Long gone were the days when he was the most-despised officer in the regiment. Burgwyn was now known as the 26th's "pride and joy." As second-in-command, Lieutenant Colonel Lane was rock-hard dependable. When Burgwyn wanted something important done, the Lieutenant Colonel liked to say, Burgwyn would "call upon Lane." Everyone could sleep soundly, Burgwyn admitted, when Lane was in charge of the regiment's picket line. The regiment's third-in-command, Major John Jones, was equally dependable. In the unlikely event that both Burgwyn and Lane should fall, the men could trust Jones to lead them competently. The strength of the regiment, however, lay not simply with able leadership, but in the quality of the troops. The 26th's commanders returned the trust of the regiment's enlisted men. When the time came, the men in the ranks would do their duty. Lane spoke for the other senior commanders when he noted that the "boys" of the 26th were good soldiers from "good blood."[27]

As they marched along the dusty road from Fredericksburg toward the northwest, Lane walked his horse alongside a small band of his "boys" who were marching under guard. The recent wave of desertion that had washed through Lee's army also affected the North Carolina troops, whose ranks included men from the mountain country where Unionist sentiment was strong. They had volunteered to defend their homeland, some told each other, but not to go along on what surely seemed like a trek to the North. The desertions crested during the first few days of the march, when a scattering of men slipped away. "Our men are deserting fast, and a great many more talks of leaving," reported one soldier. The troops under guard in the regiment's rear were men who had quit the ranks earlier. Lane had presided over their court-martial trial at Hanover Junction a couple of weeks earlier, and they had been sentenced to be shot. Now they marched glumly along, awaiting eventual execution. Lane knew some of them well, and they were all his "boys." Riding alongside in the dust of the regiment, he looked down at the men and asked a question: "Are you in sympathy with the South, and if permitted to do so, will you help us fight in this next battle?" His wayward "boys" looked up at him and spoke as one: "We will. We only wished to go home to see our folks." Lane rode off without further comment, and soon afterwards the men were pardoned.[28]

Deserters were the slim minority in the 26th North Carolina. "If you were at the point of death and I could not get to come home without desertion," one soldier wrote his wife, "I should have to stay rather than bring such a disgrace upon myself and my family. My advice to every soldier is to suffer death rather than desert." Loyalty did not prevent homesickness, however, nor soften the realization that this march would likely mean some soldiers would never go home. In their letters home to loved ones, they restated commitments and in some cases tried to prepare the folks back home for the worst. "I am sorry that I did not get my furlough to come home before this trip had taken place, for I would be so glad to be with you and the children for a little while," one soldier in the regiment wrote his wife. "You must tell my relations and my friends that I cannot write to them now." Wrote another to his wife from the road: "I am far from the imbraces of thy loving arms and have bin so separated for about 18 months. How much longer shall I stay away from you and from your sweet imbrace must I say forever[?] I hope not . . . If my lot is to fall let me be at my post. . . . If I never see you again my prayer is to meet you in heaven. Take good care of my little girl and train it to love God and tell it that its father's wish was that it would be a god loving little Girl."[29]

Colonel Burgwyn brought two horses on the march and alternated riding them. As his mount plodded alongside the troops, the methodical tread of the marching soldiers made it easy to daydream. Burgwyn found himself day-dreaming a lot these days, dwelling on thoughts of home and farm. Two years of war had sobered him. The warfare he had witnessed offered little romance or adventure. He had not yet been exposed to the war's worst bloodbaths— like Sharpsburg and Fredericksburg—but he had seen death and suffering aplenty at Malvern Hill, and he had endured numerous other tense and dangerous moments. He was determined to do his duty, but he no longer wrote of yearning for battle. "God alone knows how tired I am of this war," he had written his mother a few days before the march began. "He alone knows when it will end."[30]

His daydreams of peace and prosperity left him feeling surprisingly refreshed. He had been pondering his future after the war, and while he found himself thinking the most about "the peaceful pursuits of agriculture," the potential career that seemed most appealing was politics. Eventually, he hoped to be transferred back to North Carolina, where he believed "an opportunity for distinction is much greater than in a large army." For the present, however, he had hopes for promotion to brigadier general. He had asked his father for advice. Should he take the issue to Major General D. H. Hill, a family friend, or to Governor Vance? His father had advised patience: A 21-year-old colonel did not have to hurry. Burgwyn agreed. He would wait until the present campaign ended before seeking the general's stars. Meanwhile, despite his exceptional maturity, he was capable of youthful cockiness and competitive jealousy. "I do not believe Gen. Pettigrew will be promoted soon," he confided to his father. "He has done nothing to deserve it and he appears to hold himself too much aloof from everybody . . . [and] has never come to my camp but once or twice since I have been in the brigade." Now, however, such thoughts of promotion, peace and politics were worthy only of daydreams—action would have to await the outcome of this grand march.[31]

As his men paced themselves on the dusty lane, Burgwyn remained confident that Lee's army—"a larger army than he ever had before"—was destined to win a great victory. He was certain now that the army's destination was Pennsylvania. "Lee is certainly making a very bold movement," Burgwyn wrote home, "but I think he will strike a tremendous & a successful blow."[32]

CHAPTER 4

"May the Good Lord Take Care of the Pore Soldiers"

Major John Thomas Jones understood his enemy. The troops of the 26th North Carolina who were now kicking up the Virginia dust on the route of march had faced Northern troops before. But most were farm boys-turned-soldiers who could not be expected to fully comprehend the powers now arrayed against them in this bloody war. One who did was the twenty-two-year-old Major Jones, who was third-in-command after Lieutenant Colonel Lane. Just two and a half years earlier in 1860, while a student at the University of North Carolina, Jones had joined a classmate for a Christmas vacation to New York City. He had been impressed: The sprawling metropolis with its crowded streets, bustling businesses and towering structures was enough to leave any country boy—even a college student—wide-eyed and slack-jawed. The North, Jones had come to realize, possessed the wealth, technology and manpower to be a mighty opponent—if the Northern people had the will to fight.[1]

His trip to New York City had been a genuine eye-opener and had proven to be as frustrating as it was enjoyable. After making a celebratory round of the city's popular bars on New Year's Eve, he had brought in the New Year by ice skating in Central Park with a bevy of adoring young ladies. Later, however, while visiting Barnum's Museum, he discovered that his jacket pocket had been skillfully slit open by a pickpocket, who had lifted most of Jones's vacation cash. Only when he was near broke did he learn why he had been so popular with the Yankee girls: His traveling companion had passed him off as a millionaire Southern planter. "I thought the young ladies paid me great attention, but for a long time did not know the reason," he admitted in a letter to his father. "It would have amused you to see how those rich belles of 5th Avenue flew around me."[2]

John Jones did enjoy a relatively affluent lifestyle while growing up, but his childhood had been marked by tragedy as well as privilege. His father, Edmund W. Jones, was a prominent planter in the Yadkin Valley of western North Carolina. The oldest of six children—five boys and one girl—John Jones had grown up at Cloverhill, the family plantation, located near Lenoir in the edge of the Blue Ridge Mountains. The boys were bright, well-educated and rambunctious. All had nicknames—"Will," "Wat," "Coot," "Pat" and "Knock." John was "Knock"— so named for his scrappy childhood manner of settling disagreements. They were a close-knit family: Father and sons would routinely shoot up "a whole bag of bird shot" quail-hunting together. Then in 1856, baby brother Pat drowned in a well. Four years later, John's mother died unexpectedly at age forty-seven. John, meanwhile, enrolled at the university in Chapel Hill to make something of himself. Despite his distance from home, he remained close to his father—who had lofty aspirations for his son. "John is my brag boy," Edmund Jones told a relative, "and only hope for a judge in the family."[3]

At Chapel Hill, Jones developed a friendship with another planter's son: Henry K. Burgwyn Jr. The two had much in common—background, interests, ambitions—and so close did they become that one officer in the 26th compared their relationship to the Biblical friendship between David and Jonathan. When Burgwyn graduated and left Chapel Hill for V.M.I., Jones remained at the University—until North Carolina seceded. Then he beseeched his father to allow him to join the army. With his father's consent, Jones enrolled as a private in the Orange Light Infantry, which entered Confederate service as Company D of the 1st North Carolina Infantry Regiment. He excelled in the military. "I am highly delighted with my life as a soldier," he told his father. He developed a reputation as the "best-drilled man" in his company and saw action with his regiment at Big Bethel in the war's opening days. In August of 1861, as the 26th was organizing at Camp Carolina, Jones engineered an appointment as second lieutenant of the Caldwell Guards, which became Company I in the 26th North Carolina. In April of 1862, he was elected company captain, and when the regiment was transferred to Pettigrew's Brigade under Colonel Burgwyn's command, Jones was appointed major. He had survived action with the regiment at New Bern, Seven Days and in coastal North Carolina, and by the time the regiment deployed at Gettysburg, he was a mature and seasoned officer.[4]

Broad-shouldered and dark-haired with an athletic build, Jones was a strikingly handsome young man with an intelligent-looking face, a carefully trimmed mustache and piercing eyes. His younger brother Walter—"Wat" as Jones still called him—had transferred to the 26th from another regiment a few months before the march North began and was now serving as a private in Company I. As an officer, Jones was unable to maintain constant contact with an enlisted man, but he tried to keep up with Wat—who was two years his junior. Jones continued to write his father, although his letters tended to focus on wartime events and army activities.[5]

His personal feelings—his ambitions, worries and disappointments—he shared more openly with a fifty-nine-year-old former tutor and longtime family friend named Maria Spear. In letters written from her home in Chapel Hill, Spear assumed a motherly role in Jones's life, providing advice, counseling wisdom and dispensing praise. "We must not gain our Independence too early," she advised him during some of the South's darkest days. "We must earn it with tears & with blood." After the defeat at New Bern she offered encouragement: "I am proud of your conduct, & I could not be so, if there was anything to blame." Her greatest concern was his spiritual life. "My strongest ungratified wish & the subject of my incessant prayers," she confided to John's father, "is to see John Jones a Christian." She sent him a New Testament and challenged his priorities. "Dear John," she wrote at one point, "if you only knew what a tender, loving Savior calls you. Oh, if you only knew it, your heart would melt & lay itself down at his feet." Major Jones, however, was preoccupied with sharing the responsibility for a regiment of more than 800 men. Those men would be led into the flame of battle by Burgwyn, Lane and Jones—a twenty-one-year-old, a twenty-seven-year-old and a twenty-two-year-old. The Colonel would be in the center, the Lieutenant Colonel to the right and the Major on the left.[6]

Jones could not know if this campaign would lead them to the big battle everyone expected, but he firmly believed that he, his men and the South were in the right. After two years of war, he remained devoted to the principles of Southern independence—"those liberties & rights more dear . . . than life," he called them. More than hardly anyone in the regiment, however—with the exception of Colonel Burgwyn—Jones realized the colossal national power supporting those blue-uniformed ranks his regiment would soon face. He was confident "the old Twenty-sixth" as he called it would make a good showing, but he could not help but remember what he had seen on the teeming streets of New York City. Despite the many losses General Lee had dealt them, the armies of the North represented a mighty force that would not be thwarted easily. But whatever fate awaited the men of "the old Twenty-sixth" on some distant smoke-shrouded field, they would face it with Major John Jones commanding their left.[7]

The 26th's march from Fredericksburg had been underway only a few hours when Jones and the rest of the regiment were greeted by an ominous reminder of the horrors of war. As the regiment left Fredericksburg on June 15th, the troops followed a route that took them through the battlefield at Chancellorsville. There they trudged solemnly through an eerie scene. Bloated carcasses of dead horses littered the battered landscape. Trees were split and splintered by gunfire; the ground was blanketed with shallow graves; and a foul stench hung over the area. "[It] was difficult getting along," one soldier wrote home. "[The] yankees and some of our men [were] lying partly out of the ground." Night had fallen when Julius Lineback and the other bandsmen passed the area, but they quickly realized they were on a battlefield. "[We] could not see the signs of the fights which had occurred here," he reported, "but our noses received indisputable evidence of it."[8]

West of Chancellorsville, the troops crossed the Rapidan River, filing over a crudely built footbridge, and continued marching toward Culpeper Court House. Like the troops of the two other corps that had preceded them, the men of Hill's Corps began their march at a time when Virginia was stricken by a searing summer heat wave. All along the line of march, from the rear of the army between Fredericksburg and Culpeper to the vanguard across the Potomac, the troops suffered in the sweltering heat. Many fainted, and some died of sunstroke. The roadside was soon lined with exhausted, sweating stragglers. The officers tried to keep the troops in line, but even the well-drilled men of the 26th fell out, giving the long column a depleted, ragged appearance. "The days are so hot that it almost kild the men," James Bradshaw, an orderly sergeant in Company I, admitted in a letter to his wife. "I could see hundreds of men that was compeld to fall out of ranks . . . it looked hard to see so many men lying on the side of the road all most smothering with heat. May the Good Lord take care of the pore soldiers."[9]

To avoid the worst heat of the day, the troops were rousted awake and put on the road long before sunrise, which occurred at about 4:30 A.M. A halt was called in the early afternoon, after about twelve hours on the road. The troops were expected to cover about sixteen miles a day. The 26th could usually cover at least sixteen miles in a twelve-hour march, but heat took a toll on the men's pace during the first few days of the campaign. Dust clouds cloaked the column as the Virginia sun blazed overhead. On the regiment's third day of march—Wednesday, June 17th—the heat wave was so severe that barely fifty men remained in line when a halt was called. The rest were straggling along the route or sprawled alongside the dusty road.[10]

The regiment pitched camp the night of the 17th about two miles north-west of Culpeper Court House, a crossroads hamlet that stood amid rolling fields and forests of pine and hardwood. From the clearings west of the village, the troops of the 26th could see the high, bumpy outline of the Blue Ridge Mountains rising dramatically before them. It was enough to arouse home-sickness among the soldiers of the four companies hailing from the mountains of western North Carolina. With all the regiment's marching in North Carolina and Virginia, the men of the 26th had never marched toward mountain country. For the men from Ashe, Wilkes and Caldwell Counties—companies A, C, F and I—the country up ahead looked like home. The troops were ordered to cook more field rations that night—bacon, biscuits or whatever else they had scavenged—and expect to roll out at 1 A.M.[11]

While camped west of Culpeper, the men of the 26th paused amid the hustle and clamor of camp and took a final opportunity to write home, know-ing the army mail service would cease while they were in enemy territory. While in camp, news arrived that Ewell's Corps had routed Major General H. Milroy's garrison of Federal troops at Winchester, capturing more than 4,000 prisoners, hundreds of wagons and a huge quantity of arms, equipment and rations. Cheered by the news of Ewell's victory, Colonel Burgwyn wrote his mother an optimistic letter. "I have no idea that Lee will stop in Mary-land," he confidently predicted. "I think he will [invade] Pennsylvania. His army is admirably organized & officered & has the most implicit confidence in him. The men are all in good spirits & the whole army [now] expects to go into Pennsylvania." Burgwyn advised his family not to expect to hear from him for awhile and then closed his letter with a poignant benediction. "What will be the result of the movements now afoot God alone can tell."[12]

On June 18th, the regiment took the lead, heading up Pettigrew's Brigade on the march. They forded the Hazel River and continued to the village of Sperryville. There their route turned sharply northward. To their left, the high, hazy lines of the Blue Ridge Mountains loomed almost directly above them. An afternoon thunderstorm drenched the men but brought welcome relief from the sultry heat. At a campsite between Sperryville and Gaine's Crossroads, they slept the sleep of exhausted men. At 5 A.M. on Friday, June

19th, they resumed their march, this time in second place within the brigade, and headed toward a pass over the mountains called Chester Gap. The troops ascended the mountainside, climbing a winding switchback road that provided the men with sky-high views. "The scenery along the route was exceedingly beautiful—in some places very wild," noted one soldier. "We were struck with the luxuriant richness of the country."[13]

The 26th camped that night on the mountainside, which was covered with clouds and soaked with rain at times. The men unsuspectingly made camp in an area laced with rattlesnake dens. By nightfall they had killed at least a half-dozen rattlers, including a huge snake with sixteen rattles that was discovered beside Colonel Burgwyn's tent. "There was not much traveling around that night," recalled Lieutenant Jacob A. Bush. "Everybody got him a place and lay down on it and kept quiet for the night." In the morning some of the men proudly displayed some of the dead rattlers, but the incident left other soldiers with an uncomfortable feeling of foreboding.[14]

They crossed the Blue Ridge Mountains at Chester Gap and entered the Shenandoah Valley town of Front Royal before noon on Saturday the 20th. Harassed and intimidated by Federal forces for years, the residents of Front Royal lined the town streets and cheered Hill's Corps—and the 26th North Carolina—as if they were viewing a holiday parade. "You cannot imagine how delighted the Valley people are at our appearance," a South Carolinian in A.P. Hill's Corps wrote home. "The ladies wave their handkerchiefs from every little farmhouse we pass and cheer us onward. . . . As we marched through Front Royal this morning the people were in ecstasies and our bands played lively airs for them." The 26th's band led the regiment on its march through town, playing spirited tunes such as "Get Out the Wilderness," which was the regiment's favorite. Local boys, thrilled with excitement, ran alongside the ranks or followed behind in an imitation march. Front Royal's women beamed their welcome, waved their handkerchiefs and bombarded the troops with bouquets of flowers. The grimy-faced soldiers laughed and cheered in response, marching through town with rifles on their shoulders like conquering heroes. "The men were in splendid condition and high spirits," noted a Front Royal resident who watched the passing of Hill's Corps. "As they passed through the village they closed up ranks and the bands played as if on parade. The artillery and wagons, interspersed between the different commands, added to the impressiveness of the occasion. . . . The marching columns often were delayed and had to rest by the roadside until the line of march could be continued."[15]

North of Front Royal, the regiment forded the north and south forks of the Shenandoah River. The bridges spanning the wide, tree-lined river had been burned, but the waterway was shallow enough for easy wading at its fords. Earlier, when troops from Ewell's Corps forded the Shenandoah at the same spot, a nearby hill was covered with curious civilians who had come to watch the army wade the river. Brigadier General John Marshall Jones insisted that his Virginians ford the river naked so that they would have dry uniforms on the other side. "Strip, men, and be ready to ford!" he commanded in a booming voice. As thousands of Confederate soldiers began dropping their pants, the startled civilians on the hill scrambled away in panicked retreat. "Over the hill they went pell-mell," reported a soldier, "amidst a general yell from the men. They did not see us ford the river that day." Most men in the 26th North Carolina also shed their uniforms when crossing the two forks, but thirty-four-year-old Lieutenant Jesse L. Henry, a junior officer in Company K, deemed the procedure a waste of time. "I never pull off my clothes when I wade a little stream like this," he boasted to another officer. Halfway across the river, he stumbled over a submerged rock and disappeared into the cold mountain waters. "The water was about half-thigh deep and ran like a mill tail," recalled an observer. "He got up and shook himself and said a few words not according to scripture."[16]

When the regiment went into camp in a grove of trees south of the village of Berryville late that afternoon, the troops had marched almost 30 miles— this time with the high ridges of the Blue Ridge Mountains on their right. Despite being footsore and fatigued, they could still admire the spectacular vistas of the Shenandoah Valley. "I have had the pleasure of viewing some of the most beautiful and picturesque scenery I have beheld in my life," wrote Captain Henry Albright of Company G. "The valley has proven quite interesting to me, so much so, that I am very much pleased and instead of regretting my trip, I must say I am very much satisfied with it." That night the weary soldiers in Pettigrew's Brigade were treated to a surprise concert by the 26th's musicians and three other regimental bands. The surrounding mountain forest, fields and hollows echoed with the melodies of "Listen to the Mocking Bird," "Wait for the Wagon," "Lorena" and "Home Sweet Home."[17]

After a full day of rest on Sunday, June 21st, the regiment was up again at 4 A.M. on Monday, ready to march. Instead, the troops remained in camp for another day. On Tuesday the 23rd they were roused from their sleep at 3 A.M., were issued rations of fresh beef and hardtack and were ordered on the road again. As the regiment marched through the hamlet of Berryville, a patriotic local woman draped in the Confederate national flag suddenly appeared from a side street. "Hurrah for the rebels," she yelled excitedly—and then halted beside the marching lines, gasping for breath. "Whoop," she huffed, "I'm all out of breath." Amused and complimented, the men of the 26th saluted her with cheers as they strode past. In Charles Town the next day, the regiment was cheered by more women. They moved quickly through the town, passing the pillared brick courthouse where the controversial John Brown was tried and convicted of treason before the war. Outside of town, the regiment camped for the night.[18]

They were up again by 4:30 A.M. on Thursday, June 25th, and ordered into marching formation. The band played "The Girl I Left Behind Me," as the men marched northward in the growing light of dawn. The regiment soon reached the outskirts of Shepherdstown, a collection of brick buildings and whitewashed houses perched on a steep river bluff. Before them lay a symbolic milestone of the march: the Potomac River. Across the river lay Maryland, claimed by the Confederacy and inhabited by many Southern sympathizers, but firmly secured in the Union by Northern sentiment and military might. Although the North actually lay on the other side of Maryland's northern border, crossing the Potomac was viewed as a line of demarcation that marked the passing into enemy-held country.[19]

The bridges that spanned the Potomac at Shepherdstown had been burned earlier in the war, but a traditional crossing point known as Boteler's or Blackford's Ford lay just downstream from town. It had been used as a ford by Indian tribes in the distant past, by Colonial-era travelers who knew it as Pack Horse Ford, and by Lee's retreating army after the battle of Sharpsburg less than a year earlier. Although much of Lee's army had crossed the Potomac farther northward at Williamsport, thousands of Confederates had crossed at Shepherdstown during the preceding days. A day earlier, the advance elements of Hill's Corps had crossed here, accompanied by a division wagon train that took almost three hours to roll through the muddy waters. Now, on June 25th, it was time for Heth's Division and Pettigrew's Brigade—including the 26th North Carolina—to make the crossing.[20]

The troops of the 26th reached Boteler's Ford just after sunrise. Down the sloping bluffs to the rocky shoreline they advanced. Before them lay the Potomac, approximately 150 yards wide, marked in spots by scattered boulders, and now muddy-looking and armpit-deep in places. Some men kept on their uniforms, while others stripped. "Taking off our shoes, socks, pants, and drawers, we made a comical looking set of men," Julius Lineback would later recall. With their uniforms, blanket rolls and cartridge boxes slung on their rifles and held high above their heads, the men marched into the river, hooting and yelping as their bare legs hit the chilly waters.[21]

As the men reached the opposite shore they shouted the "Rebel yell." Someone began singing the poignant words of "Maryland, My Maryland," and other soldiers began taking up the tune. Soon the musical lament arose in a bass chorus from the long line of wading men and echoed over the broad river basin in the stillness of dawn. When the bandsmen were on the Maryland shore, an officer on General Pettigrew's staff ordered them to play the song, so the 26th's band took up the tune and continued to play it until thousands of soldiers were across. Nineteen-year-old Private Thomas Perrett of Company G would never forget that prolonged period of soldier singing. As the robust chorus echoed over the Potomac, Perrett looked back across the river toward the Virginia shoreline. How many of his comrades would never return to that distant shore?[22]

Up the road from Shepherdstown they marched, heading due north toward the hamlet of Sharpsburg. After a few miles through the rolling fields of western Maryland, the long gray column reached Sharpsburg and a fork in the road. They kept to the left, still heading northward, and soon passed by the Sharpsburg battlefield. There, less than a year earlier, more than 23,000 men had been killed or wounded in the bloodiest single day in American history. Past the tiny whitewashed Dunkard Church they marched, trying to imagine the noisy, bloody storm that had enveloped the pastoral scene that deadly September day. Little evidence could be seen from the road of the furious fighting that ended General Lee's last attempt at Northern invasion and almost destroyed his army. Nature had already repaired many of the scars of battle with the greenery of woods and the new harvest of the fields.[23]

After five more hours on the road, the regiment halted within sight of Hagerstown. There the men of the 26th were turned out to make camp in a sprawling clover field, where they were cautioned by their officers not to tear down the surrounding fence rails for firewood. General Lee had his army issued strict orders for conduct in Pennsylvania. "No private property shall be injured or destroyed by any person belonging to or connected with the army, or taken," the orders mandated. Realizing that many of his soldiers had suffered the loss of homes and property to invading Northern troops, Lee reinforced his orders with a call for restraint. "The commanding general considers that no greater disgrace could befall the army, and through it our whole people," Lee wrote, "than the perpetration of the barbarous outrages upon the unarmed and defenseless and the wanton destruction of private property, that have marked the course of the enemy in our own country." Lee wanted no revenge against Pennsylvania's unarmed civilians. "It must be remembered that we make war only upon armed men," he reminded his troops, "and that we cannot take vengeance for the wrongs our people have suffered without lowering ourselves . . . and offending against Him to whom vengeance belongeth, without whose favor and support our efforts must all prove in vain."[24]

The orders directed that sorely needed supplies and livestock should be requisitioned by the army's commissary, quartermaster, ordnance and medical officers and paid for at "the market price" in Confederate money. Resupplying Lee's depleted army was a primary goal of the invasion, and soon long wagon trains of confiscated supplies stretched along the roads leading to Virginia, followed by huge herds of horses, mules and cattle heading southward. "We are taking everything we need—horses, cattle, sheep, flour, groceries and goods of all kinds," reported one jubilant Southerner. "We gathered up thousands of beeves . . . enough to feed our army until cold weather."[25]

Colonel Burgwyn and his regiment awoke on Friday, June 26th, to a gray and drizzly morning. Not until almost 8:30 did they resume the march. In Hagerstown, the regimental band took the lead, playing sprightly tunes as the men of the 26th marched smartly through the streets. Toting his cornet through Hagerstown, Julius Lineback tried to eye the residents lining the streets as he marched and played, looking for Confederate sympathizers. He saw few. He was sure there were many and assumed they were simply outnumbered and intimidated by Unionists. Some women did wave handkerchiefs in salute to the men in gray, and several held up small Confederate flags—spurring enthusiastic cheers from the troops. One passing Confederate was certain he could spot Hagerstown's Unionists: They were the citizens, he concluded, who looked as if they were viewing a funeral procession.[26]

The cool drizzle provided welcome relief from the sweltering heat that had marked much of the march. The showers continued all morning, however, and soaked the long column of gray and butternut. The rain also turned the Maryland turnpike into a shallow slough of mud, slowing the advance and turning the ten-mile route from Hagerstown to the Pennsylvania state line into a four-hour march. At about one o'clock Friday afternoon, the men of the 26th North Carolina crossed unopposed into Pennsylvania; bandsman Julius Lineback noted the time and the route in his pocket diary. The passage into Pennsylvania lacked the drama and celebration that had marked the crossing of the Potomac. After several more hours on the road, the march was halted, and the regiment made camp at a roadside farm south of the village of Waynesboro. There the weary North Carolinians spent their first night on Northern soil.[27]

Roused long before daybreak on Saturday, June 27th, the regiment was on the road again by 4:30 that morning. They marched silently through the darkened streets of Waynesboro without the parade-like procession that had accompanied their passage through the towns and villages of Virginia. The regimental band was forbidden to play while passing through enemy towns, so even after sunrise, the 26th's march was devoid of fanfare as the troops passed through a series of Pennsylvania hamlets. After Waynesboro came Quincy, then Funkstown, then Greenwood—each "a little one-horse town," according to one veteran of the march. Hill's Corps filled several roads that ran parallel in a northeasterly direction. When passing through a town the troops were not allowed to break ranks, so the regiment's first full day's march on Northern soil moved efficiently through the Pennsylvania countryside.[28]

Like the men of the 26th, the other troops of Hill's Corps were in peak condition and displayed keen morale. "All are in the best of spirits and look for nothing but victory, although we may have bloody work ahead of us," exulted one soldier in a letter to his wife. "We will show the Yankees this time how we will fight," boasted a cocky Confederate to the folks back home. "I think we will have a big fite in a few days," predicted another. "Of course we will have to fight here," explained one soldier in a letter written from Pennsylvania. "Our men feel there is no back-out. A defeat here would be ruinous. . . . If we can come out of this country triumphant and victorious, having established a peace, we will bring back to our own land the greatest joy that ever crowned a people."[29]

"The soldiers . . . are a remarkably fine body of men and look quite sea-soned and ready for any work," noted Lieutenant Colonel Arthur J. Fremantle, a British military observer who had joined the march. Fremantle was impressed with the appearance of Lee's troops and with their abundance of weapons. Hurrying to overtake the army, he had passed through Culpeper a week earlier and had noticed a huge pile of captured Federal rifles left to deteriorate in the open. "They had been captured at Chancellorsville," he observed, "but the Confederates already have such a superabundant stock of rifles that apparently they can afford to let them spoil." Many Confederates carried captured 58-caliber Springfields—the standard-issue U.S. long arm—but Fremantle noted that a favorite weapon among Lee's infantry was the British-made .577 Enfield rifle. The men of the 26th North Carolina had been issued more than 500 converted flintlock muskets when the regiment was organized, but two years of war had provided them with ample opportunities to upgrade to Enfields, Springfields and other rifles.[30]

"The artillery," Fremantle noted, "is of all kinds—Parrots, Napoleons, rifled and smoothbores, all shapes and sizes. Most of them bear the letters U.S., showing that they have changed masters." As a military professional, Fremantle also closely studied the attitude of the men on the march. "At no period of the war," he reported, "have the men been so well equipped, so well clothed, so eager for a fight, or so confident of success—a very different state of affairs from that which characterized the Maryland invasion of last year."[31]

Buoyed by such confidence, the men of Lee's army marched through the Pennsylvania countryside boldly and unopposed, heading resolutely toward the crucial battle that most believed lay somewhere ahead. "They came in close marching order, the different brigades, divisions and corps, all within supporting distance of each other," noted an observant Pennsylvanian. "Many were ragged, shoeless, and filthy. . . . They were, however, all well-armed and under perfect discipline." Although the long columns of gun-toting soldiers in gray and butternut looked serious and imposing to nervous Pennsylvanians, Confederate troops had a reputation for humor and playfulness on the march. "The road was full of soldiers marching in a particular lively manner—the wet and mud seemed to have produced no effect whatever on their spirits, which were as boisterous as ever," noted a veteran of the march. "[Some] had got hold of colored prints of Mr. Lincoln, which they were passing about from company to company with many remarks upon the personal beauty of Uncle Abe."[32]

Officers allowed joking and talking on the march, perhaps to maintain morale, and catcalls from the ranks were routine. If an officer with a new hat rode along the line, he would be followed by cheers and quips. "Come out of that hat," the soldiers would hoot. "I know you are thar; see your toes wigglin'." Passing cavalrymen who issued the taunt "If you want to get buttermilk, jine the Cavalry" would be answered by a familiar jeer: "If you want to catch h—l, jine the Webfoot." If an unfamiliar officer appeared in a clean shirt, he would be pelted with a torrent of yells: "Ahem! Umph! Umph! Biled shirt! Ladies' man! Parlor ornament! Take him to his ma!" When weariness or boredom quieted the moving columns, the monotony might be suddenly broken by the perfect imitation of a squealing hog. "I'll kill any man's hog that bites me," someone might yell in response. "Let one cackle like a hen," veteran Johnny Reb would recall, "and [the call is answered] by the encore of 'S-h-o-o!' Then other cacklers take it up, until it sounds like a poultry yard stirred up over a mink or weasel. Let one bray like an ass, others take it up until the whole regiment will impersonate the sound, seemingly like a fairground of asses."[33]

In Pennsylvania some troops disobeyed Lee's orders and searched for booty—"flanking," they called it in the ranks—but most exercised discipline. Even Yankees who observed the passing Confederates expressed surprise at the small amount of plundering—which at least one Northerner credited to military discipline rather than Southern chivalry. "The taking of groceries, provisions, stationary, hardware, clothing, hats, boots and shoes, drugs, horses, cattle, corn, oats, hay, etc., was clearly within the rules of civilized warfare," noted a Pennsylvania civilian. "And . . . the Confederates had the right while in our country to the usages accorded to armies in an enemy's country. This, to their credit, it can be said, they exacted of us without many acts of wanton and useless plunder." Thieving "flankers" managed to rob some homes, and at least one Pennsylvania farmer was murdered by stragglers. Such incidents, however, were rare. "With the exception of a few instances," concluded Jacob Hoke, a Pennsylvania Unionist, "private houses were not entered with hostile intent." Such restraint was unexpected—even for Confederate sympathizers like the Englishman Fremantle. "To anyone who has seen as I have the ravages of the Northern troops in Southern towns," Fremantle noted, "this forebearance seems most commendable and surprising."[34]

Southern forbearance did not apply to food. "Some of the boys have been 'capturing' chickens," an Alabama soldier admitted to his diary. "It is against positive orders, but . . . it's not half as bad as [the Yankees did] in Alabama, for they not only took such things, but they took the rings from [women's] fingers, and earrings from their ears, besides cursing and abusing them." Noted a Mississippi soldier: "We had not been many hours in bivouac, until turkeys, ducks, chickens, crocks of milk, butter, apple butter and various other delicacies began to make their appearance in almost every mess." Another type of private property that was routinely appropriated by Lee's Confederates: any Yankee hat within reach. Pathetically short of headgear, the Johnny Rebs were always on the lookout for a sturdy hat, and when crowding accordion-like through the Pennsylvania towns they would nab any hat within grabbing range. "As they marched along the streets, sometimes close to the pavements, and in a few cases upon them because of the mud . . . it required but an instant to grab a hat from the wondering on-looker and place it where it could not be recognized by the owner," observed a Northern civilian. "This was repeatedly done in the presence of officers, who invariably tried to have the offending person pointed out . . . but in the similarity of the men and the necessity for the column to keep moving on, not a single one was detected." Passing through one Pennsylvania village, a soldier in the 26th North Carolina noticed a well attired Northerner sneering at the passing Confederates. "Bud, let's swap hats," the soldier called out, as he snatched the man's expensive headgear and replaced it with a battered Confederate hat. The surprised critic said nothing.[35]

Fence rails also disappeared. Georgia troops under Brigadier General John B. Gordon, a brigade commander in Ewell's Corps, beseeched the general for permission to make firewood from an old split rail fence. Figuring the fence would still be serviceable if missing the top rail, Gordon reluctantly agreed but cautioned his men to remove only the top rail. By sunrise, the fence had practically disappeared. "[Each] man declared that he had taken only the top rail!" recalled Gordon. "It was a case of adherence to the letter and neglect of the spirit; but there was no alternative except good-naturedly to admit that my men had gotten the better of me that time."[36]

Accustomed to Virginia's war-stripped countryside, the men of the 26th North Carolina—like the rest of Lee's army—were astonished at the richness of the Pennsylvania countryside. Stretching before them were seemingly endless fields of wheat, oats and hay—much of it cut and shocked. Cornfields, apple orchards, vegetable gardens and trees of ripened cherries surrounded well-built, prosperous-looking farmhouses. "The war had not hurt them like it had us," observed one Tarheel soldier. "Provisions were plenty everywhere. . . . Light bread, apple butter, buttermilk." The Pennsylvanians along the route of march "are nearly all agricultural people and have everything in abundance," marveled a South Carolinian. "I have never yet seen any country in such a high state of cultivation. Such wheat I never dreamed of, and so much of it!" Recalled another Confederate: "Oh, what a change! From the

hoof-trodden, war-wasted lands of old Virginia to a country fresh and plentiful." Soldiers and officers alike pressed Confederate money into the hands of
Pennsylvania farmers in exchange for a bounty unseen by most since the
beginning of the war. "The land is full of everything and we have an abundance," one Confederate confided to his journal, adding that "cherries are
very fine." Penned another: "Our men have purchased vast numbers of chickens, ducks, pigs, and lots of butter, milk and honey, at Yankee prices, paying
for them with Confederate money."[37]

The Southern farmers-turned-soldiers stared wide-eyed at the sturdy
Pennsylvania barns. "[The] barns in Pennsylvania were a revelation to us,"
admitted a Confederate veteran of the march. "[They] far excelled the
dwelling places of the owners." Lee's troops were also surprised by the large
number of fighting-age men who remained on the farm—a reminder of the
abundance of manpower in the North. By the time Hill's Corps passed
through southern Pennsylvania, many of the Dutch and German farmers had
concluded that they had little to fear from the passing Confederate hordes.
"The farmers along our line of march were quietly reaping and harvesting the
crops," observed the 26th's Private Thomas Perrett. "They did not, as a rule,
seem to be in the least frightened or dismayed by our presence, and were left
by us in the quiet and undisturbed possession of their crops."[38]

Along the line of march, the reaction of Pennsylvania's civilians was mixed.
Some scowled at the passing Confederates. Some watched sullenly. One bold
group joked aloud that now the Southerners were in the Union after all. Some
treated the invaders as customers, trying to barter for better prices. Many simply sought shelter as if waiting out a passing storm. Some were fearful. "[We]
entered the town of Greencastle, where the people all look scared to death, or
as melancholy as if a funeral procession were passing through the streets," a
Confederate private in Hill's Corps would report. "We find the people here
very much cowed by the presence of our army," another Southerner would
note in a letter to his wife. "The men are cringing, cowardly scoundrels and
perfect dollar worshippers. Some of the women are spirited and spunky. . . .
One of them told me she hoped not one of us would live to recross the
Potomac." Passing a group of well-dressed Northern women on the route,
Lieutenant Colonel Fremantle overheard one remark: "Look at Pharaoh's
army going to the Red Sea." Noting the tattered uniforms of a North Carolina
regiment in Ewell's Corps, one brazen Northern woman taunted the passing
Johnny Rebs. "What rags and tatters!" she spitefully commented. "Very true,

very true," replied a Tarheel soldier, "but we always put on our worst duds when we start out to butcher." The outspoken critic paled visibly and said no more. As the men of the 26th North Carolina marched by a small, roadside farmhouse, a Pennsylvania woman, who was standing guard over her onion patch, anxiously asked when the Rebel soldiers would finish passing. She would have to wait a while replied the North Carolinians, joking that the line of march extended all the way back to North Carolina. "Lord bless my soul!" she exclaimed. "I didn't know thar was half as many men in the world."[39]

Contact with Pennsylvania civilians erased the desire for revenge among some Southern troops, who had anticipated a payback for the terror and destruction their families had suffered from Northern troops back home. "I felt when I first came here that I would like to revenge myself upon these people for the desolation they have brought upon our own beautiful home . . . from which their vandalism has driven you and my helpless little ones," a Confederate officer wrote his wife. "But though I had such severe wrongs and grievances to redress and such great cause for revenge, yet when I got among these people I could not find it in my heart to molest them. They looked so dreadfully scared and talked so humble that I have invariably endeavored to protect their property." The terror on the face of a Pennsylvania farm woman unnerved Private George S. Bernard, a Virginia soldier in Hill's Corps, who entered the yard of a farmhouse with another soldier hoping to buy some milk. "Seeing us coming in, the poor woman manifested by her horror-stricken countenance, a degree of alarm that was painful to witness, seeing which both of us bade her not to be alarmed," Bernard recalled. "[My friend] called to the frightened lady and said, 'Madam, do not be alarmed! No harm is intended!' From a state of great fear, there was an instantaneous transition to one of confidence, and our canteens were soon filled with delicious milk, for which we paid in Confederate money—all we had." An attempt to barter a Confederate postage stamp for some fresh onions, however, left Bernard with nothing but rejection from a Pennsylvania farm girl. "[The] offer only brought a contemptuous curl of the lip and the declaration that she would not have one of my 'Jeff Davis' stamps," he reported.[40]

When the long lines of Confederate troops appeared in their communities, some Pennsylvanians proclaimed their desire for peace or declared personal neutrality. "The men all claim to be Democrats and non-combatants," a Confederate officer wryly observed. A few privately declared their Southern sympathies. Two Virginians in Hill's Corps were rebuked by an elderly Pennsylvania farmer. "No! No! I will not sell nor will I give you any bread," he stormed at them. "You are a vile set of rebels bent on mischief!" Moments later they were waved over to a basement window by two young girls of the house, who furtively handed them a sack filled with freshly baked bread, butter, preserves and homemade candy. "We are as good rebels as yourselves," the girls whispered as they ushered the soldiers away, "but it would not do to let the old gentleman know it."[41]

Although Lee's orders prohibited acts against "the unarmed and defenseless," some Southern officers detained or seized an undetermined number of Pennsylvania's free black residents, viewing them as escaped slaves and traitors to their homeland. Others were left unmolested. "I saw only two negroes," recalled a soldier in Ewell's Corps, "and they were a very old couple, man and woman, standing on the roadside as the army passed. One of my company asked the negro man if he was 'secesh,' and he replied, 'Yes, sir, massa; I sees you now.'" Fearing capture and enslavement, other black Pennsylvanians fled regions on the Confederate line of march. One officer in Heth's Division of Hill's Corps was repelled by an invitation to round up suspected slaves. "[My] humanity revolted at taking the poor devils away from their homes," he reported. "They were so scared that I turned them all loose." A Virginia officer was surprised by the attitude toward blacks he encountered among some Pennsylvania civilians. "A lady told me the other day that our object was to bring our slaves here and make Pennsylvania a slave state," he wrote his wife. "She says she sees too many of them in our own army for her use, and hopes we won't leave them here . . . and remarked that she would be glad if we would take every kinky head that is in Pennsylvania and carry them South."[42]

On the march through Pennsylvania, the Army of Northern Virginia included an uncounted number of black Southerners, serving as body servants to officers and performing non-combat duties in various regiments. Observed Dr. Spencer Welch, a Third Corps surgeon: "My servant, Wilson, says he 'don't like Pennsylvania at all' because he 'sees no black folks.'" Some servants were given greater responsibilities: Later in the campaign one Confederate officer reported seeing a rifle-bearing black Southerner marching a glum-looking Federal soldier to the rear. When Lee's army entered Northern territory, some slaves took the opportunity to escape. Others did not. "Simon keeps up, but is generally pretty tired after our marches," a Confederate officer informed his wife in a reference to his body servant. "He seems to be very much afraid that the Yankees may get him, but says they will have to capture the wagons before they get him. He sends his love to you and all the black ones."[43]

Among the slaves accompanying Lee's army was Kincien, Colonel Burgwyn's body servant. Bearing the name of a character from a Charles Dickens novel, he was a short, slim man with unusually large hands and a long mustache that drooped around both sides of his mouth. He cared for Burgwyn's two horses and assisted with countless mundane chores. Although granted freedom to come and go on the march—even in the North—Kincien apparently made no attempt to run away to the Yankees. Burgwyn appeared to have held no worries that Kincien would disappear once in Pennsylvania. For reasons apparently known only to himself—perhaps in respect for the treatment he received from the Burgwyn family—Kincien remained devoted to the young colonel. Back in the spring, while still in North Carolina, Burgwyn had written his father to specifically request Kincien. Although master and slave, Harry Burgwyn and Kincien shared a bond of mutual affection. Burgwyn depended on Kincien, who appeared to return the young officer's trust with genuine esteem. "I never saw fidelity stronger in anyone," marveled one of Burgwyn's fellow officers.[44]

After slogging along the muddy Pennsylvania pike for more than eight hours that Saturday, Burgwyn and the regiment were undoubtedly relieved to be called to a halt about one o'clock. They bivouacked about two miles south of the village of Fayetteville, which was located on the Conococheague River in south-central Pennsylvania. To the west lay Chambersburg, where General Lee had established temporary headquarters, and to the east, beyond Pennsylvania's South Mountains, lay the tiny community of Cashtown. Burgwyn issued orders for the troops to "clean themselves up as well as possible" from the march. Soon the campsite bustled with activity as the men of the 26th set up camp, washed clothes, built campfires, searched for hay and straw for bedding and tended to routine duties. Adding an unusual element to the camp at Fayetteville was the vast amount of food and numerous live chickens, ducks and pigs purchased or appropriated by the troops. "The boys certainly lived high now," a veteran of Hill's Corps would recall. "To say nothing of substantials, delicacies such as milk and butter, honey, molasses, delicious loaves of bread, vegetables, etc., were to be seen on all sides. To have heard the squealing of pigs, the cackling of chickens, and the quacking of ducks, the

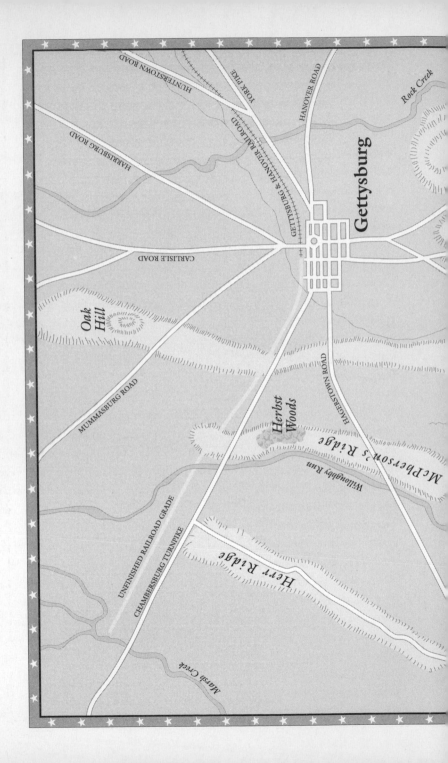

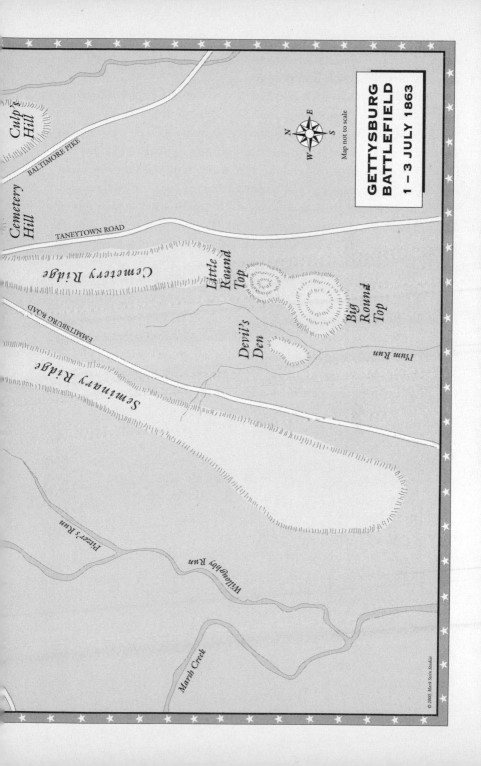

GETTYSBURG
BATTLEFIELD
1 – 3 JULY 1863

Map not to scale

Culp's
Hill

Cemetery
Hill

BALTIMORE PIKE

TANEYTOWN ROAD

Cemetery Ridge

Little
Round
Top

Big
Round
Top

Devil's
Den

Plum Run

EMMITSBURG ROAD

Seminary Ridge

Pitzer's Run

Willoughby Run

Marsh Creek

© 2000, Mark Stein Studios

luckless victims of the Confederate appetites, one for the instant might have supposed himself on some market square."[45]

Assisted by Lieutenant Colonel Lane and Major Jones, Colonel Burgwyn presided over the encamped regiment. The 26th North Carolina—and the rest of Pettigrew's Brigade—would remain in camp for the next two nights as the men rested from the long and demanding march. It was important that the men be fresh. Now that they were in enemy territory, Burgwyn knew, battle could come anytime. The advance elements of Lee's army were already deep in the heart of Pennsylvania. Surely the enemy army would soon appear. Where would the predictable battle occur? Harrisburg? York? Gettysburg? Burgwyn and his officers could only speculate. Whatever plan General Lee held at this time had not reached Burgwyn's regiment. Harrisburg was still far away, and York was more than forty miles from the 26th's Fayetteville campsite. The other potential battlefield, however, was much closer. From regimental headquarters at the Fayetteville bivouac, Colonel Burgwyn could easily see the South Mountains to the east—rising lush-green through the summer haze. It was of no consequence to him at the moment, as he busied himself with the demands of command, but beyond the distant ridges and less than twenty miles down the road to the southeast lay the town of Gettysburg.[46]

CHAPTER 5

"Summer Is Ended"

Assembled beneath the Pennsylvania sky, the soldiers of the 26th North Carolina turned their faces toward the regimental chaplain as he delivered a Sunday sermon in the field. It was their second day at the bivouac near Fayetteville, and those who had come to worship had to clear their minds of the things of war. Rumors had spread through Hill's Corps as the men rested from the long march. According to camp gossip, 150,000 Yankee troops were waiting for them up near Harrisburg—but they were all inexperienced militia troops. General Hooker's Army of the Potomac, the real threat to Lee's army, was said to be lying back, staying close to Washington to protect the Northern capital. There was also good news from the Mississippi Valley: According to Southern newspapers making the rounds in camp, the Confederates at besieged Vicksburg had soundly whipped General Grant's Yankee army.[1]

Julius Lineback dismissed the reports as unreliable. Granted, they had entered Pennsylvania unopposed—the only "action" he had heard of so far was when a company of the 26th was dispatched to round up some adventuresome Mississippi soldiers who had slipped into Fayetteville. It was generally accepted, however, among the troops that hard fighting lay ahead. While the march through Pennsylvania still seemed like a lark to some, others had begun to feel a sense of foreboding.[2]

Lineback listened intently to the sermon. The chaplain was preaching on a passage from the Old Testament book of Jeremiah, chapter eight, verse 20: "The harvest is past, the summer is ended, and we are not saved." The application was obvious: They were surrounded by Pennsylvania's rich summer harvest of wheat and oats, but soon the summer-like season of peace would end. Among the ranks of gray-clad young soldiers were men who needed to believe in Jesus Christ as Lord and Savior. After all, only the Lord knew what awaited them down that road through the peaceful-looking countryside. It was an intense sermon, especially moving under the emotional burden of pending battle. As the preacher drove home his point, Lineback glanced at Colonel Burgwyn and was struck by the look on the young commander's face: Burgwyn appeared deeply affected.[3]

When the worship service ended and the crowd of soldiers returned to camp routines that Sunday, Harry Burgwyn may have pondered the words that had so moved him. Surely he bore a far greater burden of responsibility than the typical twenty-one-year-old. Hundreds of men depended upon him for leadership even to the point of death. Some, perhaps many, might die in battle within days—Burgwyn could hardly escape that fact. He realized some kind of fight awaited them, and that it would likely be a great and decisive battle. But there were many unanswered questions. How would his men perform? How well would he lead them? Who would live and who would die? God alone knew the answers. "I hope to be able to do my duty to the best of my ability and leave the result to His infinite wisdom & justice," he had written his mother. Unlike some men in uniform, he seldom dwelt on his fears in letters home. He was not naive about the potential for death in battle—he had even arranged for a fellow officer to recover his body—but he did seem to have a sense of peace about the possibility. "Whatever may be my own fate," he had once written his mother, "I hope to be able to feel & believe that all will turn out for the best." He remained optimistic about his future. Not only did he face bright prospects for promotion and a promising political career back in North Carolina, but now he had another keen interest. Waiting for him back home, family members would attest, was a fiancée.[4]

Her name was Annie Lane Devereux—"Nan" to those closest to her. She was a nineteen-year-old Southern beauty waiting out the war in Raleigh. The oldest of eight children—six girls and two boys—Nan belonged to a prominent North Carolina family. Her father, John Devereux Jr., was a Yale-trained attorney who owned a sprawling plantation on the Roanoke River and a palatial home on the outskirts of Raleigh. He left both to volunteer for Confederate service, doing duty first as a major and staff officer but eventually accepting appointment as North Carolina's quartermaster general. Under Governor Vance's zealous direction, Devereux oversaw a busy, state-owned operation of cotton trading and blockade running, which was used to make North Carolina's troops among the best-equipped in the Confederacy. John Devereux was the classic Southern gentleman. He was known for his "fine, manly sun-burned face," noted a contemporary, "[and] quiet speech whose pure English was never marred by slang or vulgarity. His predominant trait was a genuine love of books, and his wide acquaintance with them, especially with Classic English prose and poetry." From her father, Nan had acquired a passionate interest in literature, a devotion to poetry and, perhaps, his sense of romance and humor. "[Go] and kiss mother on both eyes and the mouth and bite her ear for me," Major Devereux had joked to his daughter in a letter home from the field.[5]

From her mother, Margaret Mordecai Devereux—who was acclaimed for her loveliness—Nan had inherited beauty, charm and a tender, unselfish personality. "Patient, gentle, earnest, brave, devout," were the terms a contemporary used to describe her. Like Burgwyn, she had been raised in a cultivated environment. She was home-schooled by tutors and then educated at carefully selected schools in North Carolina and New York. The formal education was supplemented by instruction in the social graces by parents, tutors—even a dancing master. The discipline of a Biblical world view, a love of the South and a spirit of patriotism shaped her personality. She was the feminine counterpart to a Southern gentleman: a graceful, refined young Southern lady. She and Harry Burgwyn shared much in common: Both were devout Christians, both were avid readers, both delighted in intellectual pursuits, and both were raised in large and loving families.[6]

"It was a happy and delightful home in which she grew up," recalled a friend, "and those who had the privilege of knowing its gracious hospitality remember it as one of the most attractive of the many charming households to be found at that time in our Capital City." Brought home from the North after South Carolina seceded, Nan had joined the family for the war years in Raleigh at an estate called Will's Forest. Inherited by Nan's mother, Will's Forest had been the family's summer residence before the war, but Major Devereux's wartime absences made it more practical—and presumably safer—than the isolated family plantation. The estate was named for an African slave named Will, who was rescued from a shipwreck during the Colonial Era, allowed his freedom and given a cabin on the property. By the time Colonel Harry Burgwyn came calling at Will's Forest, the property was renowned for its spectacular beauty. Noted a wartime visitor: "Such glorious [roses] you never dreamed of, thousands and thousands, acres and acres . . . pale yellow roses, as big as your two hands; bright golden yellow roses not much bigger than marigolds; China roses, and climbing roses, and tea roses, and moss roses, roses everywhere, the very air is heavy with their perfume."[7]

The Devereux home at Will's Forest was a Greek revival structure that resembled an Athenian palace in design and rivaled a classic university library in scope. It was in this setting on his infrequent furloughs home that young Colonel Burgwyn came courting. He would take the looping, flower-flanked carriage road to the Devereux mansion, dismount and then climb the mansion's high front steps to pass between towering Corinthian columns. There he and Nan were free to engage in the courting courtesies customary to the Southern gentry—strolling the grounds, sharing proper expressions of affection, exchanging poetry. At Will's Forest, the courtship ritual was subject to the lively lifestyle of a large family and under the watch of a devoted family nurse. There, too, Burgwyn was exposed to the dining delights of Nan's mother, who maintained keen culinary skills despite wartime restrictions. Plum pudding, stuffed turkey, potatoes au gratin, gingerbread and chocolate cake were all favorites of the house. These moments were "precious reminders" and "happy days," recalled a contemporary, who noted that they came amid the "desolation of war and varying fortune."[8]

When Burgwyn returned to the regiment, he and Nan managed to communicate and even exchange gifts despite distance and demands of war. From some source—perhaps her father's connection with blockade runners—Nan obtained a coveted bunch of fresh lemons and sent them to Burgwyn in the field. He responded with a rare tin of sardines captured from a Yankee picket. His final furlough before the march North had allowed him more than a week at home in Raleigh, where he had the opportunity for frequent visits to the big house with the columns. Back with the regiment, preparing for the great invasion of the North, Burgwyn had said little in his letters and journal about the courtship. At home in North Carolina, however, his family had time to engage in cheerful speculation about Harry and Nan's engagement and, presumably, a wedding at war's end.[9]

Swept along in the rigors of command at the Fayetteville bivouac, however, Burgwyn had little time to ponder romantic memories or future plans. Such hopeful yearning would have to be denied for the moment. A bloody war had to be waged; a mighty battle lay ahead; and peaceful visions of love and life were only distant dreams. As Burgwyn returned to the duties of the day that Sunday in camp, Julius Lineback returned to the band tent. There he found the 26th's bandsmen discussing the chaplain's sermon. The conversation turned to Burgwyn. "Did you notice Col. Burgwyn during the preaching?" one of the men asked. "He seemed so deeply impressed." Then someone spoke words that Lineback could only hope were not prophetic: "I believe we are going to lose him on this trip."[10]

The early morning stillness at the Fayetteville bivouac was disrupted at three A.M. on Monday, June 29th: Colonel Burgwyn had received orders to resume the march. The 26th's soldiers arose groggily from their slumber and hastily began to cook breakfast. Just hours before, many of them had gathered for a Sunday night concert by the regimental band—and had been surprised by the arrival of a group of Pennsylvania ladies who had emerged from nearby Fayetteville to attend the performance. Now the brief interlude of peaceful rest had ended. The men stirred their cooking fires, struck tents and rolled up knapsacks, readying themselves to continue the march through enemy country. When thoroughly awake, they received new orders countermanding the assembly. Not until eleven o'clock that morning did they resume the march. The 26th North Carolina was placed at the head of Pettigrew's Brigade, leading Heth's Division and Hill's Corps. They headed eastward, marching under a cloudy, overcast sky toward the brushy-green South Mountains in the distance.[11]

The soldiers still did not know where they were heading. Gossip spread through the moving ranks of the 26th that Baltimore was the new target. In fact, Lee was feeling his way through enemy country almost blindly. General Stuart and most of the Confederate cavalry corps had swerved far east of Lee's army on a raid, leaving Lee without accurate knowledge of the Federal army's location. The night before, however, Lee had learned the enemy's whereabouts. The report had come from a Southern actor-turned-spy named James Harrison, who had been retained as a "scout" by General Longstreet. When the news he carried had reached army headquarters on the night of June 28th, it had altered Lee's campaign. The Army of the Potomac, more than 93,000 strong, had crossed the Potomac and was tracking Lee's army to the east—on the other side of the South Mountains. The Federal army now had a new commander: Major General George Gordon Meade. A balding, bewhiskered, forty-seven-year-old West Pointer, Meade had served as a corps commander under Generals McClellan and Hooker. After the staggering Federal defeat at Chancellorsville, Hooker had peevishly offered his resignation to President Lincoln—who had promptly accepted it. For a replacement, Lincoln had settled on Meade. He was a senior officer with solid command experience in the Army of the Potomac, and he did not dabble in politics. He could be grumpy—he was nicknamed "Old Snapping Turtle"—and he was known for an occasionally explosive temper. He was a hard worker, however, a solid military tactician and an officer respected by both superiors and subordinates. To Lincoln, Meade looked like the right man for the job—with an added bonus: He claimed Pennsylvania as his home state. Said Lincoln: "I expect Meade will fight well on his own dung hill."[12]

Armed with knowledge of the enemy's location, Lee had rethought his plans. Gone was his general strategy of moving on Harrisburg and threatening Philadelphia. From his field headquarters, located in a grove of trees just east of Chambersburg, Lee had issued new orders on Monday morning. By then the Army of Northern Virginia was spread across south-central Pennsylvania, heading toward the capital of Harrisburg. General Ewell's Corps was recalled—stopping Brigadier General Albert G. Jenkins and his advance force of cavalry almost within sight of the capital. Lee's new strategy was to concentrate his forces on the Federal army's line of march and force a confrontation. Ewell's Corps was ordered to rejoin Longstreet's Corps and Hill's Corps somewhere east of the South Mountains. There, somewhere, Lee expected to fight his great battle with the Army of the Potomac. Maybe it would be near York, but more likely it would occur at the crossroads town of Gettysburg. A quick look at the map showed Gettysburg, with its junction of roads, as a probable point of contact. "To-morrow, gentlemen," Lee told his staff on Monday, "we will not move to Harrisburg as we expected, but will go over to Gettysburg and see what General Meade is after."[13]

The men of Heth's Division, leading Hill's Corps on the march toward Gettysburg, trekked along the Chambersburg Turnpike in a long column. Couriers rode past, heading forward, then backward; small groups of soldiers hiked purposely in the opposite direction on various official errands; mounted officers trotted past; commanders and their staff officers stopped and conferred along the route. The constant activity along the way gave the marching column a bustling feeling, even while it moved slowly but resolutely toward the high ridges ahead. At the foot of the South Mountains, the regiment marched past the creekside ironworks locally known as Caledonia Furnace. It was owned by U.S. Congressman Thaddeus Stevens, a bitterly outspoken opponent of the South who maintained a law practice in nearby Gettysburg. Passing the ironworks several days earlier, Major General Jubal A. Early had declared Caledonia Furnace a Northern military industry and had ordered it wrecked. Now, as the troops of the 26th marched past, the ruins of Congressman Stevens' ironworks stood in mute contrast to the handsome and largely untouched farm buildings that had marked their route through Pennsylvania.[14]

A few miles east of Caledonia Furnace, the pike made a steep climb up the high, wooded slopes of the South Mountain range. There were no soaring peaks to scale as when they had ascended the Blue Ridge Mountains ten days earlier, but it was a steep hike to the South Mountain pass. Overhead, the rain clouds cleared to reveal a cheerfully blue sky. Along the way the narrow road curved and dipped and then rose again as it wound along the South Mountain slopes. At several points the troops could look out at a vista of farmland and woodlands. Below them, a rock-cluttered creek paralleled the road in places, and around them the terrain resembled mountain country. "Instead of the enticing field and lovely landscape," noted one Confederate, "we had now around us that which was rugged, grand and towering."[15]

It looked like home to seventeen-year-old "Jimmie" Moore, a private in Company F. Like many of the men in his company, Moore was from a rural mountain community called the Globe—a small, bowl-shaped valley that lay below the craggy heights of North Carolina's Grandfather Mountain. James Daniel Moore was tall for his age, with blond hair, gray eyes and a light complexion that reflected his Scotch-Irish and Dutch ancestry. He had gone to war at age fifteen, claiming his $50 enlistment bounty and officially joining the ranks of Caldwell County's Hibriten Guards on July 15, 1861. When he headed down the dusty wagon road to Lenoir and Confederate service, Jimmie Moore had left behind a devoted family and an idyllic boy's life.[16]

His parents, Carroll and Sarah Moore, were among the most successful of the Globe's sixty-plus farming families. Jimmie had an older sister named Rebecca and two younger brothers named William and Finley. The Moores lived in a two-story frame house, flanked by cedar trees, on a farm that stretched alongside a prong of John's River called Thunderhole Creek. Nearby was the valley watermill and the family cemetery, and outside the front gate lay a well-worn wagon road that wound up the mountain to the highland hamlet of Blowing Rock. Beneath a ledge of granite within sight of his house, Jimmie

Moore fished the creek for speckled trout, catfish and perch. On the ridges and up the hollows of the surrounding mountains, he hunted for squirrel, deer and bear. When not splitting firewood, plowing the family fields or tending to barnyard chores, he also picked huckleberries, pitched quoits with other boys from the valley or spent summer afternoons swimming in the millpond.[17]

His ancestor, Jesse Moore, had been one of the first settlers in the Globe soon after the Revolutionary War. Pioneer peers of Daniel Boone, many of the valley's early settlers had wandered down the Wilderness Road from Virginia and claimed the fertile fields along John's River. There, on rich bottomland shadowed by mountain ridges, they had built an isolated but prosperous farming community. They were a hardy, independent and somewhat reclusive people, who generally disdained slavery and remained suspicious of all government—including the Confederacy. Some chose to be politically independent, waiting out the war and hiding from the Confederate provost guard among the region's rocky ridges. Some reckoned they were for the Union and crossed the Appalachians to the Unionist stronghold of eastern Tennessee. Most, however, were like the Moore family: devoted to states' rights and Southern independence. When Jimmie Moore went to war in the summer of 1861, he had gone with a host of boys from the valley's oldest families.[18]

Moore had adopted to soldiering easily. He was a natural athlete, renowned for his success at the broad jump, and he had taken quickly to life in the field. At fifteen, he was thought to be the youngest soldier in the regiment, and had quickly become a popular figure in the 26th. "He was full of life, buoyant, happy," a contemporary would recall, "with all the frankness of a boy's nature, and with a boy's love of adventure." While posted to the North Carolina coast in 1861, he had developed a "stiffness of [the] knee joint." The problem had steadily worsened until he could hardly walk. Issued a medical discharge, he had been sent home to Caldwell County as a "recruiting officer." He had rejoined the regiment after the battle of New Bern, and he had brought new recruits along with him.[19]

Since rejoining the regiment, Moore had seen action at King's School House, Malvern Hill and Rawls' Mill, and had endured the 26th's grueling treks back and forth between Petersburg and eastern North Carolina. He had sweltered with the other troops on the march up from Virginia, hiking over the towering Blue Ridge at Chester Gap, wading the Potomac and striding through the Pennsylvania countryside. Here in the South Mountains, however, he encountered something new: Mountain ridges and hollows that resembled the terrain back home in the Globe. For a seventeen-year-old boy-soldier— even a two-year veteran—the day's march through such familiar-looking countryside had to be a mixture of adventure and reverie.[20]

Shortly after two o'clock on Monday afternoon, the regiment and the rest of Pettigrew's Brigade crossed the South Mountain pass. Just below the crest of the summit, as the route descended toward the tiny village of Cashtown, a bend in the road provided a dramatic overlook of the countryside below. The sky had temporarily cleared, and the gray-clad troops were exposed to a sunlit panorama. Julius Lineback, who was now sniffling with a summer cold, was sure he could see the distant spires of Gettysburg, which he had learned lay about seven miles ahead. The brigade wagon train rolled on down the sloping road toward Cashtown, and the regiment encamped near the summit with the sprawling view before them.[21]

The men of the 26th were up early next morning, aware that something big was happening. The brigade was issued new orders: Pile up knapsacks and leave behind everyone who was too ill to make a forced march. Julius Lineback's cold was worse, and he had awakened with a severe headache, but he was clearheaded enough to know that the activity meant the enemy was probably near. Others felt the same. Company A's Captain Samuel Wagg penned a note: "June 30 finds us at Cashtown, Penn. Here we hourly expect a fight. The enemy being near." General Pettigrew had received orders from the divisional commander, General Heth, to make a reconnaissance-in-force to Gettysburg. Although Second Corps troops from Major General Jubal Early's division had scoured Gettysburg for supplies four days earlier, Heth's orders directed Pettigrew to "search the town for army supplies (shoes especially) and return the same day." Pettigrew was ordered to conduct reconnaissance and seek supplies—and was emphatically cautioned not to stir up a battle if he encountered the enemy. To make the advance into Gettysburg, Pettigrew took three of his four regiments, Captain Victor Maurin's Donaldsville Artillery of Louisiana, and a small train of wagons for hauling back supplies. The men of the 26th were assembled on the pike for muster roll, which was necessary to measure the regiment's troop strength and get a headcount so that they could eventually receive their $11-a-month soldier's pay. The muster caused a paperwork problem for the regiment's company commanders. They had not been allowed to bring their hefty muster rolls on the campaign, so they had to struggle with makeshift records.[22]

By 6:30 A.M., they were on the road to Gettysburg. It had rained during the night and the road was soggy. As the troops marched passed the Cashtown Inn—the village's main landmark—more rain appeared imminent. Showers began sprinkling the long column, only to cease and then resume minutes later. The cloudy skies gave the day a somber appearance that added to the seriousness of the march, and the chatter in the column acquired an ominous tone. "A heavy battle expected at anytime" was the rumor muttered in ranks. Down the hill from the Cashtown Inn, General Pettigrew and the lead troops of his brigade encountered the Confederate picket line manned by troops of the 55th Virginia Infantry, which was one of Lee's most experienced regiments. The 55th's commander, Colonel William S. Christian, had just settled down to breakfast on some "confiscated chicken," when he looked up to see Pettigrew's Brigade approaching. As his troops filed through the picket line, Pettigrew summoned Colonel Christian and informed him of the reconnaissance to Gettysburg. In his typically polite manner, Pettigrew invited Christian and his regiment to join the foray even though they were assigned to Colonel J. M. Brockenbrough's brigade. Christian was reluctant: He and his men had spent a sleepless night on picket duty, and the Colonel did not relish a seven-mile morning march. Pettigrew persisted, however, and Christian submitted. Their picket duty done, the Virginians fell in with Pettigrew's troops.[23]

They covered the seven miles briskly. Rain fell in intermittent drizzles, which produced some mud but also kept summer temperatures down. Captain Wagg and others in the 26th who expected imminent battle found little that was threatening on the road to Gettysburg. The countryside looked reassuringly peaceful. The lush green fields and woodlands were punctuated by patches of yellowing wheat and oats, now nearing summer harvest. All appeared quiet and normal. The only evidence of war was the rattle of the wagons and artillery caissons and the tread of Pettigrew's marching troops. With the same keen attention he had once focused on the Spanish countryside when touring Europe, Pettigrew studied the route and the surrounding terrain so that he could make an intelligent, useful report to General Heth. Along the way, a horseman someone identified as "General Longstreet's spy" trotted by the column and disappeared down the road toward Gettysburg. He soon returned with a report that Federal cavalry from the Army of the Potomac occupied the town. The report was reinforced by a man who appeared on the road, identified himself as a Southern sympathizer and warned that Yankee troops lay ahead. Pettigrew dispatched a courier back to General Heth with the news and a request for further instructions. Heth's reply simply repeated his earlier orders: Pettigrew should proceed as planned—the "cavalry" reported in Gettysburg was probably just local militia.[24]

Obediently, Pettigrew moved his troops forward on the Chambersburg Pike to the outskirts of Gettysburg. There, on a slight ridge beside a roadside inn called Herr's Tavern, some of Pettigrew's staff officers spotted a middle-aged civilian man on horseback. He had ridden into the road from a lane that turned off to the right and had paused beside the tavern to watch the approaching Confederates. Brought over to General Pettigrew, the man identified himself as Dr. John O'Neal, a Gettysburg physician, and said he was making a sick call. He wore a gray civilian suit, carried a doctor's bag and produced a list of patients. Pettigrew dismissed the doctor, who turned his horse back down the lane on the right, and then the General rethought himself and ordered the man brought back for further questioning. By then the doctor was about two hundred yards away, but he stopped immediately when a staff orderly galloped alongside and promptly rejoined the group of Confederate officers on the road. Pettigrew probed politely. Were there any Yankee troops in town? The doctor said he had seen none at the time he had left town. Pettigrew asked other questions. The doctor responded cautiously and then grew bolder when Pettigrew persisted. "General," he said, "if I did have any matter of information, I couldn't give it to you for I'm a medical practitioner and not an informer."[25]

Pettigrew appeared to ponder the response for a long moment and then told the doctor he could leave—but only to return to town. Pettigrew and his troops then resumed their advance up the ridge toward Gettysburg, and the doctor fell in alongside. They crossed the ridge, rode down the other side, crossed a stone bridge spanning a small creek, then continued along the pike up another long ridge—and stopped. A body of mounted troops had appeared on the distant crest of the ridge. The horsemen paused, as if studying the approaching Confederates. Looking at the group, Pettigrew was certain it was a point guard of Federal cavalrymen. He turned to doctor, who sat on horseback nearby. "I understood you to say there were no Yankees in town," he said. "There are mounted men 'pointing' and are evidently from the town." The doctor appeared confused but reiterated his statement that he had seen no troops while in town. The horsemen, meanwhile, withdrew back over the ridge. Pettigrew turned away from the doctor. Although he had perhaps 2,500 troops on hand, he was mindful of Heth's command not to provoke an engagement. The brigade, he ordered, should fall back.[26]

By then his skirmish line had fanned out over the ridge and was edging toward Gettysburg's outlying buildings. Pettigrew dispatched a courier, who recalled the troops. Protected by rearguard skirmishers, the Confederate column soon reversed direction and retired back down the road toward Cashtown. On the way back, Pettigrew conferred with his officers. Some were certain the horsemen on the ridge were Federal cavalrymen: They had followed the withdrawing column for a while and the horsemen had handled themselves like veteran cavalry soldiers—not green militia troops. And there were reports from the skirmish line of drums beating in the distance, which almost certainly indicated the presence of enemy infantry. Pettigrew was convinced: Federal cavalry supported by infantry probably meant the Yankees were arriving in Gettysburg in force. Pettigrew's Brigade had found no shoes or supplies; instead, he believed, they had found the Yankee army.[27]

Back at Cashtown, Pettigrew reported his discovery to General Heth. As Heth was pondering this weighty new information, Major General A. P. Hill rode up. A superb division commander, Powell Hill had risen from colonel to major general and corps commander in little more than a year. Temperamental and sometimes argumentative, he wore his chestnut hair long, sported a thick dark beard and favored red calico shirts. His brilliance as an officer was diminished somewhat by chronic illness. During a summer break as a West Point cadet he had contracted venereal disease, which had caused him to graduate from the Academy a year late. It had also left him with lifelong health problems. Even now he remained sickly. He was taller than average, but his slender, almost gaunt appearance led him to be nicknamed "Little Powell." There was nothing lacking about his self-confidence. Raised as a member of Virginia's Piedmont aristocracy, he was opinionated, decisive and assertive— and some reckoned him cocky and impulsive.[28]

He listened to Pettigrew's report—then waved away the brigadier's concerns. "I am just from General Lee," Hill told Heth and Pettigrew, "and the information he has from his scouts corroborates what I have received from mine—that is, the enemy are still at Middleburg and have not yet struck their tents." Some of Early's Confederates had skirmished with Northern home guard troops a few days earlier near Gettysburg, and Hill apparently concluded that the Yankees spotted by Pettigrew were either militia or some wandering cavalry patrol. Pettigrew was hardly in a position to argue: He was a subordinate and a volunteer officer, while Hill was a corps commander and a West Pointer. Even so, Pettigrew believed he was right. He did not know what Hill's scouts had seen at Middleburg, which lay several hours' march away to the south, but Pettigrew was certain of what he had seen at Gettysburg. He summoned his aide-de-camp, Captain Louis G. Young, who had served with Hill during the Seven Days Campaign. Like Hill, Young was a product of the Southern gentry. A member of a prominent Charleston family, he had served with Pettigrew through much of the war and had seen a lot of combat. A year earlier at Fraser's Farm, after two horses had been shot out from under him, he had snatched up a battle flag and led a charge. Knowing General Hill respected Young, Pettigrew asked the captain to share his opinion. Young agreed with Pettigrew: Troops from the Army of the Potomac were just down the road in Gettysburg.[29]

Hill remained unpersuaded. "I still cannot believe that any portion of the Army of the Potomac is up," he declared. Despite his doubts, however, he intended to follow up on Pettigrew's reconnaissance. Third Corps was heading toward Gettysburg as part of the concentration of Lee's army anyway, so Hill decided to dispatch a much larger force of troops to the town in the morning. He issued orders for Major General Richard H. Anderson to prepare to move his division to Gettysburg, and he notified General Lee of his plans to "advance the next morning and discover what is in my front." Heth, meanwhile, appeared anxious to get to Gettysburg first and was still talking about locating supplies for his division.

"If there is no objection," he told Hill, "then I will take my division tomorrow and go to Gettysburg and get those shoes."

"None in the world," Hill replied confidently.[30]

Hill's attitude made Captain Young uneasy, and so did Heth's. Neither commander, Young believed, seemed seriously concerned about the enemy's whereabouts. Young felt as if a "spirit of unbelief" had dulled their sense of caution. "Blindness in part seemed to have come over our commanders," he would later conclude. He was dismayed to find that Brigadier General James J. Archer also seemed to hold the same casual attitude. Heth planned for Archer's Brigade to lead the march into Gettysburg the next morning, so General Pettigrew sought out Archer and briefed him on the topography between Cashtown and Gettysburg. Pettigrew had studied the series of ridges flanking Gettysburg's western approach and believed they could be easily defended by a prudent enemy. There on one of those ridges, Pettigrew predicted, Archer would probably find the enemy in the morning. Archer listened politely, but Captain Young thought the words of caution made no impression on the brigadier.[31]

That night, June 30th, most of Heth's Division encamped about three and a half miles east of Cashtown on the Chambersburg Pike. Colonel Burgwyn bivouacked the 26th North Carolina even closer to Gettysburg. The regiment was assigned responsibility for the brigade picket line for the night, so the troops were posted in advance of Heth's Division. They bivouacked on the west side of a tree-lined creek on the Chambersburg Pike about three miles from Gettysburg. Known to locals as Marsh Creek, the stream was spanned by a stone bridge and flanked by a high bluff and fenced farmland. The troops made camp in a large grove of trees on the creek bank. Captain James T. Adams, the wiry, twenty-three-year-old commander of Company D, thought the grove was beautiful. It was the kind of site that begged for a picnic, but it looked anything but peaceful when occupied by more than 800 grimy, gun-toting soldiers building campfires and setting up camp.[32]

Burgwyn placed Lieutenant Colonel Lane in command of the picket duty. He could "sleep sound," Burgwyn said, when Lane was on the picket line. Lane was complimented. He liked the trust Burgwyn placed upon him, and as the light of dusk faded into darkness, Lane remained on the line to oversee it personally. It was a peaceful summer night, softened by the occasional patter of light rain showers. At times the clouds drifted away, the skies cleared and the stars were visible around a full moon. The only disturbance occurred when two Pennsylvania women appeared on the pike, alarmed and fretting because the picket line kept them from going home. Confederate soldiers did not make war on women and children, Lane assured the women and passed them through the line.[33]

In the stillness of the night, Lane could have pondered his memories if he had been so inclined—for this was the eve of an unforgettable anniversary. Tomorrow would be July 1st—exactly one year from the regiment's near-disaster at Malvern Hill. Although the 26th had emerged relatively unscathed from the bloodbath, the battle had exposed Lane firsthand to the horrors of war. Men had been shot dead on either side of him, and a bullet had zipped by close enough to rip open the pocket of his uniform coat. He had spent the next morning prowling among the dead until he recovered the company payroll that had fallen from his torn pocket. Now it appeared obvious that he was on the eve of another bloody battle—one that seemed likely to be an even greater firestorm than Malvern Hill. Would he live to return to North Carolina's red clay country—and if so, how many of his "boys" would he be able to bring home with him?[34]

Dawn came early to the regiment's Marsh Creek encampment on Wednesday, July 1st. The sky to the east began to lighten at 4:35 A.M., but light rain showers began falling again at about six o'clock. It was a cool morning for midsummer, and as the troops of the 26th stirred around, their campfire smoke mixed with a thin mist that hung over the area. Shortly after the drizzle resumed, the men of the 26th could hear the rattle of Major William J. Pegram's artillery battalion approaching from the direction of Cashtown. Pulled by their horse-drawn caissons, Pegram's field pieces rolled through the 26th's picket line—heading toward Gettysburg in advance of Archer's Brigade. Soon afterwards the rhythmic tread of marching troops marked the approach of Archer's veteran Tennessee and Alabama troops, who were leading Heth's Division to Gettysburg. They were followed by three regiments of Davis' Brigade—Mississippians and North Carolinians under Brigadier General Joseph R. Davis. The remaining two brigades of Heth's Division—Pettigrew's and Brockenbrough's Brigades—were to follow as reserves. Behind them, as planned, Hill had dispatched Major General William Dorsey Pender's division of four brigades with another battalion of artillery. It was a powerful reconnaissance-in-force, led by Heth's Division on General Heth's declared supply-seeking mission. Neither Hill nor Heth expected to find the Yankees in force at Gettysburg, but Hill's final instructions to Heth reflected General Lee's intention to postpone fighting until his far-flung army was again concentrated. "Do not bring on an engagement," Hill had warned Heth.[35]

As the troops of Archer's Brigade tramped across the Marsh Creek bridge and up the pike toward Gettysburg, Lieutenant Colonel Lane's detachment from the 26th North Carolina was called in from picket duty, and the regiment was assembled for the march. A detachment was detailed for special duties—guarding the regiment's wagons, serving as litter bearers and performing other services—which left 800 troops available for the advance to Gettysburg. Generals Hill and Heth may have been unconcerned about what lay ahead, but at least some members of the 26th apparently believed the time for battle was finally at hand. Julius Lineback scribbled a note in his pocket diary: "Expect a fight constantly." Colonel Burgwyn obviously believed fighting lay ahead. Sometime before eight A.M., he ordered the men of the 26th to begin piling their knapsacks into the regimental wagons and to form up for the march. He also relieved the regimental band from the advance, telling the musicians they could stay with the wagons.[36]

Staying behind too was Captain Joseph Judson Young, the regimental quartermaster, who was responsible for the 26th's wagon train. The hustle and hurry of the morning's preparations kept Young busy, but he still felt a familiar sense of foreboding. Colonel Burgwyn was Young's longtime friend. The two messed together and shared the unique bond of friendship often forged among men at war. Young periodically urged Burgwyn to be more cautious, fearing the young Colonel was too bold under fire, but Burgwyn usually waved away the advice. In a serious moment, Burgwyn did extract a promise from Young: If Burgwyn were killed in battle, Young would make sure his body was sent home. Young had agreed, while continuing to advise caution. Now, with a great fight looming ominously, Young again experienced his old feeling of foreboding. He could only hope Burgwyn would follow his advice. Colonel Burgwyn, meanwhile, ordered his regiment onto the Chambersburg Pike. By then it was approaching nine o'clock. The early morning drizzle was long gone, and the morning sun had burned away the mist. Nineteen-year-old James Dorsett, a corporal in Company E, assessed the day's weather as a real "scorcher." From all the activities around him, he concluded he would see his first full-fledged battle this day. He had too little exposure to combat to know what a real battle would be like—but he would learn soon enough. Rifles on their shoulders, Burgwyn's soldiers marched as if on drill onto the Chambersburg Pike, turned toward the morning sun and tramped over the stone bridge spanning Marsh Creek. Ahead lay Gettysburg.[37]

Marsh Creek's rain-swollen waters swirled downstream beneath the stone bridge and the marching feet of the 26th North Carolina, past the regiment's creekside bivouac, alongside tree-lined banks flush with green summer growth and past furrowed fields ripening for harvest. Downstream several miles, near another bridge on the road connecting Gettysburg and the Maryland village of Emmitsburg, the same waters that had splashed by the North Carolinians' bivouac swirled past the campsite of the 24th Michigan Infantry—one of the lead regiments of the Army of the Potomac. The men from Michigan had been roused before daylight with word that the Confederates were nearby. The regiment was assigned to the First Brigade, First Division, of the army's I Corps, which was commanded by Major General Abner Doubleday. The First Division, led by Brigadier General James S. Wadsworth, was composed of two brigades. The Second Brigade, under Brigadier General Lysander Cutler, consisted of New Yorkers, Pennsylvanians and an artillery battery from Maine. The First Brigade, commanded by Brigadier General Solomon Meredith, was composed of troops from Wisconsin, Indiana and Michigan. Meredith's Brigade was known as the "Black Hat Brigade" because its troops wore the formal 1858 U.S. Army black dress hat. The prewar headgear, which was worn by few volunteer soldiers, had a tall, rounded crown and a wide brim that was normally turned up on one side and fastened with a brass eagle. It usually sported a black ostrich feather, and while it may have seemed out-of-place on the battlefield, it had become a proud symbol for the Black Hat Brigade. Within the previous year, Meredith's troops—the 24th Michigan, the 19th Indiana and the 2nd, 6th and 7th Wisconsin—had also acquired a second nickname: the "Iron Brigade." The brigade had earned the name for a tenacious defense at the battle of Groveton the previous August, and for consistently courageous conduct at Second Bull Run, South Mountain and Antietam. The men of the Iron Brigade, said some, looked like "giants with their tall black hats"—and carried with them a reputation as fighters of gigantic stature.[38]

The men of the 24th Michigan were the "green" troops of the Iron Brigade. They had been recruited from Michigan's Wayne County, and most were residents of Detroit. The regiment had been organized and trained less than a year earlier, while the men of the 26th North Carolina were still recovering from the Seven Days Battles. Unlike the 26th, which had been formed in a burst of Southern patriotism, the 24th Michigan was the product of a draft riot. On July 15, 1862, Detroit civic leaders tried to raise several new regiments with a recruitment rally, but a group of disgruntled Detroit laborers—fueled by liquor and loathing for the military draft—had disrupted the speechmaking with an attack on the speaker's platform. The mob had been turned back by Wayne County Sheriff Mark Flanagan and Detroit Judge Henry A. Morrow—who later responded to the embarrassing lack of patriotism by organizing the 24th Michigan Infantry. Judge Morrow, a former army

officer, commanded the new regiment, and Sheriff Flanagan became lieutenant colonel. After a stint of garrison duty around Washington, D.C., the
regiment joined the Iron Brigade in the field—and received an icy reception
from the veterans. The men from Michigan proved themselves a few months
later, however, when they drew their first serious fire at the Battle of Fredericksburg. Advancing under Confederate artillery fire, some men began to
waver; Colonel Morrow responded by ordering them to stop and perform the
manual of arms under fire. They did so coolly—and were afterwards treated as
equals by the rest of the Iron Brigade. Still, the regiment's battle flag—an elaborate U.S. standard adorned with "24th Michigan Infantry"—had not yet
been exposed to the worst of combat. As they prepared for the march to Gettysburg, the men from Michigan figured that would soon change.[39]

The march northward during the past few days had been somewhat like a
parade, despite the sweltering heat and sudden downpours. As the First Corps
had moved through the Maryland and Pennsylvania countryside searching for
the Rebel army, the men had been cheered by the countless Unionists along
the route, who also showered them with a bounty of food. Occasionally, the
Black Hats had added to the bounty. Some of the men from Michigan had
"confiscated" two wandering geese for the supper pot. To protect their treasures, they had persuaded one of the regimental drummers to unstring his
instrument and hide the two geese inside. Soon afterwards, the drummer was
confronted by one of the regiment's officers, who inquired why the man was
not playing his drum. "I've got a couple of geese in here," the flustered musician confided in a whisper. Assured he would be allotted a portion of roast
goose for supper, the officer straightened in the saddle and loudly proclaimed,
"Well, if you're sick and can't play, you needn't."[40]

There were no such antics this morning; the men were in a solemn mood.
"The prevailing idea among the old soldiers," one veteran would later admit,
"was that the Army was being murdered by inches. They had always been ready
and anxious to fight. When beaten they believed it was because of bad handling
by their commanders." Even in the Iron Brigade there was a hard edge of dis-
content among some troops that went beyond normal army grousing. "We have
got just enough men now to get licked every time," griped one soldier, "especially if the officers get drunk every time." Battle again seemed imminent, but
the Army of the Potomac now had a new commander, and this time its troops
would be fighting on their own soil. Assembled alongside Marsh Creek, the soldiers of the 24th Michigan quickly wolfed down a breakfast of hardtack, pork

and campfire coffee, and then gathered for a prayer by the regimental chaplain. Even as they prayed, extra ammunition was passed among the ranks.[41]

The Iron Brigade and the rest of Doubleday's I Corps prepared for the five-mile march northward to Gettysburg. The horse soldiers Pettigrew had spotted on his reconnaissance the day before *were* from the Army of the Potomac: They were two brigades of veterans from Brigadier General John Buford's division of cavalry. Like Pettigrew, Buford had sent back word that the enemy had been sighted near Gettysburg. Unlike Pettigrew, Buford had not been doubted. He had quickly surveyed the Gettysburg area, identified the most defensible positions, summoned the Federal army and prepared to hold off the advancing Confederates until the rest of the army arrived in Gettysburg. At sunup on July 1st, the Army of the Potomac, which had been trying to shadow Lee's northward march, was strung out on a twenty-two-mile-long line south of Gettysburg. The army's new commander, Major General George Meade, was moving cautiously. He hoped to engage Lee's army from a strong defensive position on Pipe Creek just south of the Maryland state line near Taneytown. But he intended to fight at Gettysburg if the full Confederate army showed up there, and—heeding Buford's reports—Meade ordered the advance elements of his army toward Gettysburg. Commanding the advance was Major General John Reynolds, who had issued the orders to get I Corps up and moving at daybreak. An aggressive officer, Reynolds intended to rush his troops to Gettysburg in support of Buford's cavalry. If the Confederate army was indeed at Gettysburg, Reynolds intended to engage the enemy there until Meade could bring up the entire Federal army.[42]

Gettysburg was a likely site for battle. The county seat of Pennsylvania's Adams County, Gettysburg, with its approximately 2,400 residents, was a medium-size crossroads community that radiated roads like the spokes of a wheel. A total of ten highways converged on the town—more roadways than the state capital could boast—and the convergence made Gettysburg difficult to avoid. Like a geographic magnet, Gettysburg drew the lumbering armies—each looking for a fight—into a crossroads conflict. A series of ridges—Herr Ridge, McPherson's Ridge, Seminary Ridge, Cemetery Ridge—rippled eastward from the South Mountain Range and stretched north-to-south through the Gettysburg area. The countryside was generally open, although it was marked in spots by patches of woodlands, coursed by a few streams, and highlighted by steep, rocky hills with dramatic, boulder-strewn shoulders. Northwest of town was a rise of land called Oak Ridge; to the east was a rocky, wooded peak known as Culp's Hill. Cemetery Ridge, named for the town cemetery on its upper end, ran southward from Gettysburg and ended in two tree-covered peaks—a smaller hill called Little Round Top and a larger, steeper eminence called Big Round Top. About a mile to the west, Seminary Ridge ran roughly parallel to Cemetery Ridge and stretched from above Gettysburg's Lutheran Seminary southward to a point opposite Big Round Top near lower Marsh Creek. Gettysburg's terrain was a military engineer's dream come true. Its numerous roads could move masses of marching men quickly; its open countryside invited maneuvering; the towering hills were perfect for artillery observers; and the well-defined ridges offered strong defensive positions. It was an admirable battlefield—for the side that managed to pick the ground.[43]

By 8:30 A.M., General Reynolds and the troops of the I Corps were on the road to Gettysburg, with the III and XI Corps soon to follow in support. Wadsworth's Division led the way with the Second Brigade marching in front, followed by the Iron Brigade. Within the brigade it was the 24th Michigan's turn to endure dust as the next-to-last regiment. Up ahead, as the brigade set out, a fife and drum detachment from the 6th Wisconsin broke into "The Campbells Are Coming," and regimental color-bearers began to unfurl their flags. As they moved up the road from their Marsh Creek campsite, the troops of the Iron Brigade passed Battery B of the 4th U.S. Artillery, which waited alongside the road for its place in the march. The battery had been attached to the brigade since the war's first year and included former Iron Brigade infantrymen who had voluntarily filled shortages in the battery's ranks. "Find a good place to camp [and] tell the Johnnies we'll be right along," joked the artillerymen, as the foot soldiers tramped past. "[Better] stay here," the infantrymen hooted back. "The climate up there may be unhealthy just now for such delicate creatures as you!"[44]

At about that time, the "Johnnies" were approaching Gettysburg. A line of skirmishers from Heth's Division headed steadily through the fields on both sides of the Chambersburg Pike, moving in advance of Archer's and Davis's Brigades. By the time the Confederate skirmishers approached Herr Ridge, some 1,600 Federal troops from Buford's cavalry division were waiting for them atop the ridge in a battle line. The horse soldiers were afoot, deployed like infantry, and although they were outnumbered by Heth's advancing Confederates, they were armed with rapid-fire breech-loading carbines. They were also supported by a battery of field artillery. They could not hope to turn back Lee's army, but their orders were to stall the Confederate advance until Federal reinforcements arrived in force. When confronted by serious fire from Herr Ridge, the troops of Heth's two brigades hustled into a battle line on both sides of the road and moved cautiously up the ridge. Major Pegram's Confederate artillerymen had already unlimbered their guns and were shelling the Yankee line. Buford's Federal soldiers—the First Cavalry Brigade commanded by Colonel William Gamble—stood their ground and poured fire down the ridge into the advancing Southerners. Expecting inexperienced Pennsylvania militia or a light force of enemy cavalry, Heth was surprised by the fierce fire. His troops pressed forward anyway—with Archer's Brigade deployed on the right side of the pike and Davis's Brigade in place on the left. Buford's hard-fighting Yankee cavalrymen fell back to the next ridge—McPherson's Ridge. There they redeployed, however, and again unleashed a fierce fire.[45]

Wadsworth's Division of Federal troops, meanwhile, hurried along the Emmitsburg Road toward Gettysburg. As the corps commander leading the Federal advance, General Reynolds had received a message from Buford that his cavalrymen were engaged with the Rebels just west of Gettysburg. Reynolds had ridden ahead of his corps to Gettysburg, and he joined Buford in the cupola of the Lutheran Seminary at about 10 A.M. As he studied the field and listened to Buford's update, Reynolds knew Wadsworth's Division with about 4,000 troops would be arriving at any moment, and that the rest of the I Corps—about 5,500 more men—would be along soon. The XI Corps—another 9,000 men plus artillery—was on the way, followed far behind by the III Corps. The ridges west of town, where the fighting was now increasing in tempo, provided good defensive ground for the Federals, and behind them was a long and formidable fallback position on what was locally known as Cemetery Ridge. The 42-year-old Reynolds was well qualified to assess the rapidly unfolding situation. A West Pointer and a highly regarded career army officer, Reynolds had recently turned down an offer from President Lincoln to command the army General Meade now headed. Reynolds had no yearning for the command slot that had been held and vacated by a parade of senior officers; yet now he was placed in the position of making decisions that would affect the entire Federal army. Studying the deadly drama before him, Reynolds concluded that Gettysburg was a good place to do battle. He sent a courier racing southward to alert General Meade and then rode back to hustle his troops forward. He found them about a mile south of Gettysburg and directed them into the fight. By now they could hear the gunfire in the distance. They left the road and moved double-quick across the fields toward the sound of the guns.[46]

The fighting that arose before him on the outskirts of Gettysburg was Henry Heth's first engagement as a major general and division commander. He was under orders to "not bring on an engagement," yet the Yankee cavalry in his front stubbornly refused to break. What enemy lay on that ridge? The Federal artillery fire did not increase as Heth's troops advanced—an indication that the enemy's strength was limited. Surely, Heth reasoned, what lay ahead was merely an enemy cavalry screen: A stronger push was bound to disperse the Yankees. Still certain he faced only light opposition, he ordered Archer's and Davis's Brigades to move against the second ridge, where the Yankee cavalry had reformed. Spread out in a half-mile battle line, the two brigades advanced. It was midmorning; the sun was up, the mist was gone, and the day was turning hot. On the north side of the Chambersburg Pike, Davis's Brigade advanced up the ridge alongside the bare roadway of an unfinished railroad now awaiting ties and rails. On the south side of the pike, Archer's troops advanced in battle formation down a slope toward a little creek known locally as Willoughby Run. They splashed through the stream and moved uphill through an open stand of timber—and were staggered by a volley of rifle fire. The crest of the hill swarmed with Federal troops advancing in a well-organized battle line. Through the smoke of battle, Archer's men could see the enemy's distinctive tall, black hats. The veterans in the Confederate ranks knew immediately what the hats meant. "There are those damned blackhatted fellows again!" one yelled. "T'aint no militia. It's the Army of the Potomac!"[47]

The Federal troops from the two brigades of Wadsworth's Division had hurried through the fields toward the fighting, trying to load and fix bayonets as they ran. Cutler's Brigade was dispatched across the Chambersburg Pike to reinforce the embattled Federal cavalrymen facing the advancing Confederates of Davis's Brigade. On the south side of the pike, the four regiments from Meredith's Iron Brigade formed a line of battle and rushed toward the stand of woods on McPherson's Ridge. Moving forward in a "long-drawn-out line of ragged, dirty blue," the men of the Iron Brigade charged through

Buford's battered cavalrymen and unleashed a sheet of rifle fire into Archer's Confederates.[48]

The Southerners returned the fire. The opposing lines were barely 50 yards apart, and the exchange was blistering. Scores of men dropped on both sides. One who went down was Major General Reynolds, who was shot from the saddle with a bullet through the head while deploying I Corps troops on McPherson's Ridge. Immediate command of the arriving Federal forces fell to General Doubleday. The 24th Michigan and the 19th Indiana, advancing across an open field to the south, moved ahead of the rest of the Iron Brigade and were able to flank Archer's Confederates. Drawing heavy fire now from their right flank and front, Archer's troops scrambled out of the woods on McPherson's Ridge, splashed back across Willoughby Run and headed back the way they had come in a crowded retreat. Some threw down their rifles and surrendered as the blue-uniformed troops surged around them. Among them was Brigadier General Archer.[49]

On the north side of the Chambersburg Pike, Davis's Confederates were doing better against the Federal troops of Cutler's Brigade. As the Federal infantry had reinforced Buford's dismounted troopers north of the pike, Davis's Brigade had met them head-on with several well-timed volleys. The fire staggered the blue wall of troops and turned them toward the rear—along with their artillery support. When Cutler's Brigade broke and retreated, Davis's troops followed up and surged forward in an attempt to turn the Federal right flank. General Doubleday saw the impending disaster unfolding and ordered in his reserves—the 6th Wisconsin Infantry and 100 other Iron Brigade troops he had held back for such an emergency. Commanded by Colonel Rufus R. Dawes, the reserves plunged into the fight, reversed the retreat and enabled Cutler's Brigade to turn back Davis's Confederates. The men in gray and butternut, who had been so close to victory, reversed direction and retreated. Most hurriedly retraced their way down the ridge, but more than 200 of them sought shelter in the gorge-like cut of the unfinished railroad and were overrun and captured. Now both Archer's and Davis's Confederates had been repulsed. Most of the field officers in both brigades had been shot down; Archer had been captured; Davis's Brigade was shattered; and Archer's men had taken serious casualties. Heth managed to check the retreat, reformed his battered troops as much as possible, held his reserves in line— and dispatched a courier requesting instructions from General Hill. Ordered to avoid a general engagement, he had not only opened a battle, but so far he was also losing.[50]

Crowded onto the Chambersburg Pike behind Archer's and Davis's Brigades that morning, the men of Pettigrew's Brigade could not ignore the sounds of fighting up the road ahead. They could hear the blasts of Pegram's artillery, joined soon by the crash of rifle fire and the added boom of enemy artillery in the distance. The 47th North Carolina led the brigade, followed by the 52nd and the 11th, with 26th bringing up the rear. The men of the 26th had heard scattered firing ahead not long after Pegram's Artillery rolled by the regiment's campsite. By the time they joined the advance up the pike, the firing had intensified. Another indication of impending battle lay beneath their marching feet: The well-trod roadway was sprinkled with playing cards. Even the most fervent poker players in the army were susceptible to fits of conscience when battle was imminent and would often drop their decks along the route of march. The road to war was paved with playing cards, and this morning the men of the 26th trod over a scattering of upturned faces—jacks, queens and kings. Their own faces unquestionably bore the grim look of men headed into battle. It was a common expression on the Chambersburg Pike this morning—"an expression of intense seriousness and solemnity," a veteran would later describe it, "[found] in the faces of men who are about to face death." From the stone bridge over Marsh Creek, they tramped up the first in a series of broad ridges on the way to Gettysburg. Just ahead of them on the left side of the pike was a blacksmith's shop. Behind it, they could see a newly constructed railroad bed, and beyond it green forested ridges that overlooked sprawling fields. Ahead, post-and-rail fences stretched along both sides of the pike. Despite the morning drizzle, the summer heat had already dried the pike's surface enough for the soldiers' scuffling feet to stir up a cloud of dust.[51]

A mile from Marsh Creek the road began a gradual rise toward the crest of Herr Ridge, where General Pettigrew had interrogated the doctor from Gettysburg the day before. A day later the landmarks remained the same—the sprawling ridge swelled hump-like to their right behind the little tavern—but the scene today was drastically different. Marching men with shouldered rifles now crowded the road, and mounted couriers raced alongside the long, gray column. Pegram's gun batteries were spread along the ridge to the right. The gun crews methodically sponged, swabbed, loaded and fired the field pieces, which emitted bursts of flame and whitish smoke with each blast. To the east, toward the midmorning sun, the smoke of battle rose from the direction of Gettysburg. Suddenly, as the 26th's lead troops crested the ridge, a Federal artillery shell rocketed down and exploded on the road just ahead. The loud blast and shattering concussion provoked an instinctive flinch among the men, and for a moment the front ranks wavered like wheat recoiling from a gust of wind.[52]

"Steady, boys, steady," Colonel Burgwyn called out, ignoring the fire. Private Albert S. Caison, a young soldier in Company I, was shaken by the first fire—until he heard Burgwyn. The colonel's command—"Steady, men!"—soothed Caison's alarm. "[It] brought every man to his place, to waver no more," he would later explain; "for we now fully realized what we must do." The regiment was directed off the pike to the left and then was moved across to the right side of the road and about a hundred yards into a field. General Pettigrew rode up, mounted on a strikingly handsome dappled gray, and issued orders for the regiment to deploy.[53]

"[Echelon] by battalion, the Twenty-sixth Regiment by the left flank," he commanded. Colonel Burgwyn repeated the command, and Pettigrew's Brigade—prompted by the 26th—formed a line of battle. The brigade moved along the back side of Herr Ridge with the 52nd North Carolina on the far right, followed in order by the 47th, 11th and 26th. When the brigade halted, the 26th North Carolina lay on the brigade's left flank directly behind Pegram's field batteries. There they waited, held in reserve with Brockenbrough's Brigade posted to their left, as Archer's and Davis's Brigades engaged the enemy.[54]

Herr Ridge spread out like a plateau to the right of the Chambersburg Pike. From their position just behind the spine of the ridge, the men of the 26th had a clear view of the fighting. "The lines extended more than a mile, all distinctly visible to us," one of the regiment's veterans would later recall. "When the battle waxed hot, now one of the armies would be driven, now the other, while neither gained any advantage." Company D's Captain James T. Adams watched the deadly drama with a peculiar fascination. He could hear the shouts of the men in battle over the artillery and rifle fire and could see the troops advancing and retreating through the shrouds of battle smoke. It was, he thought, a scene that was both grand and solemn. The regiment remained in line, waiting and watching, while Archer's Brigade and then Davis's were finally driven back by the blue-uniformed troops swarming in the distance, and the only Confederates left on the field were the dead and wounded. Atop the ridge, Pegram's Artillery continued to hammer away at the distant enemy; otherwise, a midday lull settled over the field.[55]

. Unknown to Burgwyn, Lane and the troops of the 26th North Carolina, news of General Heth's encounter and repulse was slowly echoing up the Confederate chain of command. Heth reformed the battered survivors of Archer's and Davis's Brigades, put them in a new battle line with Brockenbrough's and Pettigrew's Brigades, and covered his front with sustained artillery fire. He knew Major General W. Dorsey Pender's Division was close behind and coming up, and Pender's artillery support—a battalion of guns commanded by Major D.G. McIntosh—would soon join Pegram's Artillery in working over the Yankee positions. He was prepared for a new advance, but he would not engage the enemy again until he received orders from General Hill. Back in Cashtown, meanwhile, Hill had his own problems. He had awakened that morning feeling ill. He could hear the sound of gunfire from the direction of Gettysburg, however, and forced himself up even though his staff thought he looked pale and unsteady. Soon afterwards, General Lee and his staff officers had arrived, having worked their way through the mass of troops clogging the Chambersburg Pike. There was little Hill could tell his commander—he had no details from Heth's Division—but he intended to learn more. He pulled himself into the saddle and headed toward Gettysburg. Ahead, the boom of artillery fire continued without interruption.[56]

On the battle line overlooking the enemy positions, Lieutenant Colonel Lane had found some relief. He too had begun the day feeling ill. As the regiment left camp on Marsh Creek and moved up the road toward Gettysburg that morning, Lane had been racked by waves of nausea. He made it to the battle line, and then he took the problem to Colonel Burgwyn. He feared he needed to go to the rear, Lane explained. "Oh, Colonel, I can't, I can't," Burgwyn responded. "I can't think of going into battle without you." Burgwyn produced the flask of fine French brandy sent to him by his father, and handed it to Lane. A teetotaler, Lane was reluctant but considered the circumstances and took a swallow. Within minutes he felt better. He again sought out Burgwyn. "Colonel Burgwyn," he reported, "I can go with you." "Thank you, Colonel, thank you," Burgwyn politely replied and then turned to the battle that loomed ahead. "Colonel," he asked Lane, "do you think that we will have to advance on the enemy as they are?" From the ridge Burgwyn could see the opposing Federal line and had already assessed its strength. At the moment, the Confederate artillery was concentrating its fire in another direction. The enemy position that lay in the 26th's advance was unmarred now by artillery fire. "Oh, what a splendid place for artillery," Burgwyn commented to Lane. "Why don't they fire on them?"[57]

Burgwyn, who had posted skirmishers in front of the regiment, ordered the men on the battle line to lie down while they waited for orders. A man could better conserve his strength on his belly—and he would offer less of a target. Targets they quickly became: While in line behind the artillery, they began drawing fire from Federal sharpshooters hidden somewhere in the distance. The enemy marksmen were crack shots: One man after another was hit. Soon almost a dozen soldiers had been shot, and several were dead. Something had to be done. Eventually, sharp-eyed members of the regiment spotted Yankee sharpshooters posted behind the chimney of a large farmhouse downhill to the right. Colonel Burgwyn called for a volunteer to take out the deadly marksmen, and First Lieutenant John Anderson Lowe came forward. A twenty-three-year-old officer in Company G—Lane's old Chatham Boys Company—Lowe was also a crack shot. He headed right along the line and then crawled forward alongside a post-and-rail fence, working his way into range. Finally, he reached a spot where he could clearly see the men in blue uniforms behind the chimney. He shouldered his rifle and went to work. When he returned to the 26th's line a few minutes later, the distant rooftop was silent.[58]

After a long and tedious wait on the broad crest of Herr Ridge, the men of the 26th were ordered forward with the rest of Pettigrew's Brigade. They moved past the field artillery, advanced about 300 yards downhill and stopped more than halfway down the slope in a tree-covered swale. The Confederate battle line now stretched southward from the Chambersburg Pike for about a mile. Brockenbrough's Brigade was posted to the left; and Pettigrew's Brigade was posted to the right. The survivors of Archer's Brigade were reorganized on Pettigrew's right flank, but the remnant of Davis's Brigade—now in a "shattered condition"—was placed north of the pike and simply ordered to "collect its stragglers." The timber in which the 26th North Carolina halted was the northern end of a long, narrow stand of hardwoods, which provided welcome shade from the scorching sun. The men spread out side by side in battle formation and again lay down. The regiment formed the brigade's left flank: The 11th North Carolina was on the 26th's right, followed by the 47th North Carolina and the 52nd. The deployment placed the 26th almost exactly in the center of Heth's new battle line—a position a member of the regiment would later describe as a "bull's eye." On the opposite ridge in front of them waited the enemy—those fierce, blue-uniformed fighters in the peculiar black hats who had turned back Archer's Brigade. Burgwyn, Lane and their men had no clue when they would be called upon to advance—but they knew the order to charge would come. With Archer's and Davis's troops repulsed, there was now no one between the 26th North Carolina and the enemy.[59]

CHAPTER 6

"Like Wheat
Before the Sickle"

Private Eli Setser was the champion marbles shooter of Company F. His second cousin and fellow soldier, Thomas W. Setser, claimed Eli could "beet enybody in camp a playing marvils." Eli may have pondered those campfire games—shooting marbles amid a circle of soldiers—while he lay in line under the trees outside Gettysburg waiting to enter battle. Setser was nineteen years old. Just two years earlier, he was one of seven children growing up on his parents' thousand-acre farm in the Lower Creek section of North Carolina's Caldwell County. His daddy had served in campaigns against the Indians as a young man and had helped escort the Cherokee westward on their "Trail of Tears" to Indian Territory. When his time came, Eli Setser—like his father before him—had left the mountains to join the army. He was one of a half-dozen Setsers in the 26th North Carolina. He had an older namesake in Company I, but he spent more time with his second cousin Thomas and another cousin, Joseph, who was also a private in Company F. Like so many other youngsters in the regiment, Eli had joined the army eager for a fight. "We think we can whip six thousand yankees," he had written his father in the war's early days. "i think i can whip six my self." The Confederate defeat at New Bern, however, had tempered such bravado. "[The] yankees got everything," he had written home. "[We] haven't got a thing, only what we have got on." He killed his first enemy soldier during the Seven Days Campaign and was shocked by the battlefield horrors. "[It] was a terrible Sight to see," he had admitted to his folks. "[Men's] arms and legs and head shot off. [They were] a lying on won another. Some was Shot all to peases with canon Balls." Now he was engulfed in an even greater battle—and was waiting alongside his cousins to enter the fight. Soldiering, he had learned, was a harsh life: "It is a hard way of serving the Lord," he wrote home. Back home this day his daddy was prob-ably threshing wheat; it was harvest time in the North Carolina hills. His father had wished for Eli's help in his last letter. With all the young men away in the army, getting in the crop was difficult, and Eli's father was scared of los-ing it. The march to Pennsylvania had ended all hopes of furloughs, however, and Setser had so advised his parents in a return letter. He made it clear in his letters that he would have preferred being at home: squirrel hunting, enjoying the summer watermelon, savoring his mama's home cooking and "fancying" the girls on Lower Creek. "I have no news of interest to rite," he had penned in his last letter. He would have plenty of news to "rite" after this day—if he lived through it.[1]

Private Setser and the men of Company F were posted to the center of the line just to the left of the color guard. The company commander was Captain Romulus M. Tuttle, a twenty-year-old innkeeper's son from Lenoir, who had risen in the ranks from sergeant. Taking into account a handful of men who were ill or detailed to other duty, Tuttle counted 91 men on hand for battle in Company F—88 privates and three officers. Among them were one of his seven siblings, seventeen-year-old Private Columbus Tuttle, and a Caldwell County cousin, Sergeant John A. Tuttle. Captain Tuttle and his cousin had both enlisted on the same July day in 1861 and had been followed six months later by the captain's little brother. The regiment had numerous brothers and cousins in the ranks, but Company F may have set a record: Among the 91 men waiting in the battle line, more than 50 shared a last name with someone else in the regiment. Kinfolk were close and numerous in the mountain hills and coves from which Company F was drawn. At least three sets of twins were serving in the company, including Privates Joseph and W.E. Phillips, who had jointly enlisted after the battle of New Bern. Company F's largest clan was the Coffey family, which hailed from the hollows of the Globe. Seventeen Coffeys had served in the company. Over the past two years, three had transferred to other regiments, two had died of illness, one had provided a substitute, one had been discharged for disability, and one—Private Larkin Coffey—had deserted on the march northward. Nine members were now present—eight privates and a sergeant—ranging in age from about nineteen to almost thirty. The year before, ten members of the same family had enlisted on the same date. The old-est present at Gettysburg was Private Asbury J. Coffey, and the youngest was Private William S. Coffey. Besides Captain Tuttle, other officers also had kin in the regiment's ranks. Lieutenant Colonel Lane's twenty-two-year-old brother

Abraham was a private in Company G. Major Jones's younger brother "Wat" was a private in Company I, and Lieutenant George Wilcox of Company H commanded two of his brothers, Privates Robert and Harmon Wilcox.[2]

Waiting in Company G were the four Kirkman brothers—Bascom, Prentiss, George and Preston—all privates ages nineteen to twenty-three. Three had joined the Chatham Boys during the war's opening months, while the youngest, Private George E. Kirkman, had been drafted a year later at age eighteen. Their father was a prominent physician in St. Lawrence, North Carolina, who managed to preside over a family of fourteen despite his duties. Two of the Kirkman boys had been captured at New Bern and exchanged after stints in Northern prisoner-of-war camps. Released, they had returned to the regiment and their brothers. Together, the four had made the long, demanding march to Pennsylvania. In Company K were the three Jarman brothers—Charles, John and Elijah—who had left the family farm near Wadesboro in south-central North Carolina. Charles—a tall, red-headed twenty-three-year-old—was the oldest, and nineteen-year-old Elijah was the youngest. They too had enlisted together—exactly two years ago this day. In those early, heady days of excitement and adventure, they could not have imagined this day: sweating under the summer sun on a battle line in faraway Pennsylvania.[3]

Every man in the regiment awaiting battle on the hillside had his own story. Lying near the Kirkman brothers in Company G was Private Thomas Perrett. He had been promoted to corporal a year earlier, but after less than a year he had been reduced in rank. Now, waiting for the order to advance, Private Perrett was armed with a highly prized rifle that was the envy of the company's other soldiers. Company F's Private Jackson Gragg, a mountaineer from the Collettsville area, had been raised in a family of ten by a widowed mother, whom he had to leave back home when he joined the regiment. Another mountain boy, twenty-year-old Private Albert S. Caison of Company I, had reason to be thinking about his father as the regiment waited for action. Both father and son had entered Confederate service: Caison had joined the 26th, and his father had enlisted in the 22nd North Carolina, serving until discharged for poor health. Now, as he lay in line, knowing that his father's old regiment was somewhere to the rear with Pender's Division, Caison could only be grateful his father was not present. Lying in line with the men of Company H was Corporal Charles W. Shaw, who had joined the regiment after New Bern. A professional educator, Shaw had put aside books, students and classes to don his gray uniform. Private Elijah Flake of Company K had transferred to the 26th from the Confederate navy—after service aboard the CSS Virginia in her famous duel with the USS Monitor. Also lying in the ranks of Company K—formerly the Pee Dee Wild Cats—were the three Gathings brothers from Gum Springs near the Pee Dee River. The youngest brother, Sherwood, had joined the regiment at Camp Carolina. A year later, his three brothers—Charles, Thomas and William—had followed him. Instead of shared adventure, however, they had soon encountered unexpected tragedy when Charles was killed by his own gun near Petersburg. Now the three surviving brothers—ages thirty-five, thirty-one and twenty—were waiting to see how many of them would live through this day. In Company F, the Braswell family had already been depleted. Six Braswell men had joined the regiment: One had died a year earlier of typhoid fever, and three others had since deserted, leaving just two in the ranks—Privates Robert and R.W. Braswell.[4]

Company B's Private Isaac Mattox, a twenty-three-year-old farmer from the red clay country near Monroe, had joined the Waxhaw Jackson Guards in June of 1861, after saying farewell to his girlfriend, Rose, and his thirteen brothers and sisters. He had deserted once, but he had returned and had since stuck with the regiment. Back home, Mattox had once worked for a school teacher, and he had dubbed himself and his Company B friends the "schoolboys." Now, the "schoolboys" lay on their bellies in the narrow stand of timber and cracked jokes about what they were going to do to the enemy. The Yankees, they boasted, "were already as good as dead." Another Company B man, Sergeant Andrew Wyatt, had already learned that death was not a laughing matter. Two weeks before Christmas, Sergeant Wyatt and about ten other men of the 26th had decided to head home for a while without furloughs. They were arrested while crossing the Roanoke River, and the sergeant was sentenced to death for desertion. A few weeks later, he found himself standing in front of a firing squad, while the troops of Pettigrew's Brigade were assembled to witness the execution. Wyatt was kneeling blindfolded beside an open grave and waiting for the death bullet when a courier arrived with a stay of execution. Convinced of the sergeant's character, Burgwyn, Lane and the regiment's other officers had successfully interceded for him at headquarters. Restored to rank and command, Wyatt now waited to do his duty.[5]

Others had survived narrow escapes to see this day. Private John Vinson of Company G had also been sentenced to the firing squad for desertion. He was one of the soldiers for whom Lieutenant Colonel Lane had arranged pardons on the march. Now Vinson waited for battle with the color guard: He had volunteered to carry the regiment's battle flag through the fight if needed. Private Meredith D. Stamper of Company A had also survived a peculiar brush with death: He had killed another member of the regiment, Private H.D. Wagoner, while in camp near Kinston the year before. After the incident was investigated, Stamper was allowed to remain in the ranks. Lieutenant John B. Holloway of Company F could have avoided this day. The twenty-nine-year-old officer had been elected to a lieutenant's post in the regiment's early days, but for some reason the men of his company had not reelected him in the reorganization that had followed New Bern. He could have gone home to stay, but instead he later stood for election again—and made it. Now, Holloway waited to enter battle with the men of Company F.[6]

From his position in the center of the line, seventeen-year-old Private Jimmie Moore had a clear view of the ridge in front where the enemy was waiting. There were no encircling mountains, but the land had the roll and ridges so common to western North Carolina. Directly ahead, down the long, sloping ridge to his front lay Willoughby Run, but to Moore it was just another creek—about the size of the one running through the Moore family farm back home. On the opposite side of the creek, a steep, wooded ridge rose sharply out of the creek. The distant ridge looked much like the hilly country back home. It was covered by an open stand of hardwoods and offered a shady slope largely free of underbrush. It was from this patch of woods that the Yankees had just driven Archer's Brigade. Whenever the troops of the 26th North Carolina finally received their order to advance, this steep, tree-lined slope would be the target of their charge. Unknown to Private Moore and the rest of the regiment's men, much of the land that lay before them was known as McPherson's Ridge and was named for one of Gettysburg's most prominent citizens.[7]

Edward McPherson had inherited the property from his father, a Gettysburg banker and civic leader whose ancestors were among the region's first settlers. The property, which the senior McPherson had acquired while his son was in college, had been farmed since the 1790s—but Edward McPherson was no farmer. At age thirty-two, he had been a lawyer, newspaperman, lecturer and two-term U.S. Congressman, and he was now serving in Washington as the Chief Clerk of the U.S. House of Representatives. After suffering defeat in a re-election bid for his Congressional seat the year before, McPherson had received a boost to the Chief Clerk's post from his mentor, the fiery Congressman Thaddeus Stevens. Busy with his various occupations, McPherson had leased his inherited property on Willoughby Run to John Slentz, a forty-year-old farmer who resided in the whitewashed house with his wife Eliza and their five children. Slentz had been a successful tenant, growing wheat, corn, oats and hay on the property, and keeping a small herd of cows, a few horses, a pen of hogs and a yard full of chickens. Now the war that had ravaged so many farms down South had come to Gettysburg and had turned the old McPherson farm into a battleground. Buford's Federal cavalrymen had swarmed around the farm the night before, toting off John Slentz's fence rails, trampling his crops and scattering his chickens. Slentz had vowed to remain at home, protecting his property, but when the Confederate artillery began dropping rounds nearby, the Slentz family had frantically scrambled to safety, shooing the children away barefooted and leaving hot bread baking in the oven. Slentz had tried to herd his cattle with him, but the gunfire had spooked the livestock, sending them running in different directions. He had given up and had fled with his family.[8]

Now the blue-uniformed troops of Meredith's Iron Brigade were deployed in a defensive line near Slentz's house and barn, in his fields and across the wooded slope above the creek—a sprawling patch of open timber on McPherson's Ridge known as Herbst Woods. The stand of timber belonged to John Herbst, a middle-aged farmer who grew corn, hay, oats and wheat in nearby fields and lived in a house that lay downstream. Consisting mainly of hardwoods, Herbst Woods shaded the most defensible section of McPherson's Ridge—a steep slope that began on the east side of Willoughby Run and rose dramatically to a broad crest. To the rear of the woods a wide meadow extended eastward toward Gettysburg's thirty-seven-year-old Lutheran Seminary, visible for miles by a landmark tower and cupola.[9]

After turning back Heth's two Confederate brigades that morning, the Federals had reformed their lines and had been strengthened by reinforcements. Major General Oliver O. Howard, commander of the Federal XI Corps, had arrived in Gettysburg soon after Reynolds had been killed. "General Reynolds is dead," he was informed by a staff officer, "and you are the senior officer on the field." Until Meade and the rest of the Army of the Potomac arrived, Howard—who outranked Doubleday—would hold overall command of the two Federal corps at Gettysburg. He put Major General Carl Schurz in charge of the XI Corps with orders to hold one division of troops in reserve on Gettysburg's Cemetery Ridge and to rush the rest of the corps to the fields north of town, where they hurriedly deployed in a battle line. Deployment of Howard's Corps left Federal forces spread out in a ragged half-circle that looped around Gettysburg from the north, crossed the Chambersburg Pike on the west and then ran roughly parallel to Willoughby Run on the town-side of the stream. With Howard inheriting overall command from the fallen Reynolds, Schurz exercised immediate command over the XI Corps troops north of town, and Doubleday maintained command of the I Corps troops posted west of town.[10]

South of the Chambersburg Pike, the anchor of Doubleday's line and his strongest position was the section of the line in Herbst Woods on McPherson's Ridge—directly opposite the 26th North Carolina. There Doubleday and his First Division commander, General Wadsworth, had reformed Meredith's Iron Brigade. Forming the Iron Brigade's right wing were the troops of the 2nd and 7th Wisconsin Regiments, who were deployed on McPherson's Ridge in a battle line among the fences and fields near the Slentz house and into the edge of Herbst Woods. On the Iron Brigade's extreme right flank, Colonel Roy Stone's Brigade of Pennsylvanians had been hurriedly deployed to plug a gap in the line between the Iron Brigade and Cutler's Brigade. In the center of the Iron Brigade's line—entirely in Herbst Woods and directly opposite the left wing of the 26th North Carolina's line—lay Colonel Henry Morrow's 24th Michigan. Adjoining the Michigan men and forming the Iron Brigade's left wing was the 19th Indiana—and behind them was a reserve force composed of the 151st Pennsylvania. Posted in open fields on the Iron Brigade's left flank were Third Division troops, New Yorkers and Pennsylvanians, who were commanded by Colonel Chapman Biddle. The left flank line of Biddle's Brigade was deployed to the rear and rested in a meadow far behind McPherson's Ridge. Even though they had helped turn back the Southerners this morning, the black-hatted troops of the Iron Brigade busied themselves preparing for another Confederate assault. Then they waited.[11]

Time seemed to pass with agonizing slowness for the men of the 26th North Carolina. Noontime came and passed, and they still had not received the order to advance. The cool drizzle of the early morning was long forgotten: This Wednesday had become a steamy scorcher. Even the scattered shade of the trees above could not relieve the heat. Burgwyn, Lane and Jones kept the men quiet and on their bellies—trying to keep them as cool and comfortable as possible by detailing runners to fill canteens. The men bantered and joked with each other. Some studied pocket photographs of wives or sweethearts. Others just waited. They had hurried into battle that morning without the benefit of a worship service—the regimental chaplains were in the rear. Even so, Lane thought his "boys" were doing well: They lay calmly in line, chatting cheerfully, even though they had to realize what grim duty awaited them. They had watched Archer's and Davis's men take a licking that morning and then had been ordered into a battle line opposite those victorious black-hatted Yankees. Instead of plunging into the fighting, however, they had been ordered to wait. But they knew that the waiting would eventually end and that a deadly struggle was certain to follow. Although the swale in which they waited blocked their view of the enemy, they knew that several hundred yards to their front, past a field of waist-high oats and across the brush-lined creek, lay the wooded ridge manned by the enemy.[12]

Colonel Burgwyn was impatient. While the men waited in line, they were still drawing enemy fire. A sharpshooter's bullet had splintered the regimental flagstaff, wounding a member of the color guard. Burgwyn wondered aloud to Lane: What was the delay? Both he and Lane assumed the long wait was required to give General Hill time to deploy the rest of the corps, but more than enough time had passed for the troops to be in place. Burgwyn continued to fret. Every additional moment, he believed, the enemy on that opposite ridge was probably gaining an advantage. The Yankees were being allowed time to reorganize, rest and refit. Maybe they were being reinforced. Each passing minute was "precious time" that was lost, he told Lane. The colonel was brimming with coiled energy—Lane thought his eyes were "aflame"— and he was eager to fight.[13]

Then after hours of waiting, the men of the 26th sensed a stirring beyond the far left of the line. There, among the hazy green ridges on the northern horizon, the sound of infantry fire echoed above the countryside like a loud, slow ripping of cloth. It was as if a mighty engine was coming to life, coughing, sputtering and then raising a steady roar. To Burgwyn, Lane, Jones and the troops on the line, the meaning of such a racket had to be clear: The battle was again under way.[14]

General Hill, still sickly-looking, did not reach the Confederate artillery positions on Herr Ridge until early afternoon. He was joined there soon afterwards by General Lee and his staff. The commanding general and his officers had been forced to pick their way through the crowded pike—which now included a stream of bloodied men in gray and butternut heading rearward. Lee appeared concerned and impatient: He had stated clearly that he did not want to bring on a general engagement until his army had been fully concentrated. Now serious fighting had erupted before he could reunite his army. Longstreet's Corps was still strung out on the Chambersburg Pike to the west, and Ewell's Corps had not yet appeared from the north. Stuart and the cavalry were still missing and still unavailable to conduct reconnaissance. "In the absence of reports from him, I am in ignorance as to what we have in front of us here," Lee had told one of his officers on the road. "It may be the whole Federal army, or it may be only a detachment. If it is the whole Federal force we must fight a battle here."[15]

With Pegram's and McIntosh's batteries discharging just yards away, Lee and Hill were briefed by Heth. "I was ignorant of what force was at or near Gettysburg," Heth would state in his official report, "and supposed it consisted of cavalry, most probably supported by a brigade or two of infantry." He had been surprised by the enemy's ferocious defense, and now he had to outline the morning's failures to Lee and Hill. Heth had little good news. He had advanced Archer's and Davis's Brigades, "to feel the enemy." Archer had encountered "heavy masses" of Federal troops and was "almost surrounded by overwhelming forces in front and on both flanks." Davis's Brigade had driven back the Yankees and had captured some enemy artillery but then had been "terribly thinned" by "an overwhelming force." Both brigades had been forced to retreat, Heth had to admit. But his two fresh brigades, Pettigrew's and Brockenbrough's, were now deployed in a battle line—so Heth's Division was again prepared to assault the enemy.[16]

Hill promptly ordered Pender to deploy his division behind Heth's battle line and to stand by to support an assault. But Lee held back. He did not want to commit any more troops to battle until more of his army had arrived and he had a better understanding of the strength of those people in blue on the distant ridge. Meanwhile, the Confederate artillery continued to trade fire with the enemy—Pender's batteries had already expended several hundred rounds. The long minutes beneath the summer sun dragged on. Still Lee waited. Hill had sent a dispatch to Ewell early that morning, and ample time had passed for Ewell to reach Gettysburg. His arrival had to be imminent. So Lee waited. Then, in the early afternoon, Ewell's Corps appeared. They emerged from the wooded hills to the north—long lines of gray and butternut—and quickly deployed for battle. The first of Ewell's Corps to arrive was Rodes's Division, commanded by thirty-two-year-old Major General Robert E. Rodes, who was a seasoned, competent combat officer. From his elevated position on Oak Hill north of Heth's battle line, Rodes could see the thick dark lines of the enemy laid out before him. Knowing Early's Division was following close behind—and mindful of Lee's orders to exercise caution—Rodes at first intended to wait for Early, while positioning his troops for an assault on the Federal left flank. When the Federals seemed to be advancing to meet him, however, Rodes made the attack.[17]

From his position on Herr Ridge, General Heth could see the smoke and dust boiling to the north and could hear the stuttering crash of infantry fire as Rodes assaulted the enemy. The struggle seemed desperate. Anxious for the order to attack, Heth searched for General Hill but could not find him. Finally, he rode up to General Lee, who was watching the distant fighting in silence. "Rodes is very heavily engaged," Heth noted—and then posed the question: "Had I not better attack?" Lee was still unwilling to commit. "No," he responded, "I am not prepared to bring on a general engagement to-day—Longstreet is not up." Heth obediently turned away and rode back to his division—just as Rodes's Confederates appeared to surge forward against the Yankees. Heth quickly rode back to Lee. The commanding general was studying the distant fighting. He too could see that Rodes was pressing the enemy, who now might be overwhelmed by a two-pronged assault. Heth requested permission to attack—just as Hill rode up. Lee looked at the two officers and issued the order: Heth's Division should go in.[18]

"Attention!" The command echoed down the line, repeated by officer after officer. The men of the 26th North Carolina scrambled to their feet: Heth's Division had finally gotten orders. The regiment's officers hurried to their posts. Lieutenant Colonel Lane moved into place behind the line's right wing; Major Jones took command behind the left wing; captains and first sergeants stood to the right of their companies. Before assuming his post behind the center of the line, Colonel Burgwyn remounted his horse and rode along the rear of the line, cheering his men with a clear, commanding voice. He looked resplendent. He had chosen his uniform carefully this morning. He wore one of his officer frock coats with his sword-belt buckled over a red silk sash. Beneath his uniform he had tucked away two of his pocket-size journals and wore his treasured boyhood pocket watch on a silk cord tied around his neck. He was armed with a new, double-edged Boyle, Gamble & MacFee sword crafted in Richmond just the previous year. He wore it on his left side in a black leather scabbard that was tipped with a brass drag. As he rode down the rear of the line, Burgwyn could see his troops stand smartly at attention, awaiting orders as if on parade. Just as he had trained them, his men prepared to make their assault by the book. The common assault formation called for an advance in two lines with half a regiment's companies in the front line and the other half following about 100 yards behind. Charged with keeping the battle lines straight when men began to drop, "file-closers" took their positions behind each company. In the oat field in front, the regiment's skirmishers arose and waited for the advance. Then, from the 26th's center, the color guard stepped forward six paces to begin the assault.[19]

At the head of the nine-man color guard was Sergeant Jefferson B. Mansfield of Company E, who held aloft the deep red banner of the 26th's "Starry Cross" battle flag. A regiment's colors were considered almost sacred by the troops. The flag was the symbol of the regiment, an inspiration to the men in the ranks—and also served the vitally important purpose of guiding them into battle and keeping them in line. To effectively deliver a destructive massed fire, battle lines had to be orderly and straight. In the smoke, noise and chaos of battle, soldiers would look for the battle flag that marked the center of the line so that they could "dress on the colors"—a military phrase that meant reorder the battle line. Observed a soldier at Gettysburg: "where the colors are the regiment is supposed to be; the men rallying under these colors." Members of the color guard were chosen for the fidelity to the regiment, their courage and their coolness under fire. They were not to fire in battle with the rest of the regiment but instead were instructed to reserve their fire for attacks directly on the colors. When the regiment delivered fire, the color guard was supposed to step back several paces to avoid being hit by their own men, but the flag was to always remain aloft, signaling the center of the line and encouraging steadiness in the ranks. Should the color sergeant fall, a member of the color guard would replace him, and if heavy fighting should claim the replacement, other members of the guard would be prepared to lift up the fallen flag. Knowing the psychological and tactical importance of the flag, soldiers in battle routinely directed their fire against the enemy colors. Serving in the color guard was a distinctive honor—and one that carried with it a deadly risk.[20]

The 26th's color sergeant was well-chosen. Sergeant "Jeff" Mansfield was a twenty-five-year-old from the village of Cartersville in North Carolina's Chatham County. He had left behind two sons—a two-year-old and a new-born—and a wife named Ann whom he loved deeply. He was devout, patriotic and romantic. During his two years in service, he and his wife had composed and exchanged ballads with each other. "[There] ain't a day, no hardly an hour, but what I am thinking of you and the children," he had written Ann. "O, if this war was over [and] you and all the soldiers could come home and stay home in peace," she had replied, "I would be so glad we both [could] be with our children. . . . I look at your [photograph] and fear it is the last I shall see of you." He had sent the children seashells from the North Carolina coast, and his oldest son had cheerfully dictated a note to his father: "Mother says I am a good boy and smart too." Despite the pain of separation, Mansfield had remained faithful to his duty. "We have a long journey before us and expect hard fighting before we get back," he had written in his last letter home. "We must put our trust in God." Now the "hard fighting" was at hand, and Sergeant Mansfield was in front, holding up the regiment's "Starry Cross."[21]

"Forward, march!" The order was shouted down the lines and repeated by Colonel Burgwyn as the long line of Heth's Division—approximately 3,000 troops—moved forward. In the rear, Pender's Division prepared to advance in support. At the center of Heth's advancing line were the 800 soldiers of the 26th North Carolina. Bayonets fixed and rifles shouldered, they stepped smartly forward behind the color guard and the waving battle flag. Even amid the excitement of the moment, Lieutenant Colonel Lane noted proudly that the regiment advanced as if the men were marching in review. Ahead of them down the eastern slope of Herr Ridge lay a split-rail worm fence, and beyond it lay a field of oats. On the other side of the field, the slope led down to Willoughby Run, and—on the creek's opposite side—lay the wooded ridge where the enemy waited. The men moved briskly forward out of the wooded swale where they had been waiting, quickly scaled the rail fence, and reformed for the assault.[22]

Colonel Burgwyn then gave the order to charge. A fearsome Rebel yell erupted from the regiment's ranks. It rang down the slope, over the creek and carried into the woods where the black-hatted men from Michigan and Indiana were waiting. The soldiers of the 26th promptly advanced into the field of oats, moving steadily through the waist-high grain. They were quickly within rifle range of the men in blue, but the Black Hats held their fire. It was the calm before the storm: The double line of gray moved quietly, steadily through the field—with the command calls of officers sounding above the swish of movement. Then, Corporal Simeon P. Philyaw—a twenty-three-year-old mountaineer from Company F—suddenly broke from the ranks, ran forward and discharged his rifle at the distant line of enemy troops in the woods ahead. Philyaw's unexpected action surprised the men around him. Sergeant J.T.C. Hood wondered if the corporal's shot would provoke early fire from the Yankees.[23]

Across Willoughby Run on McPherson's Ridge, where Federal forces waited among the trees of Herbst Woods, officers of the 19th Indiana Infantry heard what they thought was a "signal gun" launching the Confederate assault. Across the creek on the opposite slope they could see the dense lines of Southern troops moving steadily toward them. The 19th Indiana's stocky, bewhiskered commander—Colonel Samuel J. Williams— ordered the Hoosier troops to prepare to deliver a volley into the advancing Confederates. Posted as they were on the left flank of the 24th Michigan, the troops of the 19th Indiana were directly opposite the right flank of the 26th North Carolina's advancing line. As Heth's Division moved toward the Federal position, Pettigrew's Brigade was heading directly toward the Iron Brigade—and the 26th North Carolina was on a line of march that would cause it to collide with the 24th Michigan and the 19th Indiana. "Boys," Colonel Williams shouted to his troops, "we must hold our colors on this line, or lie here under them."[24]

The Hoosiers were veteran troops. The regiment had been organized and trained in camp at Indianapolis at the same time the 26th North Carolina was being drilled at Camp Carolina near Raleigh. While the 26th was shuttling back and forth between Virginia and North Carolina in 1862 and 1863, the 19th Indiana was doing battle at Second Manassas, Antietam, Fredericksburg and Chancellorsville. This morning they had helped turn back two brigades of Lee's army, but they knew that Lee's troops seldom gave up easily. The Johnnies would be back, they realized, and the Black Hats from Indiana had spent the last couple of hours preparing to receive them. They were deployed on the wooded slope of McPherson's Ridge as General Meredith had ordered, but Colonel Williams believed they could do a better job defending their position by entrenching on the crest behind them. To communicate this concern, Williams had dispatched Sergeant-Major Asa Blanchard to Meredith. Wearing an elaborate sword taken from a captured Confederate officer, the sergeant-major reported to Meredith, who endorsed the request and sent Blanchard to get the approval of the division commander. But General Wadsworth disagreed. The 19th Indiana—and the Iron Brigade—should hold their position "as long as possible," he said. "[That] piece of timber," Wadsworth told Blanchard, "[is] the strongest position of the line and of the utmost importance." The wooded part of McPherson's Ridge—Herbst Woods—had the defensive strength of a natural redoubt, Wadsworth emphasized. It must be held "at all hazards," he warned. The battle-smeared sergeant-major looked Wadsworth in the face and confidently replied: "General, if that is what you want, and the Iron Brigade can't hold it, where can you find troops who can?"[25]

To the right of the Hoosiers and directly in front of the 26th North Carolina, the troops of the 24th Michigan were resting in line among the trees on McPherson's Ridge when the Confederate battle line appeared on the opposite ridge. The Black Hats from Michigan were quickly on their feet. Their commander, Colonel Henry Morrow, stood among his men and watched the long gray lines advance through the distant field of oats beneath fluttering red battle flags. Morrow had to admit it was an impressive sight: The approaching Confederates made a splendid appearance. Broad-shouldered and dark-headed—with a face full of mutton-chop whiskers—Morrow had at least one personal element in common with the advancing Rebels: He too was a native Southerner. He had been born in Virginia and had gone to school in Washington when the capital still had the feel of a Southern city. His heart, however, was firmly with the North. He had served in the prewar army during the Mexican War and had afterwards made his home in Detroit, where he had practiced law and presided as a judge. He had a wife and baby back home now, and to him these men advancing on his position—despite their common link by birth—were clearly the enemy.[26]

As the tension of impending battle steadily increased, Morrow was mindful of his orders, which had come down the chain of command with no room for interpretation: "The Iron Brigade would hold the woods at all hazards." Like his counterpart with the 19th Indiana, Colonel Morrow also thought he could better defend his portion of the line from atop the ridge. In obedience to orders, however, his men were deployed below the crest. He had placed them in a battle formation among the trees on the slope above Willoughby Run. Despite his best efforts, the rugged terrain prevented his troops from forming a precisely straight line. His right flank bent slightly backwards, following the curve of the ridge toward the 7th Wisconsin. On his left flank, the 19th Indiana's line bent back even more dramatically as it followed the terrain—and Morrow feared that beyond the Hoosiers the line was weak, disconnected and exposed. He had his orders, however, and the battle was again under way—so he would have to make the best of things. His regiment of Black Hats had taken some serious losses earlier this morning: Several members of his color guard were down, his lieutenant colonel appeared to have lost a leg, and his adjutant had been shot in the groin. His men had proved themselves, however: They had licked the Johnny Rebs, and they were now prepared to do it again. The 24th Michigan, General Hooker had once told him, was "as fine as silk." And as for Morrow himself, Hooker had praised the colonel to his face as "a most noble soldier." Would he be so "noble" when this battle was over? Would his men still earn praise? Hooker was gone now, replaced by Meade, and the ultimate time of testing for the men from Michigan had finally come. The long, gray line that advanced as if on parade was now within easy rifle range. Morrow ordered his troops to fire.[27]

The men of the 26th North Carolina brushed steadily through the waist-high oats, advancing down the slope toward Willoughby Run in perfect alignment. They were midway through the field when Corporal Philyaw had fired his unexpected opening shot, and they had taken but a few more steps when a blast of smoke and flame suddenly erupted from the Yankee line in the woods ahead. Most of the volley fell short, plowing up the oat field fifteen steps ahead of the regiment. A scattering of men dropped, but the gray lines did not waver. Seconds later, Colonel Burgwyn ordered the line to halt and return the volley. The color guard stepped back out of the line of fire. "Commence firing! Ready. Aim. Fire!" were the drill book commands. With an explosive roar, the regiment's massed rifles delivered the 26th's first fire at Gettysburg. The men coolly reloaded and resumed their advance. Another volley exploded from the opposite slope. It went high; the gray line remained intact. Colonel Burgwyn then ordered the "quick-step," and the troops picked up their pace—rifles shouldered, color guard out front, the battle flag held aloft and starkly crimson in the summer sun. They knew what awaited them, but they advanced unflinching. They headed toward the underbrush lining the creek. Now they were closer; now they were better targets. From the woods another volley erupted in smoke and flame—and this one hit true.[28]

It was a "murderous fire," one survivor would later recall. It spilled men into the oats and tore great gaps in the regiment's front line. "At our first volley," an Indiana soldier would report, "the first line in our front disappeared from view." Company F's Sergeant Hood thought the men dropped like chopped wheat. "[Volleys] of deadly missiles were sent into our ranks," he would recall, "which mowed us down like wheat before the sickle." One who went down almost immediately was Color Sergeant Jeff Mansfield. A bullet in the foot knocked him to his knees. First to bear the regiment's colors, now he was among the first to fall. Sergeant Hiram Johnson, a thirty-year-old first sergeant in Company G, was standing by in the color guard. Exactly one year earlier at Malvern Hill, Johnson had been seriously wounded. Now, he took the colors from Mansfield and moved forward. Burgwyn, Lane and Jones were unhurt. They quickly closed the gaps and reformed the line. The men of the 26th followed the colors down the slope and toward the creek ahead.[29]

CHAPTER 7

Covered with Glory

Colonel Burgwyn could see the trouble ahead. The enemy's last volley had dropped men all along his front line, but the 26th had closed ranks and kept going. Now, however, as they emerged from the oat field and approached Willoughby Run, the men faced a swath of creekside underbrush that included dense brambles with quarter-inch thorns. The obstacles would slow down the advance, cause the men to cluster together and make the regiment an easier target for the enemy on the opposite slope. There was no choice, however, and nothing to do but press on, push through the brambles, wade the stream and reform on the other side. As the straight, gray lines continued down the slope and neared the underbrush, the troops slowed down—and were suddenly hit by a deadly spray of Federal artillery fire. Somewhere to the rear of the Iron Brigade's position, Federal guns momentarily had a line of fire on the regiment. "The Yanks took advantage of that," a survivor would recall, "and began killing our men like forty."[1]

As men tumbled and dropped, wide gaps opened in the lines, and the advance slowed almost to a halt. Color-bearer Hiram Johnson was shot down as he waded through the briars, and the colors fell. Posted to the right of the color guard, Company F was hit hard. Eli Setser, the marble-shooter, went down at some point. He was hit several places in one arm and received a terrible wound to the thigh, which shattered the bone near the hip. His cousin, Private Joseph Setser, was also cut down by a leg wound that splintered his leg bone near the knee. Remarkably, Burgwyn was not hit and neither was Lane. Major Jones was struck by a spent shell fragment but was not seriously injured. A third color-bearer, twenty-year-old Private John Stamper of Company A, raised the flag but was quickly shot down. Another member of the color guard, thirty-year-old Private George Washington Kelly, grabbed the standard and resumed the lead. Stubbornly, the men advanced despite the fire, pushing through the underbrush, ignoring the thorny brambles and then splashing through the shallow, slippery, rock-bottomed creek toward the opposite bank. As he climbed out of Willoughby Run, Private Kelly stumbled and fell, seriously wounded in the ankle. "Get up, George, and come on," yelled another soldier. "Can't," Kelly called back. "I'm hit. I believe my leg is broken." The shell fragment Kelly believed had wounded him lay nearby, and in one of the oddities of war, he was determined to get it. "Give it to me, please," he yelled to another soldier. "I'm going to take it home as a souvenir." Private Larkin A. Thomas, a color-bearer from Company F, picked up the fallen flag, while the rest of the regiment splashed across the creek. Once across, the line of gun-toting men in gray paused on the creek bank to reform. At that moment—just yards away—the black-hatted troops near the base of the ridge delivered another volley of rifle fire from just yards away.[2]

Fire low! The Federal officers were shouting above the racket. Fire low! A cloud of thick white smoke rolled toward the 26th's lines, which were suddenly marked by wide gaps and piles of bodies. The black-hatted fighters quickly reloaded and resumed fire, pouring a steady, deadly rain of bullets into the North Carolinians reforming on the creek bank. First Sergeant Jacob Bush of Company I tried to close up the gaps in his company's line, motioning troops on the right and left to move in. On both sides, however, men were falling so fast he could not seem to fill the gaps. "The bullets were flying around me like hailstones in a storm," Corporal James Dorsett would later recount. It was a scene he would never forget: "Lots of men near me were falling to the ground, throwing up their arms and clawing the earth. The whole field was covered with gray suits soaked in blood." Dorsett too went down, hit in the chest and shoulder. Despite the savage fire, Burgwyn, Lane and Jones managed to reform the regiment into a single battle line. Disciplined by countless hours of drill, the troops braved the deadly onslaught, faced the enemy and unleashed a devastating fire.[3]

Blue-uniformed bodies and black hats fell to the ground. Within minutes, the Federal dead lay thick on the slope of McPherson's Ridge. "Thus we stood in the line and fired," a Michigan soldier would recall, "[until] we was all cut up." The two opposing lines—blue and gray—stood and delivered fire as rapidly as possible. On both sides the men loaded, fired, tore open another cartridge, rammed it home, fitted another percussion cap on the rifle nipple, fired again—and repeated the actions as if on a drill. Thirty feet to his front, Sergeant J.T.C. Hood of Company F could see the 24th Michigan's color

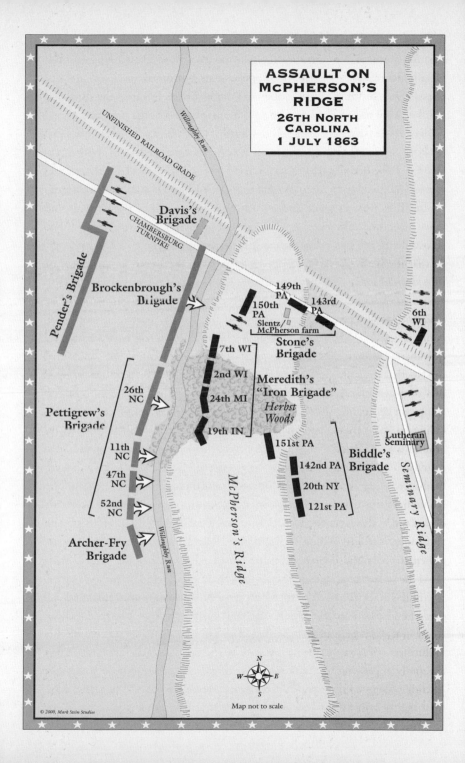

ASSAULT ON
McPHERSON'S
RIDGE
26TH NORTH
CAROLINA
1 JULY 1863

UNFINISHED RAILROAD GRADE

Willoughby Run

Davis's
Brigade

CHAMBERSBURG
TURNPIKE

Pender's Brigade

Brockenbrough's
Brigade

149th
PA

150th
PA

143rd
PA

6th
WI

Slentz/
McPherson farm

Stone's
Brigade

7th WI

2nd WI

24th MI

Meredith's
"Iron Brigade"

Herbst
Woods

Pettigrew's
Brigade

26th
NC

19th IN

151st PA

142nd PA

20th NY

121st PA

Biddle's
Brigade

Lutheran
Seminary

11th
NC

47th
NC

52nd
NC

McPherson's Ridge

Seminary Ridge

Archer-Fry
Brigade

Willoughby Run

N
W   E
S

© 2000, Mark Stein Studio

Map not to scale

guard. Hood was a tough twenty-six-year-old from the mountains near Lenoir. Moments earlier, as he had moved through the oat field, a bullet had sliced across his thigh. Despite the pain, he had made it across the creek and up the bank, adding his firepower to the firing line. Now he drew aim on the Yankee color guard and squeezed the trigger—just as another soldier stepped in front of his rifle. The hammer on Hood's rifle snapped—but the gun did not fire. Relieved but puzzled, he looked down at his rifle and saw that he had put on two percussion caps—which caused a misfire. He quickly refitted a cap and fired into the squad of Yankees. At the same instant, he was hit in the left foot. Bleeding badly, with a leg that seemed paralyzed, he turned his rifle into a crutch and hobbled across the creek and toward the rear.[4]

As the 26th moved forward, closing with the enemy, conditions became almost unbearable. The day was now sweltering hot, adding to the furnace-like fury of battle. "[The] men had difficulty in ramming down their cartridges, so slick was the iron ram-rod in hands thoroughly wet with perspiration," a Tarheel soldier would recall. "All expedients were resorted to, but mainly jabbing the ram-rods against the ground and rocks." Now that they were across the creek, they found themselves in a shallow bowl-shaped hollow—a natural killing field. To get out, they had to move uphill directly into the enemy fire. They advanced and fired, advanced and fired—unleashing the Rebel yell as they slowly climbed the hill. It rose above the roar of the fight and carried to the Yankee lines. To Colonel Morrow of the 24th Michigan, the shrill, wild battle-cry sounded simultaneously "boy-like" and "unearthly"—a feeling undoubtedly encouraged by the sight of the 26th North Carolina advancing on his lines through the smoke of battle. "Their advance was not checked," Morrow would report, "and on they came with rapid strides, yelling like demons." Raked by the steady, massed fire of the 26th, the black-hatted troops closed ranks, sealing the gaps in their front lines, and tried to stand firm—but they could not. The Federals facing the 26th's right flank—the troops of the 19th Indiana—were forced to fall back. The position of Biddle's Brigade, posted back in the field behind McPherson's Ridge, exposed the Indiana regiment's left wing to flanking fire from the 11th North Carolina. Pressed by the 26th on their right and center, meanwhile, the Hoosiers grudgingly gave ground, keeping up a steady fire as they backed up the ridge and reformed. Their withdrawal to a new position higher up on the ridge caused the Federal line to bend, which exposed the 24th Michigan's left flank to a crossfire and forced the Wolverines to fall back and re-form. They did so in good order, and it was obvious that the men of the 26th were facing excellent troops—well-disciplined, courageous and tough. Even as they re-formed, the Black Hats continued to take a terrible toll on the 26th.[5]

It was a desperate fight—far bloodier than even the night at Malvern Hill one year earlier—and already the regiment had suffered worse casualties. From his position at the center of the line, Burgwyn could assess the losses—and the progress. His men had held firm. They had steadily advanced under the deadliest fire he had ever seen. Time and again, the regiment's colors had gone down—only to be raised immediately. About the time the Federals reformed their line, Private Thomas, the fifth man to carry the flag, took a bullet in the left arm. He passed the banner over to Private John Vinson, who had been reprieved from the firing squad by Lieutenant Colonel Lane and had proved faithful. No deserter now, Vinson had been there to raise the colors when Thomas went down. Soon, Vinson too fell. Now nineteen-year-old John Marley, a private in Company G—Lane's old "Chatham Boys"—bore the regiment's Starry Cross. It quickly had become evident that to bear the colors almost certainly meant taking a Yankee bullet, but no man had hesitated. "Although they knew it was almost certain death to pick it up, the flag was never allowed to remain down," Private Caison would later report, "but as fast as it fell someone raised it up again." Burgwyn had to have been pleased with the mettle of his men. The great and long-awaited battle was as fierce and bloody as he could have feared—but so far his men had not failed him. Now they had to push the Yankees off the ridge above them.[6]

On the Iron Brigade's left flank, Colonel Williams could estimate that the 19th Indiana had more than 100 dead and wounded. Now they were reformed near the crest of the ridge, taking cover where they could find it, and unleashing a searing fire into the Confederates advancing up the slope. Fire low, Williams had ordered his men. Fire low and waste no ammunition. His losses were serious—the regiment's battle flag had fallen repeatedly—and the Rebels were still firing and still trying to close on the Iron Brigade's line. His Hoosiers were standing firm, however, and were pouring enough fire into the Confederates to turn back almost any assault. To the right, Colonel Morrow's 24th Michigan was engaged in an equally ferocious fight. How much pounding could the Rebels take? Williams and his Hoosiers could only hope the enemy would soon break and retreat.[7]

Colonel Morrow, meanwhile, reformed his battered survivors about half-way up the ridge. Herbst Woods, the section of McPherson's Ridge defended by the 24th Michigan and the 19th Indiana, was an open stand of timber with little underbrush, but the trees gave his troops some protection. The men needed it: Morrow's Wolverine regiment had also taken serious casualties. Thirty-one-year-old Captain William Speed—the city attorney when Morrow was a judge in Detroit—was dead from a bullet through the heart. He had been hit while trying to shift the regiment's left line to counter flanking fire. Also dead was one of Morrow's favorite young officers, Lieutenant Gilbert Dickey, and two members of the regimental color guard. Total dead and wounded were uncounted, but at least 50 men were already down. His troops had reformed in order, however, and they were fighting extremely well—well enough to match any of the Iron Brigade veterans. The Wolverines had to fight well: The Confederates were pressing the Michigan line. The chilling Rebel yell continued, too. "The rebels beat any people [at] shouting," Morrow would vow—and this day the Southerners were also living up to their reputation as fighters. More chilling than the Rebel yell, however, were the Confederate commands he could hear above the racket. *Fire!* Some Confederate officer would yell the command to fire in a booming voice—and immediately a blast of flame, smoke and lead would erupt from the Confederate line. Colonel Morrow's troops unleashed volleys of their own, returning an equally deadly fire. His troops had the advantage of the defense and the Confederates had to fight their way up the sloping ridge; but Morrow's men were dropping all along the line. Despite his losses, however, he was determined to obey orders: "Hold the woods at all hazards."[8]

Captain Louis G. Young—General Pettigrew's aide-de-camp—splashed through Willoughby Run on horseback to join the embattled 26th North Carolina. Events had unfolded just as he had feared. He and General Pettigrew had warned Generals Hill and Heth that the Yankees were at Gettysburg in force—and now, what Young believed was "one of the greatest battles of modern times" was under way with the Southerners so far taking a licking—all, he believed, for "want of faith" and "lack of caution." The battle was joined, however, and Captain Young had no time to ponder the decisions that had sparked it. He had left General Pettigrew back on Herr's Ridge for a close-up look at the brigade in action, and to get it he rode to the center of the line. There he found the 26th North Carolina engaged in a deadly inferno. The

26th had pressed to within twenty yards of the enemy, who had just withdrawn to a second line up the wooded ridge. The fire from both sides was volcanic—more deadly, it seemed, than any human could bear. But both sides held firm and continued to discharge a torrent of fire.[9]

"Give 'em hell, boys," Young yelled as he rode up on the 26th's line. A Yankee bullet suddenly pierced his hat, tumbling it from his head. He caught it before it hit the ground, plopped it back on his head and urged his mount in closer. Colonel Burgwyn had the troops moving up the ridge, pressing the Federals in their second line, but Young spotted a large group of soldiers from the 26th who were not moving. They were clustered at the foot of the ridge, hunkered down behind what appeared to be a marl bed—a large, dug-out section of embankment where local farmers had been digging marl for fertilizer. Beneath this manmade shelf, the troops had found protection from the awful hail of bullets, and many had paused here, as if to catch their breath before pressing forward again into the storm of lead. Young rode forward toward the huddled mass of men. Another bullet pierced his hat. Again he caught it in midair, put it back on his head and began to roust the troops from the shelter of the marl bed and back into the fight.[10]

Back on Herr Ridge, General Pettigrew watched the center of his brigade line with admiration. Things may have gone bad for the Southern forces earlier in the day, but now Pettigrew's Brigade was pressing the enemy. At the center, Colonel Burgwyn's troops especially seemed to be giving the Yankees a fit. The 26th North Carolina had marched into battle as if they were on a parade. They had taken their losses—terrible losses, he could see—and had still pressed forward, repeatedly dressing their line, delivering a devastating fire and making a slow, steady advance. Moments before, he could see movement that indicated the enemy was withdrawing back up the ridge. The 26th North Carolina appeared to have broken the Federal front line. Pettigrew turned to a staff officer, Captain William Westwood McCreery Jr., and issued an order. McCreery had openly stated at least once that he believed the men of the 26th would prove to be the best fighters in the brigade. Now Pettigrew selected McCreery to deliver an official compliment to the regiment in the midst of battle. Go find Colonel Burgwyn, the general told McCreery, and give him a message. "Tell him," Pettigrew said, "his regiment has covered itself with glory today."[11]

Captain McCreery cheerfully rode toward the smoky cauldron of battle. A twenty-six-year-old Virginian and a West Pointer, he was a relatively new member of Pettigrew's staff. He was the son of a U.S. naval officer who had gone down with his warship in 1843. His uncle, also a naval officer, had suffered the same fate—and the family's double loss to military service had been a prime consideration in President Franklin Pierce's decision to give Westwood McCreery a West Point appointment. He had graduated in the top half of his class in 1860, along with Stephen D. Ramseur, a future Confederate general, and future Federal General James H. Wilson. Despite McCreery's serious ambition to "one day gain military distinction"—as he had written U.S. Secretary of War Jefferson Davis in 1855—he was known for a fun-loving personality that may have helped him acquire 196 demerits in a single year at West Point. Upon graduation, McCreery had pulled a tour of duty at Fort Monroe until early 1861. During the Fort Sumter crisis, he had been posted to Washington's defenses and then had been dispatched to another flashpoint: Fort Pickens in the harbor of Pensacola, Florida. In June of 1861, after President Lincoln reinforced Fort Pickens with a large force of Northern troops, McCreery had resigned his commission to join Confederate service, which led Federal authorities to charge him with "having tendered his resignation in the face of the Rebels." He had begun his Confederate service as a second lieutenant and ordnance officer, assisting Lee in Virginia and South Carolina, and—promoted to captain—he had later served as assistant chief of ordnance for General John C. Pemberton. He had gained impressive authority, issuing orders in his crisp, clear handwriting on Pemberton's behalf, but he had spent the war mainly at various desk jobs, and he was eager for combat. As a West Point cadet, McCreery had happily confessed his romantic notions of war. Once, a girlfriend would later recall, he had confided that "if he was killed during the war, he wanted it to be where he had seized the colors from the dead color-bearer's hand and rallied the troops." He had joined Pettigrew's staff at Hanover Junction just seven weeks earlier, called up as acting brigade inspector just in time for the army's great invasion. Now, Westwood McCreery was on the field of what was shaping up as the war's greatest battle—and he hurried toward the fighting.[12]

As he neared the action, McCreery's horse was shot from under him. He went down but was quickly on his feet. Unhurt and amused by his plight, he hurried toward the 26th's battle line, which by now had advanced farther up the ridge toward the smoke and flame of the enemy's second line. He moved past the dead and wounded on the creek bank and started up the wooded slope near the center of the line, where he would presumably find Colonel

Burgwyn. There, just ahead of him, he spotted Captain Young—still on horseback and yelling orders to the troops huddled in the marl bed. Obediently, the men were rising and moving, heading up the slope. McCreery confronted the harried Young and jovially began recounting how he had lost his horse. Young was irritated—he felt this was no time for McCreery's "joyous way"—and he told him so. "[We have] no time to talk about such matters," Young shouted over the clamor of battle. "[We] must assist in getting the men forward." McCreery did not appear insulted; instead, Young thought, the captain acted "as tho' the danger was an enjoyment." McCreery cheerfully moved on, searching for Colonel Burgwyn so that he could deliver General Pettigrew's commendation.[13]

Colonel Burgwyn was farther up the wooded slope, where visibility was now increasingly obscured by the thick, whitish smoke of battle. His focus now had to be keeping up the regiment's fire and momentum. They had forced the Black Hats to reform in a new line. Now they had to press that line, break it and drive it back—and then, hopefully, the enemy's stubborn resistance would collapse. From the center of the 26th's battle line, Burgwyn continued to urge his men forward. On the right side of the line, Lieutenant Colonel Lane was still unhurt; and Major Jones still held command on the left. Although visibility was limited in the smoky, noisy chaos, the three officers pushed the men forward in a deadly ritual: fire, reload, advance, fire, reload, advance. The enemy's return fire was devastating. It continued to drop men dead or wounded at almost every step, steadily depleting the regiment's strength. Under Burgwyn's command the troops continued to advance, however, stepping over the blue-uniformed bodies as they moved forward.[14]

The awesome fire coming from the Yankee lines was unlike anything Burgwyn had ever experienced. Surely more of his men were down now than anyone could have predicted. Some of the wounded tried to limp to the rear; others tried to keep going. The badly wounded and the dead—scores of them now—lay where they had fallen. Their bodies formed rough lines near the creek bank and among the trees up the slope; others lay scattered individually along the line of the advance. Already, Burgwyn could have formed at least one full company from those who had fallen. More were falling around him, all along the line, and more would be falling as they moved up the slope against the deadly torrent. Under normal conditions, a man could have strolled through the woods and up the hill from the creek to the crest in about two minutes. But these were not normal conditions. The men of the 26th dressed their thinning line, closed ranks, kept up their fire—and continued their slow, steady advance. "[Up] the hill we went," Captain James T. Adams of Company D would recall. "It seemed that the bullets were as thick as hail stones in a storm." Somehow Colonel Burgwyn remained unscathed—although a Yankee bullet had taken off the brass drag that adorned the tip of his sword scabbard.[15]

On the regiment's right wing, Lieutenant Colonel Lane could see that his "boys" were pushing back the enemy, but he could also see that the 26th was paying a heavy toll in dead and wounded. How was the rest of the regiment faring? Lane decided to see for himself. Behind the slowly advancing line, he moved through the woods toward the center of the line, passing by the piles of bloody bodies in gray and blue. Through the smoke he spotted Colonel Burgwyn, sword in hand, at the center of the line. Burgwyn saw Lane coming and moved to meet him. "[It] is alright in the center and on the left," Burgwyn announced over the racket of the battle. "We have broken the first line of the enemy." The regiment was holding its own on his end, too, Lane reported. "We are in line on the right, Colonel," he told Burgwyn. Ahead, the 26th's battle line continued the charge and was applying constant pressure on the Federals.[16]

Up the slope they advanced yard by yard—moving, firing, reloading, moving, firing, reloading. Like men pushing their way through a fierce storm, they headed slowly, steadily past the battle-scarred trees, over the bodies of the dead and wounded, up the wooded slope of McPherson's Ridge. Burgwyn brought the regiment to within twenty yards of the enemy's second line, which belched forth volley after volley of gunfire. The soldiers of the 26th stoically faced the front and returned the fire, closing ranks to fill the huge gaps torn in the line. The regiment's battle standard—now with a splintered staff—was still held high at the center of the line, but it was raised at increasingly great cost. "Time after time [it was] shot down by the hot fire of the infantry," a survivor would report, "sometimes the staff being broken and sometimes a color-bearer being shot." Private Marley, the seventh color-bearer, was shot dead with the flagstaff in his hands—but the fallen standard was quickly raised again.[17]

Back at the regiment's campsite on Marsh Creek, musician Julius Lineback began to fear the worst. He had remained with the rest of the 26th's band near the regiment's wagons, preparing to aid the surgeons as needed. He had heard the cannonading in the morning and could distinctly hear the crash of small arms rise and fall after the regiment marched up the road toward Gettysburg.

After a noontime lull, the sounds of battle had picked up again and had in-creased to a sustained roar. The turnpike was packed with soldiers in gray and butternut, advancing to the sound of the guns. At one point Lineback climbed the high ridge to the rear of the creekside campsite, but all he could see was smoke rising from the distant ridges. He was mindful that this was the anniver-sary of the fighting at Malvern Hill. Even that deadly contest seemed insignif-icant compared to the struggle that now roared to the east. At about three o'clock, some of the regiment's wounded hobbled back to the rear with reports from the battlefield. The news was bad. The fighting was fierce and the 26th was engaged in the hottest of it. Casualties in the regiment were said to be dreadful. All Lineback could do was look to the east, where the smoke of bat-tle rose above the distant ridges, and pray for his friends.[18]

Colonel Morrow decided he had no choice: The 24th Michigan had to fall back again. The Confederates had advanced up the slope to within yards of his second line. Both sides were trading volleys practically in each other's faces—and his casualties were frightful. Blue-uniformed bodies lay along his line as if they had been arranged for a parade of the dead. Among them lay a disheartening number of his officers and much of his color guard. So fierce was the Rebel fire in the center of his line that Morrow wondered if the whole Confederate army was concentrating its fire on his regiment. His men were fighting nobly, but the enemy was "accumulating in our front," he concluded. To remain in line, he believed, would only invite destruction. His defense of these woods—to be held "at all hazards"—would be better served if his troops fell back and re-formed on a third line. On the broad crest of the ridge to his rear, he knew, lay a narrow but sharp ravine. He would pull his troops back again and reform on the other side of the ravine. There, hopefully, his men would stall the stubborn enemy advance. He gave the command, and his bloodied troops fell back, firing as they withdrew. Within moments they had successfully completed the tactic, and were already unleashing more punish-ment on the Rebels.[19]

As the Federals fell back through the woods, Colonel Burgwyn and the other officers ordered the 26th's thinning line forward. "While we drove on as hard as we could," one Tarheel soldier recalled, "they would step back slowly. We kept pushing them through the woods, taking a dead rest against the trees and saplings." Atop the ridge, Burgwyn and the troops on the left and center of the line found the terrain level, but their front was cut by a shallow ravine. Several yards to the rear of the ravine, the Yankees had reformed their line and were again pouring forth a deadly fire. Sunlight was obscured by the dense whitish smoke, which cast a dark, eerie pall over the woods. The setting, recalled Private Thomas Perrett, was "dark, weird, wild." A trail of dead and wounded lay behind the 26th from the crest of the ridge back to Willoughby Run. The Federal fire was especially severe at the center of the line. Posted alongside the color guard, Company F's numbers had been shredded. By now more than half the company's men were down. One of those still unhurt was James Moore, the seventeen-year-old private from the Globe. Back home he had routinely scaled ridges like this one without hesitating, but not this time: The climb had been slow and dreadful, as one man after another near him took a bullet and fell. Advancing beside the color guard, he had seen a succession of color-bearers fall, some wounded, others dead, until the color guard had been whittled down to one man.[20]

Nearby, Lieutenant Thomas J. Cureton of Company B was struggling to take charge of his company. Moments before, Cureton's company commander, Captain William Wilson, was shot dead, leaving Cureton in command of Company B. Wilson had begun the war as a captain but had lost his bid for re-election when the regiment had reorganized and he had enlisted in another regiment as a private. He had rejoined the 26th barely six months earlier to replace an ailing company commander. Now he lay among the regiment's dead. As Cureton tried to take Wilson's place, he heard commands from his rear and looked back to see Captain Young calmly ascending the ridge on horseback. Apparently unmindful of the obvious target he presented, Young motioned Cureton to close up to the right and move his company nearer the center of the line. Cureton was surprised to see one of General Pettigrew's staff officers at the battle line—and especially on horseback—but he was shocked when he focused on Young's order. Distracted by his immediate plight, he had not grasped the severity of the regiment's losses. Looking to his right, where Company F was posted beside the color guard, Cureton saw that most of the company no longer existed. Company E, posted to the other side of the colors, had also been reduced to a squad. Only a slim handful of men were still at the center of the line alongside the colors, loading and firing at the Yankees. Obediently, Cureton ordered the remnants of his company to close right and fill in the gap.[21]

* * *

Captain Westwood McCreery finally reached the crest of the ridge just as Cureton closed ranks. McCreery could see a thin line of troops systematically firing at the enemy alongside the 26th battle flag. Through the smoky haze he spotted Colonel Burgwyn, standing with sword in hand behind the line. The colonel had checked both flanks of his line and was now trying to keep the troops in the center closed up and firing. Calling Burgwyn away from the bloody work at hand, McCreery delivered General Pettigrew's message: The 26th North Carolina had "covered itself with glory." It was unquestionably encouraging praise for Burgwyn, who had seen his huge regiment mercilessly shredded in the few minutes it had taken to advance up the wooded ridge. Before Burgwyn barely had time to react to McCreery, however, another color-bearer dropped and the regimental battle flag again fell to the ground.[22]

It was the battlefield event Westwood McCreery had imagined and romanticized so long ago as a cadet at West Point: Before him lay a fallen flag and the opportunity to rally the troops in a moment of glory. He quickly retrieved the fallen standard, stepped in front of the battle line and held the flag high above his head, waving it back and forth. He then turned to lead the advance— and immediately took a bullet through the heart. Killed instantly, he fell on top of the flag, staining it with his blood. Nearby, twenty-eight-year-old Lieutenant George Wilcox of Company H saw McCreery go down. Wilcox scrambled forward, grabbed the bloodied flag and pulled it from under McCreery's body, which was lying flat and motionless on the banner. Flag in hand, Wilcox tried to lead the advance. He managed to take only a few steps, however, when he was hit in the right side. He continued anyway and seconds later was shot in the left foot. Unable to walk, he sank to the ground. As he tried to examine his wounds, the battle line moved forward around him. This time no one immediately tried to pick up the fallen flag.[23]

Ferocious fire sprayed the center of the line. The men pressed forward into the storm—and then hesitated. Seeing a crisis arise at the center of his line, Colonel Burgwyn strode up to Wilcox's fallen form and retrieved the downed battle flag. His sword in his right hand and the flag in his left, Burgwyn hurried ahead of the battle line to cheer on his troops. "Dress on the colors," he ordered in his booming voice, as he raised both flag and sword. Obediently, the surviving soldiers began closing ranks. Burgwyn then turned to Lieutenant Cureton and hurriedly asked if Company B could furnish a color-bearer to take the regiment's colors forward. Cureton called for Private Franklin L. Honeycutt, who immediately stepped forward and put down his rifle to take up the deadly task. As Burgwyn prepared to hand over the colors, Lane appeared by his side. "We are in line on the right," he reported. Burgwyn passed the battle flag to Honeycutt with orders to advance and gave Lane General Pettigrew's message: The "regiment has covered itself with glory today." Then the center of the line was struck by a blast of bullets and a blur of confusion.[24]

Private Honeycutt, who had managed to take barely two steps, was struck in the head and killed instantly. Colonel Burgwyn was hit at the same time. He was turning toward Lane—apparently to cheer on the troops—when he was struck in the side. The bullet penetrated the material of his frock coat, plowed through the two small journals he carried in his inside pocket, pierced his ribcage and passed through the lower part of both lungs. The force of the blow spun Burgwyn around and knocked him flat on his back. Lane quickly knelt by his side and grasped his hand. "My dear Colonel," he implored, "are you severely hurt?" Burgwyn could not speak. He nodded his head, motioned to his wounded side and squeezed the lieutenant colonel's hand. Responsibility for the regiment—and the assault—now fell on Lane. Looking down at Burgwyn, Lane knew he should take command immediately, but he was reluctant to leave his fallen commander. He knew, however, that Burgwyn had always put the regiment first. Lane hesitated only seconds and then moved quickly to close ranks and lead the advance.[25]

Lieutenant Wilcox was examining his wounded foot when he looked up to see Colonel Burgwyn lying flat on his back. Ignoring his wounds, Wilcox hobbled forward to help. When he reached Burgwyn, the young officer lay alone. "He motioned to his side and tried to speak," Wilcox recalled, "but seemed then in the agony of death, and amidst the terrible din and confusion of arms, I could not understand what he said." Wilcox motioned for two soldiers to help move the colonel to the rear. Privates William P. Elvington and Nevel B. Staten managed to slide Burgwyn onto a blanket and then moved him back over the brow of the hill and out of the immediate line of fire. Wilcox watched the men carry Burgwyn away—past the bullet-scarred trees, over the piles of dead and wounded and through the smoke toward the rear. Although he feared Burgwyn was mortally wounded, Wilcox could not go with him. Despite his wounds, the lieutenant had to rejoin the deadly assault: He appeared to be the only officer in his company still capable of walking.[26]

*   *   *

Lieutenant Colonel Lane took charge quickly. When Colonel Burgwyn fell, the troops at the center hesitated and the advance began to stall. Hurrying to the right, Lane confronted Captain James C. McLauchlin, the twenty-eight-year-old commander of Company K. "Close ranks and move your men quickly to the left!" the lieutenant colonel yelled. "I am going to give them the bayonet." McLauchlin promptly obeyed. He got his men moving, dressing left and closing the gaps in the line. Then he too was hit, his left thumb almost shot away, and he went down. Lane was already moving to the left, where Major Jones was still up and in command. Lane issued the same orders and then hurried back to the center of the line to lead the assault. "Shoot low men," the company commanders shouted, and the troops prepared for a bayonet charge.[27]

Back at the center of the line, Lane spotted the regiment's battle flag still lying on the ground near Private Honeycutt's body. Lieutenant Cureton was moving to pick up the banner, but Lieutenant Milton B. Blair of Company I reached it first. As Blair tried to raise the flag, he was stopped by Lane. "Blair, give me them colors," Lane ordered. "No man can take these colors and live," Blair replied. "It is my time to take them now," Lane said. "You will get tired of them," Blair responded—and handed over the banner.[28]

Lane held the battle flag high overhead to get attention. Battle smoke dimmed the sunlight on the crest of the ridge. Enemy fire continued in an uninterrupted roar, dropping more men all along the line. The once-formidable ranks of the 26th North Carolina now looked like a skeleton line of surviving soldiers shrouded in dense, hellish-like smoke. To Lane, it was a ghastly scene of horror. And defeat would make their awful sacrifice worthless. Ammunition was almost exhausted, and he realized the assault was now at a critical point. The regiment had to break through the line of black-hatted enemy troops pouring forth such deadly fire twenty yards away. Holding the battle flag high over his head, Lieutenant Colonel Lane shouted a command: "26th, follow me." The thin gray line responded wildly with a rousing Rebel yell and plunged forward toward the enemy.[29]

From his command position on the slope of Herr Ridge, General Pettigrew intently studied the center of his battle line. Although he could not know the details of the deadly drama that had enveloped McCreery, Burgwyn and Lane in the smoke-shrouded firestorm, Pettigrew could see the advance stalling. Then, for a moment he could see clearly, and at the crest of the wooded ridge an officer at the center of the line was holding aloft the colors.

Again the assault surged forward. Apparently moved, Pettigrew uttered a single observation: "It is the bravest act I ever saw."[30]

Colonel Samuel Williams and the men of the 19th Indiana were in serious trouble. After reforming on the crest of McPherson's Ridge, their ranks were torn apart by ferocious fire from their front and left flank. Colonel Williams had already lost more than half his regiment, and the men were still dropping steadily. His troops were fighting well—the "reputation of Indians as soldiers suffered nothing this day," he would later say—but he feared his regiment was on the verge of being overpowered. He was well aware of his orders to the men—that they must "hold our colors on this line, or lie here under them"—but he could only admit that it now seemed impossible to hold his position. Biddle's Brigade had been posted so far to the rear that the left flank of the 19th Indiana had been left virtually unprotected. Now, if the Hoosiers were forced back, the adjacent 24th Michigan would be uncovered on its left flank.[31]

One Hoosier officer after another had been struck down by the Confederate fire, which had also ravaged the 19th Indiana's color guard. So many color-bearers had fallen that Lieutenant Colonel William Dudley had been forced to order Sergeant Major Blanchard to find recruits. While Blanchard was rounding up another color-bearer, Dudley raised the colors himself. He was quickly shot down with a leg wound. "Colonel, you shouldn't have done this," Blanchard cried when he saw Dudley wounded and down. "That was my duty. I shall never forgive myself for letting you touch that flag." Blanchard then took the flag and, fearing it would be captured, tore the banner from its staff and wrapped it around his body under his sword belt. Within minutes, however, he too was hit. "Tell Mother I never faltered," he said as he bled to death. For a torturous twenty minutes, maybe longer, Colonel Williams and his Hoosiers had been trading the deadliest fire with the Rebels. How much longer could they sustain their fire and hold the line?[32]

The men of the 19th Indiana were being pounded and pressed on their right and center by the 26th and stricken by a scathing fire on their left by the 11th North Carolina. Now, as Colonel Williams felt the renewal of an "overwhelming force" on the right and center of his line, his left flank was suddenly threatened by the collapse of Biddle's Brigade to his left. The two regiments on the right wing of Pettigrew's Brigade—the 47th and 52nd North Carolina—had gradually flanked the poorly positioned Federal left wing defended by the Pennsylvanians and New Yorkers of Biddle's Brigade. Despite a courageous attempt to personally rally his troops, Colonel Chapman Biddle could not stop the Confederate flanking movement. The troops of the 47th and 52nd North Carolina absorbed their casualties and relentlessly pressed forward, pouring a "raking and destructive fire" into Biddle's Brigade. Biddle's battle line began breaking up. That, in turn, put pressure on the Iron Brigade's left flank, which was manned by the 19th Indiana. Despite his desperate efforts, Colonel Williams saw his thin line of Hoosiers bending backwards and at the point of breaking. He had no choice, he believed, but to order a retreat. Firing as they went, the soldiers of the 19th Indiana fell back.[33]

To the Hoosiers' right—and directly in front of the 26th North Carolina—Colonel Henry Morrow was now the only field officer still up and unhurt on the 24th Michigan's battle line. His men stubbornly continued to deliver a disciplined, destructive fire into the Rebel line across the little ravine, but the Confederate fire was equally persistent—and it had severely shrunk the ranks of the 24th Michigan. Morrow figured scarcely one-fourth of his men were still fighting. His second-in-command, Major Edwin B. Wright, was now stumbling to the rear with his right eye apparently shot out. Most other officers were dead or wounded. This was the third stand for Morrow and his Wolverines. His dead littered the line, and still the Rebels in his front were pressing him. Soon, it appeared, his troops would again have to give way. At one point, when his third color-bearer was shot down, Morrow ordered Corporal Andrew Wagner to plant the regiment's battle flag in a prominent spot in the center of the line, so the regiment could close ranks and rally. The corporal obeyed but was quickly shot. Morrow picked up the banner and called for the troops to stand firm. One of his enlisted men, Private William Kelly, took the flag from Morrow. "The colonel of the Twenty-Fourth shall never carry the flag while I am alive," he vowed—and was immediately shot dead. Another private retrieved the colors, but he too went down. Morrow again picked up the flag. Despite the bullets zipping past, he kept the banner at his side.[34]

Now, the firing in his front intensified, and from the Confederate line that "boy-like scream"—the Rebel yell—again rose shrilly over the roar of battle. In his front, the Confederates were again advancing. His men had fought the good fight, but Morrow could see that they could no longer maintain their position. The renewed fire was so fierce that his men were dropping all along the line, and the regiment's wounded were being hit again. To his left, the regiment's battle line was now unprotected by the 19th Indiana's retreat, and the pressure on the center of his line, Morrow concluded, was simply "overpower-ing." His men began backing up, firing step by step as they withdrew, but there was no stopping the retreat—the 24th Michigan's line was broken. Adding to his dilemma, just as his defense began to disintegrate, Morrow received new orders: The entire Iron Brigade was falling back. General Mere-dith was wounded; Colonel William Robinson of the 7th Wisconsin was now commanding the brigade, and General Doubleday had ordered a retreat to the ridge in the rear, where the Lutheran Seminary was located. Colonel Morrow and his Michigan Black Hats backed slowly out of the woods and off McPher-son's Ridge, withdrawing in order toward the distant seminary building.[35]

To the exhausted troops of the Iron Brigade, the men of the 26th North Carolina undoubtedly sounded ferocious as they advanced through the smoke with fixed bayonets, screaming the Rebel yell. The Tarheels' gritty willpower, however, far exceeded their numbers: The regiment had been shot to pieces. In the few minutes it had taken the 26th North Carolina to advance from Herr Ridge and across Willoughby Run up to the crest of McPherson's Ridge—little more than a half-hour—the strength of the regiment had been blasted away. The 26th's once-strong companies had been reduced to mere squads. Despite the slaughter, the survivors dressed their line, closed ranks and followed Lieu-tenant Colonel Lane, who led the charge toward the enemy line holding aloft the 26th's bloodied battle flag. Suddenly, amid the smoke and noise and confu-sion, Lane and his troops realized the Yankee battle line had again broken. The enemy troops were driven from the woods. Even as they fell back, however, the hard-fighting Black Hats poured a deadly fire into the 26th. Company G's Pri-vate Perrett went down with two wounds. Sergeant Preston Kirkman—one of the four Kirkman brothers—paused over the wounded Perrett. Since Perrett couldn't go on, would he give up his coveted rifle? Perrett handed over the weapon. Kirkman took it, advanced just a few feet and fell mortally wounded. At the center of the line, the ninety-one men of Company F had been reduced to three. Every officer was dead or wounded. Lieutenant John Holloway was dead. Captain Tuttle was down with a severe leg wound; and Lieutenant Charles Sudderth was also wounded. Sergeants Henry Coffey and Robert Hudspeth were still alive and standing. So was seventeen-year-old Jimmie Moore, who was the only Company F private still unhurt when the Federals abandoned Herbst Woods. Young Moore had seen practically his entire com-pany shot down around him. Now, as the black-hatted men in blue backed through the haze and out of the timber, the enemy fire became scattered and sporadic. Moore suddenly felt a sense of relief. Now, he congratulated himself, he was finally safe. Then he was hit—twice. Struck in the neck and left thigh, he was knocked to the ground unconscious. Sergeant Coffey was hit, too, leaving Sergeant Hudspeth as the sole unhurt survivor of Company F.[36]

Nearby, Lieutenant Colonel Lane—the fourteenth color-bearer by some accounts—presented an irresistible target as he advanced at the center of the line holding the 26th battle flag. Less than thirty yards away at the edge of the woods, Corporal Charles H. McConnell and seven other Federal soldiers were the last troops of the 24th Michigan to fall back. Behind them, they could see the Confederate battle line moving toward them through the trees with their colors out in front. "Charley," one of the black-hatted soldiers called out, "can't you bring down that Rebel color-bearer?" McConnell had a single remaining round, and he promptly loaded it. "John, that's the man that I'm laying for," he replied. "I'm loading my last cartridge and I'm going to bring him down if I know how to shoot." McConnell paused beside a sapling and steadied his rifle against the little tree. "That's right," the other soldier urged him, "take sure aim." McConnell carefully sighted down the barrel of his weapon at the tall, dark-bearded man in gray advancing toward him with the crimson Confederate battle flag. In McConnell's sights the big man looked like a giant. At thirty yards, McConnell knew he could hardly miss. He squeezed the trigger.[37]

At that instant, Lane turned back toward his thin line of troops to cheer them onward. McConnell's bullet struck the lieutenant colonel just below the base of the skull. It passed through the muscles in his neck—narrowly missing his spinal cord and his jugular vein—smashed his jaw, clipped a piece from his tongue, knocked out his front teeth and exited through his mouth. Lane was knocked flat. Lieutenant Cureton saw Lane go down—"as limber as a rag"—and felt certain he was dead. Lane lay bloody and motionless. Captain Stephen W. Brewer, the twenty-seven-year-old commander of Company E, picked up the fallen battle flag for the last time. Again shouting the Rebel yell, the regiment's thin line of soldiers moved past Lane's prostrate form to flush any lingering Yankees from the woods. "Just then," Lieutenant Cureton would later recall, "our supports [Pender's Division] came up and relieved us." The men of the 26th halted in the edge of Herbst Woods. There were no loud and lingering cheers from the battered and begrimed victors. They had won their awful and deadly duel, but they had been slaughtered in their victory. "[The] ground," one veteran would recall, "was gray with dead and disabled."

Desperately low in ammunition, the regiment's survivors began searching for cartridges on the bodies of the dead.[38]

The fresh troops of Pender's Division, who were following Heth's Division off Herr Ridge in support, moved off McPherson's Ridge into the meadow beyond in pursuit of the retreating Federals. Reserve troops of the 151st Pennsylvania had opened a brisk fire to support the Iron Brigade as it withdrew, and the Federal artillery began dropping shells in the edge of the meadow to cover the retreat. Across the meadow along the western slope of Seminary Ridge, the Iron Brigade survivors and the troops of Biddle's and Stone's brigades were regrouping in a hastily organized line of defense. They were well-supported by artillery, and as the troops of Pender's Division moved across the open land they were raked by a terrible torrent of artillery fire. A Confederate survivor would later recall: "The earth just seemed to open and take in that line which five minutes ago was so perfect." Pender's troops took their punishment and kept coming, pouring a deadly fire into the Federals. One of countless men in blue who fell was Colonel Henry Morrow of the 24th Michigan. A Confederate minié ball grazed his skull, making an ugly scalp wound, and left Morrow bloody, stunned and separated from his troops.[39]

Soon after the Iron Brigade withdrew from McPherson's Ridge, the entire Federal line west and north of Gettysburg began to unravel, forcing General Doubleday to order the entire I Corps to withdraw. To the north, meanwhile, the Federal XI Corps buckled under the relentless pressure of Early's Confederates and fled in retreat. The Iron Brigade regiments were among the last to retire, holding back Lee's army as long as possible, and—with their blood—buying time for the Army of the Potomac to rally and regroup. Troops from the Iron Brigade tried to retreat in an orderly, disciplined manner, and so did some other Federal regiments. The streets of Gettysburg, however, were soon packed with defeated and disorderly men in blue. "The streets were jammed with crowds of retreating soldiers, and with ambulances, artillery and wagons," an Iron Brigade veteran would recall. "There were cellars crowded with men, sound in body, but craven in spirit, who had gone there to surrender. . . . In one case, at least, these miscreants, mistaking us for the rebels, cried out from the cellar, 'Don't fire, Johnny, we'll surrender.'" After a bloody day of fighting on enemy soil, General Robert E. Lee's Army of Northern Virginia was triumphant. Among the ravaged ranks of the 26th North Carolina, the survivors now could tend their wounded and count their dead.[40]

CHAPTER 8

"The Sickening Horrors of War"

Private William Cheek headed back down McPherson's Ridge, trying to shake off the effects of a Federal artillery shell that had exploded nearby. The round had landed near the edge of the woods moments after the Yankee line had broken. The concussion had flattened Cheek and had temporarily clouded his vision. Dazed, he had joined other wounded from the 26th who were limping to the rear. As he retraced his steps through the shot-scarred woods, however, he encountered a sight that made him forget his condition. Two privates were trying to carry Colonel Burgwyn off the field in a blanket— and Burgwyn appeared to be seriously wounded. Cheek hurried to Burgwyn's side. The colonel looked up, recognized the private and asked him to lend a hand. Cheek promptly grabbed the blanket and helped carry the colonel down the slope.[1]

The three enlisted men decided to take Burgwyn back to the woods on Herr Ridge where the regiment had formed its battle line. They carefully headed down the steep slope toward Willoughby Run. On the way, a lieutenant from a South Carolina regiment grabbed the blanket and helped moved Burgwyn toward the rear. The lieutenant was unknown to Cheek and the other privates; he may have been a straggler from Pender's Division. The three enlisted men accepted his help without comment, however, as they descended the slope. Seeing the unidentified officer alongside, Colonel Burgwyn asked the lieutenant to pour some water on his wound. The privates stopped, placed Burgwyn on the ground, got their canteens and removed the colonel's frock coat so that they could bathe his wound. When the coat was off, Cheek spotted Burgwyn's treasured pocket watch hanging by a silk cord from his neck and reached down to remove it for safekeeping. As Cheek fiddled with the cord, the lieutenant suddenly snatched the watch, tucked it in his pocket and began striding away. Cheek yelled at the man to bring back Colonel Burgwyn's watch. When the lieutenant ignored him, Private Cheek aimed his rifle at the officer and cocked the hammer. "I demanded the watch," Cheek would later report, "telling the officer . . . that I would kill him as sure as powder would burn." The lieutenant halted, turned around and returned the timepiece. Cheek took back the watch, called the officer a thief and ordered him away. When he brought back the watch, Cheek found Burgwyn looking up at him with an expression of gratitude. "Colonel Burgwyn said to me that he would never forget me," Cheek would recall, "and I shall never forget the look he gave me as he spoke these words."[2]

Captain Louis Young, now on foot, appeared at Burgwyn's side. So did Captain Brewer. Sitting down, Young lifted Burgwyn onto his lap and cradled him in his arms. From the severity of the colonel's wound, the men around Burgwyn realized the young officer would probably die. "I regret to see you wounded as you are," Young said. "The Lord's will be done," Burgwyn replied. "We have gained the greatest victory in the war." He too seemed to realize his wound was mortal. "I have no regret at my approaching death," he told Young. "I fell in the defense of my country."[3]

The Federal artillery was now shelling the troops of Pender's Division as they moved across the meadow against the new Federal line on Seminary Ridge. An enemy shell overshot Pender's men and exploded in the woods just yards away. A shell fragment took off the top of Captain Brewer's hat, and the group decided they should move Colonel Burgwyn further to the rear. Private Cheek was dispatched to find ambulance attendants and a stretcher so that the colonel could be moved more comfortably across the creek and into the woods on Herr Ridge. While the men waited, huddled around the fallen commander, Burgwyn appeared to be lapsing into unconsciousness. In the colonel's uniform someone found the flask of French brandy Burgwyn's father had sent him. Captain Young managed to get Burgwyn to swallow some of the liquor, which seemed to momentarily revive him. He looked up at the concerned faces peering over him and wished the men good-bye. Would they please send his love to his mother and father and sisters and brothers? The small circle of soldiers watched his every breath and memorized his final sentences as the minutes slowly passed. Private Cheek, who had found it difficult to locate assistance, finally arrived with ambulance men. Colonel Burgwyn was moved to a litter, but the group gave up trying to move him to the rear—

the men could see the end was near. Impulsively, Cheek sat down beside Burgwyn and held the colonel's hand. Burgwyn's thoughts had turned to his
men—to the regiment General Pettigrew had praised for having "covered
itself with glory." He inquired about the 26th and was reassured. "I know my
gallant regiment will do their duty," he said. "Tell the General my men never
failed me at a single point." He appeared now to be failing quickly. He asked
about his sword, which someone retrieved, and his remarkable optimism
flared for a final time. He was "entirely satisfied with everything," Cheek
remembered him saying. A few minutes later, the "boy colonel" uttered a final
statement. "The Lord's will be done," he said quietly—and then he died. "I
never saw a braver man than he," Private Cheek would recall years later. "He
was always cool under fire and knew exactly what to do, and his men were
devoted to him."[4]

As darkness cloaked Gettysburg's fields and ridges, a full moon rose over
the bloodied battlefield. Its pale light bathed the dead in Herbst Woods and
cast shadows among the trees on Herr Ridge where the 26th North Carolina
was now bivouacked for the night. In Gettysburg, soldiers in gray and butternut now packed the town square and patrolled the streets. Except for prisoners and wounded, the Yankees had retreated from most of the town. Now they
were redeploying in a long defensive line along Cemetery Ridge on Gettysburg's south side. After replenishing their cartridge boxes with ammunition
picked from the dead, the men of the 26th had followed the troops of Pender's
Division into town. They had not stayed there long, however, but had been
recalled to the stand of timber on Herr Ridge where they had formed for battle
that day. There, in the woods where they had waited for battle so impatiently—
then 800 men strong—the regiment's battered survivors were now encamped.
The day's stress and terror had left them exhausted. Even so, many of them
wearily rose and made their way to field hospitals where their wounded comrades now lay. Earlier that afternoon they had passed over the battlefield in
Herbst Woods as they returned to Herr Ridge—and they had been stunned
by the carnage left by their fight.[5]

"Then it was we saw the sickening horrors of war," Lieutenant Cureton
would recall. "A great many of our wounded had not yet been carried to the hospital. The enemy's dead . . . lay mixed with their wounded—crying piteously
for water. . . . Our dead were laying where they had fallen, but the 'Battlefield
Robbers' had been there plundering the 'dead.' They seemed to have respected

neither the enemy's nor our own dead." Dead and wounded soldiers from Michigan and Indiana lay strewn among the fallen men in gray from North Carolina. "I saw many wounded Yankees, and about five hundred dead on the hill," another Tarheel would later report, "and [I] wondered how any of our men had escaped." The 26th's weary survivors had moved among the bodies, sharing water from their canteens with both friend and foe. Wandering over McPherson's Ridge, Captain Louis Young had been startled to hear some of the wounded Yankees yelling in pain. Young had seen much of the worst of the war, but he had never seen anything like this: The Yankees were not just moaning—they were howling animal-like. Hoping to calm them, Young had approached some of the fallen men in blue and had been shocked to discover they were foaming at the mouth. Realizing he could do nothing for them, he had moved on.[6]

As the regiment's survivors searched for friends and relatives on the field, they were sometimes dismayed to discover them dead and sometimes relieved to find them hurt but alive. Private Tom Setser searched until he found his cousin, the marble-shooting champion Eli Setser. "[You] may talk of this big fite and that big fite," Tom Setser would later write home, "but tha hante bin [no] sutch fiting as was dun over thair for the first days fite. I could all but walk over the field on dead and wounded. I never hav seen the like before." Setser was disheartened to find Eli with a shattered thigh and other wounds. He settled down beside his cousin, determined to stay with him all night or until medical help arrived. At a hastily established field hospital, musician Julius Lineback and the rest of the 26th's bandsmen helped treat the wounded. Lineback performed his gory chores until exhaustion overcame him. He rested a few hours and then returned to duty. Among the bloodied forms hauled into the field hospital was Lieutenant Colonel John R. Lane. Lane was still alive and received treatment for his terrible wound, but his chances for survival appeared dim. The men of the regiment soon heard the news: Lieutenant Colonel Lane would probably die soon.[7]

Major John Jones now commanded the 26th North Carolina. In the fire-lit shadows of Herr Ridge this hard night, the burden of responsibility surely weighed heavily on the young officer. At age twenty-two, he was barely a year older than the "boy colonel." He had ambition for command—"I think my knowledge will entitle me to something higher," he had once written his father—but this was not the way he had hoped to gain rank. His friend, college-mate and commander, Harry Burgwyn, was dead. There would be no more fellowship reminiscent of David and Jonathan, nor would he ever again benefit from Harry's calm and confident command. Colonel Burgwyn—who always seemed to know what to do in every situation—was gone now, and Jones could do nothing for him beyond posting a guard over his body pending burial. With Lieutenant Colonel Lane apparently near death, responsibility for the regiment now rested upon "Knock" Jones. He commanded a victorious regiment—unquestionably now a regiment of veterans—but the victory had been won at a price far costlier than anyone could have imagined. The day's devastation was obvious to Jones or anyone else who simply counted heads.[8]

When the 26th North Carolina began the assault by marching off Herr Ridge that afternoon, the regiment had numbered 800 officers and men. By the time the fighting had ended in Herbst Woods on McPherson's Ridge, 212 men were left unhurt. The charge had lasted no longer than a half-hour. In those few grueling minutes, they had marched down a gentle slope, passed through an oat field, waded a shallow creek and climbed a wooded ridge—terrain and distance that would not have rated a second thought on almost any farm back home in North Carolina. But over that short distance and in that brief period of time, the proud 26th North Carolina had suffered 588 dead and wounded—a casualty rate of more than 73 percent.[9]

The regiment's ten companies had been led by nine captains: Captain James D. McIver of Company H was on furlough. The fight for McPherson's Ridge had left three of the nine alive and uninjured. Captain Wilson of Company B had been shot dead near the spot where Colonel Burgwyn fell. Captain Jarratt of Company C had been hit in the face and hand. Company D's commander, Captain James T. Adams, had suffered a severe wound in his left shoulder. Company F's Captain Romulus M. Tuttle had taken a bullet in his right leg. Captain Nero G. Bradford, commanding Company I, was critically wounded through his left lung. Company K's commander, Captain J.C. McLauchlin, was forced to have his wounded thumb amputated. First Lieutenant Murdoch McLeod, the ranking officer in Company H, was seriously wounded in the shoulder and chest.[10]

The charge had also taken a toll on the regiment's junior officers. Two lieutenants had been mortally wounded, and as many as 14 more were casualties. Lieutenant Holloway of Company F was dead on the field, and twenty-eight-year-old Second Lieutenant William W. Richardson of Company B, who had held his rank for a little more than six months, was mortally wounded. Twenty-three-year-old Lieutenant James G. Jones of Company D was now suffering a serious wound to his right thigh. Lieutenant William G. Lane of Company G, an old-timer at age thirty-two, was nursing a foot wound. Company F's Lieutenant Sudderth was severely wounded in his right hand, and Lieutenant Ambrose B. Duvall of Company A was wounded in his left hand. Although hit twice while carrying the flag, Lieutenant Wilcox of Company H had survived. His two brothers, however, were also hit, and one, Private Harmon Wilcox, would die. He had joined his two brothers in the regiment just five months earlier.[11]

When Major Jones counted the cost among the regiment's enlisted men, he could only conclude that "the Old 26th" had suffered a "sad fate." At least two-thirds of the regiment's enlisted men were dead or wounded. Companies E and F, which had flanked the colors in the center of the line, had practically ceased to exist. Of the eighty-two men who had gone into battle that morning with Company E, only twelve were left unhurt. With only one man unharmed, Company F suffered even worse. Ninety-one men from the company—three officers and eighty-eight enlisted men—had made the charge against McPherson's Ridge, and ninety were killed or wounded. Only Sergeant Hudspeth was fit for duty when the assault had ended.[12]

Overwhelmed by the sheer number of casualties, the regiment's ambulance attendants took several hours to move the wounded. The long wait in the summer heat was excruciating for some. One was seventeen-year-old Private Jimmie Moore. "The awful thirst and the faintness of the wounded boy lying there in the open field under a July sun, growing fainter and fainter from loss of blood, was but one of [many] cruel incidents" one of Moore's friends would report. Finally, Moore was carried to a field hospital, where a surgeon poked his finger into the bullet hole in the boy's thigh and concluded that Moore had been shot by a carbine. Moore would survive, but he would be rendered unfit for infantry duty. Among those who did not survive were many of the 26th's twin brothers. Among three sets of twins in Company F—the Coffey, Phillips and Townsell families—five of the six twins were mortally wounded. Other brothers and cousins also suffered. Of the nine members of the Coffey family in Company F, two had survived unhurt: four Coffeys would die of wounds and one was already dead. Two of the four Kirkman brothers—Preston and George—were mortally wounded. Two of the three Jarman brothers in Company K had survived, but Private Elijah C. Jarman had a death wound. Privates Robert and R.W. Braswell—two of seven Braswells to join Company F—had both been hit.

Robert had been shot through the head and killed, and R.W. had been wounded in the chest. Two of Company K's Gathings brothers were unhurt, but Private Thomas C. Gathings—the middle brother—would never go home to Gum Springs. Captain Tuttle, badly wounded in his left leg, would survive—and so would his brother, Private Columbus Tuttle, who had an arm wound. Company F's Private Jackson Gragg, however, who had left eight siblings and a widowed mother back home in the North Carolina mountains, had been shot dead in the charge. Dead too was Company B's Sergeant Andrew Wyatt, who had cheated death before a firing squad only to die on McPherson's Ridge. Sergeant Wyatt had died, a fellow soldier later reported, while "bravely doing his duty." One who survived was Corporal Charles W. Shaw, the schoolteacher-turned-soldier of Company H. So did Private Isaac Mattox, leader of the "schoolboys" of Company B. Private Elijah Flake, the former sailor who had served on the CSS *Virginia,* was also unhurt. Still alive too—although seriously wounded—was Company F's Corporal Simeon Philyaw, who had fired the regiment's opening shot. Many of the wounded, Jones knew, had been hit several times.[13]

These were staggering losses for a new commander to face. Not only had Jones lost most of his regiment—his commander, his friends, his fellow soldiers—but he would lose family, too. His brother "Wat," a private in Company I—the old Caldwell Guards—had been critically wounded in the assault. Jones hoped that his younger brother would survive, but the wound appeared mortal. How would his father receive the news? "Wat" was the son he hoped would continue the family's farming tradition. He had transferred to the 26th North Carolina just four months earlier, leaving the 12th North Carolina to join the regiment where his older brother was third-in-command. What if he had stayed with the 12th? It too was at Gettysburg—part of Iverson's Brigade in Rodes' Division of Ewell's Corps—and it too had seen heavy fighting this day. But Iverson's men had not been required to make the bloody charge against the Black Hats on McPherson's Ridge. If "Wat" had not joined his brother's regiment would he now be lying in a field hospital facing death? And what was to become of the 26th North Carolina, now that it was whittled down to 212 men fit for duty? How could the regiment function at a fraction of its strength? Would it be retired from further fighting? Would it be merged into another regiment? Who would replace the dead and wounded officers? These were the kinds of previously unthinkable questions facing "Knock" Jones as he assumed command of the shattered regiment this steamy summer night.[14]

Jones could only imagine what losses the black-hatted Yankees had suffered. He had recrossed the field of battle heading back to Herr Ridge. The piles of enemy dead and wounded were unavoidable. The Black Hats in the woods had fought hard and courageously—and the number of their fallen appeared to match the horrific casualties of the 26th North Carolina. In fact, if Major Jones could have been transported across the moonlit field of battle to Cemetery Ridge, where Federal forces were digging in for the night, he would have encountered a similar scene of shock and mourning among the ranks of the two Iron Brigade regiments the 26th North Carolina had battled on McPherson's Ridge. The 24th Michigan had gone into battle with 496 officers and men; now only 97 were left—giving the regiment a casualty rate of 80 percent. Most of the casualties—dead, wounded and missing—had occurred while the Wolverines were battling the 26th North Carolina in Herbst Woods. Twenty-four of the regiment's twenty-eight officers were casualties, including Colonel Morrow, who was now a prisoner of war. Among the Michigan casualties were nine color-bearers. The 19th Indiana had suffered similar losses. The Hoosiers had gone into battle this day with 288 officers and men and had come out with only 78—giving the 19th Indiana a 73 percent casualty rate. Like the Wolverines, the Hoosiers had suffered most of their casualties on McPherson's Ridge. Mourning the loss of friends and family, a Northern newspaper reporter who visited the bloody slope of McPherson's Ridge spoke for countless bereaved relatives in North Carolina as well as the Midwest. "Stranger hands will bury our late comrades and your friends," he sadly observed, "and you will think of 'a nameless grave on the battlefield'. . . . They have no monument or memorial stone, but you can erect one to their honor in your hearts."[15]

A misting drizzle fell briefly from low, gray clouds on Thursday morning, July 2nd, dampening the woods on Herr Ridge where the men of the 26th North Carolina were bivouacked. The gray morning matched the mood of the men camped among the trees. "A gloom had settled over the entire regiment at the loss of their comrades," reported First Lieutenant Cureton. Waking up from what must have seemed like a nightmare, the surviving members of the 26th only had to think about the multitude of missing faces to be reminded of the regiment's horrendous losses. Aware of the gloom in the 26th and other regiments in his brigade, General Pettigrew issued a command that would restore order and provide distraction. "Military duties" were to be resumed immediately, he ordered. Roll calls were made, and officers were told to prepare official reports. When the troops of the 26th assembled, however, the dramatically thinned ranks and squad-size companies presented more grim evidence of the previous day's slaughter. So did burial details. Although the survivors were undoubtedly buoyed by the knowledge that the regiment had "covered itself with glory," each spadeful of earth tossed into a grave was a disheartening reminder that so many soldiers of the 26th were also now covered with a thin layer of Pennsylvania dirt.[16]

To the rear of Herr Ridge and across the Chambersburg Pike, a grave was dug for Colonel Burgwyn. His friend and messmate, Captain Joseph J. Young, helped prepare him for burial. The news of Burgwyn's death had reached Young late the night before, as he oversaw harnessing of the regiment's wagon teams back near Cashtown. Along with the dreadful news, Young had been given Burgwyn's personal effects—his wallet, his pocket journals, his binoculars and his prized pocket watch. Young looked at the journals: Each had a gaping bullet hole. Mindful of his promise to Burgwyn, Young was determined to carefully oversee the colonel's burial and mark the spot so that Burgwyn's body could someday be sent home as Young had vowed. He had hurried toward Gettysburg as soon as his duties were done. Working his way along the crowded pike past long lines of Confederate wagons, Young did not reach the regiment until almost sunrise. He immediately asked for the colonel's remains. As the morning's misty dawn lightened the battlefield, Captain Young stood over Burgwyn's body—guarded by the sentinel posted by Major Jones—and studied his dead friend's face.[17]

"How beautiful he looked even in death," Young would later write Burgwyn's father. "There was none of the usual hideous appearance generally apparent in those killed while contending in mortal strife, but he looked like one just fallen asleep. How could I doubt, looking on him, for a moment that his spirit had flown where sorrow & suffering were no more." Others would lament the loss of Burgwyn's talents to the Cause, and many would note his youthful accomplishments. Young, however, focused on the caliber of his friend's character. "I have often been struck with his high sense of honor, especially in a spiritual view," he would later tell Burgwyn's family. "He put his trust in a higher power than the puny arm of man could afford & I would say to his afflicted relatives, mourn not as those without a hope, but rather look forward to the time when they can meet him in endless happiness."[18]

Young wrapped a red woolen blanket tightly around Burgwyn's body and rounded up a large wooden gun crate to use as a coffin. A burial site was selected in the shade of a walnut tree about 75 yards north of the Chambersburg Pike. Young estimated that it lay about two miles west of Gettysburg, and he recorded directions for Burgwyn's family, believing that someday they would want the colonel's body reinterred in North Carolina. Captain Wilson of Company B was buried nearby, and so was Captain McCreery. Surviving officers and soldiers of the 26th North Carolina gathered around the gravesite for Burgwyn's burial. Before the colonel's body was lowered into the grave, one of the officers clipped a lock of his hair to send to his mother. Among those whose grief was most obvious was Burgwyn's servant, Kincian, whom Captain Young planned to send back to North Carolina with most of Burgwyn's personal possessions. "Poor Kinchen takes it bitterly enough," Young observed. Earth was shoveled back into the grave and the "Boy Colonel" was buried.[19]

"The death of one so young, so brave, so accomplished with every prospect of being at no distant period one of our greatest men has filled all with sadness and sorrow," Captain Young wrote Burgwyn's father. "His fall is universally regretted but in his regiment, now reduced to less than 200, all are filled with the greatest sorrow. . . . I can truly say, the death of Gen. Lee himself I would have preferred. But all mortal that is lovely has to fade away, but his example ought ever to be a shining light to his relatives and friends left behind. Their loss is great but I hope and believe it is his eternal gain."[20]

Private Tom Setser was also saying good-bye, and he too feared it might be a final farewell. He had spent the night alongside his severely wounded cousin Eli. Soon after daylight Thursday morning, ambulance attendants finally loaded Eli into an ambulance. When the moment of parting came for the cousins, thoughts of family were on Eli Setser's mind. He seemed to realize there would be no more home cooking, mountain watermelon or "fancying" the girls back home on Lower Creek. "Tom," he told his cousin, "tell my folks how it was." Both men could see that Eli's thighbone was shattered almost to splinters, and both knew soldiers seldom survived such a severe wound. "he said that he was a going to die and he node it," Tom Setser would later write Eli's father. "He said he was willing to die and he wanted me to tell you how it was. He was shot in too or three places in the arm, and one or too holes threw his coat, and one came went threw his thie and broke the bone all to pecis." All Tom could do was watch the ambulance creak away and perhaps wonder if the Setsers of Lower Creek would ever see Eli again.[21]

Colonel Henry K. Burgwyn, Jr., was only twenty-one years old when he took the 26th North Carolina into battle at Gettysburg. Exceptionally bright, he entered the University of North Carolina at age sixteen, graduated with honors, then joined the corps of cadets at the Virginia Military Institute—where he again distinguished himself scholastically. Despite his youthfulness, he was a capable professional officer and a proven leader. When his men entered the firestorm of battle at Gettysburg, Burgwyn would be leading them. *(Special Collections Library, Duke University)*

Back home in Raleigh, according to family members, a nineteen-year-old fiancée waited for Colonel Burgwyn. Her name was Annie Lane Devereux, pictured here in a postwar photograph, and she was the oldest daughter of a prominent North Carolina family. "Patient, gentle, earnest, brave, devout" is how a contemporary described her. She would need such character qualities by war's end. *(North Carolina Division of Archives and History)*

Will's Forest house—the Devereux family home in Raleigh—was renowned during the Civil War for its rose gardens. Here, on his last furlough before the march to Gettysburg, twenty-one-year-old Colonel Henry K. Burgwyn, Jr., was said to have come courting. The Devereux family included eight children and, according to a friend, kept a "happy and delightful home" known for its "gracious hospitality." (*North Carolina Division of Archives and History*)

Farmer-turned-soldier John R. Lane had no formal military training but had risen from corporal to lieutenant colonel of the 26th. Devout, coolheaded, and dependable, he was a popular officer with the men in the ranks, whom he described as his "boys." When the regiment was ordered into action at Gettysburg, Lane was second-in-command—and was three days away from his twenty-eighth birthday. (*Private collection of L. R. Gorrell*)

Twenty-two-year-old Major John Jones was no stranger to tragedy: As a teen he had lost his mother and his youngest brother, and he had seen the war's deadly harvest on battlefields like Malvern Hill. Nothing he had experienced, however, could have prepared him for what awaited at Gettysburg. *(Private collection of Skip Smith)*

Although he was the 26th's first colonel, Zebulon B. Vance was not present at Gettysburg. As a former U.S. Congressman, he found politics to be irresistible, and, after a year of command, he left the regiment to become North Carolina's wartime governor. *(North Carolina Collection, Pack Memorial Library)*

"We should not, therefore, conceal from ourselves that our resources in men are constantly diminishing," General Robert E. Lee wrote to Confederate President Jefferson Davis on the eve of the Gettysburg campaign. Lee knew his decision to take the war to the North involved grave risks, but he believed the South's best hope for independence lay with a major victory on Northern soil. *(Library of Congress)*

Lieutenant General A. P. Hill commanded the Army of Northern Virginia's Third Corps—which included Heth's Division, Pettigrew's Brigade and the 26th North Carolina. On the eve of battle, Hill dismissed reports that Federal forces lay ahead at Gettysburg. *(Author's collection)*

Eager to search Gettysburg for a rumored stockpile of footwear, Major General Henry Heth pressed his corps commander for permission to advance. "If there is no objection," he announced, "then I will take my division tomorrow and go to Gettysburg and get those shoes." *(National Archives)*

Fluent in six languages, Brigadier General James Johnston Pettigrew was a scientist, scholar and world traveler who had mastered the military arts well enough to earn a brigadier's commission. At Gettysburg, Pettigrew's Brigade included the 26th North Carolina, and by the battle's third day he had been placed in command of the left wing of the Pickett-Pettigrew Charge. *(Southern Historical Collection, University of North Carolina)*

Captain Louis G. Young, an aide to General Pettigrew, feared Generals Hill and Heth were incautious to dismiss reports of Federal troops at Gettysburg. "Blindness in part seemed to have come over our commanders," he concluded. (*Histories of the Several Regiments and Battalions from North Carolina*)

A hickory-tough mountain boy, Private "Jimmie" Moore of Company F had gone to war at age fifteen. By July of 1863, he was a seasoned veteran who was as ready as any man to charge into the guns of the enemy. Awaiting him at Gettysburg, however, was a hillside hike more terrible than anything he could have imagined. (*Histories of the Several Regiments and Battalions from North Carolina*)

Julius Lineback (*second from left*) and the other members of the 26th North Carolina Regimental Band left the safety of North Carolina's Moravian community to accompany the regiment to bloody fields like Gettysburg. Following the first day of battle, they would be called forth for a crucial performance. (*Southern Historical Collection, University of North Carolina*)

On Thursday, June 25, the 26th North Carolina and the rest of Pettigrew's Brigade forded the Potomac River. "Taking off our shoes, socks, pants and drawers, we made a comical looking set of men," a member of the regiment would later recall. On the opposite shore, the regimental band struck up "Maryland, My Maryland." *(Battles and Leaders of the Civil War)*

Bivouacked near Fayetteville, Pennsylvania, the men of the regiment assembled for a Sunday worship service as depicted in this soldier's sketch. "Did you notice Col. Burgwyn during the preaching?" one soldier confided to another. "I believe we are going to lose him on this trip." *(Moravian Music Foundation)*

As the Southern army advanced through the Pennsylvania countryside, President Lincoln made a surprise appointment: he put Major General George Gordon Meade in command of the Army of the Potomac. All of Meade's predeccessors had been defeated by Lee, but President Lincoln hoped for better from his new commander, who was a Pennsylvanian. Said Lincoln: "I expect Meade will fight well on his own dung hill." *(National Archives)*

The county seat of Pennsylvania's Adams County, Gettysburg in 1863 was a crossroads community of approximately 2,400 residents. Ten highways converged on the town, making Gettysburg a geographic magnet that drew the Confederate and Federal armies together from different directions. *(Adams County Historical Society)*

Advancing toward Gettysburg from the west, Burgwyn and his regiment followed the Chambersburg Turnpike up and over a series of broad ridges. Outside Gettysburg, they moved to their right onto Herr Ridge, seen here in the distance, and deployed into a battle formation. (*National Archives*)

Former U.S. congressman Edward McPherson was chief clerk of the U.S. House of Representatives and one of Gettysburg's most prominent citizens. Although his family had leased their property on Willoughby Run to a local farming family, the property still bore the family name: McPherson's Ridge. (*National Archives*)

One section of McPherson's Ridge was topped by a stand of timber and was known locally as Herbst Woods. The forested section of the ridge was the point of attack for the 26th North Carolina on Gettysburg's first day. It was defended by hard-fighting Federal troops known as the Iron Brigade. (*Library of Congress*)

Colonel Henry A. Morrow commanded the 24th Michigan, which was deployed in Herbst Woods on Gettysburg's first day. Although he was a native Virginian, Morrow's home and family were in Detroit, and his heart was with the North. To him, Colonel Burgwyn and his Tarheel soldiers were the enemy, and he was determined they would not overrun his position. (*U.S. Army Military History Institute*)

"Boys," Colonel Samuel J. Williams shouted to the men of the 19th Indiana, "we must hold our colors on this line, or lie here under them." Assaulting the wooded portion of the line Williams and his Hoosiers held on McPherson's Ridge were troops of the 26th North Carolina. (*U.S. Army Military History Institute*)

At age twenty-four, Colonel James K. Marshall was the youngest front-line brigade commander in the Pickett-Pettigrew Charge. The grandson of a U.S. Supreme Court chief justice, "Jimmy" Marshall would lead Pettigrew's Brigade—including the 26th North Carolina—in the war's most famous assault. "We do not know which of us will be the next to fall," he would tell an aide in the heat of battle. *(Virginia Military Institute)*

While the Confederate artillery pounded the distant Federal positions, the men of the 26th North Carolina waited behind the guns for the order to advance. Beneath them, the ground shook constantly, and answering enemy artillery fire shrieked overhead. "It was a time when hours are compressed into minutes, hearts cease throbbing and the blood lies dormant in your veins," a North Carolina soldier would recall. *(Battles and Leaders of the Civil War)*

Marshall's brigade would be supported by two brigades of veteran troops commanded by Brigadier General Isaac R. Trimble, an experienced, hard-fighting sixty-one-year-old officer. Watching Pettigrew's troops charge the distant Federal position on Cemetery Ridge, Trimble would marvel: "I believe those fine fellows are going into the enemy's line." *(Library of Congress)*

Brigadier General Alexander Hays commanded the division of Federal troops defending the section Cemetery Ridge in front of Pettigrew's division. "They are coming, boys," he shouted as he watched the Pettigrew-Pickett Charge advance. "We must whip them." *(U.S. Army Military History Institute)*

Major John T. Hill commanded the 12th New Jersey, which defended a section of Cemetery Ridge opposite Marshall's brigade. The regiment had limited combat experience and newly appointed officers—but the Jerseymen had improvised a deadly weapon to fell any Southerners who came their way. (*New Jersey Troops in the Gettysburg Campaign*)

A twenty-eight-year-old artillery officer, Colonel Edward Porter Alexander, was chosen to open the Confederate artillery bombardment that preceded the Pickett-Pettigrew Charge. Alexander had also been given the weighty responsibility of signaling the infantry advance. At 1:40, he hastily scribbled a dispatch: "For God's sake," it began, "come on quick." *(Library of Congress)*

Earlier in the war, Sergeant "Jake" Bush had almost been shot while raiding a farmer's potato patch. He had survived the regiment's early engagements, and had lived through the assault on McPherson's Ridge. In the Pickett-Pettigrew Charge, however, he would be shot four times. *(Private collection of Skip Smith)*

Captain Stephen W. Brewer had picked up the regiment's fallen battle flag atop McPherson's Ridge—and had escaped harm. In the Pickett-Pettigrew Charge, he would do so again, but the result would be different. *(Histories of the Several Regiments and Battalions from North Carolina)*

Captain Samuel P. Wagg of Company A had survived the first day's bloody fight on McPherson's Ridge. On July 3rd, he would again lead his company forward in a charge against the enemy—this time as part of the Pickett-Pettigrew Charge. Would he live to see his home in the Blue Ridge Mountains again? *(Histories of the Several Regiments and Battalions from North Carolina)*

The line of march awaiting the 26th North Carolina and the rest of Marshall's brigade in the Pickett-Pettigrew Charge presented a pastoral-looking scene. Sprawling fields of clover, grass, and patches of wheat, intersected by fences, led toward distant Cemetery Ridge. However, the massed firepower of Federal artillery and infantry would transform the gentle farmland into a killing field. *(Adams County Historical Society)*

The Emmitsburg Road—and its flanking fences—had to be crossed before the men of the 26th and the rest of Pettigrew's division approached Cemetery Ridge. As they scaled the fences, their ranks were raked by the massed Federal fire. "Every man that reached the road in my view sank to the ground," one of Pettigrew's officers would report. *(National Archives)*

For decades, veterans of the war would honor the 26th North Carolina for its courage and sacrifice at Gettysburg. While the regiment was justly praised for having "covered itself with glory," a shocking number of the 26th's members—like these Confederate dead at Gettysburg—were also covered with a thin layer of Pennsylvania earth. *(Library of Congress)*

At war's end, John R. Lane returned home, married Mary Ellen Siler (photographed here beside her husband) and prospered as a country businessman. He also became a regional symbol of American valor and reconciliation. "His name is known through the state and the South," proclaimed a North Carolina newspaper. *(Private collection of L. R. Gorrell)*

In 1903, Lane returned to Gettysburg for the fortieth anniversary of the battle. He delivered a major speech to a huge crowd on Cemetery Ridge, and posed for this photograph with Charles H. McConnell, a Northern veteran, atop McPherson's Ridge. Near the same spot forty years earlier, McConnell had done his best to kill Lane; in 1903 they were reconciled as friends. *(Private collection of L. R. Gorrell)*

West of the battlefield on the Chambersburg Pike, Private Thomas Perrett of Company G lay on a bed of straw in a barn that had been converted into a field hospital. Despite two wounds and the loss of his coveted rifle, Private Perrett considered himself fortunate. After receiving his wounds near the end of the charge, Perrett had hugged the earth until the Yankee line broke and the fighting seemed to have shifted away from McPherson's Ridge. He had then managed to get to his feet and was limping to the rear when he spotted a bulging Yankee knapsack. He had paused in his retreat long enough to pull on the knapsack, and as he resumed his rearward march he had been shot in the back. Happily, he later recalled, the bullet was almost spent and lodged in the knapsack. Later, after growing faint from exhaustion and loss of blood he had been picked up by ambulance attendants.[22]

Now Perrett congratulated himself on being thrice blessed. He had been saved by a Yankee knapsack, rescued relatively quickly by the ambulance corps and was now resting comfortably on a bed of straw. His contentment was interrupted, however, by a drunken Confederate surgeon who examined Perrett's wounds and vowed to conduct exploratory surgery in search of a Yankee minié ball. Perrett refused, and a shouting match erupted. The private would not back down, however, and the intoxicated surgeon finally gave up. "[A] man so obstinate ought to die," the doctor groused as he departed. Perrett felt he had scored another triumph. "I am in the greatest of luck," he told himself.[23]

Lieutenant Colonel John R. Lane may not have felt lucky, but he was still alive. Housed with other wounded officers in a brick house that had been transformed into a field hospital, Lane appeared merely to be awaiting death. He had taken no nourishment since his swig of brandy from Colonel Burgwyn's flask the morning of the battle. He was unable to eat or drink due to the damage to his mouth caused by the exiting bullet, and the wound through his neck appeared mortal. The bullet had hit no vital parts, however, and John Randolph Lane was a strong man who was determined to live. Survival was possible—if he could escape infection and endure the pain. He had a bullet hole through his neck, a sliced tongue, a mangled mouth and an unknown number of broken or missing teeth. With the valiant determination that marked his personality, he held on to life. In his misery this morning, he could hear a wounded Georgia officer who lay nearby talking deliriously. For hours, the suffering Georgian carried on. Finally, at about one o'clock in the afternoon, the officer suddenly became silent—and then spoke several sentences clearly and with lucidity. "There now, there now," Lane heard the man say.

"Vicksburg has fallen, General Lee is retreating and the South is whipped. The South is whipped." A few minutes later, Lane heard someone comment that the man had died. Days later, when news of the disastrous Confederate defeats at Vicksburg and Gettysburg were announced among the wounded, Lane would recall the wounded Georgian's prediction. For the moment, however, Lane appeared to be destined for the same fate.[24]

The morning mist soon burned away, and the summer sun raised the temperature to an estimated high of 95. By then, the skeletal ranks of the 26th North Carolina were gaining numbers. General Pettigrew had issued orders for walking wounded with minor injuries to return to their regiments. Cooks were issued rifles and put into the ranks. Soldiers who had been detailed to non-combat duties were recalled. The 26th's band members were ordered to put aside their hospital chores and report to brigade headquarters. Julius Lineback and other band members assumed that "the Gen'l was going to take their horns from them and give them muskets." Dr. Lewellyn P. Warren, the regiment's senior surgeon, sent band leader Sam Mickey to headquarters with a note excusing the musicians on grounds they could not be spared from the hospital. The surgeon's request was denied, but the bandsmen were not needed for combat—they were needed to boost morale. Their orders were to get their instruments, join the 11th North Carolina band and inspire the battle-weary troops with martial music.[25]

The musicians were put to the test. Rousing tunes like "Luto Quickstep," "Louisa Polka," "Cheer, Boys, Cheer," "Old North State," "Dixie" and "The Bonnie Blue Flag" were among the repertory. Assembled on the edge of the battlefield, the combined bands achieved what may have been a once-in-a-lifetime performance. Fighting had resumed elsewhere on the field, and the sounds of battle provided a dramatic background for the martial music. "When the cannonade was at its height," Lieutenant Colonel Fremantle would recall, "a Confederate band . . . began to play polkas and waltzes, which sounded very curious, accompanied by the hissing and bursting of the shells." The music was not "curious" to the men of the 26th North Carolina; it was inspirational. It raised spirits, provoked cheers and left some men with a memory they would never forget. "[The music] was never done more faithfully . . . and with more effect," Lieutenant Cureton would later recall. "The writer until this day has never heard music that cheered him so. [The gloom] was soon entirely dispelled by the music and by 12 o'clock noon the command could raise a cheer."[26]

As morale was reinstilled within the 26th North Carolina, the regiment was being reorganized in command structure—and so were the brigade and division to which it was attached. From the command of Heth's Division at the top to the junior officers of the regiment's ten companies, vacant positions caused by battle deaths and wounds were now being filled. General Heth had been felled by a head wound at the climax of his division's assault the day before, and General Pettigrew now took command of Heth's Division. To replace Pettigrew, Colonel James Keith Marshall, the twenty-four-year-old colonel of the 52nd North Carolina, was given command of Pettigrew's Brigade. Within the 26th, Major Jones commanded the regiment as acting lieutenant colonel. Captains Wagg, Brewer and Albright—the only unhurt company commanders—retained command of Companies A, E and G. Other companies were now led by junior officers, like First Lieutenant Cureton, who was promoted to captain of Company B to succeed Captain Wilson. Backing up Captain Isaac A. Jarratt of Company C—who had been slightly wounded in the face and hand—was Lieutenant William M. Porter. Less than a year and a half earlier, Porter had been a lowly private. Sergeant Robert Hudspeth—the sole uninjured man in Company F—acted as both commander and recruiter when he rounded up a handful of men from the ambulance and pioneer corps to maintain his company's presence in the regiment. In Company B, soldier William M. Estridge made a dramatic leap in rank when he was "elected" third lieutenant: The promotion jumped him from private to officer.[27]

While Major Jones and the surviving officers worked to reorganize and strengthen the regiment, the soldiers rested. When fighting resumed elsewhere on the field they could hear the sounds of battle, but after the previous day's slaughter in their ranks, they would not be called into action. Despite their staggering losses, they had helped the Army of Northern Virginia gain a major victory on Northern soil. Already, word of the Southern triumph on July 1 was spreading. "Our hope is all gone and we cannot expect but that a few days will determine the fate of Baltimore & Washington, that our government is not able to maintain itself," one dismayed Unionist penned in her diary. "General Grant it is said has also been defeated at Vicksburg. . . . Can it be possible that we are a nation of cowards?" Some Federal prisoners of war in Gettysburg also believed the South was on the verge of winning the war. "What added to our uneasiness," an Iron Brigade soldier would later recall, "was the fact that the rebs might clean out the Army of the Potomac and take Washington, then 'Old Abe' and the country was gone for certain." The

Federal troops who had retreated through Gettysburg the previous afternoon, however, had been rallied and reinforced—and the hard-won Confederate victory of the first day would not be repeated on July 2nd.[28]

By daylight of the 2nd, Federal forces occupied a strong defensive position. Shaped like a giant upside-down fishhook, the Federal line began at Culp's Hill just southeast of town, curved around Cemetery Hill on Gettysburg's south side and then stretched almost due south along Cemetery Ridge to the foot of Little Round Top. Major General Winfield S. Hancock, the thirty-nine-year-old commander of the U.S. II Corps, had stemmed the Federal retreat the day before and had redeployed the Federal troops into the formidable position they now held. General Meade had arrived on the field in the early morning darkness of July 2nd. A skilled military engineer, the Army of the Potomac's new commander personally inspected the defensive line Hancock had established. He liked what he saw. It was a strong line—becoming stronger as the troops piled up stone walls and built breastworks—and it provided a clear field of fire for the Federal artillery. Its convex shape also gave the defenders good interior lines that would allow Meade to rapidly shift troops from one position to another. The Army of the Potomac had been pouring piecemeal into Gettysburg through the night, and more troops continued to arrive during the day. By noon, the bulk of Meade's army was on the field except for the U.S. VI Corps, and those troops were on the way. With his troops properly deployed, Meade had good reason to believe the Federal line could hold. The Army of the Potomac would take advantage of its formidable defensive position, Meade decided, and would wait for Lee's Confederates to attack.[29]

The attack came on the afternoon of July 2nd, and its target was the left wing of Meade's line on Cemetery Ridge. The evening before, Lee had ordered General Ewell to attack the Federal right flank "if practicable"—but Ewell had deemed Cemetery Hill and Culp's Hill too strong. Lee therefore aimed at the Federal left. Longstreet urged Lee to take the defensive, leave the field, threaten Washington and lure Meade to make an attack. Lee declined, believing an attack on Meade's army was "unavoidable." At about four o'clock—far later than Lee had intended—Longstreet launched two hard-fighting First Corps divisions under Major Generals Lafayette McLaws and John Bell Hood in assaults designed to break or turn the Federal left. Horrendous casualties again occurred—and local landmarks known forever afterwards as the Wheat Field, the Peach Orchard, Devil's Den and Little Round Top became famous as sites of valor and slaughter. Although the determined

Confederates came narrowly close to penetrating the Federal line, Meade's troops stubbornly resisted. The fighting finally ended at dark. Unlike the day before, Lee's men did not break the Federal line.[30]

Captain Louis Young, General Pettigrew's aide-de-camp, received the news of the second day's failure with dismay. It was another day of "lost opportunities," he believed. Young thought the army should have pressed the attack the night before—that enough daylight and reinforcement were left after the Federal line collapsed to ensure a Southern victory. He blamed Ewell, Hill and Longstreet for doubts and delays. "If Ewell's and Hill's Divisions had pressed forward when the enemy retired to Cemetery Ridge," he would later proclaim, "the battle of Gettysburg would have ended on the day it began." He also believed Southern success had been squandered on the second day. "An early attack on either flank of the enemy," he would maintain years later, "could scarcely have failed of success."[31]

At least one Federal officer appeared to agree with Captain Young. "[T]his was no place to fight a battle in," Major General John Newton voiced in a nighttime war council with Meade and his subordinates. Meade had called the conference on the evening of July 2nd in the cramped quarters of the white-washed farmhouse that had been commandeered for his headquarters. Newton seemed to share the opinion that the Federal army had narrowly escaped defeat. The question poised among the dozen senior officers present was basic and critical. Should the Army of the Potomac withdraw? "Remain here, and make such correction in our position as may be deemed necessary," declared Major General John Gibbon, "but take no step which even looks like retreat." The other officers agreed—even Newton conceded—and also voted to remain on the defensive. "Such then is the decision," Meade concluded. The men in blue would stay and fight—and would await another attack by Lee's army.[32]

Across town at Confederate headquarters, Lee remained optimistic. "It is all well, General," he told A.P. Hill on the evening of July 2nd, "everything is all well." A crowd of Confederate officers congregated around Lee's headquarters during the night, and Lee moved among them shaking hands. Later that evening he formulated his battle plans. He was in poor health on this campaign, plagued by diarrhea and troubled by what appeared to be heart problems. Fighting in unfamiliar territory, he found his maneuverability restricted by limited reconnaissance and poor position. Instead of the sweeping movements that had produced success in the past year, Lee had hammered the enemy for two days with frontal assaults. He had no Stonewall Jackson now, and Longstreet, his chief subordinate, questioned his tactics almost to the point of insubordination. Lee still believed, however, the Army of Northern Virginia could break the Federal line. "The enemy is there," he reportedly observed, "and I am going to strike him."[33]

He still had justifiable reasons for optimism on the night of July 2nd. The enemy remained undefeated, and Confederate casualties were severe, but Lee's assaults had carried the first day and had pushed back the enemy line in some places on this day. The Army of Northern Virginia had fought hard and was ready to fight again. Morale remained high. General Stuart and his command were now located and near—finally—adding substantial cavalry to the army. Major General George E. Pickett and his division of Virginians—part of Longstreet's Corps—were also now at hand, bolstering Confederate forces with a sizable body of fresh reinforcements. The army remained strong, and the need for a Southern victory on Northern soil remained urgent. Lee acknowledged that the enemy held a formidable position—"a high and commanding ridge," he called it. Many times in the past, however, the Army of Northern Virginia had prevailed against seemingly insurmountable odds. At Gettysburg, Lee believed, the army already had come close to the victory he sought. "These partial successes," he would later report, "determined me to continue the assault the next day." He had failed to turn either Federal flank, Lee concluded, so he should next strike the Federal line near its center.[34]

The orders came in the middle of the night: Prepare to march—the brigade was moving. Major Jones had the chore of rousing the 26th's weary survivors. The men broke camp in the moonlit darkness and left the woods on Herr Ridge. With the rest of Pettigrew's brigade, now commanded by Colonel Marshall, they marched toward town and then turned southward. "Over hills, across branches, through thickets, we slowly wended our way," one North Carolinian would recall. The familiar tread of marching feet was made lighter by the absence of so many comrades. Along the way, they heard the moans of men wounded in the second day's fighting—"for God's sake don't tread on me . . . please give me some water." It was a brief trip. They were halted in a shallow, wooded area behind Seminary Ridge. Columns of troops continued to pass by their bivouac, and countless artillery pieces rumbled past. Visibility was limited in the dark, but seasoned soldiers could calculate a new location. The men of the 26th were bivouacked roughly opposite the center of the Yankee line.[35]

CHAPTER 9

"All Were Willing to Die"

Captain Thomas Cureton stood in the edge of the sprawling field and studied the distant outline of Cemetery Ridge. To do so, he had to look toward the early morning sun, which was rising through a patchy haze of ground fog and campfire smoke. The day—Friday, July 3rd—promised to be another scorcher: The morning air was already sticky warm. Cureton was accompanied by Captain Samuel P. Wagg of Company A. Together they had walked out of the regiment's wooded bivouac and onto the broad expanse of farmland that separated the Confederate and Federal lines. Behind them, the Army of Northern Virginia uncoiled along Seminary Ridge, fronted by an almost mile-long line of field artillery. In front of them, more than three quarters of a mile away, the Army of the Potomac was deployed along Cemetery Ridge, backed by formidable concentrations of Federal artillery.[1]

Cureton and Wagg had come forward to study their target. They could judge from troop deployments and rumors in the ranks that a major Confederate assault would be launched against the distant enemy line later this day. They were sure the 26th North Carolina would be involved—which meant they would be leading their undermanned and battle-torn companies over this field. For the twenty-five-year-old Cureton, the pending assault would come on his first full day as a captain. He had received a field promotion the day before, succeeding Captain Wilson—who had been shot dead on McPherson's Ridge. Cureton had been wounded himself in the first day's fighting—grazed on the left shoulder by a minié ball—but he was not seriously injured, and now he was commander of Company B. Cureton was a capable officer. He hailed from the Waxhaws, a farming region on the central border of North and South Carolina, which boasted of being the birthplace of President Andrew Jackson and had a reputation for raising men to be as tough as hickory nuts. Cureton and the thin ranks of the 26th would need a stiff dose of toughness this day: The upcoming assault appeared likely to be at least as dangerous as the charge up McPherson's Ridge.[2]

The deadly difficulty of the task was evident when Cureton studied the proposed route of assault. It was a pastoral-looking scene—sprawling fields of clover, grass and some wheat, which sloped gently downward into a shallow swale and then rose gradually to crest on the distant ridge. On the far left of the ridge stood a small barn and a white-washed cottage. Behind the ridge to the far right, he could see the dark shape of a large, wooded hill and a smaller one beside it. The route of assault would take the regiment across the open fields, through a little orchard, past a sturdy-looking barn and an adjacent farmhouse, across a fenced road, and up a gentle slope to the crest of Cemetery Ridge—where the Yankees waited behind a fortified stone wall. Pettigrew's Brigade, now commanded by Colonel Marshall, would hit the ridge somewhere between the cottage on the far left and a clump of hardwood trees near the center. Cureton thought the scene was beautiful; in peacetime the route across it would be a pleasant stroll. This day, however, the crossing would be perilous. The route through the open fields provided no protection from enemy artillery fire; it was intersected by post-and-rail fences that would have to be scaled—including a final set enclosing Emmitsburg Road—and the last leg of the charge would be uphill into the massed fire of the Federal infantry posted behind the stone wall. Based on what he had experienced on McPherson's Ridge, Cureton could imagine what horrors possibly lay ahead. But the first day's assault had ended in victory. He could hope for another triumph—at a much lower cost.[3]

Major John Jones also bore a heavier burden this July morning: The pending assault would be his first time to lead the regiment into battle. Men with their lives at stake would now look to him as they had once looked to Colonel Burgwyn. How would the men perform? Would the savagery of the first day's fighting inhibit them or embolden them? Would they respond to his leadership with the same valor they had demonstrated under Colonel Burgwyn? And how would he perform? Would he lead well or fail miserably? These were the solemn questions facing "Knock" Jones this steamy summer day. Inescapable too was the grim question of survival. Colonel Burgwyn now lay in a fresh grave; Lieutenant Colonel Lane seemed destined for the same. Would John Jones survive what lay ahead this day? Would the 26th North Carolina—what was left of it—again do its duty despite the cost?[4]

Major Jones soon learned what would be expected of him and his regiment. At noontime, brigade commanders were briefed on the upcoming assault, and the battle plan soon worked its way down to the regiment level. The Federal line on Cemetery Ridge would be assaulted just left of center by an immense attack force of more than 13,000 troops—and the 26th North Carolina would help lead the charge. Lee had placed overall command of the massive assault with General Longstreet, who in turn had given Major General George E. Pickett responsibility for coordinating it. The attack would be made primarily by Pickett's and Pettigrew's divisions. The right wing of the assault force was composed of Pickett's Division, which consisted of three brigades—fifteen fresh Virginia regiments—that had arrived on the field the night before. Pickett's troops had not been engaged in serious fighting since the battle of Sharpsburg ten months earlier, but they were seasoned veterans led by some of the most capable field commanders in Lee's army. They would be supported on their extreme right flank by two Third Corps brigades from Major General Richard H. Anderson's division—Alabama troops commanded by Brigadier General Cadmus H. Wilcox and Floridians led by Colonel David Lang.[5]

The left wing of the assault force consisted mainly of Pettigrew's division, reinforced by a two-brigade division commanded by Major General Isaac R. Trimble. Pettigrew's division, which included Marshall's brigade and the 26th North Carolina, held the post of honor—the front line. The division was still composed of the four brigades that had marched to Gettysburg under General Heth, but the ferocious fighting of July 1st had left three of the brigades headed by new commanders. Besides Colonel Marshall's promotion to head what had been Pettigrew's Brigade, Colonel Robert M. Mayo now commanded Brockenbrough's Brigade, and Archer's Brigade was led by Colonel Birkett D. Fry. Despite its "shattered condition" from the first day's fighting, Davis's Brigade, was present for duty in Pettigrew's division, and was still commanded by Brigadier General Joseph R. Davis, retained its original commander. Trimble's force, which would make the assault in a second line behind Pettigrew's division, consisted of General Alfred M. Scales's Brigade—now led by Colonel William Lowrance—and Brigadier General James H. Lane's relatively fresh brigade. The two brigades were drawn from Major General Dorsey Pender's division, but Pender had suffered a leg wound the day before. Trimble was an apt replacement for Pender: He was an experienced, hard-fighting sixty-one-year-old officer who was fresh from months of convalescing from a severe wound and a bout of mumps. Pettigrew's and Trimble's forces were to be supported on their extreme left flank by two more brigades from Anderson's Division—Brigadier General William Mahone's brigade of Virginians and Brigadier General Carnot Posey's brigade of Mississippians. Pettigrew's division now numbered about 4,600 men. Trimble commanded about 1,750 more, which gave the left wing of the assault about 6,350 troops plus supports.[6]

There had been talk earlier in the day about Pettigrew's division serving as support troops for Pickett. Instead, the placement of the division on the front line put Pettigrew's troops alongside Pickett's as equals in the upcoming assault. All would have ample opportunity to share the glory—and the gore—that the charge was expected to yield. Although composed of the same regiments Heth had headed on the battle's first day—North Carolinians, Mississippians, Tennesseeans, Alabamians and Virginians—the division Pettigrew now commanded was much different from the powerful force Heth had led into Pennsylvania. Much of its strength had been scraped away by death and wounds—perhaps 40 percent was now missing. What remained, however, was a hard-core remnant of survivors that still posed a formidable threat to any enemy. The troops of Pettigrew's division were battered, but they were also battle-tested and determined.[7]

Deployed in line with the rest of Pettigrew's division, the men of the 26th North Carolina lay in a thin patch of woods on the edge of Seminary Ridge and waited. During the night, when they slept at all, they had slept with their weapons ready. At first light, a brisk cannonading had erupted in the northeast and had continued until mid-morning. The short-lived quiet that followed was interrupted in the late morning by another cannonading—this one between III Corps artillery and opposing Federal artillery on Cemetery Ridge. The brief but heated duel was provoked by a Federal raid on the barn and farmhouse that lay in the no-man's-land halfway between Pettigrew's division and the Federal line. The structures, known locally as the William Bliss farm, had been abandoned earlier by their occupants, and had been coveted by both sides. On the morning of July 3, the buildings were occupied by Confederate sharpshooters, whose potshots against the Federal line were answered by a small force of Federals who flushed the sharpshooters and set the structures ablaze.[8]

When the late-morning outburst of artillery fire ended, a strange stillness settled over the battlefield. In the Confederate field hospitals, surgeons and attendants were still treating the multitude of wounded from the previous day's fighting. Burial details labored in the heat to dig graves for the countless Confederate dead. "The dead were being buried," Lieutenant Colonel Fremantle would note, "but great numbers were still lying about; also many mortally wounded, for who nothing could be done. Amongst the latter were a number of Yankees dressed in bad imitations of the Zouave costume. They opened their glazed eyes, as I rode past, in a painfully imploring manner." On the shady slope of McPherson's Ridge, the Federal dead of the Iron Brigade—untended by the overwhelmed Confederate burial details—still lay where they had fallen during the first day's fighting. The bodies were missing their shoes, which had been removed by footwear-desperate Confederates.[9]

The men of Pettigrew's division, waiting expectantly for orders to make an assault, may have wondered if they too soon would be lying dead or wounded on the field. Before them stretched the long and open route of assault that, their soldier's savvy told them, surely would be a bloody path to victory or defeat. "On the morning of the third," a North Carolina officer would remember, "we were aroused to a sense of our situation, and no man who viewed that ground but felt that when the charge was made that all thought *would* be, blood must flow and gallant spirits must take their final flight." Despite two days of horrific battle and the presence of a powerful enemy who remained undefeated, the men chosen for the Pickett-Pettigrew assault remained confident. "The *esprit de corps* could not have been better;" a veteran of Lee's army would recall. "The men were in good physical condition, self-reliant and determined. They felt the gravity of the situation, for they knew well the [mettle] of the foe in their front; they were serious and resolute, but not disheartened. None of the usual jokes, common on the eve of battle, were indulged in, for every man felt his individual responsibility, and realized that he had the most stupendous work of his life before him. . . . There was no straggling, no feigned sickness, no pretense of being overcome by the intense heat; every man felt that it was his duty to make that fight; that he was his own commander, and they would have made the charge without an officer of any description; they only needed to be told what they were expected to do."[10]

Many also understood what was at stake. "The intelligent soldiers of the South knew and profoundly felt that the hours were potential—that on them possibly hung the success of their cause: the peace and independence of the Confederacy," a Southern officer would later relate. "They knew that victory meant so much more to them than to the enemy. It meant to us uninvaded and peaceful homes under our own rule and under our own nationality. With us it was only to be let alone. With this end in view, all felt that victory was to be won at any cost. All were willing to die, if only their country could thereby triumph."[11]

Some in the 26th wished their chaplains were present. The clergymen were still at the field hospitals, ministering to the wounded and dying. Within earshot, however, troops to the right of Marshall's brigade held a brief worship service while waiting in line. The men of the 26th were close enough to hear the sermon and join in the prayers. As the troops were called to pray, General Lee appeared on horseback. Accompanied by Longstreet and sometimes other officers, he had ridden the lines several times since early morning. Obedient to orders not to make any demonstration that would alert the Yankees to their location, the troops suppressed their normal cheers at Lee's presence; instead they rose to their feet and removed their hats as a show of respect. When Lee saw the troops preparing to pray, he dismounted, bowed his head and waited until the prayers ended before continuing his inspection.[12]

When the same troops began singing hymns, the poignant lyrics and moving melodies wafted over the assembled warriors. Hearing the songs of faith, Captain Cureton was reminded of the 1314 battle of Bannockburn, where the Scots under Robert the Bruce won their independence from the English. Cureton's generation of Southerners knew of the victory through Robert Burns's poem "Bannockburn." It contained lines that may have stirred well-read men like Cureton: "Now's the day, and now's the hour/See the front o' battle lower . . . Lay the proud usurpers low!/Liberty's in every blow! . . . Forward! Let us do—or die!" Cureton could only hope that on this day in Pennsylvania he and the other sons of the South could duplicate the Scots' success.[13]

As the men waited, the sultry stillness of the day masked the approaching fury. A few puffy clouds were scattered across a blue summer sky. Birds chirped cheerfully. Honeybees hummed. Several cows and calves, somehow having escaped harm, grazed peacefully between the lines. Meanwhile, the men sweltered. The summer temperature rose to almost 90 degrees at midday. "It was . . . very hot," one soldier would recall, "and the air, surcharged with the smoke and vapor of two days of battle, held sort of a murky haze, which was almost sedative in its effect on the senses. What little breeze there was blew from the south, but it was not much. No sounds were heard except . . . the sharp tones of orders here and there, and the stamp of the impatient horses' hoofs as orderlies and staff officers flew up and down the line."[14]

Waiting quietly in the woods behind Seminary Ridge, the 26th North

Carolina looked starkly different from the 800-man regiment Colonel Burgwyn had led into battle two days earlier. With all the troops Major Jones had rounded up—from walking wounded to ambulance attendants—he now had no more than 230 men in line. Later, some observers would question why a regiment as drained and bloodied as the 26th would be given a front-line role in the climactic Confederate assault. Major Jones, however, had confidence in his troops. He was pleased that Marshall's brigade and the 26th again held the post of honor at the front. He was proud of the regiment's performance on McPherson's Ridge. "No troops ever fought better than ours . . ." he would say. Despite their battle-worn appearance and dramatically depleted numbers, the men of the regiment acted assured and ready for another fight—and so did the rest of the brigade. "To the great surprise of everyone," a veteran of the regiment later recalled, "the brigade seemed as ready for the fray on the morning of the third day as it had been on that of the first."[15]

Major Jones kept the regiment organized by companies, even though some companies were now squad-size. Company F, now commanded by Sergeant Robert Hudspeth—who had been appointed lieutenant—boasted only about a half-dozen soldiers. Company H had about twice as many men, but it too was commanded by a sergeant. Company D, like several other companies, was now led by a junior officer, twenty-eight-year-old Lieutenant Gaston H. Broughton, who had taken over when Captain James T. Adams was wounded on July 1st. Company D had mustered 83 officers and troops two days earlier; when Broughton counted heads this day the company had 25 soldiers. Twenty-seven-year-old Captain Stephen Brewer of Company E, counted 11 soldiers in his command. The first day's fighting had ended with Brewer holding the colors after Lieutenant Colonel Lane had been shot down. Now, as Brewer waited with his skeletal company for another assault, the regimental color guard was just steps away.[16]

Raising a color guard at all was a remarkable display of grit for the regiment, considering the parade of color-bearers shot down in the first day's assault. The newly appointed color sergeant was Sergeant William H. Smith of Company K. A twenty-six-year-old who had come to the regiment with Anson County's Pee Dee Wild Cats, Smith was unquestionably aware of the price the regiment's color-bearers had paid on McPherson's Ridge. Even so, he had accepted the colors and the responsibility for bearing them in this day's assault. Prepared to raise the Starry Cross if Smith fell were Private Thomas J. Cozart of Company F and Private Daniel Boone Thomas of Company E.

Both men were age twenty-two, and had come through the first day's fight unharmed. Cozart had been detailed to the regiment's pioneer squad, charged with toppling fences and clearing other obstacles in the regiment's way. Now he had chosen an even riskier post. Amidst the surviving fragment of the once-powerful regiment, the young men of the color guard waited calmly—as if their names were not on a death roster. In the stillness of the early afternoon, there was little breeze to stir the folds of the blood-stained banner.[17]

For approximately one mile, the line of men in gray and butternut stretched along Seminary Ridge. They were the men who would make the Pickett-Pettigrew Charge. Demonstrating the discipline of seasoned soldiers, they waited quietly, even cheerfully, despite their impatience. And many *were* impatient—eager to get the deed done. "They were restless to be 'up, and at 'em,'" a survivor would later recall, "eager to have what they knew was inevitably before them commenced and ended. . . . The great question of that campaign, perhaps of the whole war, was hanging on the next few hours." On the left wing of the long line, Pettigrew had deployed his four brigades alongside the left flank of Pickett's Division. Colonel Mayo's brigade of Virginians—formerly Brockenbrough's Brigade—was posted to the far left of Pettigrew's division. Davis' brigade—three Mississippi regiments and one North Carolina regiment—was posted to the right of Mayo's brigade. Marshall's brigade—still composed of the 52nd, 47th, 11th and 26th North Carolina regiments—was deployed to the right of Davis' Brigade. Colonel Fry's brigade—the two Alabama regiments and three Tennessee regiments formerly known as Archer's Brigade—was deployed on the far right of Pettigrew's division.[18]

Approximately 100 yards separated Pettigrew's right flank from the left flank of Pickett's Division, and Colonel Fry's command was the connecting brigade. Colonel Birkett Fry had been given temporary command of Archer's Brigade before—at Chancellorsville—and the post had resulted in his third battle wound. A forty-two-year-old Virginian who had failed out of West Point, Fry now received the challenging honor of commanding the central brigade in the Confederate assault force. The assault would target a distant stand of trees on Cemetery Ridge directly opposite Fry's position. To his right, Pickett's troops would "guide left" and angle their charge toward the stand of trees; to his left, the rest of Pettigrew's troops would "guide right" and shift their charge accordingly. The tactic would funnel the huge assault force against a single point on the faraway Federal line, which hopefully would break under the massed pressure.[19]

While Fry waited on horseback in the woods with his brigade—just yards from where the men of the 26th North Carolina lay in line—he looked up to see General Lee ride up with Generals Longstreet and Hill. The three dismounted, sat down on the trunk of a fallen tree and carefully consulted a map. After several minutes of intense discussion they remounted and rode away. Soon afterwards, Fry noticed a sudden increase in activity as couriers and staff officers rode up and down the line. General Pettigrew soon rode up to Fry, and announced that the assault would be launched following "a heavy cannonade." The Confederate barrage would hopefully reduce the threat from the Federal artillery and soften up the enemy resistance. It would also likely provoke a counter-barrage from the Federal artillery. "They will of course return the fire with all the guns they have," Pettigrew told Fry. "[We] must shelter the men as best we can, and make them lie down."[20]

Captain June Kimble was too tense to lie down. Kimble was an officer in the 14th Tennessee, which was posted with Fry's brigade not far from the 26th North Carolina. Kimble left the line of troops lying in the timber and walked to the edge of the field that he and the men of Pettigrew's Division would soon cross. He could see Big Round Top to the far right and the spires of Gettysburg to the far left. In between lay the assault route to the clump of trees on Cemetery Ridge. "I sought to locate the point on Cemetery Ridge about which our brigade and regiment would strike the enemy, provided our advance be made in a straight line," he would recall. "Realizing just what was before me and the brave boys with me . . . I asked aloud the question: 'June Kimble, are you going to do your duty to-day?' The audible answer was, 'I'll do it, so help me God.' I turned and walked back to the line. 'How does it look, June?' said Lieutenant Waters. I replied: 'Boys, if we have to go, it will be hot for us. . . .' "[21]

Three-quarters of a mile away on Cemetery Ridge, the blue-uniformed troops of the 12th New Jersey Infantry hunkered down behind a makeshift wall of piled-up field stones and fence rails. They intended to make it "hot" for any Confederates who came their way. The regiment belonged to Major General Winfield S. Hancock's II Army Corps. Two divisions from Hancock's Corps—about 5,500 troops—defended the center of the Federal line. They were deployed behind the rock wall that ran along Cemetery Ridge. Extending along the low ridge just below its crest, the wall made a sharp right turn about 100 yards north of the targeted clump of trees, extended eastward for

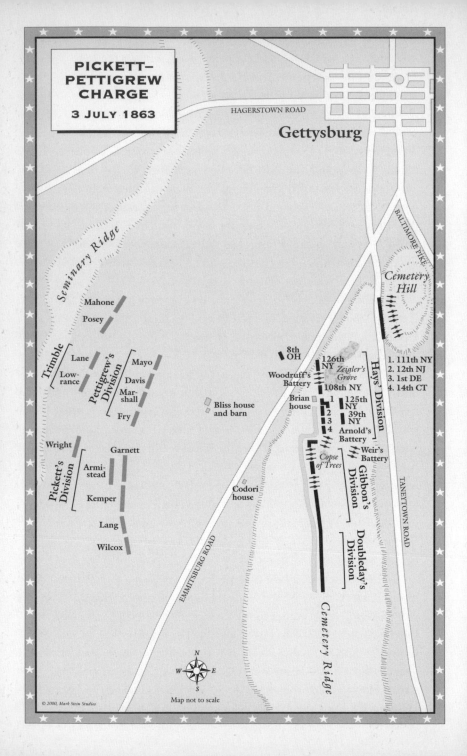

PICKETT–PETTIGREW CHARGE
3 JULY 1863

HAGERSTOWN ROAD

Gettysburg

BALTIMORE PIKE

Seminary Ridge

Cemetery Hill

Mahone
Posey

Trimble

Lane
Lowrance

Pettigrew's Division

Mayo
Davis
Marshall
Fry

8th OH

126th NY

Woodruff's Battery

Zeigler's Grove

108th NY

Brian house

Hays' Division

1. 111th NY
2. 12th NJ
3. 1st DE
4. 14th CT

Bliss house and barn

1
2
3
4

125th NY
39th NY

Arnold's Battery

Wright

Pickett's Division

Garnett

Armistead

Kemper

Codori house

Copse of Trees

Weir's Battery

Gibbon's Division

Lang

Wilcox

Doubleday's Division

EMMITSBURG ROAD

TANEYTOWN ROAD

Cemetery Ridge

N
W E
S

Map not to scale

© 2000, Mark Stein Studies

about 83 yards and then zigged northward again. Brigadier General John Gibbon's Second Division was deployed from the angle southward for about 280 yards to a point where the line was defended by I Corps troops. Two brigades of Brigadier General Alexander Hays' Third Division manned the wall from a point north of the angle for about 258 yards northward to farmer Abraham Brian's small, whitewashed barn, which stood near a stand of hardwood trees called Ziegler's Grove. Colonel George L. Willard's Third Brigade—composed of New York troops—held the right wing of Hays' Division. Troops of Colonel Thomas A. Smythe's Second Brigade—the 14th Connecticut, the 1st Delaware, the 12th New Jersey, and the 108th New York—composed the division's left wing. As planned, the Confederate assault would carry Pickett's and Pettigrew's divisions into the section of the line defended by Hancock's Corps. The route of assault for Pettigrew's division and Trimble's two following brigades would carry Pettigrew's troops—including the 26th North Carolina—into the section of the Federal line manned by Hays' Division.[22]

The 12th New Jersey was posted roughly left-of-center in the division line. To the regiment's right lay the 126th and 39th New York regiments. To the left lay the 1st Delaware and 14th Connecticut. Posted to the rear of the regiment, waiting to be called forward when needed, was another line composed of the 111th, 125th and 108th New York regiments. On the far left flank of Hays's Division—next to the 14th Connecticut—was Battery A of the 1st Rhode Island Light Artillery. Known as "Arnold's Battery" in honor of Captain William A. Arnold, its commander, the battery consisted of six three-inch rifled cannon. On the division's far right in Ziegler's Grove was Battery I of the 1st United States Artillery. Commonly called "Woodruff's Battery" for its commander, Lieutenant George A. Woodruff, the battery consisted of six 12-pounder Napolean smoothbore cannon.[23]

Among the men of the 12th New Jersey now posted on Cemetery Ridge was a dark-haired, bewhiskered young major—John T. Hill—who now commanded the regiment. As he waited among his 400-plus soldiers in the stifling heat, Major Hill had reason to wonder how his regiment would perform. The troops had limited combat experience, the regiment had recently undergone a shakeup among its officers—and Hill had held command barely two months. The regiment had been mustered in Woodbury, New Jersey less than a year earlier, and had spent its first six months pulling guard duty in Maryland and Washington, D.C. The Jerseymen had joined the Army of the Potomac in late December, and the following spring—as the army prepared for the campaign that would end at Chancellorsville—the regiment's colonel had encouraged a shuffling of officers. The changes produced a vacancy for major, and the men had expected the post to go to one of the regiment's most popular officers.[24]

Instead, it had gone to Hill. He was an outsider, who had been appointed to the major's post by New Jersey's governor—to the surprise of the regiment's troops. Hill had a strong record—he was a capable officer with combat experience—but his father was a New Jersey assemblyman, and some in the regiment suspected party politics in the appointment. It had been necessary for the major to prove himself—and he had succeeded. He had earned the respect of the men with competence, fair treatment and his conduct in combat. At Chancellorsville, where the 12th New Jersey received its baptism of fire, the regiment had been forced to retreat with the rest of the Federal army, but Hill had made a good showing. The regiment's colonel had been wounded, and with the lieutenant colonel on sick leave, Hill had found himself in command. The Jerseymen had taken serious casualties in the battle, but Hill had managed to keep at least part of the regiment in line and holding ground. Afterward, word had come that the 12th's wounded colonel would not be back for awhile, so Hill had been left in command and now was in charge of the sweating line of Jersey soldiers on Cemetery Ridge.[25]

They had arrived on the field at Gettysburg in the early morning darkness of July 2nd. Chancellorsville had left the regiment—and the brigade—seriously reduced in numbers. "Our brigade is cut up so much it ain't fit to go in the field to fite," one Jerseyman wrote home. Since deploying on Cemetery Ridge, however, troops from the regiment had been twice dispatched on raids against the Bliss farm, and had nabbed almost 100 Confederate prisoners. So far, they had proven themselves to be stout-hearted and hard-fighting. Hill could only hope that they—and he—would be "fit to . . . fite" if the Rebels came screaming forward from the distant line of trees in their front.[26]

To even the odds, the Jerseymen prepared a surprise weapon of sorts for any Confederates who came their way. The regiment had been equipped with the 69-caliber smoothbore musket, which was older and less accurate than the smaller caliber Springfield rifles commonly carried by Federal troops. To increase firepower, the men had been issued regulation "buck-and-ball" cartridges, which consisted of a large musket ball and three buckshot pellets. It was a lethal combination—especially at close quarters—but Major Hill's troops made the ammunition even deadlier. They opened the paper cartridges, tossed aside the 69-caliber ball and reloaded each cartridge with a dozen or so buckshot pellets. The rigged loads gave each firearm the short-range killing power of a shotgun. Any Johnny Rebs unfortunate enough to charge their section of the line, the Jerseymen agreed, would receive a devastating blast of hot lead.[27]

Already this morning hot lead had peppered the Northern troops manning the Federal skirmish line opposite Pettigrew's division. Posted several hundred yards in advance of Cemetery Ridge, they had drawn deadly fire from Confederate sharpshooters. "The enlisted men on both sides were all laying on the ground and had bits of fence or pits to cover them," a New York soldier would later recall. "They fired at each other by aiming at the puffs of smoke which were made by discharging the pieces." Particularly hard hit were the troops in the Federal skirmish line opposite Pettigrew's left flank. "Our dead skirmishers lay so thick where they had been killed in the line," a Northern soldier would later report, "that it was difficult for us to find a place to stretch ourselves." Particularly troublesome was a Confederate sharpshooter posted behind a large tree that stood far out in the field in front of Seminary Ridge. A wounded Northern soldier lay between the lines, begging loudly for water, but the sharpshooter's fire kept Federal troops from rescuing him. About mid-morning, however, the fire from the tree suddenly ceased with a shouted appeal: "Don't fire, Yanks!" What followed surprised the Northerner skirmishers. "A man with his gun slung across his shoulder came out from the tree," one later recounted "The man had a canteen in his hand and, when he had come about half-way to us, we saw him (God bless him) kneel down and give a drink to one of our wounded." The Yankees cheered, "Bully for you! Johnny!" and the potshots temporarily ceased. When finished, the Johnny Reb disappeared behind his tree with another shout: "Down Yanks, we're going to fire."[28]

Civility was not what Brigadier General Henry J. Hunt planned to offer the Confederates if they launched an assault on the center of the Federal line. Bewhiskered, middle-aged and thoroughly professional, Hunt was the chief of artillery for the Army of the Potomac. He had spent much of the preceding night preparing the Federal artillery for another attack. Ammunition chests had been replenished, guns and carriages had been repaired, and disabled batteries had been rearmed with replacement guns from the Federal artillery reserve. Hunt had 36 artillery batteries and 163 guns ready to use in defense of Cemetery Ridge. At least 75 guns directly supported the center of the line. More than half of them had a clear field of fire into the route of assault planned for Pettigrew's division, and so did all 55 artillery pieces posted atop Cemetery Hill. Troops following Pettigrew's intended route would come into range of the Federal artillery soon after leaving Seminary Ridge—and would remain so all the way. If General Hunt's gun crews were allowed to do their work unhampered, the line of assault proposed for Pettigrew's division would be a killing field.[29]

After several explosive exchanges with Confederate artillery in the morning, the Federal artillery had fallen silent near midday. The eerie stillness noticed by Southern troops on Seminary Ridge was also obvious to the Federal forces manning the line on Cemetery Ridge. "Hardly a shot was heard on the picket line," a Northern officer later recalled. "[It] became as still as the Sabbath day. The troops stretched upon the ground with the hot July sun pouring upon them; a hasty lunch had been eaten from the haversack [and] the soldiers were recounting the incidents of the past two days of terrible fighting. Some sat with haversack on the knee, pencil in hand, writing to the dear ones at home. The silence and the heat were oppressive. . . ." General Hunt was on Little Round Top, the rocky, wooded hill on the southern end of the Federal line. He had just finished an inspection of the entire line of Federal artillery. He was satisfied with what he found—his guns were well-placed and well-armed—but the inspection had been long and demanding in the wilting heat. Hunt had begun his tour at ten o'clock in the morning, and—someone looked at a pocket-watch—it was now almost one P.M.[30]

Standing near a line of Confederate cannon far out in front of Seminary Ridge, Colonel Edward Porter Alexander looked at *his* watch. Tall, lanky and twenty-eight years old, Alexander was acting commander of Longstreet's artillery. Officially, he was just a battalion commander; Longstreet's chief of artillery was Colonel James B. Walton. At Gettysburg, however, Longstreet had given field command of his artillery to young Alexander, whom he described as "an officer of unusual promptness, sagacity and intelligence." Preceding the assault, Longstreet's and Hill's artillery—and a few of Ewell's batteries—would follow Alexander's lead, opening fire at the sound of two signal guns. It would be the greatest field artillery barrage of the war—more than 150 guns would simultaneously bombard the targeted sections of the Federal line. The goal: to inflict destruction on the Federal artillery and doubt and despair on the Yankee infantry.[31]

When the troops in gray and butternut set out double-quick for the distant ridge, their success and survival would depend greatly on the Confederate artillery. Lee's artillerists, however, faced the same daunting question that so often plagued them. Would they have enough shot and shell to do the job? Their store of ammunition was no match for the Federal artillery, and Hill's Second Corps batteries had already burned a lot of rounds trading fire with the Federal batteries that morning. There was also a question about the reliability of the Confederate artillery fuses. These were questions, however, that could be answered only by action. Enough ammunition existed to allow the Confederate artillery to maintain a sustained barrage for at least an hour.[32]

As he had labored and fretted to unleash this unprecedented cannonade, Porter Alexander was startled to receive a remarkable dispatch from General Longstreet. "If the artillery fire does not have the effect to drive off the enemy or greatly demoralize him, so as to make our effort pretty certain," Longstreet's message read, "I would prefer that you should not advise Gen. Pickett to make the charge. I shall rely a great deal upon your judgment to determine the matter & shall expect you to let Gen. Pickett know when the moment offers." General Longstreet appeared to be putting Alexander in charge of deciding whether the great assault should even occur—a command decision presumably already made by General Lee. Suddenly, Alexander was keenly aware of his youthfulness and subordinate rank.[33]

He penciled a reply and sent it to Longstreet. "General, I will only be able to judge the effect of our fire on the enemy by his return fire," he explained, "for his infantry is but little exposed to view & the smoke will obscure the whole field." Then he diplomatically shifted responsibility for ordering the assault back to Longstreet. "If, as I infer from your note, there is any alternative to this attack it should be carefully considered before opening our fire, for it will take all the artillery ammunition we have left to test this one thoroughly, & if the result is unfavorable, we will have none left for another effort." Soon a courier galloped up with another directive from Longstreet. Alexander looked down at the scrawled meassage. It simply restated the general's order: "The intention is to advance the Inf. if the Arty has the desired effect of driving the enemy off," the note read, "or having other effect such as to warrant us in making the attack. When that moment arrives advise Gen P. . . ." Again, it was left to Alexander to signal the assault.[34]

Still puzzled, Alexander turned to Brigadier General Ambrose R. Wright, a fellow Georgian, who was standing nearby. "He has put the responsibility back upon you," Wright bluntly observed. "General," Alexander asked, "tell me exactly what *you* think of this attack." Wright's brigade of Georgians had momentarily penetrated a section of the Federal line the previous day. "Well,

Alexander," Wright replied, "it is mostly a question of supports. It is not as hard to get there as it looks. . . . The real difficulty is to stay there after you get there—for the whole infernal Yankee army is there in a bunch."[35]

Finally, Alexander sought out Pickett. The dapper Virginian appeared upbeat and confident—and certain of victory. Reassured, Alexander returned to his guns determined not to interfere with the assault already set in motion by the army's commander. "Gen. Lee had originally planned it," he concluded, "& half the day had been spent in preparation. I determined to cause no loss of time by any indecision on my part." He pondered when he should signal for the assault to begin, and concluded that the infantry should go when twenty minutes of artillery ammunition was remaining—or maybe when a fifteen-minute supply was left. His intentions now settled, Alexander dispatched a terse message to Longstreet. "When our fire is at its best," he stated simply, "I will advise General Pickett to advance."[36]

At almost one o'clock, a mounted courier dashed up to a four-gun battery of the Washington Artillery, which was posted to the Confederate right flank, and handed over a written order from General Longstreet. "Let the batteries open . . .," it read. Major Benjamin S. Eshleman gave the word and at 1:07 P.M. the first signal gun fired. A brief pause followed—the number-two gun misfired—and then another cannon fired the second round. Solitary cannon shots followed at quick intervals along the line as if the signal fire was being repeated. Then the entire line of Confederate artillery erupted in flame, smoke and an explosive roar that shattered the eerie midday stillness.[37]

"The ground fairly shook beneath the feet of the assembled armies from the terrible concussion," an eyewitness in Pettigrew's division would report. "[The] skies were clouded with smoke, and the air [was] filled with shrieking shot and shell . . . until it seemed as though hell itself had broken loose." One North Carolina soldier was reminded of the passing of an immense thunderstorm. "The lumbering of the thunder overhead," he would later write, "was but as the wail of an infant to the roar of a lion in comparison with the deafening roar that shook the ground."[38]

Captain Cureton was reminded of an earthquake. He and the rest of the 26th North Carolina lay among the trees on the backside of Seminary Ridge. Twenty paces in front of them, the Third Corps gun crews worked their field artillery, sending Southern iron hurling toward the Federal positions with every blast. Beneath them, the ground shook constantly. Smoke boiled above the line of cannon before them, as the guns crews methodically fired, sponged, swabbed, loaded and fired again. Whenever an enemy artillery caisson exploded on the distant ridge, the Confederate cannoneers whooped and yelled. "It was a time when hours are compressed into minutes, hearts cease throbbing and the blood lies dormant in your veins," a North Carolinian would later note. The men of the 26th flattened themselves and waited for the Federal artillery to return the fire.[39]

"Down! Down!" shouted the Federal troops, as the Confederate artillery fire began dropping onto Cemetery Ridge. Soldiers who seconds earlier had been lolling in the sweltering stillness suddenly jumped to their feet, rushed to their places in the battle line and flattened themselves behind the stone wall. In the rear, men sought cover anywhere or simply hugged the ground. "Shot whistled, and shell hissed and screamed and burst, scattering everywhere their deadly weapons," a Federal officer would later recall. "The wildest confusion for a few moments obtained sway among us," another would recount. "The shells came bursting all about. The horses, hitched to the trees or held by the slack hands of orderlies, neighed out in fright, and broke away and plunged riderless through the fields." Most of the Confederate fire was concentrated on the section of Cemetery Ridge occupied by Hays' and Gibbon's II Corps divisions. "The percussion shells would strike, and thunder, and scatter the earth with their whistling fragments," another Federal officer would remember. "[The] Whitworth bolts would bounce, and ricochet . . . and the great solid shot would smite the unresisting ground with a sounding 'thud.'" The incoming barrage reminded one soldier in the 12th New Jersey of "an avalanche of bursting shells." The regiment's color-bearer hastily rolled up the regimental battle flag and laid it on the ground for protection. "The roar of the guns was deafening," an Ohio officer would recall. "[The] air was soon clouded with smoke, and the shriek and startling crack of exploding shell above, around, and in our midst; the blowing up of our caissons in our rear; the driving through the air of fence-rails, posts, and limbs of trees; the groans of dying men, the neighing of frantic and wounded horses, [all] created a scene of absolute horror."[40]

"The thunder of the guns was incessant," another Federal officer would later recount, "for all of ours had now opened fire and the whole air seemed filled with rushing, screaming and bursting shells." Shells exploding among the Federal artillery, killed horses, damaged guns and blew up caissons. "We see the solid shot strike axle, or pole, or wheel, and the tough iron and heart of oak snap and fly like straws," a survivor would later write. "I had time to see one of the horses of our mess wagon struck and torn by a shell," another would later remember. "The pair plunge—the driver has lost the reins— horses, driver and wagon go into a heap by a tree. Two mules, packed with boxes of ammunition, are knocked to pieces by a shell. The shells swoop down among the battery horses, standing there apart—a half a dozen horses start, they tumble, their legs stiffen, their vitals and blood smear the ground." Watching the artillery horses go down, General Gibbon was amazed by the lack of panic among the animals: "Even when a shell, striking in the midst of a team, would knock over one or two of them or hurl one struggling in his death agonies to the ground, the rest would make no effort to struggle or escape but would stand stoically by as if saying to themselves, 'It is fate, it is useless to try to avoid it.'" Horse carcasses soon littered the area behind the targeted section of Cemetery Ridge. In the rear of the section of the line manned by Hays's Division, one soldier estimated that he saw 250 dead horses from the division's five gun batteries. Meanwhile, in the 111th New York— which was posted between the stone wall and an apple orchard in the rear— Lieutenant Samuel B. McIntyre was amazed to hear a songbird cheerfully chirping. How, he wondered, could even a bird live through such a shelling.[41]

"The air all over the wide field was fierce and heavy with the iron hail," a New Yorker in Hays's Division would report. "The greater portion of the field was swept by the fiery shot. Horses and men dropped crushed and dead." Sergeant Thomas Greer was waiting out the barrage with other troops, when an incoming shell decapitated a man beside him. "He fell over on me," Greer would later recount, "covering me with blood and brains." One Federal officer who endured the cannonade would never forget the shells bursting around the dead: "[They] hear not the roar as they stretch upon the ground, with upturned faces and open eyes, though a shell should burst at their very ears. Their ears, and their bodies this instant are only mud." As he rode along Cemetery Ridge checking his gun batteries, General Hunt saw an artillery round hit just in front of a prone infantryman: "[It] penetrated the surface and passed under him, throwing him over and over. He fell behind the rear rank, apparently dead . . ." The grisly scene reminded Hunt of the old hunter's trick of "barking squirrels" by firing just under them. To escape the barrage, a handful of soldiers from the 111th New York "slipped away" from the regiment and hid in an old barn in the rear. To their dismay, a Confederate shell tore through the barn wall, killing several men and sending the rest scurrying back to their regiment.[42]

Posted up the wall from the 12th New Jersey on the edge of Ziegler's Grove, the 108th New York took a pounding due to its proximity to one of division's gun batteries. A nearby stockpile of artillery ammunition was detonated by an exploding shell, leaving the New Yorkers severely rattled. Trees were split by the incoming fire, and huge limbs fell on the troops below. Men and animals were dismembered. Given a dispatch to deliver, a young staff officer from the regiment, Lieutenant Theron E. Parsons, reached for his horse—only to see an artillery shell pass through the animal. Moments later Parsons saw two officers and a corporal killed in quick order by exploding shells. He was shocked to see a shell fragment tear the face from one of the officers. Several New Yorkers tried to run, but a sword-waving officer forced them back in line. Posted to the rear of Cemetery Ridge, where the incoming fire was the worst, the men of the 111th New York—who had distinguished themselves in the fighting on July 2nd—now were almost paralyzed by the shelling. Their officers ordered the regiment forward to the stone wall, but the men were almost too unnerved to move. "We drove them before us up the hill more like cattle than soldiers," a New York officer would later admit. Finally, the New Yorkers were put into line just behind and to the right of the 12th New Jersey, where they "hugged the low stone wall" with the rest of the troops.[43]

On the left side of Hays's line—to the left of the 12th New Jersey—the men of the 1st Delaware and the 14th Connecticut were hugging the ground behind the wall. A detachment of the 1st Delaware was caught in the rear, helping load ambulances at a barn that had been converted into a hospital. "Men who had seemed utterly unable to move raised themselves, and crawled to some other place," a Delaware soldier would recall. "Horsemen, footmen, and wagons rushed wildly across the field. . . . The confusion, haste and cries of each one alarmed the rest. . . . " Behind the stone wall, one of the Connecticut officers felt pity when he saw some cows between the lines "torn in pieces by the shells." His concern for the cattle was soon eclipsed by his shock at the human carnage caused by the barrage. "The bodies and limbs and mangled men and horses," he would later recollect, "all made a picture for a painter, but one horrible to look upon. . . ." Near the angle of the wall, another officer was looking at an artillery-man tending to a gun caisson. "Suddenly," he later reported, "with a shriek, came a shell right under the limber box, and the poor gunner went hopping to the rear on one leg, the shreds of the other dangling about as he went."[44]

While the Yankee infantry flattened themselves beneath the barrage, the Federal artillery returned the Confederate fire. "The brave artillerymen stood gallantly at their posts and answered shot with shot," a Federal survivor would later write. "Above it all, could be heard the monotonous orders of the commander of battery. With the precision of the tick of the clock—number-one, fire! number-two, fire! The forms of the men could be seen passing through the smoke and literally through a storm of shot and shell, from caisson to gun, carrying their ammunition." The Federal artillery's targets were the faraway Confederate gun batteries—and the line of infantry waiting in the trees beyond.[45]

To the rear of the Confederate Third Corps artillery, the men of the 26th North Carolina lay on their bellies and weathered the return firestorm. While much of the Federal barrage overshot both artillery and infantry lines, some of it landed on target. "I look around," one of Pettigrew's officers would later recall, "[and] what a change, from order to chaos, from beauty to destruction, from life to death—levelled fences, splintered trees, furrowed ground, broken cannon, exploded caissons, slaughtered horses, mangled men." Private Tom Setser, one of the handful of men now left in Company F, looked up at one point and saw five artillery horses struck down by a single incoming round. In the strip of woods where the 26th and Marshall's brigade lay, incoming Federal fire split trees and knocked limbs down on the men waiting below. "The air was alive with bursting shells," a survivor would report. "Fragments of shells and limbs of trees were falling in every direction. Men were being constantly wounded." Private Caison of Company I considered the effects of the artillery duel "appalling," and he was certain there had never been anything like it. Captain Albright, the twenty-year-old commander of Company G, was sure this was "one of the most hotly contested battles of the age." Albright was one of the few officers of the regiment who had so far escaped injury at Gettysburg. He could only wonder if the "green earth"—as he called it—would still be his "place of abode" when the pending assault was over.[46]

"The atmosphere," one of Pettigrew's men would recall, "[was] a screaming, shrieking, bellowing pandemonium of shells and flying fragments." Down the line to the left from Marshall's brigade, troops of the 22nd Virginia Infantry Battalion in Mayo's brigade were panicked by the shelling. Scores of them got up and "shamefully ran away" during the bombardment. Their commander would later complain that "he did not believe that 20 men" from the battalion were still in line when the shelling ended. They were the exception among the Virginians—and other Southern troops. The Federal barrage took a bloody toll—one of Pickett's regiments recorded more than 80 casualties—but, whether with Pickett, Pettigrew or Trimble, the men in gray and butternut remained in line and in control. The discipline in the ranks was exemplified by a young private in Davis's Brigade, which was posted to the left of the 26th. Although disemboweled by an incoming round, he managed to pen a letter home, notifying his family of his death and releasing his fiancée from her commitment. "Remember that I am true to my country," he wrote, "and my greatest regret at dying is that she is not free. . . ." Far up the line to the right, meanwhile, a private was ridiculed by a junior officer for using his bayonet to make himself a man-size breastwork. Moments later, a Federal shell killed the officer and splattered the private with blood—but the men in line remained in place.[47]

Sheltered by the rise of the ridge in their front, the men of the 26th were spared serious casualties during the artillery exchange. They lay in line while shells exploded in their front and rear, and while the artillerymen of Hill's Corps hustled through their firing routine. Suddenly, the Federal artillery fire slackened and then ceased. Down the Confederate line to the right, meanwhile, Colonel Edward Porter Alexander propped himself against a tree and studied the enemy artillery with a telescope. "At first, I thought it only crippled guns," he would later explain, "but, with my large glass, I discovered entire batteries limbering up & leaving their positions. Now it was a very ordinary thing with us to withdraw our guns from purely artillery duels & save up everything for their infantry. But the Federals had never done anything of that sort before, & I did not believe they were doing it now."[48]

Alexander was mistaken: This time Federal artillery was doing exactly that—saving up everything for the expected infantry assault. From his observation, General Hunt had concluded that the Federal barrage was producing far more battle smoke than damage. A cease-fire would reserve his ammunition for the predictable Confederate assault, and might also lure the Confederates into stopping their bombardment and launching the attack while the Federal artillery was still near full strength. Meade had come to the same conclusion. With his commander's consent, Hunt had then ordered the Federal artillery to cease fire. ". . . I directed that the fire should be gradually stopped," he would later report. "I then sent orders for such batteries as were necessary to replace exhausted ones, and all that were disposable were sent to me."[49]

Despite its unprecedented ferocity, the Confederate bombardment had failed. It had shaken the earth, inflicted scores of casualties, destroyed caissons and killed horses, but much of it had overshot both man and artillery. "The safest place was just under the cover of the ridge, where the lines of infantry [were] lying flat upon the ground . . . ," one front-line Federal would later recall. "Taking into consideration the severity of the storm, and the numbers of shells in the air, the casualties among the infantry lines were comparatively few." The Confederate bombardment may have been nerve-wracking for the Federal troops, but it did not flush them into a panicky retreat or destroy their determination to fight. "In spite of the ghastly forms of mangled men and horses, in spite of the dismounted guns, exploding limbers, and other scenes of terror . . . ," a Northerner survivor would later observe, "the infantry . . . rested on their arms awaiting the bayonet-charge which they knew was sure to follow." Some artillery batteries had suffered severely, but the damage was scattered and uneven. The Federal artillery remained capable of unleashing a devastating torrent of fire into any assault against its center. "Viewed as a display of fireworks, the rebel practice was entirely successful, but as a military demonstration it was the biggest humbug of the season," a Federal artillery officer would conclude. When the Southern infantry appeared as expected, the Federal artillery would be charged and ready. "Oh, well, boys, be patient," one section commander told his gun crew. "There's going to be a [hell]—of a charge pretty soon, along the whole line. . . ." On the right side of the Federal II Corps line, directly opposite Pettigrew's division, Brigadier General Alexander Hays rode along behind his troops, cheering the men crouched behind the stone wall. "Now, boys," he shouted, "look out; you will see some fun!"[50]

Across the intervening field from Cemetery Ridge, Colonel Alexander continued to study the distant ridge through the smoke. "If they don't put fresh batteries there in five minutes," he said to those around him, "this will be our fight." Five minutes later, there was still no resumption of the Federal barrage. It was time for the infantry to go in, Alexander concluded. The Confederate bombardment, he believed, had been "generally well aimed & as effective as could be hoped." Ammunition was running low now, and the gun crews were tiring. If Longstreet intended to order the assault as planned, the time had come. Alexander hurriedly scribbled a note and dispatched it to General Pickett. "For God's sake," it began, "come on quick. . . ."[51]

CHAPTER 10

"Terrible as an Army with Banners"

Mounted on horseback, Colonel James Keith Marshall sat in front of his brigade and waited for the order to advance. At age twenty-four, "Jimmy" Marshall was the youngest front-line brigade commander in the assault force. Handsome, dark-headed and youthful-looking, he was a day away from a memorable anniversary. Just three years earlier on July 4th, he had graduated from V.M.I. Back in 1860, 36 months and several hundred thousand war deaths earlier, some young men had still viewed war as a romantic adventure. At V.M.I., he had solemnly posed for a photograph with four other cadets—all of whom had sported identically trimmed goatees. He had passed endless hours pondering mathematics and artillery tactics. He was one year ahead of Harry Burgwyn, but the younger Burgwyn had gained command of a regiment sooner than Marshall. Now, in one of the tragic ironies of war, Harry Burgwyn lay buried beneath the Pennsylvania soil and Jimmy Marshall commanded Pettigrew's former brigade—which included what was left of Burgywn's regiment.[1]

Another irony for Marshall: While he commanded the only all-North Carolina brigade in the front line of the pending assault, he was a Virginian of the Old Dominion aristocracy. His great-grandfather was a colonel in George Washington's army, and his grandfather was Chief Justice John Marshall, whose ruling in *Marbury v. Madison* had helped empower the U.S. Supreme Court. His father, Edward C. Marshall—a former Virginia legislator—was president of the Manassas Gap Railroad and lived as a gentleman farmer in the Virginia foothills. On the march to Pennsylvania a few weeks earlier, General Lee had been a dinner guest at the Marshall home. At V.M.I., Jimmy Marshall had been a mediocre student, excelling only in "moral philosophy," and after graduation, he had put aside a military career in favor of a teaching job at a private school in Edenton, North Carolina.[2]

In wartime, however, he had proven himself to be a competent commander. The war had come during his stint as a schoolteacher, so he had enlisted a local company of troops in North Carolina—the Chowan Dixie Rebels—which had joined the 1st North Carolina Infantry. Within a month, Marshall captained a company, and in less than a year he had risen to colonel of the 52nd North Carolina. Like the 26th North Carolina, Marshall's regiment had been shifted back and forth between North Carolina and Virginia for the previous year. Unlike the 26th, however, the regiment had missed the Seven Days Campaign and the bloody field at Malvern Hill. Marshall had distinguished himself in a skirmish with Federal gunboats on Virginia's Blackwater River, and had experienced serious fire and real casualties in a brief but heated engagement defending a railroad bridge near Goldsboro, North Carolina. Swept into the Army of Northern Virginia with the rest of Pettigrew's Brigade for the advance into Pennsylvania, Marshall and his regiment had performed admirably amid the fury and carnage of Gettysburg's first day. Along with the 47th North Carolina, the 52nd had driven back the Federal troops of Biddle's Brigade, which had turned the enemy's left flank and helped break the Iron Brigade's line. Although the 52nd had not suffered like the 26th North Carolina, the first day's fighting had depleted the regiment's ranks, and the head wound that had incapacitated General Heth had ultimately put Marshall in command of Pettigrew's Brigade. Now, in one of the oddities of war, Pettigrew's command had become Marshall's brigade, and General Heth's son, Captain Stockton Heth, was Marshall's aide-de-camp.[3]

Now they waited. In the fleeting moments that had followed the silencing of the Confederate cannonade, the long line of men in gray and butternut— some 13,000 strong—had been roused to their feet in the shelter of the woods atop Seminary Ridge. They knew what was coming, and they stood with a snapping, popping rattle as they fired percussion caps to field-check their weapons. A clatter of clanking metal followed the order to fix bayonets. Shaded by the green leaves of summer, the battle-tested North Carolinians of Marshall's brigade—including the 26th North Carolina—waited for Jimmy Marshall to repeat the order to advance. Some said General Lee had discouraged officers from making the assault on horseback—mounted officers made such obvious targets—but Jimmy Marshall remained mounted. Most of Pickett's brigade commanders were on foot, although Brigadier General Richard

B. Garnett, who was ill, had chosen to ride. "Dick, old fellow . . . ," Pickett had reportedly warned him, "you are going to catch hell." General Pettigrew was mounted. So was General Trimble, and Colonel Marshall intended to lead his brigade across the killing field in the same manner.[4]

The men of the 26th North Carolina and the rest of Marshall's brigade had barely gotten to their feet when Pettigrew appeared. He rode up to Colonel Marshall and stopped. Men who had served under him could tell what was coming next: He had "the bright look he always wore in the hour of danger," Captain Cureton would recall. From their position in the brigade, the men of the 26th could clearly hear Pettigrew's command. "Now Colonel," he told Marshall, "for the honor of the good Old North State. Forward."[5]

Marshall faced the brigade and repeated the command. Down the chain of command it went—from brigade to regiment to company. Like an ominous echo, it was repeated by officer after officer: ". . , for the honor of the good Old North State. Forward." Like a giant, powerful machine, the companies, regiments, brigades, and divisions all slowly cranked alive with the drill-book movements of a disciplined assault. Within the 26th North Carolina there was no hesitation— survivors would so attest in the future- -and even though there was no denying what lay ahead. "[Every] man who viewed the ground," an officer would later recall, "felt that when the charge was made . . . blood must flow and gallant spirits must take their final flight." It was time now for the thinly manned color guard to step to the front. Company commanders were in place. The men of the regiment had their orders: "Guide right" when instructed and hold all fire until close to the enemy. Now, it was time for Major Jones to take the bloodied remnant of the 26th onto the long and deadly path.[6]

Back home at Clover Hill—the Jones family farm in the North Carolina foothills—it was the season for harvesting crops. Were the fields now full of corn and wheat? Were the quail still plentiful and the bag of shot still waiting for "Knock's" return? Did his father still hold hopes for his "brag boy" to become a judge? And was Maria Spear, his surrogate mother, still praying for his salvation? What would tomorrow tell? Would he lie desperately wounded in some field hospital like brother Wat? Would he go the way of his mother and little brother Pat? Or would tomorrow find him with his men on a victory march, heading with the rest of Lee's army for Philadelphia or Washington? Across that long and open stretch of fields, beyond the fences, across the distant road, and up on that faraway ridge near the clump of trees—there awaited the answers for all of them. As Pettigrew's men moved forward from the woods, they automatically began to yell.[7]

Crouched behind the stone wall on Cemetery Ridge, the troops of Hays's Division stared toward the distant line of trees to the west and waited tensely. A light, westerly breeze slowly cleared the fields of the thick, whitish smoke from the Confederate artillery fire. The men in blue knew what was coming next, and they watched intently for the first sight of the Southern infantry. As the smoke disappeared, the green fields again basked in a bright summer sun. The long line of Hays's troops, like Gibbon's Division to their left, waited in suspense. Then, from the faraway tree line, came a high-pitched, wild and prolonged chorus—the Rebel yell.[8]

"Look!" someone shouted. "Do you see them coming?" The cry echoed along the line of Hays's Division: "They are coming! Here they come!" Then, a majestic scene appeared that would never be forgotten by those who lived through the next half hour. From the distant woods emerged Confederate skirmish lines, followed by countless men in gray and butternut, moving shoulder-to-shoulder in an assault formation that appeared to be almost a mile long. Sunlight glinted from the rifle barrels and bayonets, giving the giant mass of men an appearance of a great, flowing body of water.[9]

"The whole line of battle looked like a stream or river of silver moving towards us," one awe-struck Federal officer would later recall. "I had often read of battles and charges; had been in a few myself," another would admit, "but until this moment I had not gazed upon so grand a sight as was presented by that beautiful mass of gray, with its small, square colors, as it came on in serried array. . . ." Other men on Cemetery Ridge would later search for words to describe the remarkable scene now unfolding before them. One Federal officer was reminded of a "forest of flashing steel." The advancing Southerners resembled "an ocean of armed men sweeping upon us!" another would recall. Private William Haines of the 12th New Jersey thought it was "the grandest sight" he had ever seen. "Their lines looked to be as straight as a line could be," he would later report, "their bayonets glistening in the sun from right to left, as far as the eye could reach . . . ."[10]

Many of the Northern troops waiting to confront these sons of the South were momentarily mesmerized by the sight unfolding before them. "The order was magnificent," one would later recount. "The movement of such a force over such a field, in such perfect order, to such a destiny, was grand beyond expression. . . ." The tread of the advancing troops reverberated "step by step" like a peculiar "music and rhythm" despite the distance. "Every movement expressed determination and resolute defiance," a Connecticut soldier would later recall, "the line moving forward like a victorious giant, confident of power and victory." The steady advance of the Confederate legions looked like "an irresistible wave," to one Federal private. "On they came," a New Jersey officer would later marvel, "with flags flying . . . and arms at right shoulder shift. All in open sight of friend and foe, over the green valley they marched in 'battle's magnificently stern array.'"[11]

Captain Winfield Scott, a company commander in the 126th New York, was posted with his regiment on the right of Hays's Division opposite the approaching line of Pettigrew's troops. The Confederate artillery reopened a covering fire, and shells again began exploding over Scott's position— but the captain did not notice. "I was so absorbed with the beauty and grandeur of the scene," he would later explain, "that I became oblivious to the shells that were bursting around us." Watching the mighty, gray-clad assembly advance— marching parade-like with its straight lines and fluttering red flags —Scott found himself reciting aloud a passage from the Old Testament: *Fair as the moon, bright as the sun, and terrible as an army with banners.*[12]

Other soldiers in Hays's Division were less distracted. Posted beside Arnold's Battery on the division's far left flank, troops of the 14th Connecticut began removing ammunition from their cartridge boxes and arranging the rounds for quick loading. The Connecticut soldiers were armed with the Sharps breech-loading rifle, which gave the regiment an increased rate of fire. Although the 14th Connecticut was less than a year old, its men had been exposed to some of the war's bloodiest contests—at Antietam, Fredericksburg and Chancellorsville. They had arrived on the field at Gettysburg the day before, and earlier this morning had played a prominent role in setting fire to the Bliss house and barn. Now they prepared to turn their firepower on the Southerners marching so grandly toward them.[13]

Crouched behind the stone wall to the right of the 14th Connecticut were the troops of the 1st Delaware. The men from Delaware were getting set to make their defense under the command of a junior officer. The regiment had reached Gettysburg before dawn the day before, and had been engaged as skirmishers all day. Ammunition had run low after ten hours of skirmishing, so the 1st Delaware's commander, Lieutenant Colonel Edward P. Harris, had pulled the regiment's right wing off the skirmish line. General Hancock learned of Harris's decision; he had placed the lieutenant colonel under arrest. Captain Thomas B. Hizar had taken command of the regiment, but he had been wounded later, leaving Lieutenant John F. Dent in command. Despite their peculiar loss of leaders, the men from Delaware were ready for battle. They were veterans, mustered for duty in a divided border state, and seasoned in the same major battles as the 14th Connecticut. On orders from General Hays, they had gathered extra weapons from the dead and wounded, and detailed soldiers to keep the rifles reloaded when the fighting began. Now, heavily armed, the soldiers from Delaware hunkered down behind the stone wall and prepared to deliver a fierce and sustained fire at the proper moment.[14]

To the right of the Delaware regiment, Major Hill and the troops of the 12th New Jersey responded to the advancing gray tide by unfurling their regimental battle flag and raising it to flutter in the breeze. Nearby, the divisional flag—a huge blue cloverleaf on a field of white—was raised in the center of Hays' Division. The New Jersey troops, armed with their special loads of buckshot, had been given strict orders not to open fire until the Confederates were within close range. The men were anxious and eager—their officers repeatedly had to remind them to hold their fire. More troops were now brought up from the rear: The 39th, 125th and 111th New York were posted behind the men from Connecticut, Delaware and New Jersey—with part of the 111th New York manning the front line to the right of the Jersey troops. Farther north along Hay's line, in front of Ziegler's Grove, the 108th and 126th New York were posted near the guns of Woodruff's Battery. All along the line, the blue-clad troops of Hay's Division prepared for the approaching storm of battle.[15]

As General Hays watched Pettigrew's Confederates moving grandly on his front, he had no thought of parades or banners. He could think only of his neighbors back home in Pittsburgh. A burly, bearded giant of a man, Alexander Hays clearly understood that the approaching lines meant potential disaster for *his* troops and *his* cause. Hays was a Pennsylvanian, a Congressman's son, and this soil was *his* soil. If this spectacular assault brought another defeat to the Federal army, he told himself, he could never face his friends in Pittsburgh again. A West Pointer and a Mexican War veteran, "Alex" Hays was a man of contrasts. Robust and opinionated, cheerful and affectionate, he was an accomplished athlete, a superb horseman and a "dead shot" with a pistol. He could also quote the classics and read poetry—and he loved flowers. At West Point, his circle of friends had included Ulysses S. Grant, Winfield S.

Hancock, and James Longstreet, Hays had been a mediocre student, a loyal friend and a first-rate fighter. He was also an adventurer. After the Mexican War, he had tried a stint in the iron industry and a two-year jaunt as a California "Forty-Niner." Back home in Pennsylvania, he had built bridges as a civil engineer. In 1861, he had gone to war with characteristic zeal, rising from captain to brigadier in a year-and-a-half. Severely wounded at Second Bull Run, he had been hospitalized for months, and had received his first divisional command only a few weeks before Gettysburg. He referred to the troops of Hays' Division as the "Blue Birds"—a name inspired by the division's blue insignia—and now he intended to unleash all devastation on the Confederates heading parade-like toward *his* position. "I felt," he would later vouch, "as ironclad as if protected by railroad iron."[16]

Hays mounted his favorite horse and rode up and down his line, cheering his troops. "Boys, don't let 'em touch these pieces," he shouted to the regiments posted near the artillery on his flanks. "They are coming, boys," he yelled to the others. "We must whip them. . . ." He finally dismounted, but continued to pace the line, encouraging his Blue Birds as they prepared to meet the storm. At one point, he preoccupied some of his troops by putting them through the manual of arms. *Hold your fire until they reach the fence!* He barked the order all along the line. To the men of the 12th New Jersey he gave special orders: The Jerseymen were not to fire until the Rebels were "within forty yards."[17]

"We were ready," a New Yorker would later remember. Soldiers pulled their cartridge boxes around to the front of their bodies for easy access, then checked and rechecked their weapons. The tension was high and the minutes seemed long as they watched the Southern ranks approach. One of Hays's officers would never forget the ominous sounds of impending battle: "The click of the locks as each man raised the hammer to feel with his fingers that the cap was on the nipple; the sharp jar as a musket touched a stone upon the wall when thrust in aiming over it, and the clicking of the iron axles as the guns were rolled up by hand a little further to the front, were all the sounds that could be heard." Some Federal troops were convinced nothing could stop the approaching ranks of gray. "When I saw this mass of men . . . approaching our position," one Northerner would later admit, "I thought that our chances for Kingdom Come or Libby Prison were very good." Until ordered to fire, the troops of Hays's Division were commanded to stay down behind the wall. There they waited, flags flapping overhead, while the distant line of Southern troops advanced. "There was nothing to do," a New York officer would later recall, "but await the crash that would soon come."[18]

As Marshall's brigade advanced across the field, Major John Jones moved the 26th North Carolina forward with drill-book precision. As the regiment moved forward out of the trees, Jones could see the panorama of open fields and the long Confederate battle line stretching to his left and right. He thought the 26th and Marshall's brigade looked magnificent. General Pettigrew was also surveying the line, however and he reacted to what he saw with concern: Davis's and Mayo's brigades had not come out of the trees. Pettigrew turned to Captain Young, and told him to ride quickly to the left and fetch the missing troops. Before Young could turn away, however, Davis's brigade emerged from the trees and hurriedly caught up with the rest of the division. Pettigrew and Young still saw no sign of Mayo's Virginians, although some had reportedly advanced alongside Davis. Young offered to summon the missing brigade. "No," Pettigrew replied, ". . . it might follow, and if it failed to do so it would not matter." Mayo's brigade—formerly Brockenbrough's—had been so severely reduced by casualties on the first day that Pettigrew and Young deemed it "virtually of no value in a fight." A few minutes later, the tardy troops did emerge from the woods, but they trailed far behind the rest of Pettigrew's Division.[19]

Marching briskly at "quick-time," Pettigrew's troops advanced with their weapons held at right-shoulder-shift. Pettigrew's division—like Pickett's to the right—was preceded by two heavy lines of skirmishers. The lines were separated by about 100 yards, and the skirmishers were spaced about two paces apart. Approximately 100 yards behind the second skirmish line, came the main line of battle. The battle line was led by color guards, whose bright red Starry Cross battle flags fluttered in the afternoon breeze. The troops carried themselves with the look of seasoned soldiers. "In spite of the marked incongruity in the color and makeup of the uniforms, particularly in the manner of head dress," an observer would recall, "there was no mistaking the fact that these men were tried, disciplined veterans." Spaced in intervals behind the main battle line, regimental commanders such as Major Jones advanced on foot. Behind them, in the appropriate positon of a brigade commander, rode Colonel Marshall, accompanied by his aides. Farther back, in the division commander's post—surrounded by mounted aides and couriers—rode General Pettigrew on his handsome dapple-gray. As the battle line advanced, couriers on horseback raced back and forth between commanders. To the rear, emerging from the trees behind Pettigrew's Division, came Trimble's two brigades, which advanced in the same order as Pettigrew's troops.[20]

For most of the men in the thin ranks of the 26th North Carolina, the advance into the open fields was strikingly similiar to the way their charge had begun two days earlier. Again their target was a ridge—this one farther away and free of woods. They could remember the brief but deadly moments when artillery fire had torn through their ranks as they had approached Wiloughby Run. They knew the guns would soon open on them again—and that the long, open route of assault they now faced would prolong the deadly barrage. If they survived the artillery fire, they would face the Yankee infantry—and they had learned that those men in blue could be stubborn, hard-fighting foes. These were sobering facts, enough to tempt any man to slow his step and straggle, but the men of the 26th advanced unflinching.[21]

Captain Wagg had survived the first day's fighting unscathed. Now he again moved the men of Company A forward into battle. Two years and 47 days had passed since he had joined the Jeff Davis Mountain Rifles back home in the high country of western North Carolina. He had been mustered in as a twenty-one-year-old sergeant, but within eight months he had been elected captain. Somehow he had emerged from the bloody climb up McPherson's Ridge—one of the few captains to survive unharmed. He had studied the field this morning with Captain Cureton and surely he could image what a hellish fire would momentarily fall on these neat, gray lines. Would he ever see his home in the Blue Ridge Mountains again? Twenty-year-old Captain Henry Clay Albright—the lean, dark-haired commander of Company G—had come through *all* the regiment's combat without a scratch. His worst injury to date was a broken front tooth suffered from biting stale hardtack. Now, as he led what was left of his company onto the field, he undoubtedly hoped to retain his record of safety.[22]

Sergeant Jacob A. Bush, advancing with the remnant of Company I, may have remembered hiking back to Lenoir the year before to reenlist in the 26th. "Jake" Bush had reenlisted to get a furlough home, and when his 30 days were up, he had headed back to the war—accompanied by several local boys he had recruited. One of the boys had brought his fife, and on the way he had played "Oh, Granny, Will Your Dog Bite?" to enliven the march. Bush had come back to the regiment in time to be wounded in the Seven Days Campaign, and he had narrowly escaped being shot one night in North Carolina while raiding a farmer's potato patch. Bush had come through the fight on McPherson's Ridge unharmed, although men were shot down on both sides of him. Now, as he headed toward the Yankee artillery waiting on the distant ridge, he could also remember the time he and Major Jones had walked up on a dismembered Federal soldier during the Seven Days' fighting. The man had been hit by an artillery shell, and Bush had estimated that the Yankee's body lay in no less than 11 pieces. He had no fifer by his side now, but Jake Bush had seen enough of war to know that *this* march would need no enlivening.[23]

Marching near Bush in Company I was Second Lieutenant James C. Greer, who had risen in the ranks from corporal to lieutenant over the past two years. On the first morning at Gettysburg, as the regiment had assembled at Marsh Creek, Greer had spotted a handsome colt in a farmer's horse lot, and had tried to barter for the animal. The horse's owner, a Dutch farmer, had been intent on escaping the coming battle. "I have no time to trade horses now," he had told Greer. "I is getting to de woots." Greer had come away empty-handed, but he had also come through the day's fighting unharmed. He would be fortunate to repeat that feat this day. Advancing in the thin ranks of Company E, under Captain Brewer's command, was twenty-four-year-old Lieutenant John R. Emerson. Dark-headed and bearded, he was a good-looking man, who had left a young wife back home. Aware of the uncertainties of war, Emerson had long ago sent her his will. "I will and bequeath unto my wife Martha F. Emerson all my property of all and every kind," it read. He had been married four years, but still had fathered no children, even though he had been raised in a family with nine. He was apparently hopeful, however, and had directed his estate to include provision for an heir. As the regiment moved onto the deadly field, Lieutenant Emerson at least had the security knowing that he had prepared for the worst.[24]

They moved through the line of Third Corps artillery, flowing flood-like past the guns. Captain Louis Young, riding alongside General Pettigrew, would always remember how "beautifully clear" the day appeared. "Before us lay bright fields and a fair landscape, embracing hill and dale and mountain," he would later recall, "and beyond, fully three-fourths of a mile away, loomed Cemetery Ridge . . . its heights capped with cannon . . . ." As they moved down the slope of the shallow swale, the men of the 26th could see the ridge ahead more clearly; the enemy batteries interspersed along the distant stone wall were now distinctly visible. "We could see the mouths of the gaping cannon," one would later remember, "waiting for us to get in range to pour bushels of grape and canister into our ranks. . . ." Captain Cureton knew what lay ahead, but he too was heartened by the spectacle surrounding him: On either side as far as he could see was a perfect line of battle. The scene made a different impression on Private Albert Caison of Company I. He looked at the Federal artillery waiting ahead, and concluded that an untold number of men now marching alongside him would soon be cut down like harvested grain. Even after calculating the odds, however, he remained confident that the Yankees soon would be routed.[25]

"Steady, men, steady," the officers in Pettigrew's Division called out to their troops amid the rapid, regular tread of many feet. The men of the 26th—and the other soldiers of Marshall's brigade—came to the first of several post-and-rail fences on their route. The standard tactic called for the troops to rush against it and push it down. "The first fence," one of Pettigrew's men would later recall, "[was] quickly toppled over by hand and upon the points of bayonets." The advance continued unhindered, steady and silent. The only sound now, a veteran of the assault would later recollect, was the "tramp, tramp" of the men moving in "quick-time" over the sun-baked fields. To the rear, Trimble's brigades now began passing through the line of Confederate artillery. Trimble and his staff could see Pettigrew's Division advancing ahead "in fine style, good order and unbroken." As Trimble's troops surged around the artillery pieces, however, they encountered an ominous sign: Scattered soldiers—apparently some of Mayo's troops—*had* begun straggling and drifting backwards. Major McLeod Turner of the 7th North Carolina, one of Trimble's regiments, was startled to see what he would later describe as "crowds of stragglers coming to the rear." He promptly ordered his troops to "charge bayonets." His men levelled their fixed bayonets toward the stragglers, which forced them to either rejoin the assault or scurry out of the way.[26]

"The line moves forward," one of Pettigrew's men would later remember, "over fences, across fields, forward! forward!" In the distance, ahead of the Confederate skirmish lines, the Federal skirmishers began falling back, firing as they retreated. Scattered puffs of white smoke appeared along Pettigrew's skirmish line, and the rattle of gunfire echoed over the ranks of the 26th. As the blue-clad skirmishers arose and ran, many of them fell. When both Pettigrew's and Trimble's troops had passed the line of Third Corps artillery, some of the guns resumed fire and began lobbing shells over the long gray line and onto Cemetery Ridge. Ahead of Marshall's brigade lay a small orchard and, just beyond it, the smoldering ruins of the Bliss house and barn. "Dress to the right," Marshall's officers began shouting. It was time for three of Pettigrew's brigades to shift rightward—dressing as planned on Fry's brigade. Pickett's officers, meanwhile, began shouting, "Dress on the left." As planned, the shifting of Pettigrew's and Pickett's Divisions would funnel the huge mass of men against the Federal center, bringing irresistible force to bear on one sector of the enemy line. Ahead and still far away, the targeted clump of trees loomed above Cemetery Ridge.[27]

"The march was rapid and the columns moved on without impediment of ditch or obstacle," an observer would later report. "It was a fighting mass of trained soldiery and its movements [appeared] magnificent—perhaps irresistible." From Pickett's side, the Rebel yell began to rise from the ranks. The sound troubled one of Pettigrew's officers—Captain A.H. Moore of Fry's brigade—who wondered why the wild, familiar yell was being raised in midfield. "[We] never before failed to increase our speed when the 'yell' was started," he would later relate. This time, however, no orders for "double-time" followed: They were still too far away to sustain an increase in speed. It had already been a long charge, and they had covered only about half the distance. The entire line moved steadily, however, without hestitation—still guiding on Fry's brigade. Captain Young watched Pettigrew's troops from behind the division, where General Pettigrew had placed him with orders to help keep the brigades aligned. Young had experienced no problems keeping the troops moving—they were veterans—but now he noticed that the assault force was taking on a wedge-shaped appearance, and Pettigrew's troops were beginning to crowd together. He feared the crowding might be mistaken for wavering. It also gave the enemy a better target—especially Davis's brigade on the left flank. He tried to make the men spread out, but they were moving too quickly to heed in calls from the rear.[28]

Major Thomas W. Osborn stood near a line of cannon on Cemetery Hill and watched Pettigrew's approaching troops as they began to guide right and crowd together. Osborn commanded the Federal XI Corps Artillery Brigade. He had placed more than 50 guns on and around Cemetery Hill, which lay to the right and rear of Hays's line on Cemetery Ridge. More than a hundred pieces of Federal artillery from Cemetery Ridge to Little Round Top had been brought to bear on the advancing Confederate line—and more guns were being brought up from the rear. On the Federal left, some batteries had already begun firing on Pickett's troops, and most of the artillery on the Federal right was charged and ready. The Confederate artillery had opened a cover fire for the assault, but most of it was again overshooting the Federal line. Major Osborn ordered his gun crews to refrain from returning the Confederate artillery fire, but instead to concentrate solely on the advancing lines of infantry. His batteries still had ample long-range ammunition and the guns were charged with a variety of deadly ammunition—solid shot, explosive shell and case shot. Solid shot would plow through packed ranks of troops; shell would explode on impact, scattering deadly iron fragments; and case shot—a spherical or cone-shaped iron projectile filled with a hatful of lead balls—would explode among massed troops with devastating effect. From his elevated position on Cemetery Hill, Osborn had a clear view of Pettigrew's advancing line, which was now well within artillery range. His order was to fire at will—and now it was time. "Commence firing," came the command.[29]

The Federal artillery fire hit Pettigrew's line with savage fury, tearing great swaths through the dense ranks of men. "[They] seemed to sink into the earth under the tempest of fire poured into them," a Confederate observer would recall. The fire produced "pandemonium" among Pettigrew's troops, a Federal soldier noted, but they quickly recovered from the initial shock and plunged on through the fiery storm. "We could see our shells burst in their lines," one of Hays' officers would recall, "and it looked as though they had all been cut down in that place, but they would close up the gap and come on again." As the shot and shell blew giant holes in their lines, the men in gray and butternut closed ranks and kept going. "Guide right," Pettigrew's officers shouted to their men, and the line continued at "quick-time" across the open field. A "tremendous shower" of iron and lead sprayed the 26th North Carolina. Private Caison, advancing with company I, thought the fire was "murderous." The regiment absorbed its losses and kept going. Major Jones was knocked flat by an exploding shell at one point, but he kept the men in line and moving. As ordered, the troops held their fire even as their comrades dropped. Not until they reached the fence that flanked the Emmitsburg Road in their front would they be allowed to fire—and the road was still far away. They moved past the Bliss orchard, past the smoking ruins of house and barn, and down slightly sloping ground toward a ditch that cut through the meadow. Behind the North Carolinans now was a trail of dead and wounded.[30]

The rain of shot and shell continued relentlessly. Solid shot bounced through Pettigrew's ranks, taking down as many as a dozen soldiers at a time. Shells exploded above them, just in front of them and within their midst. As the holes were torn in their ranks, they repeatedly dressed their line, closing the gaps. "This was done under a fearful artillery fire which was cutting them down by the hundreds every minute," an amazed Federal artillery officer would remember. "They then moved forward as before, but the nearer they approached the more severe was their loss from our guns. . . . Still there was no hesitation or irregularity in the movement. The steady and firm step of the veteran soldiers continued." Captain Cureton looked to his left and right. Despite the galling storm of iron, the 26th's battle line still looked perfectly arrayed.[31]

On they charged, slowing mometarily to jump the meadow ditch and then resuming their "quick-time" march toward a field of ripened wheat that stretched all the way to the Emmitsburg Road. They pushed down another fence and surged into the field of yellow grain, heading toward the road ahead. The incoming artillery fire continued to tear into their ranks and the rest of Marshall's brigade—but the men in gray kept coming. "There was no hurry, no confusion as our shot was poured into them," a Yankee officer in their front would recall. "They came as steady and as regular as if on a parade, our guns pouring the shot into them." When shot or shell tore a swath through the ranks, the men would close up—and when another gap was blasted through the line, they would close up again. "We advanced, received their fire, and still advanced," one of Marshall's officers would later marvel. "I never saw men behave more gallantly, nor do I believe men ever did." The smoke from the Federal artillery boiled off Cemetery Ridge, rolling over the mass of advancing men. "[It] obscured the scene," a survivor would later write, "with a dreadful and darkened magnificence. . . ."[32]

As the men of the 26th moved across the field, Sergeant William Smith, the regimental color sergeant, fell with a severe head wound. Private Thomas Cozart was nearby, ready to raise the fallen battle flag. In the rear of the brigade, Colonel Marshall moved forward on horseback, cheering his troops before him. They kept their order despite the deadly artillery fire, closing ranks, filling the gaps, advancing steadily despite their losses. As Marshall and the brigade closed on the road ahead, a Federal shell exploded just feet away from man and horse. The blast knocked the young colonel from his horse. Shaken, he got to his feet. Those around him held his horse, and Marshall ordered them to help him mount. Obediently, they helped him into the saddle. Obviously rattled, but still determined, he had the men turn his horse toward the enemy—then off he went again, following his brigade toward the Emmitsburg Road.[33]

Ahead, Pettigrew's skirmishers were already at the fence that flanked the road, unleashing a brisk fire up the slope toward the enemy line. The Federal skirmishers had retreated up the slope and were climbing back over the stone wall to join their main battle line. To the rear, Trimble's brigades were closer now to Pettigrew's line, having gained ground when Pettigrew's men slowed to jump the meadow ditch. Trimble was with his troops, keeping a vow. He was a stranger to these men—Pender's troops—and when he took command earlier this day he had made a short speech, ordering them not to fire until the enemy's line was broken and promising that he would go all the way with them. Now he followed them on horseback, disregarding the target he presented. They were advancing steadily—just like Pettigrew's men out in front. They passed now over the spot where the enemy artillery had first torn into Pettigrew's line; it was marked by scores of dead and wounded. "Three cheers for the old North State," one of the wounded cried out—and Trimble's men answered with cheers. "Charley," Trimble said to an aide, "I believe those fine fellows are going into the enemy's line."[34]

The cover fire from Hill's artillery began to slacken as Pettigrew's division closed on the Emmitsburg Road. The Confederate gun crews—already low on ammunition—did not want to risk firing on their own troops. The Federal gun crews meanwhile prepared to change to short-range ammunition. Still on the front line of Marshall's brigade were the men of the 26th, battle flag aloft, moving through the wheat. Glancing to the right, looking beyond Fry's brigade, Major Jones at one point tried to catch a glimpse of Pickett's Division—but the smoke was too dense. He could only concentrate on cheering on his men, keeping them angling to the right. A few hundred yards ahead lay the road, flanked by fences, and just beyond it was the rising slope that led to the enemy line. Despite the savage Federal artillery fire, Jones believed, they were moments away from victory.[35]

On the edge of Ziegler's Grove—on the right flank of Hays's Division—Lieutenant Tully McCrea prepared to open fire on the approaching Confederate line. Never had he seen such "a splendid target for light artillery." McCrea was in charge of the right section of Woodruff's Battery. His 12-pounder

Napoleons were manned by battle-seasoned gun crews—veterans of First Bull Run, the Peninsula Campaign, Antietam, Fredericksburg, Chancellorsville—and they had taken a pounding during the Confederate bombardment. Now it was pay-back time. They had exhausted their long-range ammunition during the bombardment, so they had held their fire until the men in gray and butternut were close. They had ample short-range ammuntion—40 rounds of canister per gun—and their guns were charged and ready. On Hays's left flank, several guns in Arnold's Battery were out of ammunition and had been withdrawn, but those still in line were now also armed with canister. A large tin can packed with iron balls, canister could transform a field piece into a giant shotgun—with a murderous effect. Looking out at Pettigrew's advancing troops as they crowded to the right, McCrea knew it would be impossible to miss.[36]

"When we opened on them," Lieutenant McCrea would later recall, "one could see gaps swept down. We had forty rounds of canister to each gun and they got the most of it." From the Federal artillery in their front and on their flanks, Pettigrew's troops were blasted with canister. "A storm of grape and canister tore its way from man to man," an observer would remember, "and marked its track with corpses straight down their line." Lieutenant John Egan, commanding the right section of Woodruff's Battery, had his guns double-loaded and his gun crews could fire two rounds a minute. He would never forget the impact the double loads of canister made on Pettigrew's troops—it was like a road was instantly plowed through the mass of men. Still, to his amazement, the survivors closed ranks and kept coming.[37]

When Major Jones looked to his left—trying to catch a glimpse of the rest of Pettigrew's Division through the smoke of battle—he could see nothing. On he charged—the troops still guiding right—as they moved through the wheat field toward the road ahead. Captain Cureton moved forward with the remnant of troops from Company B. Around him, however, men were falling constantly, further shrinking the size of the regiment. The enemy line was still a far-off goal, topping the slope ahead and still more than 400 yards away. "Forward! Close together, and fill up the gaps," Pettigrew's officers shouted. Up ahead lay the rail fence, the road, the slope—and the enemy line. Soon they would return this fire. The desperation of the moment, the grim determination of the men—and the shock of being wounded—would never be forgotten by one of Pettigrew's officers. "Boom! On the right, boom! Boom! It comes down the line. Boom! Boom!" he would later recall. ". . . I feel a sudden shock as if my very soul is crushed, everything vanishes from me, and I know no more."[38]

Finally, as they neared the Emmittsburg Road, Pettigrew's troops opened fire with a powerful volley. It was "a terrific crash," according to a Yankee officer on the ridge ahead. They fired while they were advancing, and they were well within the range to do serious damage to the enemy. The Federal infantry were still crouched behind the stone wall, however, and the volley had minimal impact. Behind his advancing line, General Pettigrew galloped back and forth on horseback, shouting encouragement, apparently unmindful of the target he presented. Ahead, Colonel Marshall cheered on his brigade. If he was still shaken from the artillery blast that had toppled him, he did not show it. Still mounted, he pressed forward with the great wall of troops as they neared the Emmitsburg Road. The lane was flanked by sturdy fences—post-and-rail on the west side and post-and-slab on the east side—and they could not be toppled like the earlier fences on Marshall's line of march. Flailed unmercifully by the Federal canister, some men found cover in a ditch that ran along the west side of the fence. Most men grabbed the fence, however, hauled themselves up on it and jumped into the road. Some stopped for cover or breath in the slightly sunken roadbed, but the great majority darted across the road, and began scaling the other fence. They clambered over the slabs and dopped on the other side—now less than 200 yards from the enemy's stone wall.[39]

"Fire!" General Hays shouted at the top of his voice from behind the Federal line. "Fire! Fire!" echoed the command along Hays's line. Suddenly, ranks of blue-uniformed troops rose from behind the stone wall and unleashed a volcanic volley of gunfire. It was an explosive, shattering blast. Joined by blasts of double-charged canister from Woodruff's and Arnold's remaining artillery, it cleared the fences and dropped crowds of Pettigrew's men like a wall of falling bricks. A loud, agonizing howl of shock and pain rose from Pettigrew's line and echoed above the roar of the guns. Behind the stone wall, Hays's soldiers quickly traded their fired weapons for loaded ones and fired again. "Crack! Crack! spoke out the musketry, and the men dropped from the fence as if swept by some powerful force of nature," a survivor would recount. Piles of dead and wounded were left lying in the road and by the fence. This time the gaps in Pettigrew's line were not closed immediately.[40]

"The time it took to climb to the top of the fence seemed, to me, an age of suspense," one of Pettigrew's surviving soldiers would recall. "It was not a leaping over; it was rather an insensible tumbling to the ground, in the nervous hope of escaping the thickening missiles that buried themselves in the falling victims, the ground and in the fence. . . ." Troops who scaled the first fence clustered in the roadbed, lying flat beneath the stream of deadly fire, joined by others who jumped, tumbled or fell from the fence. The noise of bullets hitting the fence slabs and rails resounded above the gunfire, cries and curses, sounding to one of Pettigrew's men like "large rain drops pattering on the roof." Up the slope and behind the stone wall, the men of the 14th Connecticut fired round after round from their Sharps breech-loaders into the mass of men trying to climb the fences. The troops of the 12th New Jersey, meanwhile, held their fire with steely resolve, waiting to discharge their muskets-turned-shotguns when the Southerners were even closer.[41]

Still mounted on horseback, Colonel Jimmy Marshall towered above the mass of men trying to scale the fences. He cheered them onward, but was obviously appalled at the mounting carnage. "We do not know which of us will be the next to fall," he yelled to his aide. Then he took two rounds in the forehead. He toppled from his horse and landed dead at the feet of his men. Never again would he teach school, visit the family home or reminisce about days at V.M.I. His stint as a brigade commander forever would be measured in hours. The troops of the 26th North Carolina, meanwhile, were coming out of the roadside wheat field and climbing the fences when the Federal infantry opened fire. Killed at some point in the confusion was color-bearer Thomas Cozart, leaving the regiment's battle flag to again be borne by a succession of handlers. Also shot down was Sergeant Jake Bush, who fell among the trampled wheat bleeding from multiple wounds. A few feet away, Second Lieutenant James Greer—the young officer who had tried to horse-trade on the first day—also fell seriously wounded. Nearby too lay Sergeant Alexander Dunlap, now immobilized by a severe leg wound. Bush was sure he was dying. He had been hit four times—twice in the right thigh, once in his left arm, and once through his right side and lung. He lay among a pile of bodies where the field sloped away from the road, and he watched helplessly as a six-foot-long stream of blood trailed downward from his body. Just ahead, some troops were taking cover in the road; most, however, were climbing the fences so that they could get at the enemy.[42]

In the rear of the division, General Pettigrew was confronted by Captain Young—now on foot. His horse had been shot, but Young had made his way through the fire and smoke of battle with an urgent report: Pettigrew's far left flank was taking murderous fire and appeared to be breaking up. Pettigrew responded immediately. Go to General Trimble, he told Young, and get him to rush his brigades forward to shore up the assault line. Turning to another aide, Lieutenant William B. Shepard, Pettigrew ordered him to ride to the left and try to rally the troops on the flank. On horseback, Lieutenant Shepard reached Pettigrew's left flank as Captain Young was hurrying on foot to General Trimble. By the time Shepard arrived, however, Mayo's depleted brigade of Virginians had already been turned back on the far left flank—and the survivors were fleeing in retreat back toward Seminary Ridge.[43]

Unlike the rest of Pettigrew's division, Mayo's troops had been hit hard by infantry fire *before* they could approach the Emmitsburg Road. The fire had come from the 8th Ohio Infantry, which was posted near the Federal picket line far in advance of the right flank of Hays' Division. The regiment had occupied its advanced post the day before to help the Federal pickets clean out a menancing pocket of Confederate skirmishers. The Ohioans were still there when the Confederate advance began, and were unable to retire. They were veterans, and their commander, Lieutenant Colonel Franklin Sawyer, watched as Pettigrew's division approached. At first, the Confederate left flank looked as if it would sweep over the 8th Ohio's position, but the men in gray and butternut began guiding to their right and shifted away from his position. Then Sawyer looked back to his front and saw a thin line of Confederates advancing straight toward him. It was Mayo's Virginians, who were late coming out of the woods.[44]

Already reduced in strength by the defection of the 22nd Virginia Infantry Battalion during the bombardment, Mayo's brigade had started the assault with confusion. Some of the field officers had mistaken the reserve troops for Davis's brigade, and had waited for them to advance before going forward. By the time the mistake was discovered, the rest of Pettigrew's division was well out in the field. In the confusion some of the Virginians had gone forward with Davis's brigade, although scores of them had turned back—presumably to rejoin their brigade. Reduced dramatically in size, the remnant of Mayo's brigade had finally moved across the field on the far left flank—right into the path of the 8th Ohio. Lieutenant Colonel Sawyer watched them approach until they were about 100 yards away, and then the Yankee officer did the unexpected: He ordered his troops to charge.[45]

"I formed [my men] in a single line, and as the rebels came within short range of our skirmish line, charged them," he would later recall. Mayo's troops were drastically reduced, isolated from the rest of Pettigrew's Division, riddled by fresh casualties from the enemy artillery fire—and now a line of blue-uniformed troops rose before them, discharged a powerful volley, and charged. It was all too much—even for courageous veterans. "Some fell, some ran back," Sawyer would report. "Most of them, however, threw down their arms and were made prisoners." In front of the 8th Ohio's line now lay piles of dead and wounded Virginians.[46]

Sawyer quickly ordered his men to change their front to the left. They hurried toward the exposed left flank of Davis's brigade and took a position behind a rail fence running perpendicular to the Emmitsburg Road. Already there were about 75 crack shots from the 1st Massachusetts Sharpshooters. Together, they opened fire on Davis's men. After starting late, Davis's battle seasoned troops had boldly surged ahead of the rest of Pettigrew's division, and they were first to reach the Emmitsburg Road. Despite the fierce fire now poured into their left flank, Davis's North Carolinians and Mississippians ignored their losses and forged ahead. They scaled the fences, charged up the slope and headed for the enemy behind the wall. It was then that the men of Hays's Division rose up and delivered their massive opening volley. It had a devastating impact on the lead troops of Davis's brigade. "The front of the column was nearly up the slope . . . ," Colonel Sawyer would later recall, "when suddenly a terrific fire from every available gun . . . burst upon them." Davis's men fell in heaps. "That line went down like grass before the scythe," a Federal officer would later recall.[47]

Then the Rebel yell sounded over the roar of battle—it was Lane's brigade, clambering over the Emmitsburg Road fences. Composing the left wing of Trimble's division, Lane's brigade had been rushed forward by Trimble even before he received Pettigrew's summons from Captain Young. Seeing Mayo's men turned back and fearing for Davis's brigade, Trimble had ordered Lane's brigade to "oblique to the left" and hurry forward. General Lane and his North Carolina regiments had rushed in behind Davis's troops, reaching the Emmitsburg Road moments behind them. Lane's men managed to push down at least one section of the first fence, but they found the second one too sturdy and had to climb it. "Several officers, myself among the number, sprang over the fence, followed by the entire command," Lieutenant Thomas L. Norwood of the 37th North Carolina would later report. They spilled over the fences, merged with the stubborn survivors of Davis's brigade, and surged up the slope together toward the stone wall—waved onward by the fallen wounded of Davis's brigade. They poured a heavy fire into the enemy atop the slope—"with telling effect," one of Lane's men would attest—took their losses from the return fire, and pushed on toward the enemy line ahead. Seeing some Federal soldiers get up and run toward the rear, Lieutenant Norwood felt the flush of approaching victory. "I rushed forward," he would later recount, "thinking the day was ours. . . ."[48]

Major Jones had never experienced such fire. It was beyond description—not even the fury of McPherson's Ridge could equal it. The dead and wounded in the Emmitsburg Road lay in ghastly piles, while hundreds of unharmed troops paused beneath the hailstorm of deadly fire as if gathering strength for a final push forward. "Every man that reached the road in my view sank to the ground," one of Pettigrew's officers would report. They had been there only fleeting moments, but seconds seemed like minutes in such hellish conditions. Survivors would later insist that they had withstood this fire for 10 or 15 or even 20 minutes. Field officers moved through the crowded ranks of men, ordering the troops up, over the next fence and forward. Obediently, determinedly, most arose and began climbing over the second fence. Behind them, scores of dead lay unmoving where they had fallen, while countless wounded writhed or moaned. "Many of our comrades," a survivor would remember, "remained in the road. . . ."[49]

Marshall's brigade lost much of its organization in the Emmitsburg Road. Crowded together in the final stage of the assault, companies and regiments merged in the confusion. "Officers became separated from their men," a survivor would later report, "and with uplifted swords, rushed madly up and down, calling to their men to follow." Orders were muffled by the racket of battle. Major Jones looked to his right and left, but the dense smoke kept him from seeing what was happening more than a few yards away. In the smokey haze there were few choices: He could either go on or he could go back—and he was still confident of victory despite their horrendous losses. Although men were dropping constantly, the officers yelled for the troops to close up the gaps in their ranks. "When we dressed the line," a North Carolina officer would recall, "I did not see [anyone] falter. . . ." General Pettigrew was on foot now—his horse had been shot—and he was pressing into the crowded mass of men where Marshall's right flank merged with the left flank of Fry's brigade. Nearby, was Colonel Fry, pushing forward sword in hand with his troops. "I am dressing on you!" Pettigrew shouted above the roar of the guns. In response, Fry paused for a second amid the tumult of battle and saluted Pettigrew with his sword. Then they followed the troops up the slope toward the Yankee line.[50]

Most of Fry's troops approached the Federal line at the angle of the stone wall. Those who reached the wall merged with the troops of Pickett's Division who had made it up the slope on the right. Two of Pickett's brigade commanders—Garnett and Kemper—had been shot down before they could reach the wall. Brigadier Lewis Armistead, however, his hat hoisted on his saber, valiantly led about 150 troops from his brigade of Virginians over the wall near the clump of trees. When Alabamians and Tennesseeans from his brigade spilled over the wall, Colonel Fry was not with them: He had been shot down on the slope. "Go on," he yelled at his troops. "It will not last five minutes longer!" Marshall's brigade—and the men of the 26th—rushed for the wall north of the angle—where Hays's front line was defended by the troops from Connecticut, Delaware and New Jersey. There the stone wall was roughly 83 yards farther from the Emmitsburg Road. For the men of the 26th, the extra yards were deadly.[51]

When they were fifty yards from the stone wall, the Southerners in front of the 12th New Jersey received the deadly blast the Jerseymen had been saving. They had held their fire while the troops around them poured fire into the advancing Confederate ranks—and now they could wait no longer. Major Hill managed to shout a frantic reminder—*"Aim low!"*—but his command was drowned by the explosive blast of some four hundred muskets double-loaded with buckshot. Thousands of pellets tore into the gray ranks—and the sons of the South collapsed in droves. The 12th New Jersey's regimental surgeon had to look away; the carnage was more than he could bear. "It was murder," he would later observe. One North Carolina officer struggling up the slope saw visions of hog-butchering back home; he was in "a slaughter pen," he decided. Behind the stone wall, the troops of the 14th Connecticut fired their Sharps breech-loaders so rapidly that the weapons overheated; frantically, the men doused their guns with water from their canteens and kept shooting. "In vain did the Confederate commanders attempt to reform their columns," one of the Connecticut soldiers would later recall; ". . . colors were dropped and men fled in confusion." The troops of the 1st Delaware ignored orders to kneel and stood instead—unleashing "a solid sheet of withering fire" into the shrinking gray ranks advancing toward them. Watching the men of Marshall's brigade go down, the 1st Delaware's Lieutenant John Brady was reminded of frost melting beneath the sun. Above the shattering crash of gunfire, a yell rose from the Yankee line: "Come on, come on, come to death!"[52]

Major Jones saw his already thin ranks now simply shredded. Captain Cureton received a shoulder wound, but kept going. Captain Wagg was not so fortunate. He would never return to his mountain home: A blast of artillery fire killed him instantly. Lieutenant Emerson of Company E also fell, severely wounded. His commander, Captain Brewer, who had been the last man to pick up the 26th's battle flag on McPherson's Ridge, now did so again—but this time was shot down with the banner in his hands. Company I's Private Caison fell with wounds in the hand and the hip. Despite his wounds, he was confident that the Yankee line would break within moments. Major Jones was unhurt, but his men were now "going down in bunches." When halfway to the stone wall the ranks of the 26th North Carolina resembled a thin skirmish line. Still, they pressed forward and followed the colors, which were now borne by Private Daniel Boone Thomas—the remaining color-bearer. Just ahead, through the fiery storm, lay the stone wall and the Yankee line. Then, from the far left of Marshall's brigade arose a loud cry of alarm and despera-tion. Major Jones looked to his left. Through the smoky haze he could see Yankee infantry in force—and they were pouring a devastating fire into the brigade's left flank. Jones immediately realized what had happened: Marshall's brigade had been flanked by the enemy.[53]

General Hays, seeing the 8th Ohio disperse Mayo's troops and then shift its fire into the left flank of Davis's brigade, made a crucial command decision. He quickly ordered troops from two New York regiments on his right—the 108th and the 126th—to swing forward like a closing door and join the Ohioans and Massachusetts marksmen firing into the Rebel left flank. Although some men laid low, most obeyed, and were supported by two artillery pieces. Hays's quick response placed a force of more than four hundred riflemen on the Confederate left flank. Supported by the Federal artillery, this flank force unleashed "a galling fire" just as Lane's brigade surged up the slope and joined Davis's shattered ranks. Together with the furious fire from the main line, the flanking fire placed the troops on the Confederate left flank in a murderous crossfire. "They were at once enveloped in a dense cloud of smoke and dust," a Federal officer would later recount. "Arms, heads, blankets, guns and knapsacks were thrown and tossed into the clear air." Just yards away from the stone wall, Lane's men now staggered and slowed. ". . . I climbed over [the Emmitsburg Road fence] and my men were following me rapidly," Major Turner of the 7th North Carolina would recall. "I had advanced ten yards or more towards the works when I was shot down; the men who had gotten over returned to and laid down in the Pike as did the entire regiment." Lieutenant Norwood of the 37th North Carolina got even closer to the stone wall: He and two other officers were "within twenty yards of the enemy's works [when] shot down." Norwood's superior, Lieutenant Colonel William G. Morris, was certain that at least a half-dozen of his troops made it over the stone wall. Men from Davis's brigade would later say the same for themselves. Despite their desperate drive toward the wall, however, Lane's and Davis's troops were forced off the slope by the furious crossfire. As the men fell back to the Emmitsburg Road, the Federal crossfire in turn shifted to Marshall's brigade.[54]

Still returning fire, the survivors of Lane's and Davis's brigades were trying to regroup in the road when General Pettigrew's aide, Lieutenant Shepard, reached General Lane with orders "to move by brigade to the left." Lane, who was still mounted, seemed to think the courier had come from Longstreet. He was trying to figure it all out when his horse was hit by Federal fire. The wounded animal began bucking wildly. Somehow Lane held on until he could manage to dismount. Then he called for Colonel Clarke M. Avery of the 33rd North Carolina, commander of what had been Lane's left flank regiment, and ordered him to get his men up and moving against the Yankee force on their left flank. "My God!" Avery shouted back above the clamor. "General, do you intend sending your men into such a place unsupported, when the troops on the right are falling back?" Lane took a quick look around him: Lowrance's brigade was already in on the right, piling up behind Marshall's and Fry's troops, no support troops were in sight—and Marshall's battered brigade appeared to be disintegrating under the Federal crossfire. "Seeing it was useless to sacrifice my brave men," Lane would later report, "I ordered my brigade back. . . ."[55]

*   *   *

Leading the shredded remnant of the 26th North Carolina, Private Thomas waded through the deadly firestorm with the regiment's battle flag and headed up the slope toward the stone wall. Beside him was Sergeant James M. Brooks. Both were twenty-two years old, both hailed from North Carolina's Chatham County, and both were among the few survivors of Company E. Back home, two years earlier, they had enlisted on the same day. Now, together, they were going over the stone wall into the face of the Yankee fire. The men of the 26th who were still on their feet and advancing now numbered in the dozens—but they too kept going. There had been few of them left standing two days earlier, when the Federal line had finally broken atop McPherson's Ridge. Could they do the same again? Major Jones believed so. Watching his skeleton line of troops spearhead its way up the slope toward the enemy's line, Jones was certain that—despite the slaughter—victory was imminent.[56]

Up the slope to his right, Yankee gun crews on Cemetery Ridge were hurriedly pulling the serviceable guns of Arnold's Battery out of line to save them from capture. One of the Rhode Island gunners, however, was determined to take a final shot. Gun number-four was charged with a lethal double load of canister, and its gunner, Private William C. Barker, stood with lanyard in hand, waiting to fire. The gun covered the slope in front of Hays's left wing— the section defended by the men of Connecticut, Delaware and New Jersey. For some reason, as the thin gray line surged before the muzzle of his gun, Private Barker hesitated. In his line of fire were North Carolina troops—one Yankee artilleryman would claim they were from the 26th—and at such close range the double load of canister could not miss. Still the gunner hesitated. "Barker," shouted his sergeant, "why the d— l don't you fire that gun! Pull! Pull!" Finally, the gunner jerked the lanyard, and in a blast of fire and smoke, bucketsful of lead balls tore into the gray line. "The number four obeyed orders," a Federal artilleryman would recall, "and the gap made in that North Carolina regiment was simply terrible." As Arnold's artillerymen withdrew, Lieutenant Gulian Weir, commanding Battery C of the 5th U.S. Artillery, hastily filled the vacant space in the Federal line with a fresh battery of 12-pounder Napoleons. Weir had been ordered in from reserve just moments before. "Go in over there," a Federal officer advised him. "You'll come in on their flank and mow 'em down." Weir's guns were charged with double canister, and he opened fired into the Southerners surging up the slope. Delivered at almost point-blank range, the blasts of canister disintegrated the ranks of men in its line of fire.[57]

Simultaneously, the volleys of rifle fire unleashed by Hays's Federals on Pettigrew's left flank—combined with the sustained fire from the front— cleared the slope between the stone wall and the Emmittsburg Road as if a giant hand had swept aside the charging ranks. The word *annihilation* came to an officer in the 14th Connecticut, who would later describe the fire from his ranks as "murderous . . . too much for human valor. . . ." Scores of Marshall's troops fell dead or wounded. Others dropped to the ground—"dropped their guns and fell on their faces," a Yankee would recall—while countless more backed down the slope to the fences. Among the bodies carpeting the slope, some men began waving their hats—as if they could signal an end to the killing storm. Then a sprinkling of handkerchiefs appeared—held high in surrender. Despite the awful carnage, a handful of determined troops from the 26th pushed on up the slope toward the stone wall—led by Private Thomas and Sergeant Brooks. Nearby, a color-bearer from another regiment was shot dead, falling with the flagstaff in his hands. Thomas too was hit, but he and Brooks kept going. There, finally, was the stone wall—the Yankee line—that had been their goal for almost a mile of blood and death. It was time for them to scale the wall, to climb over the rocks, to lead the regiment forward and pitch into the Yankees. But behind them there was no regiment; it had been reduced to a thin scattering of desperate and determined men—and then even those had been swept away.[58]

Countless Federal rifles were free now to concentrate on the two young men still advancing beneath the 26th North Carolina's battle flag. Almost miraculously, they had survived the long, gory march, and now they were face-to-face with the enemy. Isolated at the front and made conspicuous by their flag, they had just cause to brace for a death-dealing volley like those that had felled so many of their comrades. No volley came their way, however. Instead—as if awed by the valor of the two North Carolinians—the Yankees behind the wall held their fire. "Come over on this side of the Lord!" one of the Blue Birds yelled at Thomas and Brooks. Then hands reached out and pulled the two up and over the stacked stones. The regimental colors—bloodstained, riddled with bullet holes and marked by gaping tears—became the prize of the 12th New Jersey. The 26th North Carolina had reached the wall—the regiment's colors had penetrated the Federal line—but this time the men of the 26th were captives instead of victors.[59]

Behind them, the great assault force was crumbling into a disorganized and defeated mass of men, who were retreating toward Seminary Ridge. Down the wall to the right—where Pickett's and some of Fry's troops had broken through the enemy line—the Federals had rallied in force. General Armistead had fallen mortally wounded among his Virginians, and all other Confederates had been driven out, shot down or captured. Driven back from the wall and mauled by flank fire on their right, Pickett's troops were falling back in droves. Major Jones was stunned by the sudden collapse. He had to decide in an instant what to do. Lowrance's brigade was now up to the Emmitsburg Road fences behind him, but the mighty assault appeared to be disintegrating before him. At most, he told himself, he might have 60 troops scattered among the living and the dead on the slope—and that number was shrinking every second. What should he do? What *could* be done? As he struggled for a decision, he heard a shouted order from the right: *Fall back!* Jones knew then that the great assault had failed. "At the very moment I thought victory ours," he would later report, "I saw it snatched from our hands. . . . The day was lost."[60]

CHAPTER 11

"Unconquered in Spirit"

Carpeted with bodies, the Emmitsburg Road was a bloody mess. As the troops on the Confederate left fell back under the storm of Federal fire, many halted in the lane and lay on their bellies among the fallen. "The roar of the artillery continued," one of Pettigrew's men would later recall, "and mingled with the groans of wounded and dying. . . ." A torrent of deadly fire continued to pour from the Federal troops behind the stone wall in front, from the flanking force to the left, and from the Federal artillery—and it flailed the retreating Southerners with devastating effect. "A withering sheet of missiles swept after them," an officer in the 8th Ohio would report, "and they were torn and tossed and prostrated as they ran. It seemed as if not one would escape." For the men of the 26th and other front-line troops, the retreat was almost as dangerous as the assault. "The plank, or slab, fence was splintered and riddled . . . ," a survivor would recount. "It was death or surrender to remain. It seemed almost death to retreat." Some members of the 26th were too badly wounded to retreat; some chose to lay flat and try to survive the fire. Others climbed the fences and headed for Seminary Ridge. "[On] we sped across the open field," one of Pettigrew's officers would recall, "expecting every moment to be shot to the ground." Determined not to appear cowardly—or be shot in the back—some men turned and stubbornly walked backwards across the battered fields.[1]

The men of Lowrance's brigade, who were last to reach the Emmitsburg Road, were trying to climb over the fences on Pettigrew's right when the assault broke. Retreating troops streamed by them on both sides: Pettigrew's troops falling back on their left and Pickett's men fleeing on their right. General Trimble was just behind Lowrance's left flank, still mounted and partially shielded by a large elm tree just back of the Emmitsburg Road. Captain Young found him there and delivered General Pettigrew's summons to reinforce the left flank, but it was too late. In the mounting confusion, Trimble tried to decide what to do—and then he was shot through the left leg. It was a terrible wound: The slug did severe damage to flesh and bone, and then entered his horse. His aides lifted him out of the saddle and laid him on the ground. "General, the men are falling back, shall I rally them?" one of his officers shouted. Trimble looked up from his wound, surveyed the mass of men flooding past—and knew the assault had failed. "No!" he replied. "Let them get out of this, it's all over." As Lowrance's men joined the retreat, Trimble ordered his aides to hold his bleeding mare and help him mount. Back in the saddle, the general turned the horse to the rear and rode slowly through the melee back toward Seminary Ridge.[2]

Some of Pettigrew's troops retreated in good order. "Many of these . . . would 'about-face' and fire back," a Yankee officer would recount, "taking deliberate aim, in sullen anger as it were." For most, however, the retreat was a hurried scramble to the rear. "It was a disordered and disorganized mob . . . ," a Federal officer would comment. "If they went back to the ridge from whence they emerged in any assemblence of form, it was after they were out of musketry range, and their batteries were again playing upon our position to cover their retreat." One of Pettigrew's officers, Captain June Kimble of Fry's brigade, would always remember his hasty retreat. "For about one hundred yards," he would later admit, "I broke the lightning speed record." Lieutenant Robert Hudspeth, the sole unharmed survivor of Company F in the first day's fighting, had made it almost to the stone wall and was retreating across the field when an exploding artillery shell knocked him flat. He arose and resumed his flight.[3]

The division's organizational structure collapsed along with the assault. General Pettigrew realized, like Major Jones, that the day was lost. His horse had been wounded, leaving him afoot—and he had been hit in the left arm by canister. His sleeve was soaked and blackened by blood, but unlike Generals Garnett and Armistead, he had escaped a mortal wound—even though he too had made the long and deadly trek to Cemetery Ridge. With his men in retreat around him, Pettigrew slowly retraced his steps toward the rear. Midway across the field he was joined by Captain Cureton, who had somehow survived the bloody inferno at the front. Seeing Pettigrew walking solemnly to the rear with what appeared to be a serious wound, the captain offered to help. "He thanked me," Cureton would later recall, "offered me his unwounded arm, and I assisted him up the steep little hill to the artillery."[4]

Like Major Jones, Cureton had dropped back to the Emmitsburg Road when the assault was turned back. There the regiment's surviving officers had tried to reform the 26th's battle line. It was a futile effort. On the left, the Federals had begun advancing down the road, rounding up prisoners. Cureton and the other officers had shouted a warning and then had fallen back with any troops who dared rise and join them. With Major Jones among them, the regiment's bloodied remnant of survivors retreated across the field. Jones had led the 26th all the way—across the meadows, through the wheat field, over the fences, across the road and up the slope—but this time the Yankee line before them had held firm. This time, the men in gray and butternut had broken. The Federal cross-fire had blown them away "like chaff before a whirlwind," Cureton would later conclude, leaving them only two choices: surrender or retreat. "With our thinned ranks and in such a position," he would later report, "it would have been folly to stand . . . against such odds."[5]

On both sides of the assault route, the Confederate support troops began to advance. On the right, the two brigades of Alabamians and Floridians from Anderson's Division—led by General Wilcox and Colonel Lang—advanced far enough to incur severe casualties before falling back. On the left, the two other brigades from Anderson's Division—Mahone's Virginians and Posey's Mississippians—advanced in support of Pettigrew and Trimble's men until recalled by Longstreet. As the assault troops were retreating, Lieutenant Colonel Fremantle—the British military observer—rode up to Longstreet, who was perched on a fence rail watching the retreat. "I wouldn't have missed this for anything," proclaimed Fremantle, who was unaware the assault had failed. "The devil you wouldn't!" Longstreet replied. "I would like to have missed it very much; we attacked and have been repulsed: look there!" Fremantle turned toward the Federal position. "For the first time I then had a view of the open space between the two positions," he would later recall, "and saw it covered with Confederates slowly and sulkily returning towards us in small broken parties, under a heavy fire of artillery." General Lee and his staff, meanwhile, had been awaiting the outcome of the assault at a central point on Seminary Ridge. When failure was certain, Lee rode forward to meet the survivors. "His face, which is always placid and cheerful, did not show signs of the slightest disappointment, care, or annoyance," Fremantle would later report, "and he was addressing to every soldier he met a few words of encouragement. . . ."[6]

* * *

When they saw the Confederates in full retreat, the Federal troops of Hays's Division arose behind the stone wall and broke into whoops and hurrahs. They clambered over the rocks, and rushed down the road from the left, hurrying onto the awful field of death to take prisoners. Major Hill and his Jerseymen had held their ground in the face of the mighty assault—and suffered surprisingly light casualties. They had also wound up in possession of the 26th North Carolina's battle flag. Despite their exultation, some of the victors were sobered by the carnage. "As the smoke lifted, what a horrible sight," a soldier from the 12th New Jersey would later recollect. "Dead and dying everywhere, the ground almost covered with them; their wounded and prisoners coming into our lines by the hundreds; some crawling on their hands and knees, others using two muskets as crutches. . . ." New Jersey Sergeant George Bowen would never forget one horror: In front of the stone wall he discovered a dying young North Carolinian, partially paralyzed by two bullets in his head, but stubbornly using his working hand to pull clumps of grass—which he tried fruitlessly to stuff in his head wounds. "The wounded lay scattered over the . . . field, writhing in anguish," a Delaware officer would remember, "while the gallant heroic dead, of either side, were quietly at rest, suffering neither fear nor pain." Surveying the section of Cemetery Ridge assaulted by Pettigrew's and Trimble's men, an officer in the 126th New York was stunned by the body count. "There were literally acres of dead lying in front of our line," he would later report. "I counted 16 dead bodies on one rod square, and the dead in every direction lay upon the field in heaps and scattered as far as the eye could reach." What kind of men would willingly make such a sacrifice? He could only conclude that the Southerners who had made this charge—even though they were the enemy—had to be "heroic, brave and reckless in their daring. . . ."[7]

General Alexander Hays was mounted on his third horse—two had been shot during the assault—and the animal he now rode was flecked with blood. No less than 13 of his orderlies had been killed or wounded, but big, bold Alexander Hays of Pittsburgh was unscathed—and flushed with victory. "Boys, give me a flag," he yelled to the blue-clad soldiers who were pulling fallen Southern battle standards from the mass of bodies. "Get a flag, Corts; get a flag, Dave," he ordered two of his aides. Accompanied by the two flag-bearing officers, Hays rode down to his division's right flank and jumped his horse over the stone wall. Federal artillery was still firing, and Confederate guns had reopened to cover the retreat, but Hays did not hesitate. Trailing a captured Confederate battle flag over the bloodied earth, he cantered through the fallen bodies and the wreckage of battle for the entire length of the division's front—past the New Yorkers, the Jersey troops, the men from Delaware, the soldiers of Connecticut—all the way to Arnold's Battery near the angle of the wall. Then, with his aides trailing their flags in imitation of him, he turned and dashed along the wall in the opposite direction. The Blue Birds of Hays' Division were electrified. "[The] men of the Third Division [threw] their caps high in the air as we rode along," one of his accompanying aides would later recount, "showing their admiration for their glorious division commander, some men dancing in the delirium of their joy, others hugging their comrades in close embrace, wild with the exultation of victory."[8]

General Meade rode up as Hays was making his triumphant ride. "Where is General Hays?" the army commander asked a lieutenant. The officer pointed toward Hays, but Meade ignored him and stared at the retreating Confederates as if in disbelief. "Have they turned?" he asked anxiously. "Yes, sir!" the lieutenant replied. "See there, General Hays has one of their flags." Meade responded impatiently: "I don't care about their flags, have they turned?" Reassured that the assault had failed, he sat motionless in the saddle for a few moments and watched the flood of gray and butternut recede toward Seminary Ridge. Such a sight unquestionably brought relief to Meade. The army of Robert E. Lee—viewed by some as almost invincible—had made what would prove to be the mightiest assault of the war against Meade's line— and his line had held. Now the Southerners were fleeing in full retreat. Meade moved on down his line, still asking, "Is the assault already repulsed?" Finally, he was convinced. "Thank God," he fervently muttered. Nearby, a Yankee band saluted him with "Hail to the Chief."[9]

The victorious Federal troops competed with each other to see how many fallen Confederate battle flags they could retrieve from the field, and Hays's men stacked a pile of captured banners outside his headquarters. Shortly after the repulse, Hays received a request from Brigadier General Alexander S. Webb, Second Corps brigade commander, for battle flags reportedly captured by Webb's troops. "How in h—l did I get them if he captured them?" Hays asked aloud. Then he dispatched a half-dozen banners to Webb with his compliments. "I have sent forward to headquarters seventeen of the enemy's standards, and know of at least five others which were surreptitiously disposed of," Hays would write his father. "Such a capture of flags was never known before." Tempering the general's glee was knowledge of the bloody price his men had paid for victory. He calculated that his division had suffered more than 1,200 casualties. "Only that Providence protected us I cannot account for our escape," he would confide to his mother in a letter written soon after the battle. "Women may lecture on 'The Horrors of War,' but such a scene of carnage I never imagined. . . . Dead horses, shattered carriages, dead and dying men, in all the last agonies of death for two full hours, would have paralyzed anyone not trained to the 'butcher trade.'"[10]

Private Albert Caison lay among the 26th's dead and wounded on the slope near the stone wall. The repulse had surprised him: When he went down with wounds in the hand and hip, he thought they had won again—that the Yankee line was breaking like it had on the first day. Instead, he had seen most of the troops around him shot down and the assault transformed into a retreat. Moments later, when the shooting stopped and the smoke cleared, he saw swarms of Yankees surge over the stone wall to take prisoners. "I got up and attempted to get off the field," he would later recount, "but found I was cut off, and when I saw twenty guns turned upon me, there was no alternative but to throw up my hands and surrender." Lieutenant Gaston Broughton lay nearby with a wounded foot. He figured that of the 25 men from Company D in the charge, maybe eight made it out unharmed. In a few minutes, he too was surrounded by blue-uniformed troops and became a prisoner of war. He was escorted over the stone wall that he and so many others had desperately sought to reach, and was herded to the Federal rear with Private Thomas, Sergeant Brooks and scores of other prisoners. Among them was Colonel Birkett Fry, who was prevented from retreating by his thigh wound. Although he had been shot down before reaching the stone wall, he was sure that many of Pettigrew's troops had made it before the assault collapsed. "All of the five regimental colors of my command reached the line of the enemy's works," he would later insist, "and many of my men and officers were killed or wounded after passing over it. I believe the same was true of other brigades in General Pettigrew's command."[11]

Sergeant Jake Bush would have gladly joined the prisoners who were marched at gunpoint to the Federal rear. The Northern troops were so preoccupied with handling the horde of captured Confederates that they could do little for the countless wounded lying in their front. Lying in the wheat field at the edge of the Emmitsburg Road, Bush suffered immensely from his multiple wounds. "I almost famished for water after I was shot," he would recall years later. "I had about a third of a canteen full when I was shot down. About the first thing a fellow wants after being shot is water. I drank what was in my canteen and it seemed to me I would die if I did not get more." Bush managed to rise and then collapsed from weakness and fell among the pile of dead soldiers that surrounded him. "But as luck would have it, there was a dead man lying at my feet and I discovered a canteen on him. I worked about till I got to him and the canteen was about half full of water. I got my knife and cut the strap from around his neck. I drank the water and left the knife, canteen and all with the dead man."[12]

Back on Seminary Ridge, General Lee moved among Pettigrew's troops as they streamed back to their starting point. "The fault is mine," Lee told them. "The fault is mine." Pettigrew, now accompanied by Captain Young, came through the ranks of men and stopped in front of Lee as if awaiting orders. "The fault is mine," Lee repeated, "but it will be all right in the end." He directed Pettigrew to rally his division and "protect our artillery" in case the Federals launched a counterattack and then he noted Pettigrew's bloody arm. "General, I am sorry to see you wounded," he said. "Go to the rear." The woods on Seminary Ridge were teeming with troops from Pettigrew's and Trimble's commands. They had been turned back, their great assault had failed, and their losses were fearful—but they did not act like defeated men. "Notwithstanding the failure of its efforts, the army was still unconquered in spirit," Captain Young would later recall, "and had Meade followed us back to Seminary Ridge, he would have found our troops ready to mete out to him what he had given us." Pettigrew, Jones and other surviving officers reformed the milling horde of troops to meet a Yankee assault. But the Yankees did not come.[13]

A drizzling rain dimmed the dawn on Saturday the 4th. The drizzle soon increased into a downpour—"a tremendous thunderstorm," one soldier called it. It lasted for hours, turning dirt roads into soggy mires, soaking the battlefield, bathing the still faces of the dead and bringing misery to the countless wounded men left outside. The gloomy morning matched the news that came to the field hospital where Julius Lineback and the other musicians were working. Again, they learned, the regiment had been in the forefront of the fighting—and again casualties in the regiment were extensive. The 26th North Carolina, Lineback concluded, had been "baptized in blood." He and the other musicians were still trying to tend to the multitude of wounded and dying in the regiment from the first day's fighting—and now there were scores more from the Pickett-Pettigrew Charge. Lineback had been up most of night immersed in the gore of battle, and he returned to the bloody work just after daylight. In the middle of the storm, he received more news: They would be leaving soon, one of the surgeons told him. The severely wounded and some physicians who volunteered to stay with them would be left behind, but the rest of the Confederate wounded would be loaded into wagons for the return to Virginia. The musicians did not want to leave the regiment—what was left of it—without orders, so when the wagons were almost loaded Lineback volunteered to go find Major Jones. In the rain and confusion, however, he was unable to locate the major—and then it was time to leave. "We started off in the rain . . . ," Lineback would later recall, "a motley procession of wagons, ambulances, wounded men on foot, straggling soldiers and band boys, splashing along in the mud, weary, sad and discouraged."[14]

Discouragement came easily that morning. "[We] have done very hard fighting, lost a large number of men, and yet have failed to accomplish anything material," a surviving soldier in Hill's Corps confided to his diary. "There was a general feeling of despondency in the army at our great loss," penned an officer, "though the battle is regarded as a drawn one." Throughout the night, the pitiful cries of the wounded had echoed over the lines. "[The] only sounds to be heard were the groans of the wounded, the prayers of the dying, and the strident noise of shelter tents and clothes of all kinds being torn up for bandages," an officer would later recall. General Lee had conferred with his corps commanders during the night and had announced his decision to return to Virginia. "General, this has been a hard day on you," Brigadier General John D. Imboden had told a weary-looking Lee at one point. "Yes," Lee had replied, "it has been a sad, sad day to us."[15]

The 26th North Carolina now had few men and fewer officers. Major Jones had come through the charge without injury—and was the highest-ranking officer in Marshall's entire brigade not killed or wounded. He had counted heads after the assault: The tally was 67 troops and three officers present for duty. More showed up on Saturday, but it was disheartening to look at the tiny, battered remnant. Barely a hundred troops were now on hand for Jones to command. Of the ten company commanders present on the first day at Gettysburg, only Captain Henry Albright of Company G had escaped death or wounds. Eventually, some survivors would calculate that the regiment had suffered 687 casualties at Gettysburg. Neither Major Jones nor anyone else in either army could know it this day, but some students of the battle would someday give the 26th North Carolina the bloody distinction of having incurred the greatest casualties of any regiment at Gettysburg.[16]

General Pettigrew—his wounded arm in a sling—continued to command the division. Major Jones now replaced Colonel Marshall as commander of the brigade. Within a three-day period, battlefield losses had moved him from third-in-command of one regiment to brigade commander of four regiments. Captain Albright, meanwhile, was left as the senior officer present in the 26th. "Gen. Pettigrew is in command of our division [and] Maj. Jones of our brigade," penned one of the survivors of the regiment in a letter to a friend. "This will give you an idea of the frightful loss of the officers." In his official report, Major Jones summed up the losses in the brigade: "Regiments that went in with colonels came out commanded by lieutenants."[17]

During Saturday's rainstorm, Captain Joseph J. Young, the regimental quartermaster, managed to find time to write Governor Vance back home in Raleigh. "I will trespass a few minutes upon your indulgence," he wrote the regiment's first colonel, "to communicate the sad fate that has befallen the old Twenty-sixth." He briefed the governor on the battle, calling Gettysburg "the heaviest conflict of the war," and reported the awful harvest of dead and wounded—beginning with Colonel Burgwyn and Lieutenant Colonel Lane. "We went in with over 800 men in the regiment," he estimated. "There came out but 216, all told, unhurt [on July 1st]. Yesterday they were again engaged, and now have only about 80 men for duty." Lee's army had been ravaged at Gettysburg, Young believed, the way the Yankees had suffered at Fredericksburg, where they had incurred horrendous losses. "It was another Fredericksburg," he wrote Vance, "only the wrong way."[18]

On Pettigrew's orders, Jones had deployed the survivors of the brigade into a skirmish line across the division's front on Friday night. No attack had come during the night, nor during Saturday's summer thunderstorm. The sound of sporadic firing came from the Confederate and Federal pickets during the day, but the two armies made little movement on Saturday. They lay like two great, wounded beasts, glowering at each other and waiting for the next move. Federal troops moved around Cemetery Ridge, collecting discarded weapons, and hauling off the Confederate wounded. "To one not accustomed to the sight, the scene would be sickening," a young New York officer wrote home. "At least ten thousand lay dead in all kinds of attitudes—most hideous sights, many of them youths." An officer in the 12th New Jersey, intending to give water to the Confederate wounded in the Emmitsburg Road, was shocked at what he found. "This road was filled with their dead, the ditch [beside the road] was piled up with them," he would later report. "I did not think about the water being bloody. . . . I gave some of this to a wounded man, he said, 'Can't you get some clear, cool water; that is so full of blood I cannot drink it.'"[19]

As the day passed without renewed battle, men began to notice the effect of the fighting on the landscape around them. "Dismounted guns, exploded caissons and limbers, hundreds of dead horses, piles of broken and bent muskets, splintered trees, broken tombstones at Cemetery Hill, demolished walls, riddled houses and barns met the eye," a Federal officer would remember. "The ground was plowed and cross-plowed by cannon balls . . . and the men for the greater part of the day remained quietly in their shelter tents, and sought the rest so much needed after the hardships and excitement of the last few days." Across the fields behind Seminary Ridge, Pickett's, Pettigrew's and Trimble's men sought what rest they could find amid the sobering knowledge that their sacrifices had not produced victory. "It is true that many of us shed tears at the way in which our dreams of liberty had ended," a Southern artilleryman would recall, "yet when we were permitted at length to lie down under the caissons, or in the fence corners, and realized that we had escaped the death that had snatched away so many others, we felt too well satisfied at our good fortune—in spite of the enemy still near us, not to sleep the soundest sleep it is permitted on earth for mortals to enjoy."[20]

The rain fell in torrents Saturday night. Scores of Confederate wounded still lay on the slopes of Cemetery Ridge, which remained clogged with Southern dead. "In the evening," a Northern newspaper reporter noted, "I looked over the battlefield. It was the old sad sight of other battlefields—men mangled and bloody and torn; bodies without heads and heads without brains, trunks limbless, here an arm . . . there a leg. . . . Some long since dead, some dying." Within the thin ranks of the 26th North Carolina, a rumor was repeated that had come from the picket line. Yankee pickets were boasting that Vicksburg had surrendered. It was an accurate report, and among the battle-weary men in gray it was accepted as truth. The news made the losses at Gettysburg a double blow. Even soldiers in the ranks knew that the loss of Vicksburg—splitting the Confederacy and opening the Mississippi to the Federals—was a major disaster. "I have never liked 4th July since," Captain Cureton would later proclaim. Shortly after dark, the order came to the 26th:

The army was leaving. With the rain coming down in sheets, the men of the regiment joined Lee's army on the retreat back to Virginia.[21]

"On the morning of July 5th," a Federal officer would later report, "it was found that the Confederate army had left our front and was retreating towards the Potomac." Meade dispatched cavalry in pursuit, but did not immediately put his entire army on the march. He consulted with his principal commanders and they concurred: The Army of the Potomac had been significantly reduced in strength by the three-day battle, and the men needed a rest. Meade issued orders for the general movement of the army to follow a reconnaissance-in-force.[22]

Meanwhile, a grim chore awaited Gettysburg's victors: tending to the wounded and the dead of both sides. First priority was saving those who had a chance to live. Cornelia Hancock, a Quaker nurse from New Jersey, reached Gettysburg soon after the battle—and would never forget the scene that greeted her:

> *A long table stood in [the] woods . . . and around it gathered a number of surgeons and attendants. This was the operating table, and for seven days it literally ran blood. A wagon stood near rapidly filling with amputated legs and arms; when wholly filled, this gruesome spectacle withdrew from sight and returned as soon as possible for another load. . . . We went the same evening to one of the churches, where I saw for the first time what war meant. Hundreds of desperately wounded men were stretched out on boards laid across the high-backed pews as closely as could be packed together. The boards were covered with straw. Thus elevated, these poor sufferers' faces, white and drawn with pain, were almost on a level with my own. I seemed to stand breast-high in a sea of anguish. . . . As we made our way . . . to the Field Hospital, the first sight that met our eyes was a collection of semi-conscious but still living human forms, all of whom had been shot through the head, and were considered hopeless. They were laid there to die and I hoped that they were indeed too near death to have consciousness. Yet many a groan came from them, and their limbs tossed and twitched.[23]*

Burial of the Confederate dead in front of Cemetery Ridge began on the 4th and continued for days. Burying thousands of stiffened bodies was an almost overwhelming task. "The corpses are brought into rows and counted," a jaded Federal penned in his diary, "the Confederate and Federals being separated into different rows. At the feet of each row of fifty or a hundred dead, a trench is dug about seven or eight feet wide and about three feet deep—for there is no time for normal grave depth. Then the bodies . . . are placed in the shallow ditch and quickly covered with dirt." Southern prisoners were put to work digging trenches, and many of the dead were buried where they lay. "The men were buried everywhere," another eyewitness would later recall. "When they could conveniently be brought together, they were buried in clusters of ten, twenty, fifty, or more; but so great was their number. . . . that they could not be removed. In gardens, fields, and by the roadside, just as they were found lying, a shallow ditch was dug, and they were placed in it and covered up as hastily as possible." Most of the dead from the 26th North Carolina who fell in the Pickett-Pettigrew Charge were apparently buried in the rain without ceremony or identification. Along with thousands of others, their bodies were dragged by strangers to shallow, unmarked graves and then were covered with the soil of Gettysburg.[24]

As the Army of Northern Virginia moved in columns toward the Potomac River fords, Lieutenant Colonel John R. Lane jostled along the muddy roads in a wagon of wounded. His head wound looked mortal: His face was swollen and inflamed, he was unable to speak, and he had eaten nothing for four days. The wagon train of wounded, which was under the command of Brigadier General John D. Imboden, snaked along the muddy roads for 17 miles. Orders were to keep moving at all costs, and for Lane and many other wounded men, the retreat was a grueling trip. "Very few of the wagons had even straw in them, and all were without springs," according to a contemporary account. "The road was rough and rocky; the jolting was enough to have killed strong men. As the horses trotted on, while the winds howled through the driving rain, there arose, from that awful procession of the dying, oaths and curses, sobs and prayers, moans and shrieks that pierced the darkness and made the storm seem gentle: 'Oh, stop one minute! Take me out; let me die on the roadside.'"[25]

With each roll of the wagon wheels Lane was a little closer to home, but friends who had seen his wound did not expect him to live. He was tough, however, and surprised everyone. Not only did he stay alive, he also managed to avoid becoming a prisoner of war. Federal cavalry harassed Lee's retreating columns, and on Sunday, July 5th, a force of Yankee horse soldiers raided a section of the wagon train southwest of Greencastle near the Pennsylvania-Maryland border. Lieutenant Colonel Lane was among the wounded in danger of capture by the raiders. Lane, however, mustered the strength to force himself up, and climbed down from the wagon. He was bruised, bloody and weakened, but he still had an ample store of grit—and he was determined to escape. While the Yankee cavalry dashed around the wagons, Lane managed to mount a horse and gallop off to safety.[26]

Safety was what General Lee was seeking for his army, but he did not immediately find it at the Potomac. The rains had swelled the river, making the fords impassable, and Federal raiders on the Virginia side had destroyed the pontoon bridge at Williamsport. The army was trapped. Lee's troops could do nothing but wait, deployed in a defensive position near Hagerstown. "We daily anticipated an attack from Meade in pursuit," one of Heth's officers would later report, "but none of his army put in an appearance. . . ." While a new pontoon bridge was hurriedly built, Confederate engineers directed the construction of defensive earthworks in an arc around the Williamsport crossings. Meanwhile, a serviceable flatboat was found, and was put to use ferrying the wounded across the rising river one wagon at a time. "[An] immense concourse of wagons [was] parked in the river bottom," Julius Lineback noted in his journal. "Wagons and men on foot were ordered to cross as fast as possible as the river was slowly rising from the heavy rains . . . and the whole flat on which the wagons were parked was almost like a pond." It was obvious that Lee's army was in a vulnerable, dangerous position, if the Federals arrived to do battle.[27]

They did not. Meade remained cautious, not putting the Army of the Potomac on the road in full force until July 7th. By then, the same downpour that made the Potomac unfordable also made the region's dirt roads almost impassable. Wagons and caissons became mired in the mud, and the troops sloughed along at a slow pace. To dodge the worst roads, Meade moved the army in a circuitous advance, which consumed more time. At one point, thousands of Meade's troops were halted en route until a fresh supply of shoes reached them. Meanwhile, Meade ordered more reconnaissance and convened his top commanders for another war council. Their consensus: be wary of Lee and advance with caution. Back in Washington, however, General-in-Chief Henry W. Halleck was feeling the pressure from President Lincoln, who wanted Lee's army destroyed before it escaped back into Virginia. "Call no council of war," Halleck urged Meade by telegraph. "Do not let the enemy escape."[28]

Lee's army did escape the trap—although barely. It was raining again on Monday, July 13th—eight days after the retreat began—but the Potomac was judged fordable in spots and a rickety-looking pontoon bridge was finally in place. It had been built under the oversight of Major John A. Harman, who had been Stonewall Jackson's quartermaster. Big, gruff and ill-tempered—with a booming voice to match his size—Harman had raided abandoned buildings for construction materials, and had secured the makeshift bridge downriver from Williamsport at a crossing called Falling Waters. Ewell's Corps forded the river in chest-deep waters at Williamsport, while Longstreet's and Hill's Corps used the pontoon bridge at Falling Waters. The move to the Virginia shore continued through the night. Hill's Corps followed Longstreet's, tramping over the bridge on Tuesday, July 14th. It was on this day, as the last troops prepared to cross back into Virginia, that the 26th North Carolina was witness to the Gettysburg Campaign's final tragedy.[29]

General Heth had recovered from his wound enough to take command of his division and Pender's, sending General Pettigrew back to lead the remnants of his brigade and Archer's. On the morning of the 14th, Heth's Division reached the crossing site near Falling Waters after an exhausting nighttime march from Hagerstown. "This," Heth would later recall, "was the most uncomfortable night I passed during the war; it rained incessantly; the roads were eight or ten inches deep in mud and water. My command brought up the rear of the army; we were compelled to halt every half mile, the road was blocked by wagons, artillery, etc., in our front. On one occasion we were detained two hours; as soon as we were halted the men sought the best shelter they could find—houses, barns, fence corners, and dropped to sleep." One veteran of the campaign thought the roads were the worst he had ever seen. "It appeared to me that at least half of the road was a quagmire," he would recount, "coming in places nearly to the knees." Ironically, Heth's Division—first to engage at Gettysburg—would be the last to cross the Potomac. Bringing up the division's rear was the 26th and the rest of Pettigrew's Brigade, which had been selected as the rear-guard. The post was deemed an honor by both Pettigrew and Jones, but it meant the brigade would be the last of Lee's army to cross the river—and that it might have to hold off the Federal army.[30]

Waiting for their turn to cross, the men of Heth's Division were allowed to fall out in an open field at the foot of a bluff about a mile-and-a-half from Falling Waters. Pettigrew posted pickets for his brigade, but Heth failed to post any, believing the position was protected by a squad of Confederate cavalry he had passed on the way. While they waited, the soldiers stacked arms. Many then stretched out and tried to sleep. Unknown to the weary troops, the advance elements of Meade's army—led by Brigadier General George A. Custer's brigade of cavalry—were bearing down on them. After about an hour, Heth's troops were roused and called back into line. As they were reassembling, two companies of the 6th Michigan Cavalry under Major Peter A. Weber drew up within sight and deployed into an attack formation. Seeing only part of Heth's force, Weber apparently thought he had overtaken a large group of Confederate stragglers, and did not realize his two companies of horsemen were about to attack a division of veteran troops. "While watching [my horse] enjoy his morning meal," one of the Confederate officers present would later recount, "my attention was suddenly called to a startling vision on the hill just beyond me. There on that ridge I saw a sight that for a moment paralyzed me. A long line of blue [was] rapidly forming in shape for a charge."[31]

General Pettigrew, his wounded left arm in splints and a sling, was standing in a garden near a barn, getting instructions about the crossing from General Heth, who was mounted and surrounded by his staff. Captain Louis Young, who was standing nearby, spotted the cavalry on the ridge, noted they were carrying a U.S. guidon, and called a warning to the generals. Pettigrew immediately ordered the brigade called to arms, and quickly mounted. Seconds later, a chilling order echoed off the distant ridge: "Draw sabers, charge!" The line of blue-uniformed horsemen then dashed forward down the hill at a gallop. The brigade was hurriedly forming a line of battle, and Pettigrew ordered them to fire. "No, don't fire," yelled Heth, who believed the horsemen were Confederate cavalry brandishing captured colors.[32]

Down the ridge the Federal cavalrymen charged with their sabers held aloft. "Surrender, you d—— rebels, surrender!" one of them yelled. Men scrambled for their weapons, which were stacked and unloaded. In the confusion—and perhaps in response to Heth's order—all but a few Southerners held their fire, enabling the Michigan troopers to make a first dash through the Confederate lines without many casualties. Then they turned and charged again. "The men clubbed their guns and knocked the Yankees off their horses," Major Jones would afterwards report. "One man knocked one off with a fence rail and another killed a Yankee with an ax."[33]

As the Federals made their return sweep, some of Pettigrew's troops got off a volley alongside Pettigrew's mount. The blast spooked the mare, causing her to rear. Unable to maintain control with his bad hand, Pettigrew was unhorsed. As he got to his feet he saw one of the Federal cavalrymen trying to shoot at Heth and his staff officers. Pettigrew yelled for his troops to shoot the man, but in the chaos of the attack no one heard him. The general then drew a small revolver from inside his uniform, and began walking toward the trooper. The man saw Pettigrew advancing toward him, and fired first. Petti-grew went down—shot in the abdomen. The Yankee's horse was hit, dumping its rider, who took cover in a nearby barn, firing as he ran. Private Nevel B. Staten, one of the men who had carried Colonel Burgwyn from the field, went after the soldier who had shot Pettigrew and beat him to death with a large stone. Within minutes, the fight was done. Most of the Michigan cavalrymen were shot down or captured—including Major Weber, who was killed. In the context of the campaign, it was an insignificant rearguard skirmish—except that it claimed the life of Brigadier General James Johnston Pettigrew.[34]

Bleeding badly, Pettigrew was moved across the river to a farmhouse. Confederate surgeons deemed the wound almost certainly fatal. Pettigrew's only chance, they concluded, was to remain immobile and hope for sur-vival—which meant he would have to be left behind for the Yankees. Petti-grew would not hear of it: He was determined to risk death rather than become a prisoner again. He insisted on going with the army, and was carried along on the march for several days in a litter. "Don't be disheartened," he told his sorrowful attendants. "Maybe I will fool the doctors yet." It was not to be. Pettigrew died in a borrowed bed at a house on the route, after bequeathing his horse to Captain Young and sharing his faith with an Episcopal minister. The end came at 6:25 A.M., July 17th, moments after he spoke his last words to Young. "It is time to be going," he said, and stopped breathing. "An earnest student of the scriptures, he received with childlike faith its holy teachings," Young would note soon afterwards, "and as a 'man of prayer' he had sought to prepare himself for the reception of the only true Glory." The attending cler-gyman, the Reverend Joseph Wilmer, would never forget Pettigrew's deathbed composure. "In a ministry of nearly thirty years," he would tell others, "I have never witnessed a more sublime example of Christian resignation and hope in death." Observed a sorrowful Captain Young: "Who can doubt that he has exchanged the crown of laurels for the crown of glory."[35]

Finally, they were across the Potomac. Lee's army had made the dangerously delayed retreat with comparatively few losses. Among the last troops to cross the river were the soldiers of the 26th North Carolina. As the men of Pettigrew's brigade—commanded again by Major Jones—hurried across the pontoons, Federal troops began arriving in larger numbers. A Federal cavalryman posted himself near the crossing site and began stopping Confederate stragglers at gunpoint. He had collected more than 50 prisoners when he accosted a soldier from the 26th and demanded his surrender. "Damn you," the man of the 26th replied, leveling his rifle at the horseman, "you surrender." The Yankee gave up his weapon and was escorted across the river by his former prisoners. Hundreds of Confederates *were* left behind—the slow, the stragglers and some of the rear-guard. Included among them were at least two junior officers and more than a dozen enlisted men from the 26th, who found themselves penned up as Yankee prisoners. As Federal troops swarmed the Maryland shore, supporting artillery began dropping shells across the river. With little time to spare, the pontoon bridge was cut loose to swing out in the rushing waters. The last man over—just as the bridge was cut free—was Captain Thomas J. Cureton of the 26th.[36]

Major Jones was relieved to be "again in the land of Dixie." Back on Virginia soil, he could assess losses—which were staggering. "Our brigade is in a bad fix," he would write his father in a few days, "with no other field officers but myself and very few company officers." A soldier who had been hospitalized in Virginia during the campaign was shocked at what he found when he rejoined the brigade. "The ranks had been so thinned," he would later recount, "until it seemed that only a skeleton of an army had returned." When Heth's Division had crossed the Potomac at Shepherdstown three weeks earlier, it had boasted 7,458 troops; now the division numbered 4,100 men. The 3,358 casualties amounted to almost half the division's strength. Of the 2,581 men of Pettigrew's Brigade who had gleefully waded through the river en route to Gettysburg, no more than 1,131 made it back alive and unharmed. The 1,450 soldiers now dead, wounded or left behind amounted to more than half the soldiers in the brigade.[37]

Hardest hit of any regiment in the brigade, the division, Hill's Corps and the entire Army of Northern Virginia was the 26th North Carolina. Eventually, an 85 percent figure would become the regiment's accepted casualty rate. Now, however, as company commanders counted heads on the south bank of the Potomac, some estimated that fewer than 10 percent of the regiment had made it back alive and unharmed. More men would show up, and many of the wounded would tough out a recovery and return to the regiment. At the moment, however, the 26th North Carolina seemed almost to have been shot out of existence.[38]

Company A, the Jeff Davis Mountaineers, which Captain Wagg had led north with 92 troops, now appeared to consist of four men—and Captain Wagg lay buried near Cemetery Ridge. Company K—the Pee Dee Wildcats—which had begun the campaign with 103 men, now boasted 16 present and was commanded by a second lieutenant. Captain Stephen Brewer, the commander of Company E—the Independent Guards—had gone to Gettysburg with 82 men; now two were present and the wounded Captain Brewer was in enemy hands. Company F—the Hibriten Guards—had entered the battle with 87 men; none had come back unharmed. Lieutenant Robert Hudspeth, who had been flattened by a shell-burst on the third day, was believed by some to be the single Company F man able to present himself for duty when the regiment crossed the Potomac. Excluding Captain Albright of Company G, every one of the 26th's company commanders present at Gettysburg had been killed or wounded. Of the 20-plus lieutenants who had gone to Gettysburg, two were dead and no less than 17 were wounded. As it appeared on the south bank of the Potomac, the regiment was without two of its three ranking officers, had been reduced to a single company commander, had been stripped of its junior officers, and was now smaller in numbers than a single company. Most conspicuously absent among the regiment's tiny unharmed remnant was twenty-one-year-old Colonel Henry Burgwyn Jr., who was left behind in a Gettysburg grave.[39]

Left behind too were so many others. So many faces were missing now from the regiment's campfires. Private Thomas Perrett of Company G could still visualize the boisterous, laughing young men who had forded the Potomac on the northward march—singing a rousing chorus of "Maryland, My Maryland" as they waded ashore. He had wondered then just how many of those gray-clad soldiers would return. Now he knew. "It was a trip," he concluded simply, "that didn't pay." Even so, there were few quitters in the 26th North Carolina. They judged their lot with steady-eyed realism—"tha Kill So many of us," one private would later acknowledge in a letter home—but they remained ruggedly devoted to duty. They had pulled on their gray uniforms to defend the Southern homeland, and most of them—if they lived—would stay the course until the end. They had also gained a full measure of glory from the valor they had demonstrated at Gettysburg. Glory may have been scant comfort to the grieving families back home in the hills and hollows of North Carolina. In the years to come, however, it would prove to be a precious legacy to the aging survivors of those bloody afternoons in Pennsylvania.[40]

Always in their memories, along with the smoke, the screams and the sacrifices of McPherson's Ridge and the Pickett-Pettigrew Charge, would remain another vision. It was the memory of a bright, summer morning in Virginia, when the 26th North Carolina—more than 800 strong—began the march to Gettysburg. More than a half-century later, in the twilight of his years, a veteran of the 26th would still be able to recall the heady thrill of young soldiers, cheering maidens and youthful dreams of great deeds ahead. "The long roll of the drum announced to the 'Soldier Boys' that they must take up the line of march again," he would recite. "The Regiment made a fine appearance as it marched out from its bivouac that beautiful June morning with the men beaming in their splendid gray uniforms, the colors flying, and the band playing; everything seemed propitious of success. . . . Smiling beauties, with waving banners, cheer us on to deeds of valor."[41]

"Steadfast to the Last"

Gettysburg would prove to be the high-water mark of the Confederacy. Two more years of brutal warfare would follow, but never again would Southerners come so close to achieving nationhood. The costliest battle of the war with 51,112 casualties, Gettysburg would afflict both North and South. But Federal casualties—23,049 dead, wounded and missing—could be quickly replaced in the Army of the Potomac. It was not so for Lee's army. The Army of Northern Virginia had suffered 28,063 casualties at Gettysburg, and the gaps in Lee's ranks would be difficult to fill from a Southern population already bled white. Characteristically, Lee blamed himself for the defeat. "I have no complaints to make of anyone but myself," he wrote President Davis. Soon after the battle, Lee offered to resign. So did Meade, who had incurred Lincoln's displeasure for failing to destroy Lee's retreating army. Both offers were refused.[1]

Lee made no apologies for his men. "The privations and hardships of the march and camp were cheerfully encountered, and borne with a fortitude unsurpassed by our ancestors in their struggle for independence," he noted in his official report, "while their courage in battle entitles them to rank with the soldiers of any army at any time." Lee's troops meanwhile were relieved to be back home in the South. "We are now, thank God, on Confederate soil, but oh, how many of our dear comrades have we left behind," a North Carolina soldier penned in his diary. "We can never forget this campaign. We had hard marching, hard fighting, suffered hunger and privation, but our general officers were always with us. . . . Many a general have I seen walk and a poor sick private riding his horse, and our father, Lee, was scarcely ever out of sight when there was danger. We could not feel gloomy when we saw his old gray head uncovered as he would pass us on the march, or be with us in a fight. I care not how weary or hungry we were, when we saw him we gave that Rebel yell, and hunger and wounds would be forgotten."[2]

Despite the severity of their casualties, many of Lee's troops refused to view the Gettysburg Campaign as a complete failure. "Although we did not gain a victory," noted a Gettysburg veteran, "still we did not suffer a defeat." Many believed they had dealt a serious blow to the North. "If we had not gone into [Pennsylvania] it would have been better for us," a North Carolinian wrote his family, "although I believe that the battle of Gettysburg has done more to strike terror to them than anything else." Lee's men were satisfied that they had taken the war to the North; that they had brought a season of relief to Virginia; and that they had supplied their army with an abundance of Yankee livestock. If the march north had ended abruptly, they were reassured by the fact that they had not expected to occupy Northern territory permanently. They had failed to achieve the great victory that would end the war, but they remained confident that they had made a good showing and had retained the army's hard-fighting reputation. They were consoled by the belief that they had scored a dramatic victory on Gettysburg's first day, achieved a draw on the second—and were repulsed on the third only because they had tried to take an impregnable position.[3]

A far greater calamity for the South, some soldiers believed, was the loss of Vicksburg and the Mississippi. "Our news from the west is worse than anything from Lee," a Tarheel soldier confided to his diary. "Vicksburg fell on the 4th July and that day has been for us a day of mourning and bitterness. The picture looks gloomy & casts a smoky & frightful shadow over coming events. We can only look to God and hope for the best. He can inspire us and our weary Lee or his army with courage & wisdom & cast down the arrogance of our jubilant foes." Back in Virginia, Lee's army experienced a renewed wave of desertions, but the vast majority of troops remained loyal and ready to fight again. "Our army is in splendid health and spirits, and is being increased rapidly every day by conscription and by men returning from the hospitals," a South Carolinian in Heth's Division wrote home. "We get plenty to eat now and I am beginning to get as fat as ever again." They expected to fight the Yankees again and expected to win. "The men have unbounded confidence in Gen. Lee," Major Jones wrote his father, "and have not the least doubt that we will give Meade a great thrashing when he sees fit to advance." Vowed one Confederate: "We will make them howl worse & more loudly than they are now laughing."[4]

After Gettysburg, the tattered remnant of the 26th North Carolina remained with the Army of Northern Virginia, which took up a defensive line along the Rapidan River northwest of Fredericksburg. The Army of the

Potomac, meanwhile, occupied an opposing line to the north near the Rappa-hannock. Officers were promoted and commanders were reshuffled. Colonel Thomas C. Singletary of the 44th North Carolina temporarily took com-mand of what had been Pettigrew's Brigade when his regiment rejoined the brigade from detached service. In late August, Brigadier General William W. Kirkland—a North Carolinian and a Gettysburg veteran—assumed com-mand of the brigade. Major Jones, promoted to lieutenant colonel, resumed command of the 26th pending the return of Lieutenant Colonel Lane. When Lane rejoined the regiment, Jones became second-in-command, and Com-pany D's Captain James T. Adams—who had been wounded at Gettysburg—was promoted to major and, later, to lieutenant colonel. For awhile, there was concern within the thinly manned regiment that it might be consolidated with other depleted regiments and lose its identity. Wounded veterans returned to the ranks, however, and new troops were recruited, bringing the regiment back to an acceptable strength.[5]

Rested and reorganized, Lee took the offensive again in October, moving to strike the right flank of the Federal army. At the battle of Bristoe Station on October the 14th, General A. P. Hill hurried Kirkland's and Brigadier General John R. Cooke's brigades into battle without the benefit of adequate recon-naissance. As the two brigades attacked what appeared to be the Army of the Potomac's rear-guard, they were unexpectedly raked by a savage flank fire from three Federal divisions concealed in a railroad embankment. Although severely outnumbered, the Confederates courageously turned and assaulted the Federal line. Kirkland and Cooke were badly wounded, while Cooke's brigade was mangled and turned back with 700 casualties. Kirkland's Brigade pushed on, however, led by the 26th North Carolina. The men charged into the face of another deadly firestorm, reached the Federal line, and engaged in brutal hand-to-hand combat until forced back. More than 1,300 Confeder-ates were killed, wounded or captured. The 26th suffered almost 100 casual-ties and the loss of the regimental battle flag, which was captured by the 19th Maine. "I can Say that I have Come threw a nother Storm of iron hail Safe and unhurt, while Some of our Company was kill on the field," Private Thomas Setser wrote home. "[It] is a lonsom time in Company F now. [When] I look a round and See nun of our boys, and think what has becom of them, I cante helpe but cry. . . ."[6]

The 26th wintered near Orange Court House with the rest of Lee's army. By spring of 1864, the regiment numbered 760 troops. In May, the 26th was engaged in the battle of the Wilderness. The Army of the Potomac was still commanded by General Meade, but Lieutenant General Ulysses S. Grant—newly promoted to general-in-chief—had come east to direct operations from the field. Grant boldly moved his army across the Rapidan River in an attempt to turn Lee's right flank. Lee responded promptly by advancing Ewell's and Hill's Corps—with Heth's Division and Kirkland's Brigade leading the advance. Kirkland, who had recovered from his Bristoe Station wound, put the 26th at the head of his brigade. The regiment was engaged in severe fighting on May 5th, and held its own against a series of Federal assaults. Exhausted, the men were told they would be relieved during the night. No relief came; instead the regiment and much of Hill's Corps were struck by a massive Federal assault at daybreak. Kirkland's Brigade "became very near being stampeded"—according to Major Adams—but the 26th held on until ammunition was almost exhausted. At that critical moment, the line was reinforced by Longstreet's Corps and Grant's forces were driven back.[7]

The battle ended in a draw, but Grant—whose army more than doubled Lee's 60,000-man force—shifted southward, intending to put his army between Lee's and Richmond. Anticipating Grant's actions, Lee put his army on a nighttime forced march and intercepted the Army of the Potomac at Spotsylvania Court House. The bloody battles of Spotsylvania and Cold Harbor followed. Heth's Division and Kirkland's Brigade were engaged in much of the fighting, but the men of the battered 26th were temporarily detached as support troops. At one point, the regiment drew the crucial duty of escorting a wagon train of grain needed to resupply the horses of Lee's artillery corps. At Cold Harbor, Kirkland was again wounded, and twenty-nine-year-old Colonel William MacRae of the 15th North Carolina took command of the brigade. He would soon be promoted to brigadier general, and the unit formerly known as Pettigrew's Brigade, and then Kirkland's, would finish the war as MacRae's Brigade.[8]

MacRae was a small man with a big reputation for leadership. He had risen in the ranks from private to brigadier general, so he understood the enlisted man's needs and motivation. The men of the 26th, accustomed by mid-1864 to turnovers in brigade command, quickly built a loyalty to MacRae that was reminiscent of their devotion to Pettigrew. "General MacRae soon won the confidence and admiration of the brigade, both officers and men," a veteran of the regiment would later recount. "He could place his command in position quicker and infuse more of his fighting qualities into his men, than any officer I ever saw. His presence with his troops seemed to dispel all fear, and to inspire every one with a desire for the fray."⁹

In mid-June of 1864, Grant moved his army against Petersburg, the key rail junction south of Richmond. Lee again countered by shifting the Army of Northern Virginia. On June 18th, Hill's Corps—including Heth's Division, MacRae's Brigade and the 26th North Carolina—manned the extreme right of Lee's defensive line at Petersburg. A series of engagements followed in the summer and fall, and the fighting eventually became gruesome trench warfare. Men died day after day in actions along the line that seemed to provide no advantage to either side and left the trench-bound troops demoralized. "We have to lie in our trenches day and night, rain and shine," a North Carolinian wrote his furloughed brother from Petersburg. "Thair is some killed or wounded more or less every day by mortar shells or sharpshooters. The men have become so careless they don't care much for anything. John, I don't want to give any Body bad advice but if I was at home—I would stay thair till times get better."¹⁰

At the battle of Reams' Station on August 26, 1864, the 26th was again engaged in fierce fighting. "I thought I would bee kill ever minute, for the ball giste ploude the ground all a round mee," Private Thomas Setser wrote home. "[Then] we was call too attention and ordered to charge the yankees brest works, and we did so. tha run as soon [as] we got in fronte of them. we taken a few prisners, but we coulden take the battry and we Stop at ther breste works, and I tell you tay made the grape and Canister fly. that was a lode of grape Struck the breste work rite in front of mee, kill a man on my lefte and nock mee down. . . ." While Heth's Division waited for orders to assault the Federal line, General Heth called for a battle flag to be brought forward. The 26th's color-bearer reported to him. Heth reached for the man's flag, but the soldier refused to give it up. "General, tell me where you want the flag to go, and I will take it," he vowed. "I will not surrender my colors." Heth demanded the flag, but the color-bearer refused. Finally the general gave up. "Come on," he told the soldier, taking him by the arm. "We will carry the colors together." At Heth's orders, the soldier waved the flag back and forth, signaling the charge. The Rebel yell erupted from the line, and the men dashed forward. They broke the Federal line, and Hill's Corps took more than 2,000 Yankee prisoners.¹¹

There were few such moments of gain or glory near the end. To counter the expansion of Grant's mammoth army, Lee was forced to stretch his line at Petersburg to the breaking point. Fighting erupted sporadically along the line, and the troops of the 26th were engaged "almost daily along their front and flanks" at formerly obscure Virginia locales such as Jones' Farm, Burgess' Mill, Belfield and Hatcher's Run. At Burgess' Mill on October 27, 1864, the regimental colors were again captured when several officers and a small body of troops from the 26th strayed too close to the Federal line and were captured by the 7th Michigan. The face-off at Petersburg continued until March 29, 1865, when Grant's army made a new strike against Lee's overextended line, and successfully achieved a major break-through at Five Forks on April 1st. The next day, Grant followed up with a wide-scale attack along Lee's front at Petersburg, which penetrated the Confederate defenses in a series of spots. One breakthrough occurred against MacRae's section of the line to the left of the 26th North Carolina. The Federal victory forced the fall of Richmond, and sent Lee's army on the march that ended at Appomattox.[12]

By the time he surrendered, Lee had little army left. Worn down by the attrition of battle, large-scale captures and a flood of final desertions, the Army of Northern Virginia had barely 25,000 troops on hand at Appomattox. Present at the end was the 26th North Carolina. General A. P. Hill had been killed on April 2, 1865, and his troops—the 26th included—had been merged with Longstreet's Corps. When blocked by the Army of the Potomac at Appomattox, Lee's army was outnumbered more than four-to-one. Those present were still game for a fight, however: When the ragged ranks were drawn up in a final battle line, a soldier with two badly wounded arms was spotted in line without a weapon. "What are you doing here?" an officer demanded. "You can't fight." Replied the bandaged Johnny Reb: "I know I can't, but I can still yell." Lee would not needlessly sacrifice such troops. He made terms with Grant on April 9, 1865, and surrendered on the 12th. "I shall never forget the scene that followed [the news of the surrender]," recalled a North Carolinian in Lee's army. "Some . . . threw down their guns, others broke them against trees and I saw one man thrust his musket between a forked sapling, bend the barrel, and say, 'No yankee will ever shoot at us with you. . . .'"[13]

When the time came for the 26th to stack arms at Appomattox, Colonel Lane was hospitalized with complications from his wounds, and Lieutenant Colonel Adams was temporarily commanding the brigade—so it was left to Captain Cureton to surrender the regiment. When heads were counted, the 26th North Carolina officially numbered a mere 131 officers and troops. In Company F, according to one count, there were four soldiers left. It was a heart-rending ending for a regiment that had sacrificed so much. "I saw the old ragged veterans crying," Private Columbus Tuttle would later remember, "as if their hearts would break."[14]

After the surrender, some of 26th's men joined other soldiers lining the road for a last look at General Lee. "We boys were all on the roadside," Jake Bush would later recall, "and as he rode along he saluted us, holding his hat in his left hand and saluting us with his right, never speaking a word." The regiment's survivors—men who had depended upon each other for life—who had faced death together—now turned away to face a new and uncertain future. "Next morning we hit the pike and it was every man for himself," one would later recount. "Too many together could not fare so well, so we thought it advisable to travel in less numbers so that people would not dread to feed us as we came along." In small groups, in pairs or alone, they began the long journey home.[15]

Despite its long service in campaigns and battles throughout the war, the 26th North Carolina would always be associated with Gettysburg. It was there—among the Pennsylvania ridges, woods and fields on those two torrid July afternoons—that the regiment's reputation was established in the annals of military history. The men of the regiment who lived through the firestorms of Gettysburg and survived the rest of the war would never forget the bloody climb up McPherson's Ridge and the long, deadly walk to Cemetery Ridge. The milestone of memory to which the 26th's aging veterans would inevitably return would always be the grand and awful events of Gettysburg.[16]

JAMES T. ADAMS, the Company D captain who eventually rose to lieutenant colonel, at times commanded the regiment. At one point during the fighting near Petersburg the regiment lost sight of its colors. Adams mounted a stump during the heat of battle and yelled to his troops: "Twenty-sixth, rally on your commander. He is here if the colors are lost." After Appomattox, he came home to Holly Springs, where he farmed, raised his family and contributed to his community until his death in 1918. A few years before he died, he wrote a brief history of the regiment for his niece. Otherwise, for more than a half century, he said little about his experiences in the war. "It was done," explained his grandson. "It was over. What was the use ever to think about it or talk about it again. . . . [Of] the nine children and the more than 55 grandchildren of the Adams' I know only two who even know to what command he belonged much less any of the things the command did."[17]

HENRY CLAY ALBRIGHT, the commander of Company G and the only captain in the regiment who was not killed or wounded at Gettysburg, came through Bristoe Station, the Wilderness, Spotsylvania, Cold Harbor and Reams' Station without harm. The prolonged carnage eventually convinced him, however, that he would never go home. "I know you don't like this kind of chat, but I cannot avoid it," he wrote a relative. "I never expect to survive this accursed war no how. I am just as ready to die today (and I might say as willing) as I ever shall be. . . . I am however in fine spirits and perfectly sanguine of success, ultimately." After emerging unscathed from so many major engagements, Captain Albright fell shot in the head during a minor skirmish at Squirrel Level near Petersburg on September 29, 1864. He died in a Richmond hospital a month later. He was twenty-two years old.[18]

McKESSON "KESSE" BLALOCK, the Company F private who took his wife Malinda to war disguised as a soldier, returned to the North Carolina high country with his wife after his medical discharge in 1862. There Kesse organized a gang of bushwhackers and became known "the terror of the mountains." Operating from pro-Union East Tennessee, Blalock and his outlaw band—which included wife Malinda—blended Unionist guerrilla raids with mountain-style feuding. He was wounded twice and Malinda was shot once, but the two survived more than two years of raiding, hiding and skirmishing with Confederate militia—and were never brought to justice. After the war, the couple set up shop in nearby Mitchell County, where Kesse unsuccessfully ran for the state legislature as a Republican. They relocated to Texas for a few years, but eventually returned to the North Carolina mountains where they lived unmolested into the twentieth century. Malinda suffered a natural death in 1903, but Kesse's death was more dramatic. In 1913, he was fatally injured when he crashed a railroad handcar into a mountain gorge at age 72.[19]

STEPHEN W. BREWER, the commander of Company E who was wounded carrying the regimental colors up Cemetery Ridge, made it back to the Confederate line, but was captured with other wounded near Greencastle, Maryland on the retreat from Gettysburg. He was imprisoned in the North until near the end of the war, when he was released in a prisoner exchange. He returned home to North Carolina where he became the sheriff of Chatham County.[20]

JAMES M. BROOKS and DANIEL BOONE THOMAS, the two soldiers from Company E who went over the wall at Cemetery Ridge with the regimental colors, were both imprisoned up North at Fort Delaware. Sergeant Brooks was transferred to Point Lookout and freed in a prisoner exchange in March of 1864. He returned to duty, was wounded in action, but was back with the regiment in early 1865. A week before Appomattox he was captured again and sent back North to prison. He was released in June of 1865, and made his way home to North Carolina. He eventually took a job teaching school in Texas, where he reportedly died of tuberculosis. Daniel Boone Thomas survived more than a year-and-a-half at the notorious Fort Delaware prison before he was freed in a prisoner exchange in February of 1865. He moved back to North Carolina and faded into the obscurity of daily life.[21]

GASTON H. BROUGHTON, the Company D lieutenant who was wounded in the foot near the climax of the Pickett-Pettigrew Charge, spent the remainder of the war in Northern prisons. Somehow he survived the deadly diseases and harsh winters that claimed so many Confederate prisoners in the North and was released in June of 1865. After living as a farmer back home in North Carolina's Wake County, he took up a job in nearby Raleigh as the custodian of the State Supreme Court building. Eventually, age dimmed the vigor that had enabled him to charge up Cemetery Ridge. At age sixty-eight, he was granted a veteran's pension by the State of North Carolina. A stroke had left him "wholly incapacitated," his physician attested. Broughton had no other source of income, the doctor noted, but was "worthy in every respect to receive a pension."[22]

JACOB "JAKE" BUSH lay on the battlefield for two nights after being wounded in the Pickett-Pettigrew Charge. Taken prisoner, Sergeant Bush was treated well by the Federal soldiers, not by a Yankee surgeon—who ordered him out of a hospital tent for Northern troops. "The doctor said, 'Get out of here or I will kick you out right now,'" Bush recalled, "so I went out and sat down by the root of a tree and got as wet as if I had been dipped in a creek. . . . I never went into another Yankee tent while I stayed there." Bush survived his soaking, recovered from his four wounds, endured imprisonment at David's Island in New York Harbor, and was returned South in a prisoner exchange two months after Gettysburg. He was granted an extended furlough and went home to North Carolina's mountain country. There he nursed his wounds, taught school and got married. He returned to the regiment, was wounded again at the battle of Reams' Station, but was promoted to lieutenant and remained with the 26th until Appomattox. Almost sixty years later, his account of Gettysburg was published by his hometown newspaper, the *News-Topic* of

Lenoir. "I went into the army at 19 years of age," Bush concluded, "and came out with a little more experience than I had when I left home. . . ."[23]

WILLIAM M. CHEEK, the Company E private who redeemed Colonel Burgwyn's pocket watch at gunpoint, was wounded in the Pickett-Pettigrew Charge and became a prisoner of war. He spent several months at the David's Island prison in New York Harbor and at Point Lookout before he was exchanged. He returned to duty in mid-1864, but was captured again near Petersburg. He was sent back to Point Lookout until war's end, when he went home. Thirty-seven years after Gettysburg, he attended a Confederate Memorial Day address in Raleigh where the keynote speaker was William H.S. Burgwyn—Colonel Burgwyn's brother. Cheek shared his account of Colonel Burgwyn's last moments with Burgwyn's brother, who produced the late colonel's sash, gauntlets and sword. Holding the artifacts and remembering the colonel's final moments on McPherson's Ridge, Cheek was moved to tears.[24]

GEORGE W. COFFEY and JESSE P. COFFEY were the only members of the Coffey family in Company F who survived Gettysburg unharmed. The seven other Coffeys in the company were wounded, and five died. Several months after Gettysburg, George was captured at the battle of Bristoe Station and was imprisoned at Point Lookout until near the end of the war. Jesse deserted on the retreat from Gettysburg, but later rejoined the regiment. On June 11, 1864, he deserted again. This time he went over to the enemy, was briefly imprisoned at Point Lookout, then joined the U.S. Army. Despite its horrendous losses at Gettysburg, the Coffey family survived and continued to farm the mountain country around John's River well into the 20th century.[25]

THOMAS J. CURETON, the newly promoted captain who led Company B in the Pickett-Pettigrew Charge, remained with the regiment for the rest of the war. Less than a year after Gettysburg, he was seriously wounded while commanding a skirmish line following the battle of Spotsylvania. He recovered, however, and at Appomattox oversaw the regiment's surrender. He returned home to the Waxhaws region after the war, and pursued a career as a cotton merchant. In 1890, he penned an account of the regiment's actions at Gettysburg for John R. Lane. "I was engaged in every battle or engagement the 26th was in from New Bern to Appomattox," he reminded Lane. "I am getting old and . . . would like to see it all written up for the truth of history."[26]

JOSEPH R. DAVIS, whose brigade was ravaged by crossfire in the Pickett-Pettigrew Charge, was present at Appomattox. After the war he moved to the Gulf Coast of Mississippi, where he practiced law until his death in 1896.[27]

JOHN R. EMERSON, the lieutenant from Company E who sent his wife a formal will when he went off to war, never recovered from the wound he received in the Pickett-Pettigrew Charge. Left on the field and captured, he died in the Federal prison at David's Island, New York, of complications from his wound. Back in North Carolina, his wife Martha received the letter so dreaded on the home front: "It becomes my painful duty to inform you of the death of your husband. . . ." Like numerous other Southern survivors of Gettysburg, Lieutenant Emerson became a prison camp statistic, buried in grave # 773, Cypress Hill Cemetery, Brooklyn, New York. At the time of his death, he and his wife were still childless.[28]

ALEXANDER HAYS, the Federal division commander who played such a pivotal role in the repulse of the Pickett-Pettigrew Charge, saw his Blue Birds merged with other divisions when Grant took command of the Army of the Potomac. The reorganization left Hays in command of a single brigade. At the battle of the Wilderness, Hays was shot through the head and killed. He was buried in Allegheny Cemetery in Pittsburgh. Fort Hays, Kansas and nearby Hays City were named for him.[29]

THE 12th NEW JERSEY, whose troops captured the 26th's battle flag on Cemetery Ridge, remained with the Army of the Potomac after Gettysburg. The regiment was present at Bristoe Station, the Wilderness, Spotsylvania, Cold Harbor and the siege of Petersburg. When the Confederate line was broken at Five Forks, the 12th New Jersey joined in the pursuit of Lee's army, was present at Appomattox, and was mustered out of service on July 15, 1865. During the Confederate surrender at Appomattox, the troops of the 12th refrained from cheering or taunting the defeated Confederates. "Such plucky, brave fighters had won our respect," a New Jersey veteran explained, "and we gladly shared with them our hardtack and coffee, as we swapped reminiscences of the times when we were foemen— now friends." Major John T. Hill, the officer who commanded the Jerseymen on Cemetery Ridge, suffered poor health after Gettysburg and was discharged from the army in early 1864.[30]

ROBERT N. HUDSPETH, the sole member of Company F to survive the charge up McPherson's Ridge unharmed, kept the lieutenant's rank given to him on Gettysburg's third day. He remained with the regiment through Bristoe Station, the Wilderness, Spotsylvania, Cold Harbor and Reams' Station.

After surviving so much deadly combat, he "was taken sick with fever" in November of 1864 and died in a Richmond hospital. His epitaph: "Cause of death not reported."[31]

PRENTISS KIRKMAN, one of the four Kirkman brothers in Company G, was the only brother to survive Gettysburg unharmed. George and Preston died at Gettysburg, and Bascom succumbed to his wounds in a Federal field hospital two months later. Prentiss survived the battle, but was captured by Federal forces on July 5th. He was imprisoned at Fort Delaware and then was transferred to Point Lookout. There he contracted scurvy—an illness his physician father could have cured—and died in prison one month before Lee surrendered. The Kirkman family was left to mourn four brothers who never returned from the war.[32]

JAMES H. LANE, the brigadier general whose troops surged up Cemetery Ridge on the left until raked with a crossfire, lost almost half his brigade at Gettysburg. After the war he went home to Virginia, where he found the family plantation in ruins. A former college engineering instructor, he returned to the classroom and ended his career as a department chairman at Alabama Polytechnic Institute.[33]

JULIUS LINEBACK and the 26th North Carolina Band remained with the regiment until the retreat to Appomattox. At least twice during the Virginia campaigns, the band serenaded General Lee, who complimented the musicians on each performance. "I don't believe we can have an army without music," Lee observed. The band members also continued to serve as hospital attendants. "I could amputate a man's leg as well as some of the doctors . . . ," Lineback later recalled. On the retreat to Appomattox, the band was separated from the regiment. After securing some food at a house along their way, the musicians played a tune in appreciation for the handout. It proved to be the band's farewell performance. After trying to hide for several days, the musicians finally surrendered to Federal troops. "Our instruments were taken from us and that seemed to be the bitterest experience of all," Lineback recollected. "I had learned to love my B-flat cornet more than all the rest of my few possessions and to see it go into the hands of another and know that I would never see it again, was a very hard thing to endure." Imprisonment for three months at Point Lookout proved even harder. "Here we soon learned what poverty, misery, helplessness and dependence meant," recalled Lineback. "Dirt and filth made our tent or whatever shelter we might have, almost unendurable. We had scarcely any opportunity to wash either our persons or clothing, privacy was impossible and our condition was as near that of brutes as could well be imagined. . . ." Back home in Salem after the war, Lineback married Anna Vogler, the daughter of Moravian missionaries, and together they parented five children. He returned to bookkeeping until 1876. That year he became an administrator in the Moravian Church, rising eventually to church treasurer—a post he held until he retired in 1914 at age eighty.[34]

JEFFERSON B. MANSFIELD, the color sergeant wounded during the opening minutes of the assault on McPherson's Ridge, also was captured and imprisoned. "I am here in the hospital; am shot in the foot," he wrote home from prison on David's Island, "but I think that I can save my foot . . . I am getting good fare, am treated very well, but would like to get home." He was freed in the same prisoner exchange as Jake Bush, was restricted to "light duty" for the rest of the war and survived to become "father to many children and the ancestor to many, many more."[35]

JAMES D. "JIMMIE" MOORE, the seventeen-year-old private who was the eighty-fifth soldier from Company F to be shot down on McPherson's Ridge, eventually became a prominent textile executive. After Gettysburg, he went home to the Globe to recover from his wounds. While recuperating, his family home was raided by Keese Blalock and his gang. Moore and the rest of the family fought off the raiders, and during a second assault one of them managed to shoot out one of Blalock's eyes. Back with the regiment, Moore fought at the battle of the Wilderness, but was unable to march because of his leg wound. Instead of going home, he joined the 1st North Carolina Cavalry, was involved in numerous actions and, by war's end, was serving as a courier to Confederate General Wade Hampton.[36]

After the war, he worked for several years as a storekeeper in Indiana and then joined his brother in a mercantile business in North Carolina's Gaston County. There he married Martha Lewis, the daughter of the local clerk of court, and raised eight children. He also raised up a series of cotton mills and became a leading citizen in Gastonia. He served as a town alderman, cashier of the First National Bank and Sunday school teacher of the First Baptist Church. Exceeding his reputation as a businessman was his reputation for Christian charity. In a season of bloody fighting late in the war, a fellow Confederate, B.M. Tuttle, had shared the Gospel with Moore one night. "A while after they had lain down, father awoke and noticed that young Moore was gone from his side," recounted the Rev. D.H. Tuttle in 1905. "He soon heard groaning in prayer and found him in a fence corner, face in hands and on the ground, earnestly crying to God for mercy. . . . Father then got down by him, directing him by God's word in the way to the kingdom."[37]

Respected and revered, Moore died at age fifty-nine—stricken at his Gastonia home by an apparent aneurysm. His death was front page news in the *Charlotte Observer*. "The whole town is in mourning," the *Observer* reported. "He never needed to be reminded of a case of want," recalled a colleague. "He knew every house in this town where there was trouble or need and he was at their service . . . " Back in the Globe, the hunting trails Moore had followed as a boy disappeared in new forests, the old family home washed away in a flood, and the Globe's population shriveled away in size when the farming community was by-passed by a modern highway. By the end of the twentieth century, there were few reminders of Jimmie Moore and his wartime saga even in the Globe—except for the wooded mountainsides that faintly resembled faraway McPherson's Ridge.[38]

HENRY A. MORROW, the colonel of the 24th Michigan, was captured with other Federal wounded on Gettysburg's first day. On July 3rd, Morrow asked Confederate Brigadier General John B. Gordon for assistance in treating the Iron Brigade's wounded, many of whom had lain untended on the field for two days. That night Gordon provided Morrow with a dozen Confederate ambulances, ample litter-bearers and permission to move the wounded Black Hat troops to a field hospital. "It was a weird sight," Morrow would later recall, "that long train of army hearses, as by the fitful light of a half-clouded moon . . . this party threaded its way among the blackened and swollen corpses. . . . [The] moans and cries of the wounded for assistance, and their supplications for water were heart-rending. Some were delirious and talked of home and friends. . . . But by midnight they were all tenderly borne away to receive the care they so much needed and so many a valuable life was saved."[39]

Morrow escaped being swept South into imprisonment with Lee's retreating army by posing as a Federal surgeon. He recovered from his wound and rejoined his regiment. He was given a brigade command in January of 1864, but was wounded again at the battle of the Wilderness—and required a six-month recovery. He returned to the front during the siege of Petersburg and was brevetted a brigadier general by Meade's order. Morrow continued intermittently to hold brigade command, but he was disturbed by the increasingly brutal nature of the war in Virginia. "The burning of private dwellings, churches etc. deserves to be reprobated as neither politic nor in accordance with civilized warfare," he wrote in his diary in December of 1864. "It exasperated the People & makes the struggle more cruel & bloody. It carries one back to a less enlightened & civilized age."[40]

On February 6, 1865, while again in command of the Iron Brigade, Morrow was wounded a third time at the battle of Dabney's Mill. It was a severe wound, but he recovered in time to rejoin the brigade when it was mustered out of service. At the close of the war, he was brevetted major general for valor in combat. In peacetime he resumed his law practice in Detroit, but soon rejoined the military. Commissioned as a lieutenant colonel in the Regular Army in 1866, he rose to colonel and commander of the 21st Infantry. Two of his sons also became army officers. While posted to Fort Sidney, Nebraska, Colonel Morrow developed a fatal illness and died on January 31, 1891. He was buried with military honors in Niles, Michigan.[41]

Colonel Morrow's counterpart with the 19th Indiana, Colonel Samuel J. Williams, was praised by General Doubleday for his "promptness, courage and skill" in defending the Iron Brigade's left flank on McPherson's Ridge. After Gettysburg, Williams remained in command of his Hoosier regiment during the fighting in Virginia. Like General Hays and Colonel Morrow, he too was struck down at the battle of the Wilderness—where he was hit by a cannonball and instantly killed on May 6, 1864. He left behind a wife and six children.[42]

THE IRON BRIGADE—with which Colonels Morrow and Williams would forever be associated—never fully recovered from the dreadful losses it suffered on Gettysburg's first day. The casualty rate among the Black Hats at Gettysburg was calculated to be 65 percent, which included the 19th Indiana's 73 percent casualty rate and the 80 percent casualty rate of the 24th Michigan. Like the troops of the 26th North Carolina within Lee's army, the men of the 24th Michigan achieved a lamentable distinction at Gettysburg: They were said to have incurred the highest number of losses of any Northern regiment engaged in the battle. The brigade remained with the Army of the Potomac until near the end of the war, but lost its Western character when its depleted ranks were filled by regiments from the East. In October of 1864, the 19th Indiana was consolidated with another regiment and ceased to exist. The troops of the 24th Michigan remained with the reorganized Iron Brigade. In February of 1865, a few days after Colonel Morrow received his last wound, most of the brigade was detached from Grant's army and sent to New York and Illinois to keep order among new Northern draftees. The 24th Michigan was pulling guard duty in Springfield, Illinois when its long-time opponent, the Army of

Northern Virginia, surrendered at Appomattox. The regiment served as military escort at President Lincoln's funeral and then was mustered out of Federal service on June 30, 1865. For the Gettysburg veterans of the Iron Brigade, the long and bloody first day of fighting would remain the brigade's principal expression of duty and sacrifice. At McPherson's Ridge, it too "covered itself with glory."[43]

THOMAS PERRETT, the private who never forgot the sight of so many young soldiers singing "Maryland, My Maryland" at the Potomac Crossing, recovered from his Gettysburg wound, returned to the regiment and was promoted to sergeant. He was wounded again in the summer of 1864, recovered, and again returned to duty. In early 1865, during the prolonged, deadly fighting at Petersburg, he gave up and "went over to the enemy." He was confined in Washington, D.C., until after Lee's surrender, when he was released. After the war, he lived in Faison, North Carolina, where he worked as a life insurance agent. In his last years, he engaged in a letter-writing campaign to preserve the history of the regiment's action at Gettysburg. In 1905, he penned an account of the Gettysburg Campaign, which he entitled "A Trip That Didn't Pay." In it, he recalled the regiment's river crossing into Maryland. "Many of my comrades, companions of my youth, were then looking for the last time upon the receding shores of their beloved Southland," he wrote. "The incident has lingered with me all these sad years as the sad memory of a troubled dream."[44]

JAMES JOHNSTON PETTIGREW was mourned by a multitude of Southern leaders as "the brightest star in that galaxy that North Carolina sent to Virginia." Pettigrew's body lay in state in North Carolina's capitol, and business was suspended in Raleigh during his funeral. After temporary burial in a Raleigh cemetery, his body was reinterred in the family's burial ground at Bonarva Plantation. "I want no higher honor," vowed a North Carolina officer, "than to have been a member of his command."[45]

SIMEON PHILYAW, the Company F corporal who prematurely fired the regiment's first shot in the assault on McPherson's Ridge, survived a battle wound at Gettysburg and incarceration in a Northern prison camp. After he was exchanged in 1864, he went home to the North Carolina mountains on furlough, and joined Kesse Blalock's gang of outlaws. Soon afterwards, he was accidentally killed when his handgun prematurely discharged.[46]

ELI SETSER, the champion marbles player of Company F, died of the wounds he received in the first day's fighting. "Eli requested me to write to you," a North Carolina officer wrote Setser's father after Gettysburg. "I went by and saw him as we fell back. . . . He told me that he was willing to die and that he hoped to meet me in heaven. It was hard for me to leave the boys, and if I had not been an officer I would have been taken with them. Jo Setser lay close to Eli with his leg amputated above the nee, and Dan Courtenay lay near them with his leg broke below the nee. . . . I told them I must go, that the yankees was coming and with a heavy heart I took their hands, and a tear fell from our eyes and we parted."[47]

THOMAS W. SETSER, Eli's cousin, was also wounded at Gettysburg, but survived and returned to Virginia with the regiment. He lived through the fierce fighting at Bristoe Station and was promoted to sergeant. Wounded in the spring campaign of 1864, he returned to duty in the summer and experienced more combat at Reams' Station. "When I found the Regiment tha was on the front lines in too hundred yards of the yankees, a shooting at each other all the time," he wrote his parents, "and a man couden look over the breste works with oute beeing shot in the head. . . ." By March of 1865, Thomas Setser was among a handful of Company F men who had survived almost four years of war. On March 29th—less than two weeks before Appomattox—he deserted to the enemy.[48]

ISAAC R. TRIMBLE, whose two brigades followed Pettigrew's division in the assault against Cemetery Ridge, was so badly wounded that one of his legs had to be amputated. Left at Gettysburg with the severely wounded, he became a prisoner of war, and was not exchanged until February of 1865. After the war, he lived in Baltimore, and worked as an engineering consultant for a Northern railroad. He died in 1888 at age 86.[49]

ROMULUS M. TUTTLE, the captain who commanded Company F in the charge up McPherson's Ridge, recovered from the wound he suffered in the assault and returned to duty in early 1864. He was wounded again at the Wilderness and on two other occasions during the Petersburg Campaign. Finally, he was placed in the Invalid Corps, where he remained until war's end. After the war he graduated from Davidson College, accepted a call to the ministry and pastored Presbyterian churches in Texas and Virginia.[50]

GEORGE W. WILCOX, the Company H lieutenant who picked up the 26th's fallen battle flag after Captain McCreery was killed, recovered from his wounds. He was captured by captured by Federal troops twice, and escaped both times. He was wounded again at the Wilderness, but survived and stayed with the regiment until late 1864, when he was appointed captain in the 46th

North Carolina. After the war he went home to Moore County, married a local girl, and was elected to the state legislature, serving first as a house member and later as a state senator.[51]

JOSEPH J. YOUNG, the regimental quartermaster who prepared Colonel Burgwyn's body for burial, was appointed brigade quartermaster in 1864. He survived the war and returned home to North Carolina, where he married, raised a family and enjoyed a long career as a prominent planter.[52]

LOUIS G. YOUNG, Pettigrew's aide-de-camp at Gettysburg, survived the war, married, moved to Savannah and excelled in his family's cotton export business. Six months after Gettysburg, his fellow officers persuaded him to write a brief history of the brigade's actions in the battle. In 1875, his account was published in *Our Living and Our Dead,* a journal specializing in Southern war memoirs. About a quarter-century later, his profiles of Pettigrew's brigade appeared in Walter Clark's epic *Histories of the Several Regiments and Battalions From North Carolina in the Great War.* Young died on May 31, 1922, almost 70 years after Gettysburg. His skillfully crafted accounts eventually became obligatory sources for historians studying Pettigrew's men.[53]

ZEBULON B. VANCE, the 26th North Carolina's first colonel, became famous as his state's war governor. His determined efforts to keep Tarheel soldiers equipped and fed were remarkably successful, although his policies often grated on Confederate officials. At the war's end he was taken into custody by Federal authorities, who imprisoned him without charges or trial. After a month and a half in Washington's Old Capitol Prison, he was released without explanation or apology. He was elected to the U.S. Senate in 1870 but was not permitted to serve. In 1876, he was again elected governor, but halfway through his term the state legislature elected him to the U.S. Senate. This time he was allowed to take his seat. He served for three terms, and died in office in 1894 at age sixty-three. After a funeral service in the U.S. Senate, Vance's body was returned to North Carolina for services in the state capitol and burial in Asheville's Riverside Cemetery. As the funeral cortege moved by rail across the state, Zeb Vance drew a final crowd: Thousands of grateful Confederate veterans lined the tracks in his honor. Almost a century after Vance's Civil War service, his birthplace near Asheville was restored and designated as a state historic site.[54]

HENRY K. BURGWYN JR., was mourned throughout his home state. "The life, career, and death of young Burgwyn," eulogized the *Raleigh Observer,* "convey a lesson to the youth of this Confederacy which cannot be too well studied and thoroughly profited by." His parents were heartbroken, but bore the news nobly. After a long and dangerous trek from Gettysburg, Colonel Burgwyn's grieving servant, Kincian, arrived at the family plantation with Burgwyn's two horses and his personal belongings. Long after emancipation, Kincian continued to share a bond of friendship with the Burgwyn family.[55]

Burgwyn's parents continued to speak and write about Harry for the rest of their lives. They tried to recover his body during the war, but U.S. Secretary of War Edwin M. Stanton reportedly refused to allow it. In 1867, they were successful. Burgwyn's remains were removed from the Gettysburg burial site and reinterred in Raleigh's Oakwood Cemetery. After the war, Burgwyn's family suffered from indebtedness. Henry Senior eventually filed for bankruptcy and moved with wife Anna to a house in Richmond. He suffered a series of strokes and died in 1877, followed ten years later by Harry's mother. Although revered as a war hero by contemporaries, Burgwyn's fame faded with the passing of his generation. Eventually, he was known only to serious students of the war. In 1985, however, he regained a measure of recognition when the University of North Carolina Press published his biography. Aptly told by a banker-turned-historian, Archie Davis, the book was titled *Boy Colonel of the Confederacy*.[56]

Annie "Nan" Devereux, Colonel Burgwyn's fiancée, never married. Like Burgwyn's sister Maria, she dressed in mourning attire the rest of her life. The Devereux family lost most of its fortune in the war. Major John Devereux, Nan's father, died in 1893, and a few years later the family sold Will's Forest. The stately home was torn down and the land was developed as North Carolina's capital city expanded. Within a century, only a few street names—Devereux Street, Will's Forest Street—survived as evidence of "the happy and delightful home" where a twenty-one-year-old Colonel Henry Burgwyn came calling on a nineteen-year-old Nan Devereux. For almost a half-century following the war, Nan taught school and lived with her widowed mother. Eventually, observed a Raleigh old-timer, "the widowed mother and her elder daughter, drawn nearer together by the circumstances of their loving dependence, [became] to the minds of their many dear friends and relatives, a precious reminder of the happy days of the past."[57]

The mother, Margaret Devereux, died at age eighty-eight. Two years later, sixty-eight-year-old Nan followed her, passing away at her Raleigh home on April 29, 1912. Her modest two-inch obituary in the local newspaper was obscured by reports about the recent sinking of the *Titanic*, presidential candidate Woodrow Wilson's warnings of socialism, and Roald Amundsen's expedition to the South Pole. The day's sports news reported Cincinnati's lead in the National League; a weather map charted the nation's high pressure systems; and advertisements trumpeted products ranging from new automobiles to Wrigley's chewing gum. Among such modern marvels who could imagine Confederate cavaliers, refined Southern belles and death-dealing volleys on a Pennsylvania hillside? After a funeral in Raleigh's Christ Church, Miss Devereux was buried in the family plot at Oakwood Cemetery.[58]

Left behind among her treasured effects was a small envelope, yellowed with age, which was addressed to "Miss Annie Devereux—At Home." In it, written in a youthful script, was a meticulously rendered poem typical of a nineteenth-century courtship between an educated antebellum maiden and a Southern gentleman:

> *None so humble, none so weak*
> *But may flush his father's cheek*
> *And his Maiden's dear and true*
> *With the deeds that he may do.*
> *Be his days as dark as night*
> *He may make himself a light.*

Was the anonymously penned poetry a farewell from her young colonel, when he was bound for Gettysburg? If so, Nan took the secret to her grave. Ironically, just as death separated the two, it reunited them somewhat almost a half century later. Across the field of stones from Nan Devereux's grave stood a granite monument inscribed *Semper Fidelis*—"Always Faithful"—which marked the final resting place of Colonel Henry K. Burgwyn Jr.[59]

JOHN "KNOCK" JONES, the major who commanded the 26th North Carolina in the Pickett-Pettigrew Charge, was promoted to lieutenant colonel after Gettysburg. His promotion was back-dated to July 1, 1863—the day he had taken command of the regiment following the loss of Burgwyn and Lane. When General Pettigrew was shot at Falling Waters, Jones temporarily led the brigade. "I understand Gen. Heth was pleased at the manner in which I brought up the brigade at Fallings Waters," Jones wrote his father. "Had Gen. Pettigrew lived I think I would have been Col. of the 26th without a doubt. He as good as told me so several times after the battle." Jones faced a challenging job after Gettysburg: maintaining a regiment that had been almost destroyed in battle. He also had to deal with personal loss. Not only had he lost his close friend and commander—Harry Burgwyn—along with numerous friends in the regiment, but he had also lost a brother. A few weeks after returning to Virginia, Jones learned that Wat had died of the wound he had received at Gettysburg.[60]

Jones led the regiment through the battle of Bristoe Station and then assumed second-in-command when Lane returned to the regiment as colonel. He remained dedicated to the 26th, and bristled in defense when rumors blamed the failure of the Pickett-Pettigrew Charge on North Carolina troops. "That we never came up is all a lie," he wrote his father in August of 1863. "Tell a man in this army that North Carolinians failed to go where Virginians went and he would think you a fool." Jones also remained optimistic that the South would eventually win its independence. On the eve of the bloody battle of the Wilderness, he wrote his father a cheerful letter in which he predicted a Confederate victory. "Our army certainly was never in so fine a condition and they feel confident of success," he reported. "I had a long conversation with Gen. Lee a day or two since. He is in the highest of spirits, and seems to think our prospects have never been so very good. . . . If we are only successful this campaign, I think as Gen. Lee that another winter will find us all at home."[61]

Knock Jones never saw home again. He was mortally wounded at the Wilderness on May 6, 1864, when Grant's army assaulted the line defended by Hill's Corps. Colonel Lane had been wounded the day before, and Jones had again resumed command of the regiment. The men of the 26th were exhausted from the previous day's fighting. In the morning, instead of being relieved, they were hit by a surprise assault. The men were lying in line when the Federals attacked. Throughout the war, Jones had habitually avoided lying down on the battle line. This time he made exception—and was struck by enemy fire while lying down. After he was hit, he was moved back from the front line. His best friend, Surgeon William Gaither, removed the bullet from Jones's body and confessed that the wound was mortal. "It must not be," Jones replied. "I was born to accomplish more good than I have done." He remained composed, however, and complained only that he wished he could live long enough to see Southern nationhood. He died at 10:40 the next morning.[62]

In a letter similar to the one he had written Colonel Burgwyn's father, Captain Joseph Young offered condolences to Jones's father. "He had been so long connected with us," Young wrote, "had been in so many fights and always came out unhurt that all hoped he would be spared. But, alas, death has deprived us of one never to be forgotten. He fell where the true patriot could only wish—at the heart of the command in the face of danger. . . . His sense of honor, truth and virtue was of the purest type." Jones's surrogate mother, Maria Spears, who had written that "the subject of her incessant prayers was to see John Jones a Christian," apparently had her prayers answered. Beginning in 1862 and increasing after the defeats at Gettysburg and Vicksburg, a spiritual revival had swept through the Southern armies. "We have a large number of preachers here now from home who are preaching to the soldiers," a Confederate in Lee's army wrote home in September of 1863, "and we have religious services in camp almost every day." Noted another: "We sometimes feel more as if we were in a camp-meeting than in the army expecting to meet an enemy." In this season of revival, one who appeared to profess Jesus as Lord was John Jones. "You spoke to me in your last letter on the subject of religion," he had written to his father shortly before the Wilderness. "I can tell you this much—I often think seriously of such things and think I would be confirmed if an opportunity should offer." After Jones's death, Captain Young reported how the young officer had come to demonstrate "great reliance and trust in Him who controls all things." After temporary burial in a soldier's graveyard, Jones's body was reinterred near his mother's grave back home in Happy Valley.[63]

JOHN RANDOLPH LANE never fully recovered from the head wound he received at Gettysburg. The wound continued to drain for the rest of his life and it also left him with a slight speech impediment—problems Lane dismissed as minor. He returned to the regiment in November of 1863, and was promoted to colonel. His commission was back-dated to July 1, 1863, when command of the regiment had fallen to him on McPherson's Ridge. He officially led the 26th North Carolina for the rest of the war, although his command was interrupted several more times by battle wounds. He was wounded three more times after Gettysburg—at the Wilderness, at Yellow Tavern near Petersburg, and at Reams's Station. His fourth wound, caused by an exploding artillery shell, appeared mortal, but he again surprised the surgeons and returned to his regiment. During the siege of Petersburg in the spring of 1865, complications from his wounds forced him to seek more medical treatment. He was in a military hospital in Danville, Virginia, when the 26th North Carolina and the rest of the Army of Northern Virginia surrendered at Appomattox.[64]

When the war ended, Lane went home to Ore Hill in North Carolina's Chatham County and became rich. He did it, according to the *Raleigh News and Observer,* by "untiring energy, business ability and thrift." With the same determination and devotion to duty that had propelled him up McPherson's Ridge, he built a prosperous real estate, mercantile and livestock company. By 1900, his Ore Hill firm, the Brookside Farm and Land Company, boasted a new-fangled telephone, a grist-mill and a mercantile store—and was advertising "good farms for sale" along with "fine jacks and brood mares." Success did not erase his characteristic humility. Lane was described as "a quiet, unimposing and unpretentious gentleman . . . of the Old South." Along the way, he married Mary Ellen Siler—daughter of the founder of nearby Siler City—and raised a son and a daughter. "There was about him a grand simplicity," observed a contemporary. "Without the advantage of a college education, without any previous military training, and without the aid of influential friends, Colonel Lane obtained his position in life."[65]

As the twentieth century approached and the number of Civil War veterans began to diminish rapidly, Americans began paying an increasing amount of tribute to the old warriors. In 1889, a retired Northern officer, William F. Fox, caught the nation's attention when he published a compilation of the war's terrible harvest—*Regimental Losses in the American Civil War.* In it, he cited the unique sacrifice of the 26th North Carolina at Gettysburg. "This loss of the 26th North Carolina at Gettysburg," he wrote, "was the severest regiment loss during the war." Other publications, including the South's influential *Confederate Veteran,* reported the regiment's dramatic story, and attention focused on Lane as the 26th's surviving colonel. In 1900, he was invited to appear as a headliner at a Louisville convention of the United Confederate Veterans. Erect, dignified and humble, Lane electrified his audience. "I presented him in the convention hall to all his comrades," recalled his host, "and, standing in his worn and tattered regimentals, stained in many places with his blood, he received an ovation that is accorded but to few men."[66]

In his last years, John Randolph Lane became a regional symbol of Southern valor and national reconciliation. "His name is known throughout the State and the South," proclaimed the *News and Observer,* "as the valiant leader of the famous Twenty-Sixth North Carolina Regiment in the Confederate army." He served as commander of his local U.C.V. camp, appeared at veterans' assemblies, and encouraged mutual respect and cordiality with the Grand Army of the Republic—the G.A.R.—which was the Northern counterpart to the U.C.V. As late as 1907, when age seventy-two, he mounted one of his horses and rode in a parade to unveil a Confederate monument at his county seat. "Colonel Lane wore his old uniform," noted a reporter, "and although seventy-two years old, he rode a spirited horse at the head of the procession, erect as an Indian, with all the ease and grace of an accomplished cavalier."[67]

As he packed for another veterans' convention in the fall of 1908, he fell ill. By year's end he was obviously failing. Typically, he met his end calmly and fearlessly. "With a sublime physical courage and strong Christian faith he met the great Conqueror without a tremor," observed a friend. "I never knew a kinder, braver, or more knightly man." At 4 P.M., on December 31, 1908, Lane uttered his last words—"I am nearing the shore"—and died at age seventy-three. He was buried in the cemetery of his beloved Brush Creek Baptist Church, and was eulogized throughout the South. "Wealth, social position and political honors were not what he strove for," observed a relative, "but to live for the good of his fellow-man, and to follow in the footsteps of his Master. This was the ambition of his life."[68]

Five years before his death, Lane returned to Gettysburg. It was the 40th anniversary of the battle, and he was invited by the North Carolina Society of Baltimore to be a keynote speaker at a commemoration of the Pickett-Pettigrew Charge. Accompanying him was a Chicago pharmaceutical executive named Charles H. McConnell—the man who had shot Lane on McPherson's Ridge four decades earlier. McConnell, who was president of the Iron Brigade Association, had been introduced to Lane by Colonel Burgwyn's brother, William, who had met McConnell while on a trip North. Now, addressing each other as "dear old friend," they were borne by a procession of carriages to a stage erected near the "High-Water Mark of the Confederacy" on Cemetery Ridge. There, before a crowd of several thousand, the two former enemies again greeted each other. "I thank God I did not kill you," McConnell told Lane. Then the two old soldiers heartily shook hands. In response, the heavily Southern crowd sent the Rebel yell echoing again over the battleground at Gettysburg.[69]

When Lane spoke, the crowd hushed. Looking down into the faces of his audience, he saw many who had witnessed the excitement, tragedy and horror on those unforgettable fields of fire. There too were many who could never imagine what he described; they were a new generation for whom those three days were merely history. "I was once a soldier . . . ," he began, and then spoke at length—an old man telling a young man's story of smoke and fire and death. He tried to tell them about the shouts and the volleys, about brave enemies in Black Hats, about dressed lines and fallen color-bearers. He tried to tell them about the courage and the confusion, about McCreery and Wilcox and Honeycutt—and about Colonel Burgwyn, down and dying. He tried to tell them what it was like to look into the face of a twenty-one-year-old when the boyish light in his eyes was fading. He spoke of exhilarating victory and searing losses. "On the third day," he told them, "the remnant with colors flying stepped out, with hearts of oak, to take part in that memorable third day's charge." He gave them brutal numbers and awful statistics of bloody subtraction: 800 young and healthy men with homes and families and futures— reduced to so few and then reduced again to nearly nothing.[70]

Always, he came back to his men. "Your valor is coming to be regarded as the common heritage of the American nation," he told them. "It no longer belongs to your State alone; it no longer belongs to the South; it is the high-water mark of what Americans have done and can do." He wept. In front of everyone and without apology, the old warrior looked at the tiny, aged remnant of the 26th North Carolina and he wept. "I give you the highest tribute," he told them, "—a comrade's tears." A blue-uniformed band of Pennsylvania veterans then broke into a spirited rendition of "Dixie," and the audience— Northerners, Southerners, Americans all—erupted in cheers. In that rare moment of reflection—on the battleground at Gettysburg—surely John Randolph Lane again heard the guns, saw the faces, recalled the horrors, mourned the fallen and remembered the words: *covered with glory . . . covered with glory.*[71]

Notes

Abbreviations in the Notes

BHNC *Biographical History of North Carolina From Colonial Times to the Present.* Edited by Samuel A. Ashe, Stephen B. Weeks and Charles L. Van Noppen. Vol. 8. Greensboro, N.C.: Charles L. Van Noppen Publisher, 1917.

DAB *Dictionary of American Biography.* Edited by Allen Johnson and Dumas Malone. New York: Charles Scribner's Sons, 1928–1936.

DNCB *Dictionary of North Carolina Biography.* Edited by William S. Powell. Chapel Hill, N.C.: University of North Carolina Press, 1991.

DU Special Collections Library. Duke University.

EOC *Encyclopedia of the Confederacy.* Edited by Richard Current. New York: Simon and Schuster, 1993.

GHM Greensboro Historical Museum.

HKB Henry K. Burgwyn Jr.

HTECW *Historical Times Illustrated Encyclopedia of the Civil War.* Edited by Patricia Faust. New York: Harper & Row, 1986.

JRL John Randolph Lane.

JTJ John Thomas Jones.

LOC Manuscript Division. Library of Congress.

NA National Archives.

NCDAH North Carolina Department of Archives and History.

NCMOH North Carolina Museum of History.

NCT *North Carolina Troops, 1861–1865: A Roster.* Compiled by Weymouth T. Jordan Jr. Unit Histories by Louis H. Manarin. Raleigh: North Carolina Department of Archives and History, 1979.

OR *War of the Rebellion: The Official Records of the Union and Confederate Armies.* Washington, D.C.: Government Printing Office, 1880–1901.

SHC Southern Historical Collection. University of North Carolina at Chapel Hill.

SHSP   *Southern Historical Society Papers.*

USAMHI   U.S. Army Military History Institute. Carlisle, Pennsylvania.

INTRODUCTION
"I Was Once a Soldier"

1. "At Gettysburg on Old Battleground"; *DNCB* 4:12–13; "Confederate Monument": 504.
2. "Address by Lane"; "Colonel John R. Lane," John R. Lane Papers, SHC; "Col. Lane Has Passed Away."

CHAPTER ONE
Good, Honest American Stock

1. "Address by Lane"; "Colonel John R. Lane," Unpublished Manuscript in John R. Lane Papers, SHC; *DNCB* 4. 12–13; Bennett Young, "Col. Lane and His Regiment": 110–111; "At Gettysburg"; Underwood, "Twenty-Sixth Regiment": 342–343; Henry Besancom Diary, 1 July 1863, Henry Besancom Papers, DU.
2. "At Gettysburg"; "Colonel Lane," Lane Papers, SHC; *DNCB* 4:12–13; Dorsett, "Fourteenth Color-Bearer," 8; Underwood, "Twenty-Sixth Regiment": 342–343.
3. "Address by Lane"; Underwood, "Twenty-Sixth Regiment," 279–281; Coddington, *Gettysburg Campaign,* 17.
4. Caison, "Southern Soldiers": 159; Underwood, "Twenty-Sixth Regiment": 323, Olds, "Brave Carolinian": 247; *DNCB* 1: 276.
5. Olds, "Brave Carolinian": 247; Caison, "Southern Soldiers": 159; "Address by Lane."
6. Underwood, "Twenty-Sixth Regiment": 304–305; HKB Journal, 27 Aug 1861, Burgwyn Family Papers, SHC; *NCT* 7: 455.
7. Underwood, "Twenty-Sixth Regiment": 305; *NCT* 7: 548.
8. HKB Journal, 27 Aug 1861, Burgwyn Family Papers, SHC.
9. Davis, *Boy Colonel:* 9–19; *DNCB* 1: 276; *BHNC* 8: 67.
10. Haldeman, "Henry K. Burgwyn": 19–20; Davis, *Boy Colonel:* 25; *BHNC* 8: 67; *DNCB* 1: 276.
11. *BHNC* 8: 67; "Reflections of Judge W.H.S. Burgwyn," Burgwyn Family Papers, SHC; Davis, *Boy Colonel:* 22–27.
12. *DNCB* 1: 276; *BHNC* 8: 67–68; Davis, *Boy Colonel:* 32–33; H.A. Jacob to W.H.S. Burgwyn, 14 Apr 1960, Henry K. Burgwyn, Jr. Papers, Records of the Superintendent, Virginia Military Institute Archives.
13. Henry Burgwyn Sr. to L.O.B. Branch, 31 December 1859, Branch Family Papers, DU; *HTECW:* 536; Randall and Donald, *The Civil War and Reconstruction,* 35–37, 46–49, 182–187.
14. Henry Burgwyn Sr. to L. Branch, 31 Dec 1859, Branch Family Papers, DU; Davis, *Boy Colonel:* 51–55, 68–71.
15. *BHNC* 8: 68; *DNCB* 1: 76; Davis, *Boy Colonel:* 71–80; "Judge Burgwyn Reflections," Burgwyn Family Papers, SHC; Joseph Judson Young to HKB Sr., 31 July

1863, W.H.S. Burgwyn Papers, NCDAH; HKB Journal, 27 Aug 1861, Burgwyn Family Papers, SHC; Haldeman, "Henry K. Burgwyn, Jr.": 19.

16. Henry C. Albright to Thomas C. Dixon, 10 Aug 1861, Henry C. Albright Papers, GHM; James McDaniel to brother, 27 July 1861, Lewis Leigh Collection, USMHI; "Closing Sketch": 4–5; *NCT* 7: 455.

17. Underwood, "Twenty-Sixth Regiment": 18–21; "Address by Lane"; Martha J. Moore, *James Daniel Moore:* 9–15.

18. "Address by Lane"; Underwood, "Twenty-Sixth Regiment": 18–21; *NCT* 7: 455; McGee, "History of the Twenty-Sixth": 26–27.

19. *HTECW:* 536; Alexander, *Here Will I Dwell:* 126–127; "Address by Lane."

20. Albright to Dixon, 10 Aug 1861, Albright Papers, GHM; *NCT* 7: 466, 481, 493–494, 506, 519, 533, 548, 561, 573, 589; Underwood, "Twenty-Sixth Regiment": 303–304.

21. *Heritage of Caldwell County:* 195; Alexander, *Here Will I Dwell:* 126–127; Van Noppen and Van Noppen, *Western North Carolina:* 6; "Setser Letters," 1: 29.

22. Alexander, *Here Will I Dwell:* 128–129, 132–133; McGee, "History of the Twenty-Sixth": 29.

23. "Closing Sketch"; Alexander, *Here Will I Dwell:* 128–129, 132–133.

24. North Carolina Adjutant General's Office, Ordnance Department, Record of Issue 1861–1862: 166–167, NCDAH; "Letters of Jefferson Mansfield," 1:18; John Jones to father, 8 May 1861, Edmund W. Jones Papers, SHC; James McDaniel to brother, 27 July 1861, Lewis Leigh Collection, USMHI; "Setser Letters," 1: 29; "Daniel Liles Letters": 8–9.

25. Underwood, "Twenty-Sixth Regiment": 19–20; "Mansfield Letters" 1:18; "Daniel Liles Letters": 8–9; HKB Journal, 27 Aug 1861, Burgwyn Family Papers, SHC; *DNCB* 6: 85–86.

26. *EOC* 4: 1649–1651; *DNCB* 6: 85–86; *Irishman in Dixie:* 35–36; *North Carolina Civil War Documentary:* 23.

27. *DNCB* 6: 85–86; Underwood, "Twenty-Sixth Regiment": 404.

28. HKB Journal, 28 Aug–6 Sep 1861, Burgwyn Family Papers, SHC; *OR* I, 4: 574–575; *DNCB* 6: 85–86; Elizabeth Collier Diary, Collier Family Papers, SHC; Underwood, "Twenty-Sixth Regiment": 307.

29. HKB Journal, 2 Sep–6 Sep 1861, Burgwyn Family Papers, SHC; *HTECW:* 275–276.

30. HKB Journal, 1 Sep–5 Sep 1861, Burgwyn Family Papers, SHC; Regimental History, James T. Adams Papers, NCDAH; N.A. Ray to cousin, 13 Oct 1861, Hugh Ray to sister, 28 Oct 1861, Hugh Ray to father, Nov 1861, Nevin Ray Papers, DU.

31. "Mansfield Letters" 1:19; "First Lieutenant John Emerson": 80; Regimental History, Adams Papers, NCDAH; "Setser Letters" 1: 31.

32. Regimental History, Adams Papers, NCDAH; "Setser Letters" 1: 31; N.A. Ray to cousin, 28 Dec 1861; Nevin Ray Papers, DU.

33. Hugh Ray to sister, 28 Oct 1861, Nevin Ray Papers, DU; "Setser Letters" 1:28; Albright to sister, 23 Dec 1861, Albright Papers, GHM; Noah Denton to friend, 7 Oct 1861, Nevin Ray Papers, DU; "Mansfield Letters" 1: 22.

34. Christian Ray to brother, 30 Jul 1861, Nevin Ray Papers, DU; "Mansfield Letters" 1: 22–30.

35. Christian Ray to brother, 30 Jul 1861, Nevin Ray Papers, DU; "Mansfield Letters" 1: 22–30; "Setser Letters" 1: 28–31.

36. HKB Journal, 6 Sep–25 Sep 1861, 23 Jan 1862, Burgwyn Family Papers, SHC; Underwood, "Twenty-Sixth Regiment": 307; N.A. Ray to cousin, 28 Dec 1861, Nevin Ray Papers, DU; "Mansfield Letters" 1: 28–31.

37. Underwood, "Twenty-Sixth Regiment": 328–329; N.A. Ray to cousin, 28 Dec 1861, Nevin Ray Papers, DU; "Address by Lane."

38. "Setser Letters" 1: 28–31; Eggleston, *Rebel's Recollections:* 70–74.

39. HKB Journal, 18 Oct 1861, Burgwyn Family Papers, SHC; Underwood, "Twenty-Sixth Regiment": 328–329.

CHAPTER TWO

Into the Jaws of Certain Death

1. Barrett, *Civil War in North Carolina,* 95–98; *NCT* 7: 455; *HTECW:* 524; *Atlas to Accompany the Official Records,* plate 71; Underwood, "Twenty-Sixth Regiment": 308; HKB Journal, 4 Feb 1862, Burgwyn Family Papers, SHC.

2. *NCT* 7: 455; *OR Atlas,* plate 171; McGee, "History of the Twenty-Sixth": 10; Barrett, *Civil War in North Carolina:* 95–96.

3. *NCT* 7: 455; Underwood, "Twenty-Sixth Regiment": 308; HKB Journal, 24 Jan. 1862, Burgwyn Family Papers, SHC.

4. Underwood, "Twenty Sixth Regiment": 308; HKB Journal, 18 Oct 1862; *NCT* 7: 455.

5. Underwood, "Twenty-Sixth Regiment": 308; HKB to mother, 12 Mar 1862, Burgwyn Family Papers, SHC.

6. *OR* I, 9: 255 256; Barrett, *Civil War in North Carolina:* 102–103; 26NC History, Adams Papers, NCDAH.

7. *OR* I, 9: 255–266; Barrett, *Civil War in North Carolina:* 103–104.

8. *OR* I, 9: 255–256; Regimental History, Adams Papers, NCDAH; Underwood, "Twenty-Sixth Regiment": 316–317, 322–323, 327; Stepp, "Dedication of Gravestone": 6–7.

9. Underwood, "Twenty-Sixth Regiment": 322–323; Davis, *Boy Colonel:* 124–125.

10. HKB to mother, 17 Mar 1862, Burgwyn Family Papers, SHC; Underwood, "Twenty-Sixth Regiment": 324–326, 329.

11. *OR* I, 9: 255–256: Underwood, "Twenty-Sixth Regiment": 324–329.

12. HKB to mother, 17 Mar 1862, Burgwyn Family Papers, SHC; Underwood, "Twenty-Sixth Regiment": 324–329.

13. HKB to mother, 17 Mar 1862, Burgwyn Family Papers, SHC; Underwood, "Twenty-Sixth Regiment": 324–329; Regimental History, Adams Papers, NCDAH.

14. Lineback, "Civil War Diary"; Barrett, *Civil War in North Carolina:* 106–108.

15. *OR* I, 9: 246; Davis, *Boy Colonel:* 127–129; HKB to father, 18 and 20 Mar 1862, Burgwyn Family Papers, SHC; *Papers of Zebulon Vance* 1: 128–130; Stepp, "Dedication of Gravestone": 7–8.

16. Lineback, "Civil War Diary"; Hall, *Johnny Reb Band:* 4–9.

17. Lineback, "Civil War Diary"; Hall, *Johnny Reb Band:* 4–9.

18. *OR* I, 9: 460; Warner, *Generals in Gray:* 253–254; Davis, *Boy Colonel:* 134–138; Underwood, "Twenty-Sixth Regiment": 328.

19. Alexander, *Here Will I Dwell:* 136–137; "Old North State": 202; Mast, *State Troops* 1: 215; "Old North State": 202; Undated Interview with Charles L. Gragg, Globe, N.C.; Albright to sister, 28 Apr 1862, Albright Papers GMH; Underwood, "Twenty-Sixth Regiment": 330–331.

20. *NCT* 7: 456; Underwood, "Twenty-Sixth Regiment": 330–331; Lineback, "Civil War Diary."

21. Underwood, "Twenty-Sixth Regiment": 328, 330; Davis, *Boy Colonel:* 140, 142; HKB to father, 22 Apr 1862, Burgwyn Family Papers, SHC.

22. Lineback, "Civil War Diary"; Underwood, "Twenty-Sixth Regiment": 330–331; *NCT* 7: 456; *HTECW:* 571.

23. *DAB* 10: 120–129; *EOC* 2: 916–919; Warner, *Generals in Gray:* 179–181.

24. Albright to Dixon, 19 June 1862, Albright Papers, GHM; Underwood, "Twenty-Sixth Regiment" 7: 417.

25. *NCT* 7: 417; *OR* I, 9 (2): 791–793; Regimental History, Adams Papers, NCDAH; *EOC* 2: 799; Gus Jarratt to mother, 24 Jul 1862, Jarratt-Puryear Papers, DU.

26. *OR,* I, 9 (2): 793–795; HKB to mother, 14 Jul 1862, Burgwyn Family Papers, SHC.

27. Underwood, "Twenty-Sixth Regiment": 334; Lineback, "Civil War Diary"; HKB to mother, 14 Jul 1862, Burgwyn Family Papers, SHC.

28. *OR,* I, 9 (2): 795; HKB to mother, 14 Jul 1862, Burgwyn Family Papers, SHC; Z.B. Vance to W.L. Scott, 25 Jul 1862, William Lafayette Scott Papers, DU; Albright to Dixon, 6 Jul 1862, Albright Papers, GHM; I.A. Jarratt to mother, 24 Jul 1862, Jarratt-Puryear Papers, DU.

29. HKB to mother, 14 Jul 1862, Burgwyn Family Papers, SHC; Regimental History, Adams Papers, NCDAH; I.A. Jarratt to mother, 24 Jul 1862, Jarratt-Puryear Papers, DU.

30. HKB to mother, 14 Jul 1862, Burgwyn Family Papers, SHC; Albright to Dixon, 6 Jul 1862, Albright Papers, GHM.

31. HKB to mother, 14 Jul 1862, Burgwyn Family Papers, SHC; *OR* I, 9 (2): 504–505; Underwood, "Twenty-Sixth Regiment": 333–334; Vance to Scott, 25 Jul 1862, Scott Papers, DU; I.A. Jarratt to mother, 24 Jul 1862, Jarratt-Puryear Papers, DU.

32. Lineback, "Civil War Diary"; Albright to Dixon, 6 Jul 1862, Albright Papers, GHM; HKB to mother, 14 Jul 1862, Burgwyn Family Papers, SHC; Untitled Article, *Wadesboro (N.C.) Argus,* 10 Jul 1862; I.A. Jarratt to mother, 24 Jul 1862, Jarratt-Puryear Papers, DU.

33. *OR* I, 9 (2): 504–505; *NCT* 7: 457; Vance to Scott, 25 Jul 1862; Scott Papers, DU; Albright to Dixon, 6 Jul 1862, Albright Papers, GHM; Lineback, "Civil War Diary."

34. Underwood, "Twenty-Sixth Regiment": 333; HKB to mother, 14 Jul 1862, Burgwyn Family Papers, SHC.

35. *North Carolina Civil War Documentary:* 312–313; *EOC* 4: 1650; *DNCB* 6: 86; Vance to Scott, 25 Jul 1862, Scott Papers, DU; Lineback, "Civil War Diary."

36. Davis, *Boy Colonel:* 185–189; Underwood, "Twenty-Sixth Regiment": 335; Lineback, "Civil War Diary."

37. Davis, *Boy Colonel:*185–189; Joseph J. Young to HKB, 22 Aug 1862, and JTJ to HKB, 21 Aug 1862, Burgwyn Family Papers, SHC.

38. Davis, *Boy Colonel:* 185–189.

39. Underwood, "Twenty-Sixth Regiment": 334–335; Davis, *Boy Colonel:* 188–189; "Setser Letters" 2: 24.

40. Wilson, "James J. Pettigrew": 13–17; *DAB* 7: 516.

41. Wilson, *Carolina Cavalier:* 41–44, 98–106, 109–114; *Mary Chestnut's Civil War:* 366–367.

42. Wilson, "James J. Pettigrew":15–18, 135; *DNCB* 5: 77–79; F.W. Pickens to W.S. Pettigrew, 18 May 1864, Samuel Wylie Crawford Papers, LOC.

43. *NCT* 7: 457; "Setser Letters" 2: 29; Davis, *Boy Colonel:* 197; "A Bandsman's Letters to Home from the War," *Moravian Music Journal,* 36:1; Lineback, "Civil War Diary."

44. Davis, *Boy Colonel:* 196; *NCT* 7: 506; JRL to W.H.S. Burgwyn, 5 May 1900, W.H.S. Burgwyn Papers, NCDAH; Unpublished manuscript in John R. Lane Papers, SHC.

45. *NCT* 7: 457–459; *OR* I, 18: 192–194; I.A. Jarratt to mother, 17 Mar 1863, Jarratt-Puryear Papers, DU.

46. Underwood, "Twenty-Sixth Regiment": 340–341; *NCT* 7: 459; JTJ to father, 21 Apr 1863, Edmund W. Jones Papers, SHC; HKB to father, 21 Apr 1863, Burgwyn Family Papers, SHC; "Setser Letters" 3: 11–12; Albright to sister, 21 Nov 1862, Albright Papers, GHM; I.A. Jarratt to father, 26 Apr 1863, Jarratt-Puryear Papers, DU.

47. HKB to father, 21 Apr 1863, HKB to N.C. Hughes, 26 Apr 1863, HKB to mother, 23 Apr 1863, HKB to father, 6 Apr 1863, Burgwyn Family Papers, SHC.

48. HKB Journal, 1 May 1863, Burgwyn Family Papers, SHC; HKB to mother, 30 Apr 1863, Burgwyn Family Papers, SHC.

CHAPTER THREE
We Are on Our Way

1. Lineback, "Civil War Diary"; Regimental History, Adams Papers, NCDAH; "A Trip That Didn't Pay," Thomas Perrett Papers, NCDAH.

2. Lineback, "Civil War Diary."

3. HKB to mother, 28 May 1863, Burgwyn Family Papers, SHC; *NCT* 7: 459; Underwood, "Twenty-Sixth Regiment": 407.

4. *Gettysburg Nobody Knows:* 4–11; Gordon, *Reminiscences:* 137–142; *EOC* 2: 916–919.

5. Robertson, *Stonewall Jackson:* 701; *HTECW:* 126–129.

6. *Fremantle Diary:* 197.

7. Gordon, *Reminiscences:* 137–142; *HTECW:* 126–129.

8. "General Lee Decides to Take the Offensive," *The Blue and the Gray:* 591–592.

9. Coddington, *Gettysburg Campaign:* 8–11; Foote, *Civil War* 2: 442–443.

10. Coddington, *Gettysburg Campaign:* 8–11; Gordon, *Reminiscences:* 137–142.

11. Freeman, *Lee's Lieutenants,* 3: 44–45; Coddington, Gettysburg Campaign: 244–250; *Gettysburg Nobody Knows:* 4–5.

12. Foote, *Civil War* 2: 434–435; Coddington, *Gettysburg Campaign:* 6–18.

13. HKB to father, 21 May 1863, Burgwyn Family Papers, SHC.

14. Lafayette McLaws, "Gettysburg," *SHSP* 7: 64–65.

15. Lineback, "Civil War Diary"; Hall, *Johnny Reb Band:* 30; *NCT* 7: 459; *OR* I, 26 (3):1061; *EOC* 2: 769; *HTECW:* 358–359; Hassler, *Crisis at the Crossroads:* 10.

16. Lineback Journal, 15 Jun 1863, Julius Lineback Papers, SHC; Coddington, *Gettysburg Campaign:* 80–81; HKB to father, 13 Jun 1863, and HKB to mother, 14 Jun 1863, Burgwyn Family Papers, SHC.

17. Lineback Journal, 15 Jun 1863, Julius Lineback Papers, SHC; HKB to father, 13 Jun 1863, and HKB to mother, 14 Jun 1863, Burgwyn Family Papers, SHC.

18. Coddington, *Gettysburg Campaign:* 80–81; Toney, "Opening Moves": 18.

19. Lineback, "Civil War Diary"; HKB to father, 13 Jun 1863, Burgwyn Family Papers, SHC.

20. Lineback, "Civil War Diary"; "A Trip That Didn't Pay," Thomas Perrett Papers, NCDAH.

21. McLaws, "Gettysburg"; *SHSP:* 64–65; Hunt, "First Day at Gettysburg": 257–259, 265; Lineback, "Civil War Diary."

22. Worsham, *One of Jackson's Foot Cavalry:* 155; *Fremantle Diary:* 180, 216; Hoke, *Great Invasion:* 208.

23. *Fremantle Diary:* 180, 205, 216; Tucker, "North Carolina in the Gettysburg Campaign," *NCHR:* 198–199; "James Wright Letters" 1: 69.

24. *Fremantle Diary:* 205; James Bradshaw to wife, 18 Jun 1863, Samuel S. Biddle Papers, DU; Welch, *Confederate Surgeon's Letters:* 39–40; "James Wright Letters" 1: 68.

25. "Address by Lane"; Lineback, "Civil War Diary"; Tucker, "North Carolina in the Gettysburg Campaign": 198–199, 211; HKB Journal, 5 Jun 1863, Burgwyn Family Papers, SHC.

26. Rose, *Colours of the Gray:* 31, 38; HKB to father, 14 May 1863, Burgwyn Family Letters, SHC.

27. Tucker, "North Carolina at Gettysburg": 211; "Address by Lane"; Underwood, "Twenty-Sixth Regiment": 401; "James Wright Letters" 1: 68–69; JRL to W.H.S. Burgwyn, 14 May 1900, W.H. S. Burgwyn Papers, NCDAH.

28. "Address by Lane"; Underwood, "Twenty-Sixth Regiment": 401; "James Wright Letters" 1: 68–69.

29. "Jefferson Mansfield Papers" 2: 6, 12; Bradshaw to wife, 18 Jun 1863, Samuel S. Biddle Papers, SHC.

30. HKB to mother, 17 Jun 1863, HKB to father, 21 and 31 May 1863, Burgwyn Family Papers, SHC.

31. HKB to father, 21 and 31 May 1863 and HKB to mother, 5 and 13 Jun 1863, Burgwyn Family Papers, SHC; Davis, *Boy Colonel:* 270–271.

32. HKB to mother, 13 Jun 1863, Burgwyn Family Papers, SHC.

CHAPTER FOUR
"May the Good Lord Take Care of the Pore Soldiers"

1. JTJ to father, 11 Feb. 1861, Edmund Jones Papers, SHC.

2. *Ibid.*

3. Family Profile, Edmund Jones Papers, SHC; "Explanation of Mallett Family Names," Charles Mallett Papers, SHC; Hickerson, *Happy Valley:* 132.

4. Underwood, "Twenty-Sixth Regiment": 410; JTJ to father, 8 May 1861, 31 Aug 1861, Edmund Jones Papers, SHC; *NCT* 7: 573.

5. McGee, "Twenty-Sixth North Carolina": 43; *NCT* 7: 580–581; JTJ to father, 21 Apr 1863, Edmund Jones Papers, SHC; Hickerson, *Happy Valley:* 132.

6. Maria Spear to E.W. Jones, 6 Jun 1861, and to JTJ, 20 Mar 1862, Edmund Jones Papers, SHC; Underwood, "Twenty-Sixth Regiment": 410.

7. JTJ to father, 8 May 1861, 31 Aug 1861, 21 Apr 1863, Edmund Jones Papers, SHC.

8. HKB to mother, 17 Jun 1863, Burgwyn Family Papers, SHC; Bernard, "Gettysburg Campaign"; J. Bradshaw to wife, 18 Jun 1863, Samuel S. Biddle Papers DU; Lineback, "Civil War Diary."

9. Bernard, "Gettysburg Campaign"; *Life for the Confederacy,* 151; *Make Me a Map:* 153; Bush, "From 1861 to 1865"; J. Bradshaw to wife, 18 Jun 1863, Samuel Biddle Papers, DU.

10. "Almanac of 1863," Lyman C. Holdford Diary, Lyman C. Holdford Papers, LOC; Lineback, "Civil War Diary"; Bush, "From 1861 to 1865."

11. Lineback Journal, 17 Jun 1863, Julius Lineback Papers, SHC; Lineback, "Civil War Diary"; Bush, "As I Remember."

12. *OR Atlas,* plate 100:1; J. Bradshaw to wife, 18 June 1863, Samuel S. Biddle Papers, DU; Bernard, "Gettysburg Campaign"; HKB to mother, 17 Jun 1863, Burgwyn Family Papers, SHC.

13. Lineback, "Civil War Diary"; Bush, "From 1861 to 1865"; Bernard, "Gettysburg Campaign"; Jesse L. Henry to "Bet," 20 Jun 1863, Jesse L. Henry Papers, DU.

14. "Trip That Didn't Pay," Thomas Perrett Papers, NCDAH; Bush, "From 1861 to 1865"; Lineback, "Civil War Diary"; Lineback Journal, 19 Jun 1863, Julius Lineback Papers, SHC.

15. *OR Atlas*, plate 100:1; Bernard, "Gettysburg Campaign; Lineback, "Civil War Diary"; Welch, *Confederate Surgeon's Letters:* 55; Hale, *Four Valiant Years:* 268.

16. Worsham, *One of Jackson's Foot Cavalry:* 150–155; Bush, "From 1861 to 1865"; *NCT* 7: 589; J. Henry to "Bet," 20 Jun 1863, Jesse L. Henry Papers, DU.

17. *OR Atlas,* plate 100:1; H. Albright to T. Dixon, 23 Jun 1863, GHM; Lineback, "Civil War Diary."

18. Lineback, "Civil War Diary"; Lineback Journal, 21 Jun 1863, Lineback Papers, SHC; Bush, "As I Remember"; H. Albright to T. Dixon, 23 Jun 1863, Albright Papers, GHM.

19. Lineback, "Civil War Diary"; Lineback Journal, 22 Jun 1863, Lineback Papers, SHC; Bush, "From 1861 to 1865,"

20. "Battle of Shepherdstown": 1; *Make Me a Map,* 153; Lineback, "Civil War Diary."

21. "A Trip That Didn't Pay," Thomas Perrett Papers, NCDAH; *Civil War Memoirs of Captain Seymour:* 64–67; Lineback, "Civil War Diary"; *Gettysburg Nobody Knows:* 8; Bernard, "Gettysburg Campaign."

22. Lineback, "Civil War Diary"; "A Trip That Didn't Pay," Thomas Perrett Papers, NCDAH.

23. *OR Atlas*, plate 85: 1; *Make Me a Map:* 154; " A Trip That Didn't Pay," Thomas Perrett Papers, NCDAH; Lineback, "Civil War Diary"; Lineback Journal, 25 Jun 1863, Julius Lineback Papers, SHC; Bernard, "Gettysburg Campaign."

24. *OR* I, 27 (3): 912, 942–943; Lineback, "Civil War Diary."

25. *OR* I, 27 (3): 912; Gordon, *Reminiscences:* 135–142; Hoke, *Great Invasion:* 177–178; *Gettysburg Nobody Knows:* 9; Julia Chase Diary, 23 Jun 1863, Julia Chase Papers, Handley Library; Mrs. Hugh Lee Diary, 25 June, 1863, Mrs. Hugh Lee collection, Handley Library; Bernard, "Gettysburg Campaign."

26. Lineback Journal, 26 Jun 1863, Julius Lineback Papers, SHC; Lineback, "Civil War Diary"; Bernard, "Gettysburg Campaign."

27. Lineback Journal, 26 Jun 1863, Julius Lineback Papers, SHC; Bernard, "Gettysburg Campaign."

28. Lineback Journal, 27 Jun 1863, Julius Lineback Papers, SHC; Bernard, "Gettysburg Campaign"; Loyd, "Second Louisiana": 417; Hunt, "First Day at Gettysburg": 595–596.

29. "A Rebel Letter," Newspaper File, Edward McPherson Papers, LOC; J. Bradshaw to wife, 18 Jun 1863, Samuel S. Biddle Papers, DU; Hunt, "First Day at Gettysburg": 595; Gordon, *Reminiscences:* 137.

30. *Fremantle Diary:* 176; Ordnance Dept. Files, Adjutant General's Office Papers, NCDAH.

31. *Fremantle Diary:* 180, 185.

32. "A Trip That Didn't Pay," Thomas Perrett Papers, NCDAH; Hoke, *Great Invasion,* 208; *Fremantle Diary,* 223.

33. B.L. Ridley, "Ridley's Journal": 143.

34. Lineback, "Civil War Diary"; Hoke, *Great Invasion:* 176; *Fremantle Diary:* 196.

35. Patterson, *Yankee Rebel:* 111–112; William Peel Diary as quoted in Long, "General Orders No. 72": 14; Gordon, *Reminiscences:* 144–145; Hoke, *Great Invasion:* 176; "Pee Dee Wild Cats."

36. Gordon, *Reminiscences:* 144–145.

37. Strikeleather, "Recollections": 17; Blackford, *War Years With Jeb Stuart:* 223; *Make Me a Map,* 155; Worsham, *Jackson's Foot Cavalry:* 150.

38. Bernard, "Gettysburg Campaign"; "A Trip That Didn't Pay," Thomas Perrett Papers, NCDAH.

39. *Make Me a Map,* 155; Bernard, "Gettysburg Campaign"; *Fremantle Diary:* 191; "Rebel Letter," Newspaper File, Edward McPherson Papers, LOC; Strikeleather, "Recollections": 17.

40. Hunt, "First Day at Gettysburg": 595; Bernard, "Gettysburg Campaign."

41. "Rebel Letter," Newspaper File, Edward McPherson Papers, LOC; Gordon, *Reminiscences:* 143; Bernard, "Gettysburg Campaign."

42. *OR* I, 27 (3): 243; Loyd, "Second Louisiana": 417; Hunt, "First Day at Gettysburg": 595; *Fremantle Diary:* 186; "Rebel Letter," Newspaper File, Edward McPherson Papers, LOC.

43. Welch, *Confederate Surgeon's Letters:* 58; *Fremantle Diary:* 191; "Rebel Letter," Newspaper File, Edward McPherson Papers, LOC.

44. Davis, *Boy Colonel:* 258, 336–338; "Kincian," *Oxford English Dictionary;* Joseph J. Young to Henry Burgwyn Sr., 11 Jul 1863, Burgwyn Family Papers, SHC.

45. Lineback, "Civil War Diary"; Lineback Journal, 27 Jun 1863, Julius Lineback Papers, SHC; Bernard, "Gettysburg Campaign."

46. Lineback Journal, 27–29 Jun 1863, Julius Lineback Papers, SHC; *Make Me a Map:* 155; Hoke, *Great Invasion:* 184; *Gettysburg Nobody Knows:* 146; *OR Atlas,* plate 85: 1.

CHAPTER FIVE

Summer Is Ended

1. Lineback, "Civil War Diary"; Regimental History, Adams Papers, NCDAH; "A Trip That Didn't Pay," Thomas Perrett Papers, NCDAH; *NCT* 7: 464.

2. Lineback, "Civil War Diary"; Underwood, "Twenty-Sixth Regiment": 407.

3. Lineback, "Civil War Diary"; Betts, "Chaplain Service": 611; Jeremiah 8:20; *NCT* 7: 459; Underwood, "Twenty-Sixth Regiment": 407.

4. HKB to mother, 18 May and 28 May 1863, Burgwyn Family Papers, SHC; J.J. Young to HKB Sr., 31 Jul 1863, W.H.S. Burgwyn Papers, NCDAH; "Reflections of Judge Burgwyn," Burgwyn Family Papers, SHC; Davis, *Boy Colonel:* 247–248.

5. T.P. Devereux to sister, 30 Sep 1864, Thomas P. Devereux Papers, NCDAH; Eighth Census of the United States, 1860: Wake County, N.C., U.S. Census Department, NA; *Death Notices:* 78–79; *Journal of a Secesh Lady,* xxvii, 711, 739; Davis, *Boy Colonel:* 247–248, 382; Oliver, *Blockade Running by North Carolina:* 1–2; Obituary of Annie Lane Devereux, "Clippings 1884-1922," Devereux Family Papers, DU; Kenneth J. Zorgy to William R. Erwin Jr., Aug 1996, William Erwin Jr. Files, DU; John Devereux Jr. to Nell Devereux, 5 Jun 1862, "Correspondence 1859–1864," Devereux Family Papers, DU.

6. *Journal of a Secesh Lady:* 33; Obituary of Annie Lane Devereux, "Clippings 1884–1922," Devereux Family Papers, DU; Davis, *Boy Colonel:* 247–248, 382; Annie Lane Devereux Composition Book, Devereux Family Papers, DU.

7. Obituary of Annie Lane Devereux, Devereux Family Papers, DU; K.J. Zorgy to W. R. Erwin Jr., Aug 1996, William Erwin Jr. Files, DU; David S. Libbey to "Dear May," David S. Libbey Papers, DU.

8. Davis, *Boy Colonel:* 248; "Recipes—Mrs. J. Devereux": Obituary of Annie Lane Devereux, Devereux Family Papers, DU.

9. HKB to father, 22 Mar 1863, and HKB to mother, 23 Mar 1863, Burgwyn Family Papers, SHC; Davis, *Boy Colonel:* 247–248.

10. Lineback, "Civil War Diary."

11. Lineback Journal, 29 Jun 1863, Julius Lineback Papers, SHC; *Memoirs of Henry Heth:* 173.

12. Lineback, "Civil War Diary"; Hoke, *Great Invasion:* 169; Coddington, *Gettysburg Campaign:* 244–250; *First Day at Gettysburg:* 41; Robertson, *General A.P. Hill:* 204; *HTECW:* 307–308; *Gettysburg Nobody Knows:* 110–111; Gorham, *Life of Edwin M. Stanton* 2: 99.

13. *Bachelder Papers 2:* 926–927; *First Day at Gettysburg:* 41–42; Fulton, "Fifth Alabama at Gettysburg": 379; *Make Me a Map:* 156; Hunt, "First Day at Gettysburg": 267–268; *Gettysburg Nobody Knows:* 110–111.

14. Lineback Journal, 29 June 1863, Julius Lineback Papers, SHC; Welch, *Confederate Surgeon's Letters:* 61; Miller, "Perrin's Brigade": 22; *HTECW:* 232, 718; "Caledonia Furnace."

15. *OR Atlas,* plate 85:1; Lineback Journal, 29 Jun 1863, Julius Lineback Papers, SHC; Welch, *Confederate Surgeon's Letters:* 61; *Fremantle Diary:* 202.

16. James D. Moore Service Record, Compiled Service Records of the 26th N.C. Infantry, NA; Moore, *James Daniel Moore:* 9–10, 44–45, 48; *NCT 7:* 543.

17. Eighth Census of the United States, 1860: Caldwell County, N.C., U.S. Census Department, NA; Moore, *James Daniel Moore:* 44–45, 48; *Heritage of Caldwell County:* 195; Alexander, *Here Will I Dwell:* 126–127; Confederate Gravestone Records 1: 118, NCDAH.

18. Van Noppen and Van Noppen, *Western North Carolina:* 3–7; Moore, *James Daniel Moore:* 44; Oral history, Charles L. Gragg, Globe, N.C., Private Collection of Rod Gragg; *NCT 7:* 543.

19. Moore, *James Daniel Moore:* 44–48; James D. Moore Service Record, Compiled Service Records of the 26th N.C. Infantry, NA; *NCT 7:* 543.

20. James D. Moore Service Record, Compiled Service Records of the 26th N.C. Infantry, NA.

21. Lineback Journal, 29 June 1863, Julius Lineback Papers, SHC; W.S. Christian Memoir, John W. Daniels Papers, University of Virginia; *Fremantle Diary:* 201–202; Meredith, "First Day at Gettysburg": 183; Young, "Pettigrew's Brigade": 114–116.

22. Lineback Journal, 30 Jun 1863, Julius Lineback Papers, SHC; Coddington, *Gettysburg Campaign:* 263–264, 683; *OR* I, 27 (2):637; *Gettysburg Nobody Knows:* 58; Underwood, "Twenty-Sixth North Carolina": 342; Katcher, *Army of Robert E. Lee:* 221, 293; Davis, *Boy Colonel:* 155; Regimental History, James T. Adams Papers, NCDAH; Muster Rolls of the 26th N.C., 30 Jun 1863, NCDAH.

23. Lineback Journal, 30 Jun 1863, Julius Lineback Papers, SHC; *OR Atlas,* plate 85: 1; Wilson, *Carolina Cavalier:* 91; Muster Rolls of the 26th N.C., Company B, NCDAH; W.S. Christian Memoir, John W. Daniels Papers, University of Virginia; Meredith, "First Day at Gettysburg": 188; Young, "Pettigrew's Brigade": 114.

24. Lineback Journal, 30 Jun 1863, Julius Lineback Papers, SHC; Beveridge, "First Gun at Gettysburg": 172–173; Wilson, *Carolina Cavalier:* 191–192; Young, "Pettigrew's Brigade": 114–116.

25. "Battle 42 Years Ago," *Gettysburg Compiler,* 5 Jul 1905; John O'Neal Memoir, Civilian Accounts File, Gettysburg National Military Park.

26. Coddington, *Gettysburg Campaign:* 263–264, 683; John O'Neal Memoir, Civilian Accounts File, Gettysburg National Military Park.

27. W.S. Christian Memoir, John W. Daniels Papers, Alderman Library, University of Virginia; Coddington, *Gettysburg Campaign:* 263–264, 683; Morrison, "Memoirs of Henry Heth": 173; Young, "Pettigrew's Brigade": 116.

28. Robertson, *General A.P. Hill:* 11, 205; *EOC 2:* 770–771; Warner, *Generals in Gray:* 134–135; Robertson, *Stonewall Jackson:* 463, 519.

29. Young, "Pettigrew's Brigade": 114–115; *Memoirs of Henry Heth*: 173; Robertson, *A.P. Hill*: 205–206; *First Day at Gettysburg:* 42; Coddington, *Gettysburg Campaign:* 264; "Brilliant War Record of Louis G. Young," Robert N. Gourdin Papers, DU.

30. Robertson, *A.P. Hill*: 205–206; Coddington, *Gettysburg Campaign:* 264; "Letter From Major General Henry Heth": 157.

31. Young, "Pettigrew's Brigade": 117; Coddington, *Gettysburg Campaign:* 264.

32. "Address by Lane"; Underwood, "Twenty-Sixth Regiment": 342; "A Trip That Didn't Pay," Thomas Perrett Papers, NCDAH; Regimental History, James T. Adams Papers, NCDAH.

33. "Address by Lane"; Lineback Journal, 30 Jun 1863, Julius Lineback Papers, SHC; JRL to W.H.S. Burgwyn, 14 May 1900, W.H.S. Burgwyn Papers, NCDAH; Almanac for 1863, Lyman C. Holdford Papers, LOC; Elmore, "Torrid Heat and Blinding Rain": 10–13.

34. Underwood, "Twenty-Sixth Regiment": 333; "Address by Lane."

35. Almanac for 1863, Lyman C. Holdford Papers, LOC; Elmore, "Torrid Heat and Blinding Rain": 10–13; Lineback Journal, 1 Jul 1863, Julius Lineback Papers, SHC; *OR* I, 27 (2): 607, 649; Robertson, *A.P. Hill*: 207.

36. Regimental History, James T. Adams Papers, NCDAH; Lineback Journal, 1 Jul 1863, Julius Lineback Papers, SHC; Busey and Martin, Regimental Strengths and Losses: 174; Burgwyn, "Unparalleled Loss of Company F": 200. Troop strength of the 26th North Carolina varies, according to sources, from 800 to more than 900. The number of troops from the regiment engaged in battle on July 1, 1863, is generally accepted to have been 800. For a selection of sources on troop strength, see Busey and Martin, *Regimental Strengths and Losses at Gettysburg:* 174.

37. J.J. Young to HKB, 3 Jul 1863, 11 Jul 1863, 31 Jul 1863, Burgwyn Family Papers, SHC; Elmore, "Torrid Heat and Blinding Rain": 10–13; Dorsett, "Fourteenth Color-Bearer": 5; Lineback Journal, 1 Jul 1863, Julius Lineback Papers, SHC.

38. *OR Atlas,* plate 85:1; *OR* I, 27 (1): 155; Nolan, "Paper Trail of the Iron Brigade": 43; Clemmons, "Black Hats Off": 50–51; Dyer, *Compendium* 3: 1291; Nolan, *Iron Brigade:* 232; "Twenty-Fourth Regiment": 438–439.

39. Nolan, *Iron Brigade:* 232–233; "Twenty-Fourth Regiment": 438–441; Smith, *Twenty-Fourth Michigan:* 1–3, 40–41, 111–112; Clemmons, "Black Hats Off": 50–51; Nolan, "Paper Trail of the Iron Brigade": 43.

40. Nolan, *Iron Brigade:* 232–233; Smith, *Twenty-Fourth Michigan:* 115; "Twenty-Fourth Regiment": 449.

41. Buell, *The Cannoneer:* 60; J.E. Ryder to father, 24 Jun 1863, Ryder Family Papers, Bentley Historical Library, University of Michigan; Nolan, *Iron Brigade:* 232–233.

42. Hassler, *Crisis at the Crossroads:* 19–20; Coddington, *Gettysburg Campaign:* 238–239.

43. *OR Atlas,* plate 95:1; Hassler, *Crisis at the Crossroads:* 21–24; Balch, *Battle of Gettysburg:* 33–37; Coddington, *Gettysburg Campaign:* 265; Love, *Wisconsin in the War:* 405; Gross, *Battle-Field of Gettysburg:* 20–21.

44. Nolan, *Iron Brigade:* 233–234; 357; *OR* I, 27 (1): 155, 265, 273; Felton, "Iron Brigade Battery": 57; Buell, *The Cannoneer:* 63–64.

45. *OR* I, 27 (2): 67, 637; Coddington, *Gettysburg Campaign:* 266–267; *OR* I, 27 (1): 934–935; *Memories of Henry Heth:* 173–174; Robertson, *A.P. Hill:* 206–207.

46. Nolan, *Iron Brigade:* 235–236; Coddington, *Gettysburg Campaign:* 266–267; *HTECW:* 625–626; *OR* I, 27 (1):265–267.

47. *OR* I, 27 (2): 637; Robertson, *A.P. Hill:* 207–208; Coddington, *Gettysburg Campaign:* 266–268; Hassler, *Crisis at the Crossroads:* 52.

48. Nolan, *Iron Brigade:* 236–237; *OR* I, 27 (1): 281–282; Quiner, *Military History of Wisconsin:* 459; Hassler, *Crisis at the Crossroads:* 51.

49. *OR* I, 27 (1): 244–245, 265–268; Nolan, *Iron Brigade:* 237–238; Hassler, *Crisis at the Crossroads:* 53.

50. *OR* I, 27 (1): 288–289; Hassler, *Crisis at the Crossroads:* 52–53; Nolan, *Iron Brigade:* 238–239; Robertson, *A.P. Hill:* 209; *OR* I, 27(2): 637–638.

51. Julius Lineback Journal, 1 July 1863, Julius Lineback Papers, SHC; Warren, *Map of Gettysburg; OR Atlas,* plate 95:1; *Irishman in the Iron Brigade:* 93; Miller, "Perrin's Brigade": 22; Taylor, "Col. James Keith Marshall": 84; Frassanito, *Early Photography at Gettysburg:* 57; Beveridge, "First Gun at Gettysburg": 171–173.

52. *OR Atlas,* plate 95:1; Caison, "Southern Soldiers": 159; Underwood, "Twenty-Sixth Regiment": 343; Miller, "Perrin's Brigade": 22; *OR* I, 27(2):643.

53. Underwood, "Twenty-Sixth Regiment": 343; *OR* I, 27 (1): 642; *NCT* 7: 576; Caison, "Southern Soldiers": 159.

54. Underwood, "Twenty-Sixth North Regiment": 343; *OR* I, 27 (2):642–643; Miller, "Perrin's Brigade": 12; Caison, "Southern Soldiers": 159.

55. *OR Atlas,* 95:1; Regimental History, James T. Adams Papers, NCDAH; Underwood, "Twenty-Sixth North Regiment": 350; Hassler, *Crisis at the Crossroads:* 53.

56. *OR* I, 27 (2): 637, 649, 656, 674–675; Freeman, *Lee's Lieutenants* 3:79; Robertson, *A.P. Hill:* 206–209.

57. Underwood, "Twenty-Sixth Regiment": 368–369; Regimental History, James T. Adams Papers, NCDAH; Hood, "26th Regiment."

58. *OR* I, 27 (2): 642-643; "Address by Lane"; Underwood, "Twenty-Sixth Regiment": 350.

59. *OR* I, 27 (2): 638–639, 638–649, 642–643; Young, "Pettigrew's Brigade": 119; Hadden, "The Deadly Embrace": 23; Underwood, "Bull's Eye at Gettysburg," W.H.S. Burgwyn Papers, NCDAH.

Chapter Six

Like Wheat Before the Sickle

1. "Setser Letters"1: 29, 33 and 2: 26-28; Eighth Census of the United States, 1860:Caldwell County, N.C., U.S. Census Department, NA; W.E. Setser Service Record, Compiled Service Records of the 26th North Carolina, NA; Confederate Gravestone Records, 12: 5, NCDAH.

2. "Address by Lane"; Burgwyn, "Unparalleled Loss of Company F": 201; Eighth Census of the United States, 1860: Caldwell County and Chatham County, N.C., U.S. Census Department, NA; Tuttle, "Company F": 109; *NCT* 7: 465, 533-548,

555, 572, 580; Underwood, "Twenty-Sixth Regiment": 421; Tuttle, "Thrilling and Awful Account": 312.

3. Kirkman papers, Private Collection of John Bass; *NCT* 7: 544, 595; Mast, *State Troops:* 185–187; "Pee Dee Wildcats."

4. *NCT* 7: 549, 557, 570, 591, 593-594; "A Trip That Didn't Pay," Thomas Perett Papers, NCDAH; Eighth Census of the United States, 1860: Caldwell County, N.C., U.S. Census Department, NA; "Albert Caison": 107.

5. "Pee Dee Wild Cats"; *NCT* 7: 479–480, 488–489, 493; Isaac Mattox Papers, Private Collection of Herman Starnes; Underwood, "Twenty-Sixth Regiment": 400–401.

6. Underwood, "Twenty-Sixth Regiment": 401; *NCT* 7: 479–480, 493, 533.

7. Moore, *James Daniel Moore:* 8–9; Frassanito, *Early Photography at Gettysburg:* 56–59; Gross, *Battle-Field of Gettysburg:* 21–23; Balch, *Battle of Gettysburg:* 32–33.

8. *OR* I, 27 (2): 643; Kathy G. Harrison, Unpublished Manuscript on McPherson Farm, McPherson Farm and Tract File, Gettysburg National Military Park Archives; Frassanito, *Early Photography at Gettysburg:* 56–59; Newspaper File, Edward McPherson Papers, LOC; Warren, *Map of Gettysburg;* Louis G. Young to W. Burgwyn, 22 Aug 1903, W.H.S. Burgwyn Papers, NCDAH.

9. Warren, *Map of Gettysburg;* Battlefield Photography Album, vol. 87, #4363, Adams County Historical Society; "Claims of John Herbst in the County of Adams, Oct. 21, 1868," Adams County Historical Society.

10. Martin, *Gettysburg July 1:* 197–198; Howard, *Autobiography of Oliver Otis Howard* 1: 413.

11. Dudley, "Sgt. Mjr. Blanchard at Gettysburg": 4; *OR* I, 27(1):155–156, 254, 267; Hassler, *Crisis at the Crossroads:* 50–51; Smith, *Iron Brigade:* 129; Underwood, "Twenty-Sixth Regiment": 346.

12. "Address by Lane": 2–3; Dawes, "Sixth Wisconsin at Gettysburg": 381; Dorsett, "Fourteenth Color-Bearer"; Wheeler, *Witness to Gettysburg:* 135; Regimental History, James T. Adams Papers, NCDAH.

13. Hood, "26th Regiment"; "Address by Lane": 2–3; Underwood, "Twenty-Sixth Regiment": 351, 368–369.

14. *OR* I, 27 (2): 552–553, 607; Young, "Pettigrew's Brigade": 118; Freeman, *Lee's Lieutenants* 3: 82–86; Hassler, *Crisis at the Crossroads:* 63.

15. *Fremantle Diary:* 203; Freeman, *Lee's Lieutenants* 3: 81-82; Longstreet, *From Manassas to Appomattox:* 357.

16. *OR* I, 27 (2): 607, 637; Robertson, *General A.P. Hill:* 209; Coddington, *Gettysburg Campaign:* 281–282.

17. *OR* I, 27 (2): 552–553, 607; Freeman, *Lee's Lieutenants* 3: 83–87; Warner, *Generals in Gray:* 263; Coddington, *Gettysburg Campaign:* 286, 289; *HTECW:* 640; Robertson, *General A.P. Hill:* 209–211.

18. *OR* I, 27 (2): 552–553, 607, 637; Robertson, *General A.P. Hill:* 211; "Letter From Major-General Heth": 158; Freeman, *Lee's Lieutenants* 3: 84–87.

19. "Address by Lane"; Underwood, "Bull's Eye at Gettysburg," W.H.S. Burgwyn Papers, NCDAH; "Fortieth Anniversary of Gettysburg"; "Foot Officer's Sword," Henry K. Burgwyn Jr. Collection, NCMOH; J.J. Young to "My Dear Sir," 31 Jul

1863, W.H.S. Burgwyn Papers, NCDAH; Casey, *Infantry Tactics* 2: 148–161; Stewart, *Pickett's Charge:* 87; Harrison and Busey, *Nothing but Glory:* 136.

20. "Address by Lane"; Casey, *Infantry Tactics* 2: 149–151; Rollins, *"Damned Red Flags:* 76–77, 81; Underwood, "Twenty-Sixth Regiment": 423; Coppee, *Field Manual for Battalion Drill:* 11, 105, 117.

21. Jefferson B. Mansfield file, Compiled Service Records of the 26th North Carolina Infantry, NA; *NCT* 7:527; "Letters of Jefferson Mansfield" 1:18–19, 22–23, 29–30; "Address by Lane": 3.

22. *OR* I, 27(1): 268; "Address by Lane"; *OR* I, 27 (2): 643; Hood, "26th Regiment"; Young, "Pettigrew's Brigade": 119; Emerson, "Most Famous Regiment": 352–353; Regimental History, James T. Adams Papers; NCDAH; *NCT* 7: 544; Warren, *Map of Gettysburg;* H.S. Huidekoper, *Bird's Eye View of the Battlefield of Gettysburg,* Edward McPherson Papers, LOC.

23. Hood, "26th Regiment"; Warren, *Map of Gettysburg;* "Address by Lane."

24. Dudley, "Sgt. Mjr. Blanchard": 4; *OR,* I, 27 (1): 155–156, 254, 267; Smith, *Iron Brigade:* 129; Underwood, "Twenty-Sixth Regiment": 346; Gaff, "Here Was Made Our Last Stand": 25–29.

25. Dyer, *Compendium of the War* 3: 1126–1127; Dudley, "Sgt Mjr. Blanchard at Gettysburg": 3–4; Gaff, "Here Was Made Our Last Stand": 25–29.

26. *OR* I, 27 (1): 268; Curtis, *History of the Twenty-Fourth Michigan:* 188; "To Chancellorsville with the Iron Brigade": 12–13; "Death of Gen. Morrow"; Boatner, *Civil War Dictionary:* 570.

27. "To Chancellorsville with the Iron Brigade": 17; *OR* I, 27 (1): 268; Smith, *Twenty-Fourth Michigan:* 128–129; Nolan, *Iron Brigade:* 242–243.

28. T.J. Cureton to JRL, 15 Jun 1890, John R. Lane Papers, SHC; "Address by Lane"; Hood, "26th Regiment"; Underwood, "Twenty-Sixth Regiment": 361; Coppee, *Field Manual for Battalion Drill:* 10–13; Gaff, "Here Was Made Our Last Stand": 29.

29. Caison, "Southern Soldiers": 159; Hood, "26th Regiment"; Dudley, "Sgt. Mjr. Blanchard": 3–4; "Jefferson Mansfield Letters"; *NCT* 7: 553; Emerson, "Most Famous Regiment": 352–353.

CHAPTER SEVEN

Covered with Glory

1. "Address by Lane"; "A Trip That Didn't Pay," Thomas Perrett Papers, NCDAH; Bush, "From 1861 to 1865"; Emerson, "Most Famous Regiment": 353; Dorsett, "Fourteenth Color-Bearer": 5.

2. Bush, "From 1861 to 1865"; T.J. Cureton to JRL, 15 Jun 1890, John R. Lane papers, SHC; Personal field observations at Willoughby Run, 1995–1999; "Setser Letters" 2: 14; *NCT* 7: 545, 513, 547; Louis T. Young to W.J. Baker, 10 Feb 1864, Francis Winston Papers, NCDAH; Emerson, "Most Famous Regiment": 353; Regimental History, James T. Adams Papers, NCDAH.

3. Dudley, "Sgt. Major Blanchard": 4; Bush, "From 1861 to 1865"; Dorsett, "Fourteenth Color-Bearer," 5; James D. Dorsett Service Records, Compiled Service Records of the 26th N.C., NA; *NCT* 7: 523; Hood, "26th Regiment."
4. Nolan, *Iron Brigade:* 245; R. Root to grandfather, 23 Aug 1863, Harrisburg Civil War Round Table Collection, USAMHI; "Address by Lane"; Hood, "26th Regiment."
5. Thorp, "Forty-Seventh Regiment": 84; Personal field observations at Gettysburg, 1995–1999; "Iron Brigade," *Bachelder Papers:* 142; Martin, *Gettysburg July 1:* 354–355; *NCT* 7: 547; *OR* I, 27 (1): 268; "Address by Lane."
6. Emerson, "Most Famous Regiment": 352–354; *NCT* 7:547, 555, 560; Underwood, "Twenty-Sixth Regiment": 401; Lane, "Address by Lane"; Caison, "Southern Soldiers": 159.
7. Martin, *Gettysburg July 1:* 354–355; Dudley, "Sgt Mjr. Blanchard": 3–4; Mash, Henry C. "The Nineteenth Indiana at Gettysburg," Robert L. Brake Collection, USAMHI; Gaff, "Here Was Made Our Last Stand": 25; Dunn, *Iron Men Iron Will:* 188–191.
8. *OR* I, 27 (1): 268; "Twenty-Fourth Regiment": 448; Louis G. Young to W.H.S. Burgwyn, 22 Aug 1903, W.H.S. Burgwyn Papers, NCDAH; Rosentreter, "Those Damned Black Hats": 29; "Report of Lt. Col. William W. Dudley": 941; Gaff, "Here Was Made Our Last Stand": 29–30; Curtis, *History of the Twenty-Fourth Michigan:* 88; Hadden, "Deadly Embrace": 28; Nolan, *Iron Brigade:* 243.
9. Young, "Pettigrew's Brigade": 117–120; Louis G. Young to W.H.S. Burgwyn, 22 Aug 1903, W.H.S. Burgwyn Papers, NCDAH.
10. Smith, *Twenty-Fourth Michigan:* 130; Louis G. Young to W.H.S. Burgwyn, 22 Aug 1903, W.H.S. Burgwyn Papers, NCDAH; R. Young to "My Dear Robert," 8 Jun 1864, Robert N. Gourdin Papers, DU; Bush, "From 1861 to 1865."
11. "Address by Lane"; Regimental History, James T. Adams Papers, NCDAH; Louis G. Young to W.H.S. Burgwyn, 22 Aug 1903, W.H.S. Burgwyn Papers, NCDAH.
12. Cullum, *Biographical Register of the U.S. Military Academy:* 746; W.W. McCreery Jr. to "The Honorable Secretary of War," 3 Mar 1855, Cadet Application Papers, 1805–1866, U.S. Military Academy; *Official Register of the U.S. Military Academy:* 13; W.W. McCreery Service Records, Compiled Service Records of Confederate Officers, NA; North Carolina Confederate Veteran Grave Locator, NCDAH: 343; W.W. McCreery Letterbook, Pocataligo Headquarters, 10 Jan–30 Apr 1861, South Caroliniana Library, University of South Carolina; L.C. Davison to "Dear Kittie," 27 Sep, Kate Mason Rowland Collection, Museum of the Confederacy.
13. Louis G. Young to W.H.S. Burgwyn, Aug 1903, W.H.S. Burgwyn Papers, NCDAH; Louis G. Young to W.J. Baker, 10 Feb 1864, Francis D. Winston Papers, NCDAH.
14. "Address by Lane"; "A Trip That Didn't Pay," Thomas Perrett Papers, NCDAH; *OR* I, 27 (2): 643; Young, "Pettigrew's Brigade":121; Underwood, "Twenty-Sixth Regiment": 358.
15. Louis G. Young to W.J. Baker, 10 Feb 1864, Louis G. Young Papers, NCDAH; *OR* I, 27 (2): 643; Personal field observation at Gettysburg, 1995–1999; Regimental History, James T. Adams Papers, NCDAH; "A Trip That Didn't Pay," Thomas Perrett Papers, NCDAH; J.J. Young to Henry Burgwyn Sr., 31 Jul 1863, W.H.S. Burgwyn Papers, NCDAH.

16. T.J. Cureton to JRL, 15 Jun 1890, John R. Lane Papers, NCDAH; "Address by Lane"; Olds, "Brave Carolinian": 245; *OR* I, 27 (2): 643; Emerson, "Most Famous Regiment": 354.

17. *OR* I, 27 (2): 643; Emerson, "Most Famous Regiment": 354; JRL to W.H.S. Burgwyn, 20 Oct 1900, W.H.S. Burgwyn Papers, NCDAH; *NCT* 7: 555.

18. Lineback Diary, 1 Jul 1863, Julius Lineback Papers, SHC; Hood, "26th Regiment"; Lineback, "Civil War Diary."

19. *OR* I, 27 (1): 268; "Twenty-Fourth Regiment": 444; Smith, *Twenty-Fourth Michigan:* 131–132; Nolan, *Iron Brigade:* 245; Dorsett, "Fourteenth Color-Bearer": 5. (In his official report, Colonel Morrow recorded defending three lines of battle on McPherson's Ridge; some observers believe the 24th Michigan established even more lines before withdrawing.)

20. "A Trip That Didn't Pay," Thomas Perrett Papers, NCDAH; Dorsett, "Fourteenth Color-Bearer"; Young, "Pettigrew's Brigade": 121; Louis G. Young to W.J. Baker, 10 Feb 1864, Francis D. Winston Papers, NCDAH; Moore, "Interesting Narrative."

21. Louis G. Young to W.J. Baker, 10 Feb 1864, Francis D. Winston Papers, NCDAH; *NCT* 7:481; *OR* I, 27 (1): 268; T.J. Cureton to "Dear Sir," John R. Lane Papers, SHC; "A Trip That Didn't Pay," Thomas Perrett Papers, NCDAH; Moore, "Interesting Narrative."

22. T. J. Cureton to "Dear Sir," 15 and 22 Jun 1890, John R. Lane Papers, SHC; *NCT* 7:481; Underwood, "Twenty-Sixth Regiment": 418.

23. "Address by Lane"; Regimental History, James T. Adams Papers, NCDAH; Emerson, "Most Famous Regiment": 354; L.C. Davison to "Dear Kittie," 27 Sep, Kate Mason Roland Papers, Museum of the Confederacy; George Wilcox to W.H.S. Burgwyn, 21 Jun 1900, W.H.S. Burgwyn Papers, NCDAH.

24. "Address by Lane"; T.J. Cureton to "Dear Sir," 15 Jun 1890, John R. Lane Papers, SHC; Regimental History, James T. Adams Papers, NCDAH; L.C. Davison to "Dear Kittie," 27 Sep, Kate Mason Roland Papers, Museum of the Confederacy; George Wilcox to W.H.S. Burgwyn, 21 Jun 1900, W.H.S. Burgwyn Papers, NCDAH.

25. "Address by Lane"; George Wilcox to W.H.S. Burgwyn, 21 Jun 1900, W.H.S. Burgwyn Papers, NCDAH; T.J. Cureton to "My Dear Sir," 15 Jun 1890, John R. Lane Papers, SHC; Joseph J. Young to "Col.," 11 Jul 1863, Burgwyn Family Papers, SHC; Regimental History, James T. Adams Papers, NCDAH; Moore, "Interesting Narrative"; "A Trip That Didn't Pay," Thomas Perrett Papers; NCDAH; Emerson, "Most Famous Regiment": 354. (Some accounts claim that Colonel Burgwyn was "caught in the folds of the flag" when he fell. However, Captain Joseph J. Young, who wrote to Burgwyn's father within days of the colonel's death, did not mention it. Neither did Lt. Col. Lane, Lt. Cureton or Lt. George Wilcox, who were within a few feet of Burgwyn when he was shot. In a letter to Burgwyn's brother in 1900, Wilcox praised Colonel Burgwyn but noted that some details reported about his death were not "literally true.")

26. George Wilcox to W.H.S. Burgwyn, 21 Jun 1900, W.H.S. Burgwyn Papers, NCDAH; "Address by Lane"; T.J. Cureton to "My Dear Sir," 15 Jun 1890, John R. Lane Papers, SHC; Olds, "Brave Carolinian": 245–246; *NCT* 7: 492, 524.

27. "Address by Lane"; Underwood, "Twenty-Sixth Regiment": 418; *NCT* 7: 589.

28. T.J. Cureton to "My Dear Sir," 15 Jun 1890, John R. Lane Papers, SHC; "Address by Lane": *NCT* 7: 573.

29. "Address by Lane"; T.J. Cureton to "My Dear Sir," 15 Jun 1890, John R. Lane Papers, SHC; Underwood, "Twenty-Sixth Regiment": 352–353; *OR* I, 27 (2): 643.

30. Underwood, "Twenty-Sixth Regiment": 409.

31. Gaff, "Here Was Made Our Last Stand": 30–31; Stevenson, *Indiana's Roll of Honor* 1: 376–377; Dunn, *Iron Men Iron Will:* 190–192.

32. Gaff, "Here Was Made Our Last Stand": 30–31; Marsh, "The Nineteenth Indiana," Robert L. Brake Collection, USAMHI; Stevenson, *Indiana's Roll of Honor:* 376–377; Dudley, "Sgt. Mjr. Blanchard": 3–4; Roswell L. Root to "Dear Grandfather," 23 Aug 1863, Harrisburg Civil War Round Table Collection, USAMHI; Nolan, *Iron Brigade:* 245; Dunn, *Iron Men Iron Will:*188–191.

33. *OR* I, 27 (2): 642; Martin, *Gettysburg July 1:* 358–362; Gaff, "Here Was Made Our Last Stand": 30–31; Nolan, *Iron Brigade:* 245.

34. *OR* I, 27 (1): 268–269; Smith, *Twenty-Fourth Michigan:* 132; Curtis, *Twenty-Fourth Michigan:* 162; Way, "From the 24th Regiment"; Roswell L. Root to "Dear Grandfather," 23 Aug 1863, Harrisburg Civil War Round Table Collection, USAMHI; "Twenty-Fourth Regiment": 448.

35. *OR* I, 27(1): 252, 268–269; Gaff, "Here Was Made Our Last Stand": 30–31; Martin, *Gettysburg July 1:* 362–364; "Record of Events," Company F, Compiled Service Records of the 24th Michigan Infantry, NA.

36. "Address by Lane"; Moore, "Interesting Narrative"; Burgwyn, "Unparalleled Loss of Company F": 201–203; *NCT* 7: 533, 537.

37. "Fortieth Anniversary of Gettysburg"; "Address by Lane"; Emerson, "Most Famous Regiment": 354.

38. "Address by Lane"; "Fortieth Anniversary of Gettysburg"; *OR* I, 27 (2): 643; T.J. Cureton to "My Dear Sir," 15 Jun 1890, John R. Lane Papers, SHC; Coddington, *Gettysburg Campaign:* 294; "Battle of Gettysburg, July 1, 1863": 903; Olds, "Brave Carolinian."

39. Nolan, *The Iron Brigade:* 247–249; "Extract From Letter of M.C. Barnes": 937; Thorp, "Forty-Seventh Regiment": 89–90; Hassler, *Crisis at the Crossroads:* 117–120; "Twenty-Fourth Regiment": 449; Curtis, *Twenty-Fourth Michigan:* 188.

40. Coddington, *Gettysburg Campaign:* 294–296; Martin, *Gettysburg July 1:* 448-450; Dawes, "With the Sixth Wisconsin": 381; *OR* I, 27 (2): 643.

CHAPTER EIGHT

The Sickening Horrors of War

1. Olds, "Brave Carolinian": 246.

2. W.M. Cheek to W.H.S. Burgwyn, 18 Apr 1906, W.H.S. Burgwyn Papers, NCDAH; Olds, "Brave Carolinian": 246.

3. W.M. Cheek to W.H.S. Burgwyn, 18 Apr 1906, W.H.S. Burgwyn Papers, NCDAH; Olds,"Brave Carolinian": 246.

4. George P. Collins to "H.K. Burgwyn, Esquire," 3 Jul 1863; Burgwyn Family Papers, SHC; Joseph J. Young to H.K. Burgwyn, 31 Jul 1863, W.H.S. Burgwyn Papers, NCDAH; T.J. Cureton to "Dear Sir," 22 Jun 1890, John R. Lane Papers, SHC; "Foot Officer's Sword," Henry K. Burgwyn Jr. Collection, NCMOH; Regimental History, James T. Adams Papers, NCDAH; W.M. Cheek to W.H.S. Burgwyn, 18 Apr 1890, W.H.S. Burgwyn Papers, SHC; Olds, "Brave Carolinian": 246.

5. *OR* I, 27 (2): 643; T.J. Cureton to "Dear Sir," 22 Jun 1890, John R. Lane Papers, SHC; 1863 Almanac, Holdford Diary, Lyman C. Holdford Papers, LOC; Elmore, "Torrid Heat and Blinding Rain": 10–11.

6. T.J. Cureton to "Dear Sir," 22 Jun 1890, John R. Lane Papers, SHC; Samuel Mickey Diary quoted in Hall, *Johnny Reb Band:* 48; Young, "Pettigrew's Brigade": 121.

7. Underwood, "Twenty-Sixth Regiment": 358–359; Tom Setser to cousin, 17 Jul 1863; "Setser Letters" 3: 14; Lineback, "Civil War Diary"; "Address by Lane."

8. JTJ to father, 20 Jun 1861, Edmund W. Jones Papers, SHC; R. Root to grandfather, 23 Aug 1863, Harrisburg Civil War Round Table Collection, USAMHI; Underwood, "Twenty-Sixth Regiment": 410–411; Joseph J. Young to W.H.S. Burgwyn, 31 Jul 1963, W.H.S. Burgwyn Papers, NCDAH.

9. *OR* I, 27 (2): 645; "Address by Lane"; Underwood, "Twenty-Sixth Regiment": 360; Emerson, "Most Famous Regiment": 354; Mast, "Tha Kill So Many of Us": 29; Hadden, "The Deadly Embrace": 32–33; Fox, *Regimental Losses:* 555–556. (Assistant Quartermaster Joseph Young and Lt. Col. Lane both reported 216 survivors from the July 1st assault. Civil War casualty authority William F. Fox calculated 212. The Army of Northern Virginia casualty return for the 26th N.C. [*OR* I, 27 (2): 344] lists 588 casualties—leaving 212 survivors—but lists these as the total casualties for Gettysburg and is thus inconclusive.)

10. *OR* I, 27 (2): 645; *NCT* 7:467, 481, 494, 506–507, 513, 519–520, 533, 548, 561–562, 573, 589; Regimental History, James T. Adams Papers, NCDAH; Norris, "Now Growing Old": 509; Burgwyn, "Unparalleled Loss of Company F": 202; Underwood, "Twenty-Sixth Regiment": 418; "Address by Lane."

11. *NCT* 7: 467, 481–482, 494, 506–507, 519–520, 533, 561–562, 572–574, 589; *OR* I, 27 (2): 645.

12. *OR* I, 27 (2): 344, 645; Fox, *Regimental Losses:* 555–556; Underwood, "Twenty-Sixth Regiment": 360–361; Emerson, "Most Famous Regiment": 354.

13. T.J. Cureton to "Dear Sir," 22 Jun 1890, John R. Lane Papers, SHC; Moore, "Interesting Narrative"; Tuttle, "Company F": 109; Moore, *James Daniel Moore:* 16; *NCT* 7: 537–558, 595, 536, 593–594, 547, 540, 493, 570, 488–489, 593, 591, 544; Underwood, "Twenty-Sixth Regiment": 400–401; Burgwyn, "Unparalleled Loss of Company F": 202–203; Henry C. Kirkman to "Dear Father," 6 Aug 1863, Kirkman Papers, Private Collection of John Bass.

14. Confederate Gravestone Records, N.C. Division of the United Daughters of the Confederacy, 12: 436, NCDAH; Hickerson, *Happy Valley:* 99, 132; JTJ to father, 17 Jul 1863, 17 Aug 1863, Edmund W. Jones Papers, SHC; *NCT* 7: 580–581.

15. *OR* I, 27 (1): 269; Nolan, *Iron Brigade:* 365–366; Rosentreter, "Damned Black Hats": 31; Gaff, "Here Was Made Our Last Stand": 30-31; "From the Twenty-Fourth," *Detroit Free Press*, 17 Jul 1863.

16. *OR* I, 27 (1): 643; Elmore, "Torrid Heat and Blinding Rain": 12–13; T.J. Cureton to "Dear Sir," 22 Jun 1890, John R. Lane Papers, SHC; Caison, "Southern Soldiers": 161.

17. J.J. Young to W.H.S. Burgwyn, 3, 11, and 31 Jul 1863, W.H.S. Burgwyn Papers, NCDAH; George P. Collins to Henry Burgwyn Sr., 3 Jul 1863, Burgwyn Family Papers, SHC.

18. George P. Collins to Henry Burgwyn Sr., 31 Jul 1863, Burgwyn Family Papers, SHC.

19. J.J. Young to Henry Burgwyn Sr., 3, 31 Jul 1863, W.H.S. Burgwyn Papers, NCDAH; George P. Collins to Henry Burgwyn Sr., 3 Jul 1863, Burgwyn Family Papers, SHC; Archie K. Davis to "Dear Ms. Georg," 15 Jun 1982, 26th N.C. File, Administrative Archives, Gettysburg National Military Park; Davis, *Boy Colonel:* 338; Underwood, "Twenty-Sixth Regiment": 408.

20. J.J. Young to Henry Burgwyn Sr., 11 Jul 1863, Burgwyn Family Papers, SHC.

21. "Setser Letters" 3:14; *NCT* 7: 545.

22. "A Trip That Didn't Pay," Thomas Perrett Papers, NCDAH.

23. Ibid.

24. Underwood, "Twenty-Sixth Regiment": 369; *DNCB* 4: 14.

25. T.J. Cureton to "Dear Sir," 22 Jun 1890, John R. Lane Papers, SHC; Lineback, "Civil War Diary"; Underwood, "Twenty-Sixth Regiment": 362; *NCT* 7: 464.

26. Lineback Journal, 2 Jul 1863, Julius Lineback Papers, SHC; Lineback, "Civil War Diary"; Hall, *A Johnny Reb Band:* 49–50; Leinbach, *Regiment Band:* 229, 234; *Fremantle Diary:* 208; T.J. Cureton to "Dear Sir," 22 Jun 1890, John R. Lane Papers, SHC.

27. *Memoirs of Henry Heth:* 175; Krick, *Lee's Colonels:* 243; *NCT* 7: 467, 481, 494, 506–507, 519, 533, 548, 561, 573, 589; *OR* I, 27 (2). 645; Burgwyn, "Unparalleled Loss of Company F": 201.

28. T.J. Cureton to "Dear Sir," 22 Jun 1890, John R. Lane Papers, SHC; Julia Chase Diary, 5 Jul 1863, Julia Chase Papers, Handley Library; *Irishman in the Iron Brigade:* 100.

29. Coddington, *Gettysburg Campaign:* 321–333; Warner, *Generals in Blue:* 202–203; Hunt, "First Day at Gettysburg": 283–284.

30. *OR* I, 27 (2): 308; Hunt, "First Day at Gettysburg": 284; Freeman, *Lee's Lieutenants* 3: 93–110; Robertson, *General A.P. Hill:* 213; Coddington, *Gettysburg Campaign:* 360–369; *First Day at Gettysburg:* 34–35.

31. Young, "Pettigrew's Brigade": 120–121.

32. Gibbon, "Council of War": 313–314; Warner, *Generals in Blue:* 345; Hoke, *The Great Invasion:* 352–353.

33. *OR* I, 27 (2): 308; Hoke, *The Great Invasion:* 305; Freeman, *Lee's Lieutenants* 3:144; Robertson, *General A.P. Hill:* 220; *Annals of the War:* 429.

34. *OR* I, 27 (2): 308; Freeman, *Lee's Lieutenants* 2: 144–148; Robertson, *General A.P. Hill:* 220; Coddington, *Gettysburg Campaign:* 454.

35. *OR* I, 27 (2): 643; T.J. Cureton to "Dear Sir," 22 Jun 1890, John R. Lane Papers, SHC; Almanac for 1863, Holdford Diary, Lyman C. Holdford Papers, LOC; "Record of Events," Compiled Service Records of the 24th Michigan, NA; "Lee's Army in Pennsylvania": 43–44; "Letter of Capt. Frank E. Moran": 776.

CHAPTER NINE

"All Were Willing to Die"

1. T.J. Cureton to "Dear Sir," 15 Jun 1890 and 22 Jun 1890, John R. Lane Papers, SHC; Elmore, "Torrid Heat and Blinding Rain": 14; Haines, *History of Co. F:* 39; *OR* I, 27 (2): 308.

2. T.J. Cureton to "Dear Sir," 22 Jun 1890, John R. Lane Papers, SHC; *NCT* 7: 481; Underwood, "Twenty-Sixth Regiment": 415–416..

3. T. J. Cureton to "Dear Sir," 22 Jun 1890, John R. Lane Papers, SHC; Warren, *Map of Gettysburg;* Huidekoper, *Bird's Eye View of the Battle of Gettysburg,* Edward McPherson Papers, LOC; Bachelder, *Map of Gettysburg Battlefield;* "Lee's Army in Pennsylvania": 44; Frassanito, *Early Photography at Gettysburg:* 232–234; "Letter of Capt. David Shields": 1068; Coddington, *Gettysburg Campaign:* 484–485; Rollins, *Pickett's Charge: Eyewitness Accounts:* 250.

4. JTJ to father, 17 Jul 1863, and D.M. Key to "Edmund Jones Esq.," 14 May 1864, Edmund W. Jones Papers, SHC; Underwood, "Twenty-Sixth Regiment": 410–411.

5. Southern Commanders and Staff Officers File, Robert L. Brake Collection, USAMHI; *OR* I, 27 (2): 283–290, 308–309, 607–608; Freeman, *Lee's Lieutenants* 3: 146–148; Katcher, *Army of Robert E. Lee:* 289–294; Coddington, *Gettysburg Campaign:* 462, 777.

6. *OR* I, 27 (2): 283–290, 607–608, 657–661; Louis G. Young to W.J. Baker, 10 Feb 1864, Francis Winston Papers, NCDAH; Young, "Pettigrew's Brigade": 123; Underwood, "Twenty-Sixth Regiment": 362–363; Freeman, *Lee's Lieutenants,* 3:146–148; Coddington, *Gettysburg Campaign:* 489–492; Robertson, *General A.P. Hill:* 220–221; Katcher, *Army of Robert E. Lee:* 289–294; Warner, *Generals in Gray:* 95, 233–234; *EOC* 4: 1621–1622; Reardon, *Pickett's Charge:* 7–8; Foote, *The Civil War* 2: 535–536.

7. *OR* I, 27 (2): 283–290; Young, "Pettigrew's Brigade": 133–135; Warner, *Generals in Gray:* 95, 233–234; Louis G. Young to W.J. Baker, 10 Feb 1864, Francis Winston Papers, NCDAH.

8. Caison, "Southern Soldiers": 160; *OR* I, 27 (1): 237; *OR* I, 27 (2): 643; Coddington, *Gettysburg Campaign:* 484–485; Frassanito, *Early Photography at Gettysburg:* 181.

9. Thompson, "A Scrap of Gettysburg": 101–102; Lineback Journal, 3 Jul 1863, Julius Lineback Papers, SHC; *Fremantle Diary:* 209–210; "From the Twenty-Fourth."

10. Rollins, *Pickett's Charge: Eyewitness Accounts:* 63; Martin, "Rawley Martin's Account": 184–194.

11. Rollins, *Pickett's Charge: Eyewitness Accounts:* 54; Underwood, "Twenty-Sixth Regiment": 362.

12. T.J. Cureton to "My Dear Sir," 22 Jun 1890, John R. Lane Papers, SHC; Taylor, "North Carolina in the Pickett-Pettigrew-Trimble Charge": 81; Caison, "Southern Soldiers": 160–161; Freeman, *Lee's Lieutenants* 3: 147; Bush, "From 1861 to 1865": Foote, *The Civil War* 2: 534–535.

13. Caison, "Southern "Soldiers": 160–161; Bush, "From 1861 to 1865"; Smith, *Complete Works of Robert Burns:* 227.

14. T.J. Cureton to "My Dear Sir," 22 June 1890, John R. Lane Papers, SHC; "Petti-grew's Old Brigade," Southern Commanders and Staff Officers File, Robert L. Brake Collection, USAMHI; Elmore, "Torrid Heat and Blinding Rain": 14; Thompson, "Scrap of Gettysburg": 101–102; Buell, *The Cannoneer:* 92; Browne, *Experiences in the Army:* 202–203.

15. Caison, "Southern Soldiers": 160; John T. Jones, "Pettigrew's Brigade at Gettys-burg": 133–135; *OR* I, 27 (2) 645; Foote, *The Civil War* 2: 536; Underwood, "Twenty-Sixth Regiment": 361.

16. Moore, "Interesting Narrative"; "Address by Lane"; "North Carolina at Gettys-burg"; Taylor, "North Carolina in the Pickett-Pettigrew-Trimble Charge": 86, 87; "Capt. Stephen Brewer": 5.

17. Regimental History, James T. Adams Papers, NCDAH; *NCT* 7: 531, 538, 599; Buell, *The Cannoneer:* 92; Brooks W. Gilmore to author, 10 Oct 1996, Rod Gragg collection; Thomas Cozart Service Record, Compiled Service Records of the 26th North Carolina, NA.

18. Shultz and Rollins, "Measuring Pickett's Charge": 114; Ashe, "Charge at Gettys-burg": 5–7; McFarland, Baxter, "Casualties of the Eleventh Mississippi": 410. (The evidence concerning the 26th North Carolina's location within Marshall's brigade is contradictory. In a letter written soon after the battle, Major Jones stated that the regiment was posted on the brigade's far right and was adjacent to the left flank of Fry's brigade. See Jones, "Pettigrew's Brigade at Gettysburg": 132. Other evidence places the regiment left of center in Marshall's brigade. See Trinque, "Arnold's Bat-tery and the 26th North Carolina": 63.)

19. *OR* I, 27 (2): 360, 608; Coddington, *Gettysburg Campaign:* 490–491; *HTECW:* 294; Fry, "Pettigrew's Charge at Gettysburg": 92–93; Freeman, *Lee's Lieutenants* 3:148.

20. Fry, "Pettigrew's Charge at Gettysburg": 92–93.

21. Kimble, "Tennesseans at Gettysburg": 460–461.

22. *OR* I, 27 (1): 158–159, 417–418, 464–466, 470–471; Coddington, *Gettysburg Campaign:* 476–477; Shultz and Rollins, "Measuring Pickett's Charge": 111, 116; Frassanito, *Early Photography at Gettysburg:* 180, 232–234; Trinque, "Arnold's Bat-tery and the 26th N.C.": 64; Shultz, *"Double Canister":* 73.

23. *OR* I, 27 (1): 464–466; Dyer, *Compendium of the War* 3: 1361–1362; Haines, *His-tory of Co. F:* 38–39; Thompson, "Scrap of Gettysburg": 102–105; Scott, "Pickett's Charge": 902–904.

24. Toombs, *New Jersey Troops:* 175; Longacre, *To Gettysburg and Beyond:* 79–82; *OR* I, 27 (1): 464–466; Dyer, *Compendium of the War* 3: 1361–1362; Haines, *History of Co. F:* 38–39; Thompson, "Scrap of Gettysburg": 102–105; Scott, "Pickett's Charge": 902–904.

25. Longacre, *To Gettysburg and Beyond:* 79–82, 92–99, 104; Dyer, *Compendium of the War:* 1361–1362.

26. Garrett V. Deacon to sister, 13 Jun 1865, as quoted in Longacre, *To Gettysburg and Beyond:* 106; *OR,* I, 27 (1): 465.

27. Thompson, "Scrap of Gettysburg": 105; Longacre, *To Gettysburg and Beyond:* 131; *HTECW:* 710.

28. Galwey, *Valiant Hours:* 109–110; Benjamin W. Thompson, as quoted in Campbell, "Remember Harper Ferry": 100.

29. *OR* I, 27 (1): 228–243; Warner, *Generals in Blue:* 242; Shultz, *"Double Canister":* 67; Shultz and Rollins, "Measuring Pickett's Charge": 108–114.

30. Scott, "Pickett's Charge": 904; *OR* I, 27 (1): 238-239.

31. *Fighting for the Confederacy:* 253–257; Warner, *Generals in Gray:* 3–4; Jorgenson, "Edward Porter Alexander": 44–45.

32. Wise, *Long Arm of Lee:* 664–665; Foote, *The Civil War* 2: 539.

33. *Fighting for the Confederacy:* 254–255.

34. E.P. Alexander to J. Longstreet, 3 Jul 1863, Edward Porter Alexander Papers, LOC; Foote, *The Civil War,* 2: 539–541; *Fighting for the Confederacy:* 254–255.

35. *OR* I, 27 (2): 288; *Fighting for the Confederacy:* 255; Warner, *Generals in Gray:* 345.

36. E.P. Alexander to G. Pickett, 3 Jul 1863, Edward Porter Alexander Papers, LOC; *Fighting for the Confederacy:* 255; Wise, *The Long Arm of Lee:* 674.

37. *Fighting for the Confederacy:* 257; *OR* I, 27 (1): 239; Wise, *Long Arm of Lee:* 677; Banes, *History of the Philadelphia Brigade:* 187; Foote, *The Civil War* 2: 541.

38. Brown, *University Greys:* 37; Wheeler, "Reminiscences of Gettysburg": 213; "Our Army Correspondence," Thomas Goreman Papers, NCDAH; Gibbon, *Personal Recollections:* 146.

39. T.J. Cureton to "Dear Sir," 22 Jun 1890, John R. Lane Papers, SHC; "Setser Letters" 2:15; "Our Army Correspondence," Thomas Goreman Papers, NCDAH.

40. Thompson, "Scrap of Gettysburg": 959; Scott, "Pickett's Charge": 904–905; Harwell, *Two Views of Gettysburg:* 175; Sawyer, *History of the 8th Ohio Infantry:* 130.

41. Scott, "Pickett's Charge": 905; Rollins, *Pickett's Charge: Eyewitness Accounts:* 110; Harwell, *Two Views of Gettysburg:* 174–175; Gibbon, *Personal Recollections:* 148; "Letter of Lt. Samuel B. McIntyre": 1744.

42. Simons, *History of the 125th N.Y.:* 134; Rollins, *Pickett's Charge: Eyewitness Accounts:* 110; Hunt, "Third Day at Gettysburg": 369–372; "Burning of the Bliss Buildings": 1188; "Letter of Lt. Samuel B. McIntyre": 1744, 1754.

43. Washburn, *History of the 108th N.Y.:* 50–52; "Letter of Capt. David Shields": 1069; *OR* I, 27 (1): 189, 466, 474–475; Campbell, "Remember Harpers Ferry": 103–104.

44. Murphey, *History of the 1st Delaware:* 120–121; Brown, *Experiences:* 202–203; Rollins, *Pickett's Charge: Eyewitness Accounts:* 100.

45. *OR* I, 27 (1): 239; Rollins, *Pickett's Charge: Eyewitness Accounts:* 112.

46. "Setser Letters," 3: 15; Turney, "First Tennessee at Gettysburg": 536; "Lee's Army in Pennsylvania": 43–44; Bernard, "Gettysburg Campaign"; Caison, "Southern Soldiers": 160; H.C. Albright to "Dear Sir," 12 Jul 1863, Henry C. Albright Papers, GHM; *NCT* 7: 548.

47. H. Heth to S. Cooper, 18 Oct 1864, Compiled Service Records of the 22nd Battalion of Virginia Infantry, NA; Coddington, *Gettysburg Campaign:* 498; Brown, *University Greys:* 38; Rollins, *Pickett's Charge: Eyewitness Accounts:* 96–97.

48. T.J. Cureton to "Dear Sir," 22 Jun 1890, John R. Lane Papers, SHC; *OR* I, 27 (1): 239; *Fighting for the Confederacy:* 258; *Gettysburg Nobody Knows:* 125–126; Coddington, *Gettysburg Campaign:* 498–499.

49. *OR* I, 27 (1): 239; Coddington, *Gettysburg Campaign:* 498.

50. Scott, "Pickett's Charge": 9–10; Coddington, *Gettysburg Campaign:* 495; Banes, *History of the Philadelphia Brigade:* 188; Rollins, *Pickett's Charge: Eyewitness Accounts:* 114, 116; Buell, *The Cannoneer:* 94.

51. *Fighting for the Confederacy:* 258–259; Jorgensen, "Edward Porter Alexander": 52–53; Coddington, *The Gettysburg Campaign:* 500–501; *Gettysburg Nobody Knows:* 125; E.P. Alexander to G. Pickett, 3 Jul 1863, Edward Porter Alexander Papers, LOC.

CHAPTER TEN

Terrible as an Army with Banners

1. Krick, *Lee's Colonels:* 243; Warner, Ezra, *Generals in Gray:* 11, 68, 95, 99, 165; Sifakis, *Who Was Who in the Civil War:* 439–440; Taylor, "Col. James Keith Marshall": 78; T.J. Cureton to "Dear Sir," 22 Jun 1890, John R. Lane Papers, SHC; H.A. Jacob to "Dear Judge Burgwyn," 14 Apr 1960, HKB Papers, V.M.I. Archives.

2. Krick, *Lee's Colonels:* 243; Taylor, "Col. James Keith Marshall": 78–80, 84.

3. Young, "Pettigrew's Brigade": 556; Taylor, "Col. James Keith Marshall": 80–82, 87.

4. "Pettigrew's Old Brigade," Southern Commanders and Staff Officers File, Robert L. Brake Collection, USAMHI; Berkeley, "Rode With Pickett": 175; "Letter of Capt. Frank E. Moran": 776; T.J. Cureton to "Dear Sir," 22 Jun 1890, John R. Lane Papers, SHC; "Letter of Maj. Gen. Isaac R. Trimble": 933.

5. T.J. Cureton to "Dear Sir," 22 Jun 1890, John R. Lane Papers, SHC; "Pettigrew's Old Brigade," Southern Commanders and Staff Officers File, Robert L. Brake Collection, USAMHI; Underwood, "Twenty Sixth Regiment": 365; Taylor, "Col. James Keith Marshall": 87.

6. T.J. Cureton to "Dear Sir," 22 Jun 1890, John R. Lane Papers, SHC; H.K. Burgwyn to "Editors of the Enquirer," Southern Commanders and Staff Officers File, Robert L. Brake Collection, USAMHI; Taylor, "Col. James Keith Marshall": 87; Underwood, "Twenty-Sixth Regiment": 365; Fry, "Pettigrew's Charge": 92–93; "Letter From Gen. Lane."

7. Hickerson, *Happy Valley:* 131–132; Introduction to Edmund W. Jones Papers, SHC; Maria Spear to JTJ, 20 Mar 1862, Edmund W. Jones Papers, SHC.

8. Galwey, *Valiant Hours:* 115; Goss, *Recollections of a Private:* 214; "Battle of Gettysburg."

9. Haines, *History of Co. F:* 41; Galwey, *Valiant Hours:* 115; Goss, *Recollections of a Private:* 214; Driver, "Pickett's Charge at Gettysburg": 353–354.

10. Harwell, *Two Views of Gettysburg:* 189; Driver, "Pickett's Charge at Gettysburg": 353–354; Rice, "Repelling Lee's Last Blow": 387; Haines, *History of Co. F:* 42.

11. Scott, "Pickett's Charge": 10–11; Goss, *Recollections of a Private:* 214; Rollins, *Pickett's Charge: Eyewitness Accounts:* 273; Simons, *History of the 125th New York:* 135–136.

12. Scott, "Pickett's Charge": 10–11; Song of Solomon 6:10.

13. Rollins, *Pickett's Charge: Eyewitness Accounts:* 273; HTECW: 672; Brown, *Experiences in the Army:* 202–203; Dyer, *Compendium of the War:* 1012–1013; OR I, 27 (1): 466–467.

14. *OR* I, 27 (1): 464–466; "1st Delaware Regiment": 1388, 1391; Seville, *History of the First Delaware:* 81–82; Dyer, *Compendium of the War* 3: 1017.

15. *OR* I, 27 (1): 158–159, 464–466, 468–470, 472–477; Thompson, "Scrap of Gettysburg": 103–104; Seville, *History of the First Delaware:* 81–82.

16. Fleming, *Life and Letters of Alexander Hays:* 3–4, 14–15, 28–29, 418, 421, 474–475; *DAB* 4 (2): 460–461; Warner, *Generals in Blue:* 223–224.

17. Washburn, *History of the 108th New York:* 52; Haines, *History of Company F:* 41; "1st Delaware Regiment": 1397; Fleming, *Life of Alexander Hays:*, 439; Thompson, "Scrap of Gettysburg": 103–104.

18. Harwell, *Two Views of Gettysburg:* 189–190; W.S. Christian, "55th Virginia," John W. Daniel Papers, University of Virginia; Rollins, *Pickett's Charge: Eyewitness Accounts:*, 271; Fleming, *Life of Alexander Hays:* 457–458.

19. *OR* I, 27 (2): 643–644; Rollins, *Pickett's Charge: Eyewitness Accounts:* 64, 251; "Letter From Colonel Jones"; Stewart, *Pickett's Charge:* 87; Bush, "From 1861 to 1865"; Scott, "Pickett's Charge": 10–12; Thompson, "Scrap of Gettysburg":103; Young, "Pettigrew's Brigade": 124–125; W.S. Christian, "55th Virginia," John W. Daniel Papers, University of Virginia.

20. "Letter From Hon. Jos. J. Davis"; Thompson, "Scrap of Gettysburg": 103; Scott, "Pickett's Charge": 10–12; Wilson, *Carolina Cavalier:* 203–204; "Letter of Maj. Gen. Isaac R. Trimble": 1200.

21. "Lee's Army in Pennsylvania": 43–44; Caison, "Southern Soldiers": 160.

22. *NCT* 7: 467, 548; T.J. Cureton to "Dear Sir," 22 Jun 1890, John R. Lane Papers, SHC; H.C. Albright to "Dear Sir," 8 Jun 1863, Henry C. Albright Papers, GHM; Underwood, "Twenty-Sixth Regiment": 417.

23. Bush, "From 1861 to 1865"; *NCT* 7: 573.

24. Bush, "From 1861 to 1865"; *NCT* 7: 574, 478; Emerson, *Lieutenant John Emerson:* 3–7.

25. "Lee's Army in Pennsylvania": 44; Hazlewood, "Gettysburg Charge"; Scott, "Pickett's Charge": 11; "Battle of Gettysburg"; T.J. Cureton to "Dear Sir," 22 Jun 1890, John R. Lane Papers, SHC; Caison, "Southern Soldiers": 160.

26. Rollins, *Pickett's Charge: Eyewitness Accounts,* 248, 273; "Letter From Lt. Col. Turner"; Warren, *Map of Gettysburg;* "Letter of Maj. Gen. Isaac R. Trimble": 1200.

27. "Lee's Army in Pennsylvania": 44; T.J. Cureton to "Dear Sir," 22 Jun 1890, John R. Lane Papers, SHC; Rollins, *Pickett's Charge: Eyewitness Accounts:* 247; Fleming, *Life of Alexander Hays:* 457.

28. Young, "Pettigrew's Brigade at Gettysburg": 127; Fleming, *Life of Alexander Hays:* 457; Moore, "Heth's Division": 390.

29. *OR* I, 27 (1): 159, 238–240, 748–749; Shultz, *"Double Canister":* 37–39, 67, 74–77; Shultz and Rollins, "Measuring Pickett's Charge": 109–117; Coddington, *Gettysburg Campaign,* 506.

30. Washburn, *History of the 108th N.Y.:* 52; "Lane's Brigade"; Haines, *History of Co. F:* 42; Fry, "Pettigrew's Charge": 92–93; Rollins, *Pickett's Charge: Eyewitness Accounts:* 269; Caison, "Southern Soldiers": 160; Warren, *Map of Gettysburg; OR* I, 27 (2): 643; Goss, *Recollections of a Private:* 241; *NCT* 7: 463; "Letter From Colonel Jones."

31. T.J. Cureton to "Dear Sir," 22 Jun 1890, John R. Lane Papers, SHC; Rollins, *Pickett's Charge: Eyewitness Accounts:* 264–265.

32. Bush, "From 1861 to 1865"; Warren, *Map of Gettysburg;* "Letter of Maj. Gen. Isaac R. Trimble": 1199; Goss, *Recollections of a Private:* p. 214; W.S. Christian, "55th Virginia," John W. Daniel Papers, University of Virginia; Ashe, *Charge at Gettysburg:* 10–11; "Pettigrew's Old Brigade," Southern Commanders and Staff Officers File, Robert L. Brake Collection, USAMHI; Rollins, *Pickett's Charge: Eyewitness Accounts:* 269, 77; Moore, "Heth's Division": 391.

33. Burgwyn, "Unparalleled Loss of Company F": 201; *NCT* 7: 538, 599; Rice, "Repelling Lee's Last Blow": 387; Rollins, *Pickett's Charge: Eyewitness Accounts:* 269; Taylor, "Col. James Keith Marshall": 87; Dowdy, *Death of a Nation:* 319–320.

34. Scott, "Pickett's Charge": 11–12; "Lane's Brigade"; "Letter of Isaac R. Trimble": 1199.

35. Scott, "Pickett's Charge": 11–12; Goss, *Recollections of a Private:* 214; Underwood, "Twenty-Sixth Regiment": 366; Bush, "From 1861 to 1865"; Moore, "Heth's Division"; *OR* I, 27 (2): 644; "Letter from Colonel Jones."

36. Crary, *Dear Belle:* 209; Shultz, *"Double Canister".* 73, 77; Brown, *Cushing of Gettysburg:* 243–244; Trinque, "Arnold's Battery and the 26th North Carolina": 65–66; *OR* I, 27 (1): 479–481; Dyer, *Compendium of the War* 3: 1695.

37. Haskin, *History of the First Artillery:* 168–169; Crary, *Dear Belle:* 209; Brown, *Cushing of Gettysburg:* 256: "Lee's Army in Pennsylvania": 44.

38. *OR* I, 27 (2):644; "Letter From Colonel Jones"; Bush, "From 1861 to 1865"; Warren, *Map of Gettysburg;* T.J. Cureton to "Dear Sir," 22 Jun 1890; John R. Lane Papers, SHC; "Lee's Army in Pennsylvania": 44.

39. Haskin, *History of the First Artillery:* 168; "Testimony About Gettysburg": 524; Turney, "First Tennessee at Gettysburg": 536; Moore, "Heth's Division": 390; "Letter of Maj. Gen. Isaac R. Trimble": 1199, "1st Delaware Regiment": 1397–1399.

40. Seville, *History of the First Delaware:* 87, Rollins, *Pickett's Charge: Eyewitness Accounts:* 274–275; Sawyer, *History of the 8th Ohio:* 130–131; Thompson, *History of Co. F:* 105; "1st Delaware Regiment": 1397–1399.

41. Moore, "Heth's Division": 391; Fleming, *Life of Alexander Hays:* 461; Rollins, *Pickett's Charge: Eyewitness Accounts:* 269, 271, 274–275; Thompson, "Scrap of Gettysburg": 105.

42. Taylor, "Col. James Keith Marshall": 87; *NCT* 7: 538, 564, 573, 574; Regimental History, James T. Adams Papers, NCDAH; Bush, "From 1861 to 1865"; J.A. Bush File, 1901 Confederate Pension Applications for North Carolina, NCDAH.

43. Young, "Pettigrew's Brigade": 127; Young, "Pettigrew-Kirkland-McRae Brigade": 556; "Letter From Lt. W.B. Shepard"; Moore, "Heth's Division": 391; Rollins, *Pickett's Charge: Eyewitness Accounts:* 274–275.

44. *OR* I, 27 (1): 461–462; Galwey, *Valiant Hours:* 116–117; "Letter of Lt. Col. Franklin Sawyer": 1132–1133; Sawyer, *History of the 8th Ohio:* 130–132; Campbell, "Remember Harper's Ferry!": 106; "From the 8th Ohio"; Dyer, *Compendium of the War* 3: 1499.

45. H. Heth to S. Cooper, 18 Oct 1864, Compiled Service Records of the 22nd Battalion of Virginia Infantry, NA; Young, "Pettigrew's Brigade": 127; W.S. Christian, "55th Virginia," John W. Daniel Papers, University of Virginia. *OR* I, 27 (1): 461–462; Sawyer, *History of the 8th Regiment Ohio:* 130–132; "Letter of Lt. Col. Franklin Sawyer": 1132–1133.

46. *OR* I, 27 (1): 461–462; "Letter of Capt. Samuel C. Armstrong": 1001–1002; "Letter of Lt. Col. Franklin Sawyer": 1132–1133; Galwey, *Valiant Hours:* 116–117; Sawyer, *History of the 8th Ohio:* 131–132; Rollins, *Pickett's Charge: Eyewitness Accounts:* 272–273; Campbell, "Remember Harper's Ferry!": 106.

47. Sawyer, *History of the 8th Ohio:* 131–132; *OR* I, 27 (1): 461–462; "Letter of Capt. Samuel C. Armstrong": 1000–1002; "Letter From General Lane"; Scott, "Pickett's Charge": 12–13; *OR* I, 27 (2): 651.

48. Scott, "Pickett's Charge": 13; *OR* I, 27 (2): 659–660; "Letter From General Lane"; "Letter From Lt. Col. J. McLeod Turner"; "Letter From Captain P.C. Carlton"; "Letter From Lt. Col. W.G. Morris"; "Letter From Col. Lowe"; "Letter From Lt. Col. Jos. H. Saunders"; "Letter From Lt. Thos. L. Norwood."

49. "Letter From Col. Jones"; *OR* I, 27 (2): 641; Rollins, *Pickett's Charge: Eyewitness Accounts:* 253; "Letter From Adjutant H.C. Moore"; "Letter From General Lane."

50. "Testimony About Gettysburg": 524; Aldrich, *History of Battery A: First Rhode Island:* 216; "Letter From Colonel Jones"; T.J. Cureton to "Dear Sir," 22 Jun 1890, John R. Lane Papers, SHC.

51. *OR* I, 27 (1): 360; Coddington, *Gettysburg Campaign:* 514–517; Foote, *The Civil War,* 2: 562; Fry, "Pettigrew's Charge": 93; Shultz and Rollins, "Measuring Pickett's Charge": 111, 116.

52. Longacre, *To Gettysburg and Beyond:* 131–135; Martin, "Eleventh North Carolina": 45; Rollins, *Pickett's Charge: Eyewitness Accounts:* 274; "1st Delaware Regiment": 1398; Thompson, "Scrap of Gettysburg": 106; Scott, "Pickett's Charge": 13–14.

53. "Letter From Colonel Jones"; *OR* I, 27 (2): 645; Caison, "Southern Soldiers": 160; Emerson, *Lieutenant John R. Emerson:* 11; "Testimony About Gettysburg": 524; T.J. Cureton to "Dear Sir," 22 Jun 1890, John R. Lane Papers, SHC; Regimental History, James T. Adams Papers, NCDAH; *NCT* 7: 463, 481; Underwood, "Twenty-Sixth Regiment": 374, 417.

54. Foote, *The Civil War* 2: 560; Campbell, "Remember Harper's Ferry!": 107; Simon, *History of the 125th N.Y.:* 137; Sawyer, *History of the 8th Ohio:* 131; "Letter From General Lane"; "Letter From Lt. Col. J. McLeod Turner"; "Letter From Lt. Thos. L. Norwood."

55. "Letter From General Lane"; *OR* I, 27 (2): 667; "Letter From Lt. W.B. Shepard"; "Letter From Adjutant H.C. Moore."

56. Underwood, "Twenty-Sixth Regiment": 366; *OR* I, 27 (2): 644;"Letter From Colonel Jones"; Regimental History, James T. Adams Papers, NCDAH; *NCT* 7: 521, 531.

57. *OR* I, 27 (1): 480, 879–880; Shultz, *"Double Canister":* 55–57; Aldrich, *History of Battery A: First Rhode Island Artillery:* 216.

58. "Letter From Colonel Jones": Aldrich, *History of Battery A: First Rhode Island Artillery:* 216; Simons, *History of the 125th N.Y.:* 138; Haines, *History of Co. F:* 42; Underwood, "Twenty-Sixth Regiment": 366, 374; Browne, *Experiences in the Army:* 199.

59. Underwood, "Twenty-Sixth Regiment": 366, 374; Foote, *The Civil War* 2: 563; Rose, *Colours of the Gray:* 31, 38.

60. *OR* I, 27 (2): 644; Coddington, *Gettysburg Campaign:* 506–508, 513–519; Freeman, *Lee's Lieutenants* 2: 160–161; "Letter From Colonel Jones."

CHAPTER ELEVEN
"Unconquered in Spirit"

1. Moore, "Heth's Division": 392; *OR* I, 27 (2): 644; "Letter From Colonel Jones"; Sawyer, *History of the 8th Ohio:* 132; "Letter From Lt. Col. J. McLeod Turner."

2. "Maj. Gen. Isaac R. Trimble": 934; "Letter of Maj. Gen. Isaac R. Trimble": 1199; Rollins, *Pickett's Charge: Eyewitness Accounts:* 233.

3. *OR* I, 27 (2): 644; Fleming, *Life of Alexander Hays:* 462–463; Kimble, "Tennesseans at Gettysburg": 451; Moore, "Interesting Narrative."

4. T.J. Cureton to "Dear Sir," 22 Jun 1890, John R. Lane Papers, SHC; *NCT* 7: 481; Wilson, *Carolina Cavalier:* 197–198; Young, "Pettigrew's Brigade": 128.

5. T.J. Cureton to "Dear Sir," 22 Jun 1890, John R. Lane Papers, SHC; *OR* I, 27 27 (2): 608.

6. Hazelwood, "Gettysburg Charge": 234–235; Driver, "Pickett's Charge": 356; Foote, *The Civil War* 2: 564; *Fremantle Diary:* 212–215.

7. *OR* I, 27 (1): 467, 469; Foster, *New Jersey and the Rebellion:* 305; Rose, *Colours of the Gray:* 38; Haines, *History of Ca F:* 42; Longacre, *To Gettysburg and Beyond:* 137; "1st Delaware Regiment": 1400–1401; Scott, "Pickett's Charge": 15.

8. Fleming, *Life of Alexander Hays:* 410, 424–425, 464; Washburn, *History of the 108th Regiment N.Y.:* 53; "1st Delaware Regiment": 1399.

9. Shultz, *"Double Canister":* 64–65; "Letter of Lt. Egan to George Meade Jr.": 389; Foote, *The Civil War* 2: 566.

10. Fleming, *Life of Alexander Hays:* 409, 421, 433; Warner, *Generals in Blue:* 545.

11. Caison, "Southern Soldiers": 160; "Letter From Lt. Gaston Broughton"; *NCT* 7: 506–507; Fry, "Pettigrew's Charge at Gettysburg": 93.

12. Bush, "From 1861 to 1865."

13. Moore, "Heth's Division": 392–393; Young, "Pettigrew's Brigade": 128.

14. William C. Byrnes Diary, 4 Jul 1863, William C. Byrnes Papers, DU; *Make Me a Map:* 159; Banes, *History of the Philadelphia Brigade:* 196; Lineback, "Civil War Diary."

15. Bernard, "Gettysburg Campaign"; *Make Me a Map:* 158; "Letter of Capt. Samuel Armstrong": 1002; Galwey, *Valiant Hours:* 120; Imboden, "Confederate Retreat From Gettysburg": 421.

16. *OR* I, 27 (2): 644–645; MacKay, "Hampton's Duel": 123; H.C. Albright to "Dear Sir," 12 Jul 1863, Henry C. Albright Papers, GHM; T.J. Cureton to "Dear Sir," 22 Jun 1890, John R. Lane Papers, SHC; *NCT* 7: 533; Moore, "Interesting Narrative"; Busey and Martin, *Regimental Strengths and Losses at Gettysburg:* 173, 236, 308–309, 313; Fox, *Regimental Losses:* 555–556.

17. J.J. Young to "Col.," 3 Jul 1863, W.H.S. Burgwyn Papers, NCDAH; *OR* I, 27 (2): 645.

18. *OR* I, 27 (2): 645.

19. T.J. Cureton to "Dear Sir," 22 Jun 1890, John R. Lane Papers, SHC; William C. Byrnes Diary, 4 Jul 1863, William C. Byrnes Papers, DU; Henry P. Clare to "Dear William," 5 Jul 1863, Henry C. Clare Papers, DU; Rollins, *Pickett's Charge: Eyewitness Accounts:* 340.

20. Sawyer, *History of the 8th Ohio:* 133–134; Imboden, "Confederate Retreat From Gettysburg": 420–424; *The Blue and the Gray:* 638–639.

21. William C. Byrnes Diary, 4 Jul 1863, William C. Byrnes Papers, DU; Banes, *History of the Philadephia Brigade:* 196; "Our Special Dispatches," Newspaper Clippings File, Edward McPherson Papers, LOC; T.J. Cureton to "Dear Sir," 22 Jun 1890, John R. Lane Papers, SHC.

22. Banes, *History of the Philadelphia Brigade:* 196; Coddington, *Gettysburg Campaign:* 544–546.

23. William C. Byrnes Diary, 4 Jul 1863, William C. Byrnes Papers, DU; *Letters of a Civil War Nurse:* 4–5; Gross, *Battle-Field of Gettysburg:* 20.

24. Balch, *Battle of Gettysburg:* 107–108; Galwey, *Valiant Hours:* 121; William C. Byrnes Diary, 4 Jul–5 Jul 1863, William C. Byrnes Papers, DU.

25. Underwood, "Twenty-Sixth Regiment": 370; Balch, *Battle of Gettysburg:* 92; "Address by Lane."

26. Foote, *The Civil War* 2: 584–585; Underwood, "Twenty-Sixth Regiment": 370.

27. Coddington, *Gettysburg Campaign:* 550–551; Foote, *The Civil War* 2: 585–586; Moore, "Heth's Division": 394; Lineback, "Civil War Diary."

28. Coddington, *Gettysburg Campaign:* 555–557; Foote, *The Civil War* 2: 591.

29. Robertson, *Stonewall Jackson:* 224; Foote, *The Civil War* 2: 592.

30. *OR* I, 27 (2): 644; "Letter From Colonel Jones"; "Unpublished Memoirs of Henry Heth," Henry Heth Papers, Alderman Library, University of Virginia; Welch, *Confederate Surgeon's Letters:* 70.

31. "Unpublished Memoirs of Henry Heth," Henry Heth Papers, Alderman Library, University of Virginia; Fulton, "Fifth Alabama at Gettysburg": 379; Young, "Pettigrew-Kirkland-MacRae Brigade": 560–561; Wilson, *Carolina Cavalier:* 201–202 *OR* I, 27 (1): 990, 1000.

32. "Unpublished Memoirs of Henry Heth," Henry Heth Papers, Alderman Library, University of Virginia; Fulton, "Fifth Alabama at Gettysburg": 379; Young, "Pettigrew-Kirkland-MacRae Brigade": 560–561; Wilson, *Carolina Cavalier:* 201–202.

33. Young, "Pettigrew-Kirkland-MacRae Brigade": 560–561; Wilson, *Carolina Cavalier:* 201–202; "Unpublished Memoirs of Henry Heth," Henry Heth Papers, Alderman Library, University of Virginia; Moore, "Heth's Division": 394–395.

34. JTJ to father, 17 Jul 1863, Edmund W. Jones Papers, SHC; Underwood, "Twenty-Sixth Regiment": 376; Wilson, *Carolina Cavalier:* 204–205; Young, "Pettigrew-Kirkland-MacRae Brigade": 560–561; *NCT* 7: 492; *OR* I, 27 (1): 990.

35. Wilson, *Carolina Cavalier:* 204–205; Louis Young to "My Dear Sir," 10 Feb 1864, Francis Winston Papers, NCDAH.

36. Underwood, "Twenty-Sixth Regiment": 378; *OR* I, 27 (1): 1000–1001; *NCT* 7: 467, 470, 472, 478, 513, 514, 517, 591, 594, 597, 599-600; Moore, "Heth's Division": 394–395.

37. JTJ to father, 17 Jul 1863, Edmund W. Jones Papers, SHC; Bartlett, "From Yorktown to the Appomattox," North Carolina Collection, Pack Memorial Library; Busey and Martin, *Regimental Strengths and Losses:* 173, 236, 308–309, 313.

38. *OR* I, 27 (2): 643–644; T.J. Cureton to "Dear Sir," 22 Jun 1890, W.H.S. Burgwyn Papers, SHC.

39. Underwood, "Twenty-Sixth Regiment": 373; *NCT* 7: 467, 481–482, 494, 506–507, 520, 533, 548–549, 561–562, 574, 589.
40. "A Trip That Didn't Pay," Thomas Perrett Papers, NCDAH; "The Setser Letters" 1: 15; JTJ to father, 17 Jul 1863, Edmund W. Jones Papers, SHC: "Address by Lane."
41. "A Trip That Didn't Pay," Thomas Perrett Papers, NCDAH.

<hr>

Epilogue

"Steadfast to the Last"

1. *HTECW:* 307–308; Foote, *The Civil War* 2: 494–657; *OR* I, 27 (2): 324–325.
2. Carmichael, "We Will Make Them Howl": 46–48; James T. Morehead Diary, 13 Jul 1863, James T. Morehead Papers, SHC.
3. William Hill to "My Dear Mother," 5 Jul 1863, Private Collection of Robert H. MacIntosh Jr.; Carmichael, "We Will Make Them Howl": 46–48; *Voices From Cemetery Hill:* 110.
4. Samuel H. Walkup Journal, 10 Jul 1863, Samuel H. Walkup Papers, DU; JTJ to father, 17 Jul 1863, Edmund W. Jones Papers, SHC; Welch, *Confederate Surgeon's Letters:* 74–75; Carmichael, "We Will Make Them Howl": 48.
5. *NCT* 7: 460–461; Underwood, "Twenty-Sixth Regiment": 379–381; JTJ to father, 17 Jul 1863, Edmund W. Jones Papers, SHC; Warner, *Generals in Gray:* 172.
6. *OR* I, 29 (1): 280–282; *NCT* 7: 461; *HTECW:* 80–81; Foote, *The Civil War* 2: 792–793; Freeman, *Lee's Lieutenants* 3: 244–247; Regimental History, James T. Adams Papers, NCDAH; *OR* III, (4): 816; "The Setser Letters" 4: 13; Terry, "The Mystery Flags of Bristoe Station": 13.
7. *NCT* 7: 461–462; Underwood, "Twenty-Sixth North Carolina": 383–384; *HTECW:* 709, 825–827; Regimental History, James T. Adams Papers, NCDAH.
8. Underwood, "Twenty-Sixth Regiment": 384–385; *HTECW:* 709, 149–150; *NCT* 7: 461–463; Warner, *Generals in Gray:* 206–207; Regimental History, James T. Adams Papers, Civil War Collection, NCDAH.
9. Warner, *Generals in Gray:* 206–207; *NCT* 7: 462; Underwood, "Twenty-Sixth Regiment": 385; Regimental History, James T. Adams Papers, NCDAH.
10. *NCT* 7: 462; Underwood, "Twenty-Sixth Regiment": 387–388; R.M. Tuttle to "My Dear Friend," 29 Sep 1900, W.H.S. Burgwyn Papers, NCDAH; Anonymous to "Sir," 29 Jul 1864, Nevin Ray Papers, DU.
11. *NCT* 7: 462; "Setser Letters" 3: 16; Regimental History, James T. Adams Papers, NCDAH.
12. *OR* I, 29 (1): 343; *NCT* 7: 462–463, 502, 504, 507–508, 518, 520–522, 525, 591; *Deeds of Valor:* 452–453; 26th N.C. Battle Flag File, NCMOH; Regimental History, James T. Adams Papers, NCDAH.
13. Freeman, *Lee's Lieutenants* 3: 752, 767–768; *HTECW:* 20–21; Regimental History, James T. Adams Papers, NCDAH; Thomas P. Devereux Memoir, Family Correspondence 1885–1936, Devereux Family Papers, DU.
14. *NCT* 7: 466–601; Underwood, "Twenty-Sixth Regiment": 394–395; Regimental History, James T. Adams Papers, NCDAH; Leinbach, "Regiment Band of the 26th

North Carolina": 226; Kilmer, "Food for Powder": 62–66; Tuttle, "'F' and 'I' of the 26th Regiment."

15. Regimental History, James T. Adams Papers, NCDAH; Bush, "From 1861 to 1865."

16. Fox, *Regimental Losses:* 556–560; Martin, *Gettysburg July 1:* 349–353; "Address by Lane."

17. Norris, "Now Growing Old": 509; Underwood, "Twenty-Sixth Regiment": 411–412; "Unpublished Manuscript by Leary W. Adams," Private Collection of Rita A. Simpson; Confederate Gravestone Records, N.C. Division of the United Daughters of the Confederacy, 3: 523, NCDAH.

18. Underwood, "Twenty-Sixth Regiment": 418; *NCT* 7: 548; Introduction and H.C. Albright to "My Dear Sir," 29 Mar 1864, Henry Clay Albright Papers, GHM.

19. Underwood, "The Twenty-Sixth Regiment": 330; "The Old North State": 202; Tuttle, "Incidents in Caldwell County in 1864"; Moore, *James Daniel Moore:* 16; Mast, *State Troops and Volunteers* 1: 215.

20. *NCT* 7: 519; Underwood, "Twenty-Sixth Regiment": 416.

21. *NCT* 7: 521, 531; Brooks W. Gilmore to "Dear Mr. Gragg," 10 Oct 1996, Private Collection of Rod Gragg.

22. Underwood, "Twenty-Sixth North Carolina": 419; *NCT* 7: 506; Gaston Broughton File, Confederate Pension Applications for 1907, NCDAH.

23. Bush, "From 1861 to 1865"; *NCT* 7: 573–574.

24. *NCT* 7: 523; Olds, "A Brave Carolinian": 245–247.

25. *NCT* 7: 537–538.

26. *NCT* 7: 481; T.J. Cureton to JRL, 22 June 1890, John R. Lane Papers SHC; Underwood, "Twenty-Sixth Regiment": 415– 416.

27. "General Joseph R. Davis": 63; Warner, *Generals in Gray:* 68–69.

28. *NCT* 7: 520; Emerson, *Lieutenant John R. Emerson:* 11–12.

29. Warner, *Generals in Blue:* 224; Oliva, *Fort Hays:* 12.

30. Dyer, *Compendium of the War* 3: 1361–1362; Longacre, *To Gettysburg and Beyond:* 283, 317.

31. Moore, "Interesting Narrative"; *NCT* 7: 533.

32. W.P. Kirkman to "Dear Parents," 21 Oct 1863, Private Collection of John Bass, *NCT* 7: 554–555.

33. Warner, *Generals in Gray:* 172–173; "Gen. James H. Lane": 469–470.

34. Lineback, "Civil War Diary"; Underwood, "Twenty-Sixth Regiment": 399–400; Hall, *Johnny Reb Band:* 96, 102–108; *History of North Carolina:* 6.

35. "Jefferson B. Mansfield Letters": 12; *NCT* 7: 527.

36. *NCT* 7: 543; Moore, *James Daniel Moore:* 21; Tuttle, "Incidents in Caldwell County in 1864."

37. Moore, *James Daniel Moore:* 17, 53, 57; "Capt. Moore Dead"; Moore, "Interesting Narrative."

38. "Capt. Jas. Moore Dead"; "Capt. Moore Dead"; Moore, *James Daniel Moore:* 58; Anderson, *Heritage of Caldwell County* 1: 61–62, 78; "I Was Born at the Head of John's River," Oral History Account of Lemuel Wallace Gragg, Globe, N.C., Private Collection of Rod Gragg.

39. "Notes Regarding the 24th Michigan Vols." *Bachelder Papers* 1: 333–335; "Twenty-Fourth Regiment": 449; Boatner, *Civil War Dictionary:* 570.

40. "Notes Regarding the 24th Michigan Vols." *Bachelder Papers* 1: 334–335; "Last of the Iron Brigade": 18–21.

41. Smith, *Twenty-Fourth Michigan:* 3, 264; "Last of the Iron Brigade": 18–21; Boatner, *Civil War Dictionary:* 570; Curtis, *History of the 24th Michigan:* 477–478; "Death of Gen. Morrow."

42. *OR* I, 27 (1): 254; Gaff, "Here Was Made Our Last Stand": 29.

43. *OR* I, 27 (1): 254, 267–273; Busey and Martin, *Regimental Strengths and Losses at Gettysburg:* 313; Fox, *Regimental Losses:* 390; *HTECW:* 385; Dyer, *Compendium of the War* 3: 1126–1127, 1291–1292; Stevenson, *Indiana's Roll of Honor* 1: 381; "Last of the Iron Brigade": 21; Rosentreter, "Those Damned Black Hats": 31; "Record of Events for June 1865," Record of Events Cards, Compiled Service Records of the 24th Michigan Infantry, NA.

44. *NCT* 7: 557; "A Trip That Didn't Pay," Thomas Perret Papers, NCDAH.

45. F.W. Pickens to "Dear Sir," 18 May 1864, Samuel Wylie Crawford Papers, LOC; Wilson, *Carolina Cavalier:* 205; *DAB* 7: 516; Young, "Pettigrew's Brigade": 131; "Pettigrew's Old Brigade," Southern Commanders and Staff Officers File, Robert L. Brake Collection, USAMHI.

46. *NCT* 7: 544; Tuttle, "Incidents in Caldwell County in 1864."

47. "Setser Letters" 3: 16; *NCT* 7: 545.

48. "Setser Letters" 3: 13–17; *NCT* 7: 545.

49. "Gen. Isaac R. Trimble" *New York Times,* 5 Jan 1888; Warner, *Generals in Gray:* 310–311.

50. Moore, "Interesting Narrative"; *NCT* 7: 533; Tuttle, "Company F, 26th N.C.": 109; Moore, "Rev. Romulus Tuttle": 296–297.

51. Underwood, "Twenty-Sixth Regiment": 420–421; *NCT* 7: 420–421.

52. *History of North Carolina* 5: 312; *NCT* 7: 464, 519; Confederate Gravestone Records, N.C. Division of the United Daughters of the Confederacy, 5: 212, NCDAH.

53. Morgan, "Capt. Louis Young": 306; L.G. Young to "My Dear Sir," 10 Feb 1864, Francis Winston Papers, NCDAH; Young, "Pettigrew's Brigade": 113–159, 552–558; "Battle of Gettysburg"; Young, "Pettigrew-Kirkland-MacRae Brigade": 555–568.

54. *DNCB* 6: 85–86; *EOC* 4:1649–1651; "Death of Vance."

55. "Southern Telegraph Companies," 3 Jul 1863, Burgwyn Family Papers, SHC; W.H.S. Burgwyn to "Dearest Mother," 14 Jul 1863, Burgwyn Family Papers, SHC; *DNCB* 1: 276–277; "Reflections of Judge W.H.S. Burgwyn," Burgwyn Family Papers, SHC.

56. Davis, *Boy Colonel:* 342–344, 346–347; "Reflections of Judge W.H.S. Burgwyn," Burgwyn Family Papers, SHC; *Confederate Military History* 4: 414.

57. "Reflections of Judge W.H.S. Burgwyn," Burgwyn Family Papers, SHC; Mackay, K.J., "Sketch of Will's Forest," Margaret Mordecai Devereux Papers, SHC; Kenneth J. Zorgy to William Erwin Jr., Aug 1996, William Erwin Papers, DU; *Death Notices From the* Raleigh State *Chronicle:* 78–79; Annie Lane Devereux Obituary, Clippings File 1884–1922, Devereux Family Papers, DU.

58. Mackay, "Sketch of Will's Forest," Margaret Mordecai Devereux Papers, SHC; "Mrs. Devereux Passes": Clippings File 1884–1922, Devereux Family Papers, DU; Cemetery Archives, Oakwood Cemetery, Raleigh, N.C.

59. "Miss Annie Devereux—At Home," Box 3, Devereux Family Papers, DU; Devereux Family File, Cemetery Archives, Oakwood Cemetery.

60. NCT 7: 463; JTJ to father, 17 Aug 1863, Edmund W. Jones Papers, SHC.

61. NCT 7: 463; JTJ to father, 17 Aug 1863 and 26 Apr 1864, Edmund W. Jones Papers, SHC.

62. Z. Vance to "Dear Sir," 9 May 1864, D.M. Key to "Dear Sir," 14 May 1864, J.J. Young to "My Dear Sir," 25 May 1864, and W.W. Gaither to "My Dear Sir," 26 May 1864, Edmund W. Jones Papers, SHC; Lineback, "Civil War Diary."

63. M. Spear to "Sir," 6 Jun 1861, JTJ to father, 26 Apr 1863, and J.J. Young to "My Dear Sir," 25 May 1864, Edmund W. Jones Papers, SHC; Welch, *Confederate Surgeon's Letters:* 78; *From That Terrible Field:* 13.

64. Underwood, "Twenty-Sixth Regiment": 386, 409; *DNCB* 4: 12–13; *NCT* 7: 463.

65. "Col. Lane Has Passed Away"; JRL to W.H.S Burgwyn, 20 Oct 1900, W.H.S. Burgwyn Papers, NCDAH; "Col. John R. Lane," John R. Lane Papers, SHC.

66. Fox, *Regimental Losses:* 556; Kilmer, "Food For Powder": 62–66; "Confederate Veterans in Old N.C.": 229; "Col. Lane and His Regiment": 111.

67. "Col. Lane Has Passed Away"; "Confederate Veterans in Old N.C.": 229; *DNCB* 4: 409.

68. "Col. Lane and His Regiment": 111; "Col. Lane Has Passed Away"; Confederate Gravestone Records, N.C. Division of the United Daughters of the Confederacy, NCDAH; "Col. John R. Lane," Private Collection of L. R. Gorrell.

69. "At Gettysburg on Old Battleground"; Dorsett, "Fourteenth Color-Bearer": 4–5, 8.

70. "Fortieth Anniversary of Gettysburg"; "Address by Lane."

71. "Fortieth Anniversary of Gettysburg"; "Celebration of the Great Charge."

Bibliography

Books and Articles

"A Bandsman's Letters to Home from the War." *Moravian Music Journal.* 36 (Spring 1991).

"Address at Gettysburg by Col. John R. Lane." *Raleigh News and Observer.* 6 July 1903.

"Albert Stacey Caison." *Confederate Veteran* 29 (March 1921).

Aldrich, Thomas M. *The History of Battery A, First Regiment Rhode Island Light Artillery.* Providence, R.I.: Snow and Farnham Printers, 1904.

Alexander, Nancy. *Here Will I Dwell: The Story of Caldwell County.* Lenoir, N.C.: n.p., 1956.

The Annals of the War Written by Leading Participants, North and South. Dayton, Ohio: Morningside Press, 1988.

Ashe, S.A. "The Charge at Gettysburg." *North Carolina Booklet* 1 (March 1902).

"At Gettysburg on Old Battleground." *Raleigh News and Observer.* 6 July 1903.

Atlas to Accompany the Official Records of the Union and Confederate Armies. Compiled by Capt. Calvin D. Cowles. Washington, D.C.: U.S. Government Printing Office, 1889–1895.

Bachelder, John. *Map of the Gettysburg Battlefield.* Boston: John B. Bachelder, 1863.

Balch, Ralston W. *The Battle of Gettysburg: An Historical Account.* Harrisburg, Pa.: Gettysburg and Harrisburg Railroad, 1885.

Banes, Charles H. *History of the Philadelphia Brigade.* Philadelphia: J.B. Lippincott Co., 1876.

Barrett, John G. *The Civil War in North Carolina.* Chapel Hill, N.C.: University of North Carolina Press, 1963.

"Battle 42 Years Ago." *Gettysburg Compiler.* 5 July 1905.

"The Battle of Gettysburg." *Richmond Morning News.* 4 April 1900.

"Battle of Gettysburg, July 1, 1863." *The Bachelder Papers: Gettysburg in Their Own Words.* Vol. 2. Edited by David L. Ladd and Audrey J. Ladd. Dayton, Ohio: Morningside House, Inc., 1994.

"The Battle of Shepherdstown." Antietam National Battlefield: National Park Service, n.d.

Berkeley, Edmund. "Rode with Pickett." *Confederate Veteran* 23 (May 1915).

Bernard, George S. "The Gettysburg Campaign." *Petersburg Enterprise*. 3 March 1894.

Betts, A.D. "The Chaplain Service." *Histories of the Several Regiments and Battalions from North Carolina in the Great War 1861–1865*. Vol. 4. Edited by Walter Clark. Goldsboro, N.C.: Nash Brothers, 1901.

Beveridge, John L. "The First Gun at Gettysburg." *The Gettysburg Papers* 1.

Biographical History of North Carolina From Colonial Times to the Present. Edited by Samuel A. Ashe, Stephen B. Weeks and Charles L. Van Noppen. Vol. 8. Greensboro, N.C.: Charles L. Van Noppen Publisher, 1917.

Blackford, W. W. *War Years With Jeb Stuart*. New York: Charles Scribner's Sons, 1945.

The Blue and the Gray: The Story of the Civil War as Told by Participants. Edited by Henry Steele Commager. New York: Fairfax Press, 1982.

Boatner, Mark Mayo III. *The Civil War Dictionary*. New York: David McKay Co., 1959.

Brown, Kent Masterson. *Cushing of Gettysburg: The Story of a Union Artillery Commander*. Lexington, Ky.: University of Kentucky, 1993.

Brown, Maud M. *The University Greys: Company A, Eleventh Mississippi Regiment, Army of Northern Virginia, 1861–1865*. Richmond: Garrett and Massie, 1940.

Browne, Dunn. *Experiences in the Army*. Boston: Nichols and Noyes, 1866.

Buell, Augustus C. *The Cannoneer: A Story of a Private Soldier*. Washington, D.C.: National Tribune, 1890.

Burgwyn, William H.S. "Unparalleled Loss of Company F." *Southern Historical Society Papers* 28 (1900).

"Burning of the Bliss Buildings." *The Bachelder Papers: Gettysburg in Their Own Words*. Vol. 2. Edited by David L. Ladd and Audrey J. Ladd. Dayton, Ohio: Morningside House, Inc., 1994.

Busey, John W. and David G. Martin. *Regimental Strengths and Losses at Gettysburg*. Hightstown, N.J.: Longstreet House, 1994.

Bush, Jacob A. "From 1861 to 1865 as I Remember." *Lenoir (N.C.) Topic*. 25 March 1922.

Caison, Albert S. "Southern Soldiers in Northern Prisons." *Southern Historical Society Papers* 23 (1895).

"Caledonia Furnace." Caledonia State Park, Penn.: n.d.

Campbell, Eric A. "Remember Harpers Ferry." *Gettysburg Magazine* 8.

Cannon, Devereaux D. Jr. *Flags of the Confederacy: An Illustrated History*. Wilmington, N.C.: Broadfoot Publishing, 1988.

"Capt. Jas. Moore Dead." *Charlotte Daily Observer*. 7 August 1905.

"Capt. Moore Dead." *Gastonia Gazette*. 8 August 1905.

"Capt. Stephen W. Brewer, Co. E, 26th N.C. Troops." *Company Front* (June 1984).

Carmichael, Peter S. "We Will Make Them Howl Worse Than They Are Now Laughing." *Civil War Magazine* (February 1997).

Casey, Silas. *Infantry Tactics for the Instruction, Exercise and Manoeuvres of Corps D'Armee*. New York: Van Nostrand, 1862.

"Celebration of the Great Charge at Gettysburg." *Raleigh News and Observer*. 7 July 1903.

The Civil War Memories of Captain William J. Seymour. Edited by Terry L. Jones. Baton Rouge: Louisiana State University Press, 1991.

Clemmons, Tom. "Black Hats Off to the Original Iron Brigade." *Columbiad* 1 (Summer 1997).

"Closing Sketch." *Company Front* (September 1984).

Coddington, Edwin B. *The Gettysburg Campaign: A Study in Command.* New York: Charles Scribner's Sons, 1984.

"Col. John R. Lane and His Regiment." *Confederate Veteran* 17 (March 1909).

"Col. John R. Lane Has Passed Away." *Raleigh News and Observer.* 1 January 1909.

"Company F, 26th N.C. Infantry." *Confederate Veteran* 3 (April 1895).

Confederate Military History. Edited by Clement A. Evans. Atlanta: Confederate Publishing Co., 1899.

"Confederate Monument at Pittsboro." *Confederate Veteran* 15 (November 1907).

"Confederate Veterans in Old N.C." *Confederate Veteran* 2 (August 1894).

Coppee, Henry. *Field Manual for Battalion Drill for the Use of Officers in the U.S. Infantry.* Philadelphia: J.B. Lippincott, 1862.

Crary, Catherine S. *Dear Belle: Letters From a Cadet and Officer to His Sweetheart, 1858–1865.* Middletown, Conn.: Wesleyan University Press, 1965.

Crocker, J.F. *Gettysburg: Pickett's Charge and Other War Addresses.* Portsmouth, Va.: n.p., 1915.

Cullum, George W. *Biographical Register of the Officers and Graduates of the U.S. Military Academy at West Point, N.Y.* Boston: Houghton Mifflin and Co., 1891.

Curtis, O.B. *History of the Twenty-Fourth Michigan of the Iron Brigade.* Detroit: Winn and Hammon Co., 1891.

"Daniel Liles Letters." *Company Front* (April–May 1991).

Davis, Archie K. *Boy Colonel of the Confederacy: The Life and Times of Henry King Burgwyn Jr.* Chapel Hill, N.C.: University of North Carolina Press, 1985.

Dawes, Rufus. "With the Sixth Wisconsin at Gettysburg." *The Gettysburg Papers* 1.

Death Notices from the Raleigh State Chronicle, *September 15, 1883–June 30, 1893.* Edited by Stephen B. Massengill and Robert M. Topkins. Raleigh: n.p., 1992.

"Death of Gen. Morrow." *New York Times.* 2 February 1891.

"Death of Vance." *Asheville Daily Citizen.* 16 April 1894.

Deeds of Valor: How America's Heroes Won the Medal of Honor. Edited by W.F. Beyer and O.F. Keydel. Detroit: Rerrien-Keydel Co., 1905.

"Diary of Samuel E. Burgess, 1860–1862." Edited by Thomas W. Chadwick. *South Carolina Historical and Genealogical Magazine* 48 (Oct. 1947).

Dictionary of American Biography. Edited by Allen Johnson and Dumas Malone. New York: Charles Scribner's Sons, 1928–1936.

Dictionary of North Carolina Biography. Edited by William S. Powell. Chapel Hill, N.C.: University of North Carolina Press, 1991.

Dorsett, Wilbur. "The Fourteenth Color-Bearer." *The Carolina Magazine* (1932).

Dowdy, Clifford. *Death of a Nation.* New York: Alfred A. Knopf, 1958.

Driver, William R. "Pickett's Charge at Gettysburg." *The Gettysburg Papers* 1.

Dudley, William W. "Sgt. Mjr. Blanchard at Gettysburg." *Indiana Magazine of History* (June 1938).

Dunn, Craig L. *Iron Men, Iron Will: The Nineteenth Indiana Regiment of the Iron Brigade.* Indianapolis: Guild Press of Indiana, 1995.

Dyer, Frederick H. *A Compendium of the War of the Rebellion.* New York: Thomas Yoseloff, 1959.

Eggleston, George Cary. *A Rebel's Recollections.* Baton Rouge: LSU Press, 1997.

Elmore, Thomas. "Torrid Heat and Blinding Rain: a Meteorological and Astronomical Chronology of the Gettysburg Campaign." *Gettysburg Magazine* 13.

Emerson, John H. *Lieutenant John R. Emerson, Company E, 26th Regiment, N.C.T.* Cary, N.C.: n.p., 1997.

Emerson, Mrs. B.A.C. "The Most Famous Regiment." *Confederate Veteran* 25 (October 1917).

Encyclopedia of the Confederacy. Edited by Richard Current. New York: Simon and Schuster, 1993.

"Extract From Letter of M.C. Barnes." *The Bachelder Papers: Gettysburg in Their Own Words.* Vol. 2. Edited by David L. Ladd and Audrey J. Ladd. Dayton, Ohio: Morningside Press Inc., 1994.

Felton, Silas. "The Iron Brigade Battery at Gettysburg." *Gettysburg Magazine* 11.

Fighting for the Confederacy: The Personal Recollections of General Edward Porter Alexander. Chapel Hill, N.C.: University of North Carolina Press, 1989.

The First Day at Gettysburg. Edited by Gary W. Gallagher. Kent, Ohio: Kent State University Press, 1992.

"First Delaware Regiment." *The Bachelder Papers: Gettysburg in Their Own Words.* Vol. 3. Edited by David L. Ladd and Audrey J. Ladd. Dayton, Ohio: Morningside House, Inc., 1994.

"First Lieutenant John R. Emerson." *Company Front* (November–December 1990).

Fleming, George T. *Life and Letters of General Alexander Hays.* Pittsburgh: n.p., 1919.

Foote, Shelby. *The Civil War: A Narrative.* New York: Random House, 1958.

"Fortieth Anniversary of the Battle of Gettysburg." *Raleigh News and Observer.* 6 July 1903.

Foster, John M. *New Jersey and the Rebellion: A History of the Services of the Troops and People of New Jersey in Aid of the Union Cause.* Newark, N.J.: Martin R. Dennis and Co., 1868.

Fox, William F. *Regimental Losses in the American Civil War, 1861–1865.* Albany, N.Y.: Randow Printing Co., 1889.

Frassanito, William. *Early Photography at Gettysburg.* Gettysburg: Thomas Publications, 1995.

Freeman, Douglas Southall. *Lee's Lieutenants: A Study in Command.* New York: Charles Scribner's Sons, 1942.

———. *R.E. Lee: A Biography.* New York: Charles Scribner's Sons, 1934.

The Fremantle Diary. Edited by Walter Lord. Boston: Little, Brown and Co., 1954.

From That Terrible Field: Civil War Letters of James M. Williams, Twenty-First Alabama Infantry Volunteers. Edited by John Kent Folmer. Tuscaloosa, Ala.: University of Alabama Press, 1981.

"From the Eighth Ohio." *Cleveland Plain Dealer.* n.d.

"From the Old North State." *Confederate Veteran* 6 (August 1894).

"From the Twenty-Fourth: On the Battle-Field at Gettysburg." *Detroit Free Press.* 17 July 1863.

Fry, Birkett D. "Pettigrew's Charge at Gettysburg." *Southern Historical Society Papers* 7 (1879).

Fulton, W.F. "The Fifth Alabama at Gettysburg." *Confederate Veteran* 31 (October 1923).

Gaff, Alan D. "Here Was Made Out Our Last and Hopeless Stand: The 'Lost' Gettysburg Reports of the Nineteenth Indiana." *Gettysburg Magazine* 2.

Galwey, Thomas F. *The Valiant Hours.* Edited by W. S. Nye. Harrisburg, Pa.: The Stackpole Co., 1961.

"Gen. Isaac R. Trimble." *New York Times.* 5 January 1888.

"Gen. James H. Lane." *Confederate Veteran* 16 (September 1908).

"General Joseph R. Davis." *Confederate Veteran* 5 (February 1897).

The Gettysburg Nobody Knows. Edited by Gabor S. Borritt. New York: Oxford University Press, 1997.

Gibbon, John. *Personal Recollections of the Civil War.* New York: G.B. Putnam's Sons, 1928.

———. "The Council of War on the Second Day." *Battles and Leaders of the Civil War.* Vol. 3. Edited by Robert U. Johnson and Clarence C. Buell. New York: The Century Company, 1884.

Gordon, John B. *Reminiscences of the Civil War.* New York: Charles Scribner's Sons, 1903.

Gorham, George C. *The Life and Public Services of Edwin M. Stanton.* Boston: Mifflin and Co., 1899.

Goss, Warren L. *Recollections of a Private: A Story of the Army of the Potomac.* New York: Thomas Y. Crowell, 1890.

Gross, George J. *The Battle-Field of Gettysburg.* Philadelphia: Collins Printers, 1866.

Hadden, R. Lee. "The Deadly Embrace." *Gettysburg Magazine* 5.

Haines, William P. *History of the Men of Co. F of the 12th New Jersey Vols.* Mickleton, N.J.: n.p., 1897.

Haldeman, Bruce. "Henry K. Burgwyn Jr., 1861: The 'Boy Colonel' of the 26th North Carolina." *Virginia Military Institute Alumni Review* 54 (Spring 1978).

Hale, Laura Virginia. *Four Valiant Years in the Lower Shenandoah Valley.* Strasburg, Va.: Shenandoah Publishing, 1973.

Hall, Harry. *A Johnny Reb Band from Salem.* New York: DaCapa Press, 1980.

Harrison, Kathy George and John W. Busey. *Nothing but Glory: Pickett's Division at Gettysburg.* Gettysburg: Thomas Publications, 1993.

Harwell, Richard. *Two Views of the Battle of Gettysburg.* Chicago: Lakeside Press, 1964.

Haskin, William L. *The History of the First Regiment of Artillery.* Fort Preble, Me.: Thompson and Co., 1879.

Hassler, Warren W. Jr. *Crisis at the Crossroads: The First Day at Gettysburg.* Tuscaloosa, Ala: University of Alabama Press, 1990.

Hazlewood, Martin W. "Gettysburg Charge." *Richmond Dispatch.* 26 January 1896.

The Heritage of Caldwell County, North Carolina. Edited by Carl E. Anderson Jr. and John O. Hawkins. Winston-Salem, N.C.: Hunter Publishing Company, 1983.

Hickerson, Thomas F. *Happy Valley: History and Genealogy.* Chapel Hill, N.C.: n.p., 1940.

The History of North Carolina. Chicago: Lewis Publishing Co., 1919.

Historical Times Illustrated Encyclopedia of the Civil War. Edited by Patricia Faust. New York: Harper and Row, 1986.

Histories of the Several Regiments and Battalions From North Carolina in the Great War, 1861–'65. Edited by Walter Clark. Goldsboro, N.C.: Nash Brothers, 1901.

Hoke, Jacob. *The Great Invasion.* New York: Thomas Yoseloff, 1959.

Hood, J.T.C. "The 26th Regiment at Gettysburg." *Lenoir News Topic.* 8 April 1896.

Howard, Oliver O. *The Autobiography of Oliver Otis Howard.* New York: Baker and Taylor, 1908.

Hunt, Henry J. "The First Day at Gettysburg." *Battles and Leaders of the Civil War.* Vol. 3. Edited by Robert U. Johnson and Clarence C. Buell. New York: The Century Company, 1884.

Imboden, John D. "The Confederate Retreat from Gettysburg." *Battles and Leaders of the Civil War.* Vol. 3. Edited by Robert U. Johnson and Clarence C. Buell. New York: The Century Company, 1884.

An Irishman in Dixie: Thomas Conolly's Diary of the Fall of the Confederacy. Edited by Nelson Lankford. Columbia, S.C.: University of South Carolina Press, 1988.

An Irishman in the Iron Brigade: The Civil War Memoirs of James P. Sullivan. Edited by William J.K. Beaudot and Lance J. Herdegen. New York: Fordham University Press, 1993.

"The Iron Brigade." *The Bachelder Papers: Gettysburg in Their Own Words.* Vol. 1. Edited by David L. and Audrey J. Ladd. Dayton, Ohio: Morningside House, Inc., 1994.

"J. Moore on Roster of North Carolina Troops." *Confederate Veteran* 6. (September 1898).

"The James W. Wright Letters." Pt. 1. Edited by David H. McGee. *Company Front* (1992).

Johnston, David. *A Confederate Boy in the Civil War.* Radford, Va.: n.p., 1914.

Jones, John. "Pettigrew's Brigade at Gettysburg." *Histories of the Several Regiments and Battalions from North Carolina in the Great War, 1861–'65.* Vol. 4. Edited by Walter Clark. Goldsboro, N.C.: Nash Brothers, 1901.

Jorgenson, Jay. "Edward Porter Alexander, Confederate Cannoneer at Gettysburg." *Gettysburg Magazine* 17.

Journal of a Secesh Lady: The Diary of Catherine Ann Devereux Edmondston, 1860–1866. Edited by Beth G. Crabtree and James W. Patton. Raleigh: North Carolina Division of Archives and History, 1979.

Katcher, Phillip. *The Army of Robert E. Lee.* London: Arms and Armour Press, 1994.

Kilmer, George L. "Food for Powder: How the Twenty-Sixth North Carolina Caught Hot Bullets." *The Racket* (June 1892).

Kimble, June. "Tennesseans at Gettysburg." *Confederate Veteran* 18. (September 1910).

Krick, Robert K. *Lee's Colonels: A Biographical Register of the Field Officers of the Army of Northern Virginia.* Dayton, Ohio: Morningside Press, 1979.

"Lane's Brigade." *Raleigh News and Observer.* 29 November 1877.

"The Last of the Iron Brigade: The H.A. Morrow Diary." *Civil War Times Illustrated* 14 (February 1976).

"Lee's Army in Pennsylvania." *The Land We Love* 2 (November 1866).

Leinbach, Julius. *Regiment Band of the 26th North Carolina.* Edited by Donald M. McCorkle. Winston-Salem, N.C.: Moravian Music Foundation Publications, 1958.

"Letter From Adjutant H.C. Moore." *Raleigh Observer.* 29 November 1877.

"Letter From Capt. P.C. Carlton." *Raleigh Observer.* 29 November 1877.

"Letter From Col. Jones." *Raleigh Observer.* 29 November 1877.

"Letter From Col. Lowe." *Raleigh Observer.* 29 November 1877.

"Letter From Gen. Lane." *Raleigh Observer.* 29 November 1877.

"Letter From Hon. Jos. J. Davis." *Raleigh Observer.* 29 November 1877.

"Letter From Lt. Col. J. McLeod Turner." *Raleigh Observer.* 29 November 1877.

"Letter From Lt. Col. Jos. H. Saunders." *Raleigh Observer.* 29 November 1877.

"Letter From Lt. Col. W.G. Morris." *Raleigh Observer.* 29 November 1877.

"Letter From Lt. Gaston Broughton." *Raleigh Observer.* 29 November 1877.

"Letter From Lt. Thos. L. Norwood." *Raleigh Observer.* 29 November 1877.

"Letter From Lt. W.B. Shepard." *Raleigh Observer.* 29 November 1877.

"Letter From Major-General Henry Heth, of A.P. Hill, A.N.V." *Southern Historical Society Papers.* Vol. 4 (1877).

"Letter of Capt. David Shields." *The Bachelder Papers: Gettysburg in Their Own Words.* Vol. 2. Edited by David L. Ladd and Audrey J. Ladd. Dayton, Ohio: Morningside House, Inc., 1994.

"Letter of Capt. Frank E. Moran." *The Bachelder Papers: Gettysburg in Their Own Words.* Vol. 2. Edited by David L. Ladd and Audrey J. Ladd. Dayton, Ohio: Morningside House, Inc., 1994.

"Letter of Capt. Samuel C. Armstrong." *The Bachelder Papers: Gettysburg in Their Own Words.* Vol. 2. Edited by David L. Ladd and Audrey J. Ladd. Dayton, Ohio: Morningside House, Inc., 1994.

"Letter of Lt. Col. Franklin Sawyer." *The Bachelder Papers: Gettysburg in Their Own Words.* Vol. 2. Edited by David L. Ladd and Audrey J. Ladd. Dayton, Ohio: Morningside House, Inc., 1994.

"Letter of Lt. Egan to George Meade Jr." *The Bachelder Papers: Gettysburg in Their Own Words.* Vol. 1. Edited by David L. Ladd and Audrey J. Ladd. Dayton, Ohio: Morningside House, Inc., 1994.

"Letter of Lt. Samuel B. McIntyre." *The Bachelder Papers: Gettysburg in Their Own Words.* Vol. 2. Edited by David L. Ladd and Audrey J. Ladd. Dayton, Ohio: Morningside House, Inc., 1994.

"Letter of Maj. Gen. Isaac R. Trimble." *The Bachelder Papers: Gettysburg in Their Own Words.* Vol. 2. Edited by David L. Ladd and Audrey J. Ladd. Dayton, Ohio: Morningside House, Inc., 1994.

Letters of a Civil War Nurse. Edited by Henrietta S. Jaquette. Lincoln: University of Nebraska Press, 1998.

"Letters of Jefferson B. Mansfield." Edited by Randal Garrison. *Company Front.* Pt. 1 (September/October 1995).

A Life for the Confederacy: As Recorded in the Pocket Diaries of Pvt. Robert A. Moore. Edited by James W. Silver. Wilmington, N.C.: Broadfoot Publishing, 1987.

Lineback, Julius. "Extracts From a Civil War Diary." *Twin Cities Daily Sentinel.* 14 June 1914–3 April 1915.

Long, Roger. "General Orders No. 72." *Gettysburg Magazine* 7.

Longacre, Edward G. *To Gettysburg and Beyond: The Twelfth New Jersey Volunteer Infantry, II Corps, Army of the Potomac.* Hightstown, N.J.: Longstreet House, 1988.

Longstreet, James. *From Manassas to Appomattox: A Memoir of the Civil War in America.* Philadelphia: J.B. Lippincott, 1895.

Love, William Deloss. *Wisconsin in the War of the Rebellion: A History of All Regiments and Batteries.* Chicago: Church and Goodman, Publishers, 1866.

Loyd, W.G. "The Second Louisiana at Gettysburg." *Confederate Veteran* 6. (September 1898).

MacKay, T.J. "Hampton's Duel." *Southern Historical Society Papers* 22.

"Maj. Gen. Isaac R. Trimble." *The Bachelder Papers: Gettysburg in Their Own Words.* Vol. 2. Edited by David L. Ladd and Audrey J. Ladd. Dayton, Ohio: Morningside House, Inc., 1994.

Make Me a Map of the Valley: The Civil War Journal of Stonewall Jackson's Topographer. Edited by Archie McDonald. Dallas: Southern Methodist University Press, 1988.

Martin, David G. *Gettysburg July 1.* Conshohocken, Pa.: Combined Books, 1995.

Martin, Rawley. "Rawley Martin's Account." *Southern Historical Society Papers* 39 (1911).

Martin, W.J. "The Eleventh North Carolina Regiment." *Southern Historical Society Papers* 23.

Mary Chestnut's Civil War. Edited by C. Vann Woodward. New Haven, Conn.: Yale University Press, 1981.

Mast, Greg. *State Troops and Volunteers: A Photographic Record of North Carolina's Civil War Soldiers.* Raleigh: North Carolina Division of Archives and History, 1995.

———. "Tha Kill So Many of Us": The 26th North Carolina Troops at Gettysburg." *Company Front* (April/May 1988).

McCarthy, Carlton. *Detailed Minutiae of Soldier Life in the Army of Northern Virginia, 1861–1865.* Richmond: Carlton McCarthy and Company, 1882.

McFarland, Baxter. "Casualties of the Eleventh Mississippi Regiment at Gettysburg." *Confederate Veteran* 24. (September 1916).

McGee, David. "History of the Twenty-Sixth North Carolina." *Company Front* (April 1993).

McLaws, Lafayette. "Gettysburg." *Southern Historical Society Papers* 7.

The Memoirs of Henry Heth. Edited by James L. Morrison Jr. Westport, Conn.: Greenwood Press, 1974.

Meredith, Jaquelin Marshall. "The First Day at Gettysburg." *Southern Historical Society Papers* 24 (1896).

Miller, J. Michael. "Perrin's Brigade on July 1, 1863." *Gettysburg Magazine* 13.

Moore, A.H. "Heth's Division at Gettysburg." *Southern Bivouac* 3 (May 1885).

Moore, James Daniel. "Interesting Narrative of the Civil War." *Raleigh Morning Post.* 11 February 1900.

Moore, J. Scott. "Rev. Romulus Morris Tuttle." *Confederate Veteran* 12 (June 1904).

Moore, Martha J. *James Daniel Moore.* Raleigh: Edwards and Broughton Printing Co., 1907.

Morgan, B. "Capt. Louis Young." *Confederate Veteran* 30.

"Mrs. Devereux Passes." *Raleigh News and Observer.* 30 April 1912.

Murphey, Thomas G. *History of the 1st Delaware Infantry.* Philadelphia: Alfred Martien, 1866.

Nolan, Alan T. *The Iron Brigade: A Military History.* New York: Macmillan Publishing Co., 1961.

———. "The Paper Trail of the Iron Brigade." *Columbiad* 1 (Summer 1997).

Norris, Mrs. M.T. "Now Growing Old Gracefully." *Confederate Veteran* 11 (November 1912).

"North Carolina at Gettysburg." *Raleigh Observer.* 30 November 1877.

North Carolina Civil War Documentary. Edited by W. Buck Yearns and John G. Barrett. Chapel Hill, N.C.: University of North Carolina Press, 1980.

North Carolina Troops, 1861–1865: A Roster. Compiled by Weymouth T. Jordan Jr. with Unit Histories by Louis H. Manarin. Raleigh: North Carolina Department of Archives and History, 1979.

"Notes Regarding the 24th Michigan." *The Bachelder Papers: Gettysburg in Their Own Words.* Vol. 1. Edited by David L. Ladd and Audrey J. Ladd. Dayton, Ohio: Morningside House, Inc., 1994.

Official Register of the Officers and Cadets of the U.S. Military Academy, June 1856–1860. West Point: U.S. Military Academy, n.d.

"The Old North State." *Confederate Veteran* 4 (May 1898).

Olds, Fred A. "Brave Carolinian Who Fell at Gettysburg." *Southern Historical Society Papers* 36 (1908).

Oliva, Leo E. *Fort Hays, Frontier Army Post, 1865–1889.* Topeka: Kansas State Historical Society, 1980.

Oliver, William H. *Blockade Running by the State of North Carolina, 1863–1864.* New Bern, N.C.: n.p., n.d.

Oxford English Dictionary. Oxford: Clarendon Press, 1989.

Papers of Zebulon Baird Vance. Edited by Frontis W. Johnston. Raleigh: North Carolina Department of Archives and History, 1963.

Patterson, Edmund DeWitt. *Yankee Rebel.* Chapel Hill, N.C.: University of North Carolina Press, 1966.

"The Pee Dee Wildcats." *Anson County (N.C.) Messenger and Intelligencier.* 18 September 1863.

Pennsylvania at Gettysburg. Edited by John P. Nicholson. Harrisburg, Pa.: William S. Ray, 1904.

Quiner, E.B. *The Military History of Wisconsin in the War for the Union.* Chicago: Clarke Company, Publishers, 1866.

Randall, J.G. and David Donald. *The Civil War and Reconstruction.* Boston: D.C. Heath, 1961.

Reardon, Carol. *Pickett's Charge in History and Memory.* Chapel Hill, N.C.: University of North Carolina Press, 1997.

"Report of Lt. Col. William W. Dudley." *The Bachelder Papers: Gettysburg in Their Own Words.* Vol. 2. Edited by David L. Ladd and Audrey J. Ladd. Dayton, Ohio: Morningside House, Inc., 1994.

Rice, Edmund. "Repelling Lee's Last Blow at Gettysburg." *Battles and Leaders of the Civil War.* Vol. 3. Edited by Robert U. Johnson and Clarence C. Buell. New York: The Century Company, 1884.

Ridley, B.L. "B.L. Ridley's Journal." *Confederate Veteran* 3. (May 1895).

Robertson, James I. Jr. *A.P. Hill: The Story of a Confederate Warrior.* New York: Random House, 1987.

———. *Stonewall Jackson: The Man, The Soldier, The Legend.* New York: Macmillan Publishing Co., 1997.

Rollins, Richard. *The Damned Red Flags of the Rebellion: The Confederate Battleflag at Gettysburg.* Redondo Beach, Calif.: Rank and File Publications, 1997.

———. *Pickett's Charge: Eyewitness Accounts.* Redondo Beach, Calif. Rank and File Publications, 1994.

Rollins, Richard, and Dave Shultz. *Guide to Pennsylvania Troops at Gettysburg.* Redondo Beach, Calif.: Rank and File Publications, 1996.

Rose, Rebecca Ansell. *Colours of the Gray: An Illustrated Index of Wartime Flags From the Museum of the Confederacy's Collection.* Museum of the Confederacy, 1998.

Rosentreter, Roger L. "Those Damned Black Hats: The Twenty-Fourth Michigan at Gettysburg." *Michigan Historical Magazine* (July–August 1991).

Sawyer, Franklin. *A Military History of the 8th Regiment Ohio Volunteer Inf'ry.* Cleveland: Fairbanks and Co., 1881.

Scott, Winfield. "Pickett's Charge as Seen From the Front Lines." *Gettysburg Magazine* 2.

"The Setser Letters." Pts 1–3. Edited by Greg Mast. *Company Front* (December 1988–July 1989).

Seville, William. *History of the First Regiment, Delaware Volunteers.* Baltimore: Longstreet House, 1986.

Shultz, David. *"Double Canister at Ten Yards": The Federal Artillery and the Repulse of Pickett's Charge.* Redondo Beach, Calif.: Rank and File Publications, 1995.

Shultz, David, and Richard Rollins. "Measuring Pickett's Charge." *Gettysburg Magazine* 17.

Sifakis, Stewart. *Who Was Who in the Civil War.* New York: Facts on File, Inc., 1988.

Simons, Ezra D. *A Regimental History of the One-Hundred-and-Twenty-Fifth New York State Volunteers.* New York: Ezra D. Simons, 1888.

Smith, Alexander. *The Complete Works of Robert Burns.* London: Macmillan Publishing Co., 1914.

Smith, Donald L. *The Twenty-Fourth Michigan of the Iron Brigade.* Harrisburg, Pa.: The Stackpole Co., 1962.

Stepp, Jeff. "Dedication of the New Gravestone for Major Abner Carmichael." *Company Front* (May–June 1995).

Stevenson, A.M. *Indiana's Roll of Honor.* Indianapolis: A.D. Streight, Publisher, 1864.

Stewart, George R. *Pickett's Charge: A Microhistory of the Final Attacks at Gettysburg, July 3, 1863.* Boston: Houghton Mifflin Co., 1959.

Strikeleather, J.A. "Recollections of the Late War." *Company Front* (October 1993).

Taylor, Michael W. "Col. James Keith Marshall: One of Three Brigade Commanders Killed in the Pickett-Pettigrew-Trimble Charge." *Gettysburg Magazine* 15.

———. "North Carolina in the Pickett-Pettigrew Trimble Charge at Gettysburg." *Gettysburg Magazine* 8.

Terry, Mark. "The Mystery Flags of Bristoe Station." *Company Front* (September 1999).

"Testimony About the Battle of Gettysburg." *Confederate Veteran* 18 (November 1910).

Thompson, Richard S. "A Scrap of Gettysburg." *The Gettysburg Papers* 2.

Thorpe, John H. "Forty-Seventh Regiment." *Histories of the Several Regiments and Battalions From North Carolina in the Great War 1861–'65.* Vol. 3. Edited by Walter Clark. Goldsboro, N.C.: Nash Brothers, 1901.

"To Chancellorsville With the Iron Brigade: The Diary of Colonel Henry W. Morrow." *Civil War Times Illustrated* 14 (January 1976).

Toney, Keith. "Gettysburg: Opening Moves." *Civil War Art* 1 (Summer 1996).

Toombs, Samuel. *New Jersey Troops in the Gettysburg Campaign.* Orange, N.J.: Evening Mail Publishing House, 1888.

Trinque, Bruce A. "Arnold's Battery and the 26th North Carolina." *Gettysburg Magazine* 12.

Tucker, Glenn. "Some Aspects of North Carolina's Participation in the Gettysburg Campaign." *North Carolina Historical Review* 35 (April 1958).

Turney, J.B. "The First Tennessee at Gettysburg." *Confederate Veteran* 3 (April 1885).

Tuttle, C.A. "'F' and 'I' of the 26th Regiment From 1861 to 1865." *Lenoir News Topic.* 11 May 1922.

———. "Incidents Which Happened in Caldwell County in 1864." *Lenoir News Topic.* 4 May 1922.

Tuttle, R.M. "A Thrilling and Awful Account. . . ." *Confederate Veteran* 4 (September 1896).

———. "Company F, 26th N.C. Infantry." *Confederate Veteran* 3 (April 1895).

"Twenty-Fourth Regiment Infantry." *Michigan in the War.* Compiled by John Robertson. Lansing, Michigan: W.S. George and Co., 1882.

Underwood, George C. "The Twenty-Sixth Regiment." *Histories of Several Regiments and Battalions From North Carolina in the Great War, 1861–'65.* Vol. 2. Edited by Walter Clark. Goldsboro, N.C.: Nash Brothers, 1901.

Untitled article. *Wadesboro (N.C.) Argus.* 10 July 1862.

Van Noppen, Ina W., and John J. Van Noppen. *Western North Carolina Since the Civil War.* Boone, N.C.: Appalachian Consortium Press, 1973.

Voices From Cemetery Hill: The Civil War Diary, Reports and Letters of Colonel William Henry Asbury Speer, 1861–1864. Edited by Allen P. Speer. Johnston City, Tenn.: Overmountain Press, 1997.

War of the Rebellion: The Official Records of the Union and Confederate Armies. Washington, D.C.: Government Printing Office, 1880–1901.

Warner, Ezra. *Generals in Blue.* Baton Rouge: Louisiana State University Press, 1964.

———. *Generals in Gray.* Baton Rouge: Louisiana State University Press, 1959.

Warren, G.K. *Map of the Battlefield of Gettysburg.* Washington, D.C.: U.S. Army Engineers Department, 1873.

Washburn, George H. *A Complete Military History and Record of the 108th Regiment N.Y. Vols. From 1862 to 1894.* Rochester, N.Y.: n.p., 1894.

Way, William C. "From the 24th Michigan." *Detroit Advertiser and Tribune.* 16 July 1863.

Welch, Spencer G. *A Confederate Surgeon's Letters to His Wife.* New York: Neale Publishing Co., 1911.

Wheeler, Cornelius. "Reminiscences of the Battle of Gettysburg." *The Gettysburg Papers* 1.

Wheeler, Richard. *Witness to Gettysburg.* New York: Harper and Row, 1987.

Whitten, Clayte H. "Arkansan, 97, Recalls Civil War Experiences." *Monroe (N.C.) Enquirer Journal.* n.d.

Wilson, Clyde N. *Carolina Cavalier: The Life and Mind of James Johnston Pettigrew.* Athens, Ga.: University of Georgia Press, 1990.

———. "The Most Promising Young Man of the South: James Johnston Pettigrew." *Civil War Times Illustrated* 11 (February 1973).

Wise, Jennings Crooper. *The Long Arm of Lee.* Lynchburg, Va.: J.P. Bell Co., 1915.

Worsham, John H. *One of Jackson's Foot Cavalry.* New York: Neale Publishing Co., 1912.

Young, Bennett. "Col. John R. Lane and His Regiment." *Confederate Veteran* 17 (March 1909).

Young, Louis G. "The Pettigrew-Kirkland-MacRae Brigade." *Histories of the Several Regiments and Battalions From North Carolina in the Great War 1861–'65.* Vol. 4. Edited by Walter Clark. Goldsboro, N.C.: Nash Brothers, 1901.

———. "Pettigrew's Brigade." *Histories of the Several Regiments and Battalions From North Carolina in the Great War 1861–'65.* Vol. 5. Edited by Walter Clark. Goldsboro, N.C.: Nash Brothers, 1901.

———. "Pettigrew's Brigade." *Our Living and Our Dead* 1 (February 1875).

Manuscript Sources

ADAMS COUNTY HISTORICAL SOCIETY. GETTYSBURG, PENNSYLVANIA
  Battlefield Photography Album
  John Herbst Claims File

JOHN BASS COLLECTION. SPRING HOPE, NORTH CAROLINA
  Kirkman Papers

DUKE UNIVERSITY. SPECIAL COLLECTIONS LIBRARY. DURHAM, NORTH
    CAROLINA
  Henry Besancom Diary
  Samuel S. Biddle Papers
  Branch Family Papers
  William C. Byrnes Papers
  Henry C. Clare Papers
  Devereux Family Papers
  William Erwin Jr. Files
  Robert N. Gourdin Papers
  Jesse L. Henry Papers
  David S. Libbey Papers
  Jarratt-Puryear Papers
  Nevin Ray Papers
  William Lafayette Scott Papers
  Samuel Walkup Papers

GETTYSBURG NATIONAL MILITARY PARK. ADMINISTRATIVE ARCHIVES.
    GETTYSBURG, PENNSYLVANIA
  Civilian Accounts File
  McPherson Farm File
  Twenty-Sixth North Carolina File

L.R. GORRELL COLLECTION. RALEIGH, NORTH CAROLINA
  John R. Lane Manuscript

ROD GRAGG COLLECTION. CONWAY, SOUTH CAROLINA
  Brooks L. Gilmore File
  Globe Valley File
  Charles L. Gragg File
  Lemuel Wallace Gragg File

GREENSBORO HISTORICAL MUSEUM. GREENSBORO, NORTH CAROLINA
  Henry C. Albright Papers

HANDLEY LIBRARY. WINCHESTER, VIRGINIA
  Julia Chase Papers
  Mrs. Hugh Lee collection

LIBRARY OF CONGRESS. MANUSCRIPT DIVISION. WASHINGTON, D.C.
  Edward Porter Alexander Papers
  Samuel Wylie Crawford Papers
  Lyman C. Holdford Papers
  Edward McPherson Papers

ROBERT H. MacINTOSH JR. COLLECTION. COLUMBIA, SOUTH CAROLINA
William Hill Letter

MUSEUM OF THE CONFEDERACY. ELEANOR BROCKENBROUGH LIBRARY
Confederate Battle Flags File
Kate Mason Roland File

NATIONAL ARCHIVES. WASHINGTON, D.C.
Compiled Service Records, Confederate Officers
Compiled Service Records, 19th Indiana Volunteer Infantry
Compiled Service Records, 22nd Battalion of Virginia Infantry
Compiled Service Records, 24th Michigan Volunteer Infantry
Compiled Service Records, 26th North Carolina State Troops
Eighth Census of the United States, 1860

NORTH CAROLINA DEPARTMENT OF ARCHIVES AND HISTORY. RALEIGH,
        NORTH CAROLINA
James T. Adams Papers
Adjutant General's Office Papers
W.H.S. Burgwyn Papers
Confederate Pension Applications (1901)
Confederate Pension Applications (1907)
Thomas P. Devereux Papers
Thomas Goreman Papers
Edmund W. Jones Papers
Muster Rolls, 26th North Carolina State Troops
Thomas Perrett Papers
U.D.C. Confederate Gravestone Records
Francis D. Winston Papers

NORTH CAROLINA MUSEUM OF HISTORY. RALEIGH, NORTH CAROLINA
Henry K. Burgwyn Collection
26th North Carolina Battle Flag File

OAKWOOD CEMETERY ARCHIVES. RALEIGH, NORTH CAROLINA
Henry K. Burgwyn Jr.
Annie Devereux File

PACK MEMORIAL LIBRARY. ASHEVILLE, NORTH CAROLINA
North Carolina Collection

RITA A. SIMPSON COLLECTION. CHARLOTTE, NORTH CAROLINA
Leary W. Adams Manuscript

HERMAN STARNES COLLECTION. MONROE, NORTH CAROLINA
Isaac Mattox Papers

UNIVERSITY OF MICHIGAN. BENTLEY HISTORICAL LIBRARY. ANN ARBOR,
        MICHIGAN
Ryder Family Papers

UNIVERSITY OF NORTH CAROLINA. SOUTHERN HISTORICAL COLLECTION.
        CHAPEL HILL, NORTH CAROLINA
Burgwyn Family Papers

Collier Family Papers
Margaret Mordecai Devereux Papers
Edmund W. Jones Papers
John R. Lane Papers
Julius Lineback Papers
Charles Mallett Papers
James T. Morehead Papers
Louis G Young Papers

UNIVERSITY OF SOUTH CAROLINA. SOUTH CAROLINIANA LIBRARY. COLUMBIA,
SOUTH CAROLINA
W.W. McCreery Letterbook

UNIVERSITY OF VIRGINIA. ALDERMAN LIBRARY. CHARLOTTESVILLE, VIRGINIA
John W. Daniel Papers
Henry Heth Papers

U.S. ARMY MILITARY HISTORY INSTITUTE. CARLISLE, PENNSYLVANIA
Robert L. Brake Collection
Harrisburg Civil War Round Table Collection
Lewis Leigh Collection

U.S. MILITARY ACADEMY. U.S. MILITARY ACADEMY LIBRARY. WEST POINT, NEW
YORK
Cadet Application Papers, 1805–1866
Official Register of Officers and Cadets, 1856–1860

VIRGINIA MILITARY INSTITUTE. PRESTON LIBRARY. LEXINGTON, VIRGINIA
Henry K. Burgwyn Jr. Papers
Records of the Superintendent

Index